Simulation Operations in Healthcare Education
A Primer into the Role of Operations in Medical and Nursing Training

KEITH A. BEAULIEU

Porthos Press

KEITH A. BEAULIEU

Simulation Operations in Healthcare Education
A Primer into the Role of Operations in Medical and Nursing Training

Copyright © 2025 by Keith A. Beaulieu, Porthos Press
All Rights Reserved.

No part of this document may be reproduced or transmitted in any form or by any means, electronic, mechanical, photocopying, recording, or otherwise, without prior written permission.

Requests for permission to make copies of any part of the work should be submitted to the publisher.

Published by Keith A. Beaulieu, Porthos Press
Cape51@yahoo.com

Printed in the United States of America
First Printing: January 2025

ISBN 978-1-7360792-6-3 (Paperback)
ISBN 978-1-7360792-7-0 (hardback)

First edition, 2025
10 9 8 7 6 5 4 3 2 1

Acknowledgments

I want to thank the **UC Irvine Sue & Bill Gross School of Nursing** for allowing me to continue contributing and growing in healthcare simulation operations and accreditation.

I would like to thank the **Society for Simulation in Healthcare**, especially the **Accreditation Council,** for allowing me to follow in the footsteps of some of healthcare simulation's biggest champions.

KEITH A. BEAULIEU

PAGE INTENTIONALLY LEFT BLANK

Contents

Chapter 1
Introduction to Medical and Nursing Simulation Operations   2

Chapter 2
Shaping Healthcare Competencies Through Simulation   25

Chapter 3
Simulation Design and Implementation in Healthcare Education   38

Chapter 4
Operations Management in Medical and Nursing Simulation Centers   67

Chapter 5
Staff Management in Medical and Nursing Simulation Centers   102

Chapter 6
Implementing Effective Simulation-based Education Programs   136

Chapter 7
Assessing Program Outcomes in Simulation Center Operations   151

Chapter 8
Emerging Technologies in Healthcare Simulation   163

Chapter 9
Research and Continuous Improvement in Simulation Operations   171

Chapter 10
Careers and Professional Development in Healthcare Simulation Operations   197

Chapter 11
Standards of Best Practice in Simulation   216

Chapter 12
Aligning Simulation Curriculum and Operations to Accreditation Standards   223

Chapter 13
Simulation Operations for Systems Integration   230

Chapter 14
Contingency and Continuity Operations in Simulation   247

Chapter 15
Conclusion and Next Steps: Advancing Healthcare Simulation Operations   260

Appendices   277

SIMULATION OPERATIONS IN HEALTHCARE EDUCATION: A PRIMER INTO THE ROLE OF OPERATIONS IN MEDICAL AND NURSING TRAINING

Introduction

Simulation has become a game-changer in today's fast-paced and ever-evolving healthcare world, transforming how medical and nursing professionals learn and grow. Picture this: students and clinicians immersed in lifelike scenarios, making critical decisions, performing intricate procedures, and collaborating under pressure—all without jeopardizing patient safety. This is the transformative power of healthcare simulation. It bridges the gap between theoretical knowledge and real-world practice, offering a safe yet challenging environment to cultivate skills, confidence, and critical thinking.

Nevertheless, while the high-tech mannequins, virtual reality (VR) environments, and detailed patient scenarios often steal the spotlight, the true heart of a successful simulation program lies in its operations. These behind-the-scenes efforts ensure every detail runs like clockwork—from maintaining cutting-edge technology to crafting realistic, immersive scenarios that align with educational objectives. Without these operational foundations, even the most sophisticated tools and designs would fall short of their potential.

This book is your gateway into the intricate world of healthcare simulation operations. It is a practical guide for educators, administrators, and operators who aim to design, manage, and elevate their simulation programs. From planning and resource allocation to technical troubleshooting and program evaluation, you will discover strategies to build and sustain impactful simulation initiatives that meet the highest standards of modern healthcare education.

As healthcare education continues to evolve, simulation is not merely a tool but a necessity. With technologies like artificial intelligence (AI) and augmented reality (AR) pushing boundaries, the opportunities for innovation are endless. This book explores how to harness these advancements while staying grounded in the principles that make simulation effective: realism, interactivity, and meaningful feedback. You will learn how to create scenarios that foster technical skills, teamwork, communication, and resilience—qualities essential for navigating the complexities of today's healthcare environment.

Whether you are a seasoned professional or new to the field, this book equips you with the knowledge and tools to transform healthcare simulation from a good idea into a powerful, game-changing reality. Together, we will delve into the strategies that make simulation operations a cornerstone of healthcare education, ensuring learners are prepared to provide safe, compassionate, and expert care. Let us redefine the future of healthcare training—one simulation at a time.

Chapter 1

Introduction to Medical and Nursing Simulation Operations

1.1 The Evolution of Simulation in Healthcare Education

Simulation in healthcare education has a rich history, evolving alongside advancements in technology and pedagogy. Traditionally, medical training relied on the apprenticeship model, where students observed and practiced under the supervision of experienced clinicians. While foundational, this approach was limited by patient availability, ethical considerations, and the variability of real-world cases.

Simulation can be traced back to the Renaissance when wax anatomical models provided early visual aids for medical instruction. By the mid-20th century, educational tools became more specialized. The introduction of *Resusci Anne* in 1960 revolutionized CPR training, while the *Harvey cardiology simulator*, developed in 1968, allowed students to learn about heart sounds and pathologies without patient involvement (Gaba, 2004). These innovations marked a shift from theoretical instruction to interactive, hands-on learning.

The 1980s and 1990s saw significant technological advancements, ushering in high-fidelity simulators like *SimMan*, which debuted in the late 1990s. These mannequins could simulate physiological functions in real-time, enabling learners to practice complex procedures such as intubation and trauma management in controlled environments. The proliferation of computing power and robotics during this period laid the groundwork for the following immersive technologies (Bradley, 2006).

In the 21st century, simulation has expanded dramatically by integrating cutting-edge technologies. Virtual reality (VR), augmented reality (AR), and artificial intelligence (AI) have created highly immersive and adaptive training experiences. Virtual patient platforms like *Body Interact* enable learners to engage with dynamic, case-based scenarios entirely online, transforming traditional Objective Structured Clinical Examinations (OSCEs) into virtual formats. These platforms reduce logistical challenges, lower stress levels, and provide automatic performance feedback, enhancing learner outcomes and instructional efficiency (*Body Interact*, 2024).

AI-powered tools like *Nasco Healthcare's ALEX* and *SimConverse* have revolutionized communication skills training. These innovations support asynchronous and inclusive learning environments by simulating real-time patient interactions and delivering tailored feedback (HealthySimulation, 2023). Additionally, advancements in wearable technology and haptic feedback devices have enhanced the realism of physical skill practice by replicating tactile sensations during clinical procedures (Advances in Simulation, 2023).

Theoretical models, such as Kolb's experiential learning cycle and Schön's reflective practice theory, have reinforced the pedagogical framework of simulation-based education. These models emphasize the iterative process of performing, reflecting, and improving—an approach that aligns seamlessly with the simulation's objectives. Research consistently demonstrates that simulation enhances technical skills, critical thinking, decision-making, and interprofessional collaboration, making it a cornerstone of modern healthcare education (Advances in Simulation, 2023).

Beyond its traditional applications, simulation now plays a critical role in addressing global healthcare challenges. It provides scalable training solutions for underserved regions, prepares healthcare teams to respond to emerging public health crises, and fosters interprofessional collaboration to improve systemic outcomes. These advancements underscore simulation's ongoing evolution as an indispensable tool in healthcare education and practice.

1.2 Pioneers of Healthcare Simulation and the Influence of Aviation's CRM

Healthcare simulation, as we know it today, owes much to the vision and efforts of early pioneers who recognized its potential to enhance medical training and patient safety. These pioneers not only pushed technological boundaries but also adapted interdisciplinary methodologies, particularly from aviation, to address the complex challenges of healthcare. A defining influence in this journey was the aviation industry's Crew Resource Management (CRM), which set a precedent for teamwork, communication, and safety in high-stakes environments.

The Pioneers of Healthcare Simulation

The roots of healthcare simulation date back to the 1960s and 1970s when innovative educators began integrating mechanical and electronic devices into medical training. Dr. Michael Gordon stands out as a trailblazer with his development of *Harvey*, a cardiology patient simulator introduced in 1968. *Harvey* replicated over 30 cardiac conditions, offering learners a realistic yet controlled environment to practice diagnostic skills (Gordon, 1974). This innovation allowed medical students to practice auscultation and palpation techniques on a simulator before encountering real patients, reducing the risk of error in clinical settings.

Similarly, SimOne emerged as a groundbreaking innovation in the realm of anesthesia. Designed in the late 1960s by a team led by Dr. Stephen Abrahamson, this full-body patient simulator gave anesthesiology residents a realistic platform to practice intubation, ventilation, and other critical skills (Abrahamson, Denson, & Wolf, 1969). Although costly and limited in distribution, *SimOne* was a proof-of-concept that demonstrated the feasibility and benefits of simulation-based medical training.

In the 1980s, Dr. David Gaba's work took healthcare simulation to new heights. Often regarded as the "father of simulation-based training in anesthesia," Dr. Gaba pioneered high-fidelity simulators to train clinicians in crisis management. His development of the *Stanford Anesthesia Simulator* in 1986 provided an immersive experience where participants could simulate real-world scenarios, including life-threatening emergencies, without jeopardizing patient safety. Dr. Gaba's subsequent introduction of Crisis Resource Management (CRM) training tailored specifically for healthcare teams marked a pivotal moment in integrating aviation-inspired methodologies into medicine (Gaba, 1992).

The Early Use of CRM in Healthcare Simulation

The aviation industry's CRM emerged in the late 1970s following a series of tragic accidents attributed to human error. NASA's research into the causes of these incidents revealed that poor communication, decision-making, and teamwork among flight crews were significant contributors (Helmreich & Foushee, 1993). CRM was introduced as a training paradigm to address these issues, emphasizing the importance of non-technical skills like leadership, situational awareness, and assertiveness in ensuring operational safety. This comprehensive approach significantly reduced accidents in aviation, inspiring its adaptation into other high-risk industries, including healthcare.

Dr. Gaba was instrumental in bringing CRM principles into the medical field. He recognized the parallels between aviation and healthcare: both industries involve complex systems, high-pressure environments, and the need for flawless coordination among team members. In his seminal work on crisis resource management for anesthesia teams, he emphasized clear communication, task delegation, and adaptive leadership during emergencies (Gaba, 1994). His training programs used simulation to recreate high-stakes medical scenarios, allowing teams to practice these essential skills risk-free.

Studies demonstrating CRM's effectiveness further bolstered the adoption of CRM in healthcare simulation. For example, early research showed that surgical teams trained in CRM principles experienced improved communication and reduced preventable errors during operations (Grogan et al., 2004). High-fidelity simulation centers like Stanford and Harvard became hubs for testing and refining CRM-based training curricula. These programs emphasized interdisciplinary collaboration, breaking down traditional hierarchies that often hindered effective communication in healthcare settings.

The Legacy of Integration

Integrating CRM into healthcare simulation has profound implications for patient safety and medical education. Today, simulation-based training programs are a standard component of curricula in many medical and nursing schools and in continuing education for practicing clinicians. Modern simulators, from task trainers to full-body manikins and virtual reality systems, incorporate CRM principles to train healthcare professionals in technical procedures and critical non-technical skills.

The legacy of early healthcare simulation pioneers and the adoption of aviation's CRM methodology underscores the power of interdisciplinary collaboration. Healthcare has evolved to prioritize safety, teamwork, and continuous learning by leveraging insights from aviation and other industries. These foundational contributions continue to shape the future of medical education and patient care.

1.3 The Importance of Simulation in Modern Healthcare

Healthcare is an inherently high-risk field where errors can have life-threatening consequences. Simulation provides a risk-free environment for learners to practice and refine their skills, preparing them for real-world clinical scenarios. The Institute of Medicine's landmark report To Err is Human (2000) highlighted that preventable medical errors accounted for thousands of deaths annually in the United States. Simulation has emerged as a critical tool to enhance training, reduce errors, and foster a safety culture (Kohn, Corrigan, & Donaldson, 2000).

- Enhancing Clinical Competence
- Improving Non-technical Skills
- Fostering Critical Thinking and Decision-making
- Promoting a Culture of Safety
- Enhancing Interprofessional Collaboration
- Addressing Psychosocial Aspects of Care
- Supporting Life-long Learning and Adaptability

Enhancing Clinical Competence

Simulation offers opportunities to master technical and procedural skills in a controlled environment. From basic tasks such as catheter insertions to advanced interventions like trauma resuscitation or laparoscopic surgery, simulation ensures learners gain proficiency without risking patient safety. Virtual and augmented reality technologies, such as VR tools like SimX, allow trainees to encounter complex and rare clinical conditions, enhancing their competence and confidence (Body Interact, 2024; HealthySimulation, 2023).

Improving Non-Technical Skills

Beyond technical expertise, simulation addresses non-technical competencies critical to patient care, such as communication, teamwork, and decision-making. Scenarios like cardiac arrest or trauma resuscitation involve interdisciplinary team simulations that mimic real-life challenges. These exercises have shown measurable improvements in team dynamics, collaboration, and patient outcomes (Weaver et al., 2010; TeamSTEPPS, 2024). Advanced tools like SimConverse use AI to provide tailored feedback on communication, further supporting the development of these vital skills.

Fostering Critical Thinking and Decision-Making

Simulations often present dynamic, evolving scenarios requiring learners to assess, prioritize, and act under pressure. High-fidelity simulators recreate real-time physiological responses, challenging learners to make accurate clinical decisions quickly. Studies have shown that such exposure improves the speed and accuracy of critical thinking in high-stakes environments like emergency medicine and intensive care (Advances in Simulation, 2023).

Promoting a Culture of Safety

Simulation-based training instills a safety-first mindset in learners. Simulation reduces the likelihood of preventable mistakes in clinical practice by allowing repeated practice of complex procedures and error-prone tasks. For example, training healthcare professionals on central line insertion using simulation significantly lowered hospital infection rates (Gaba, 2004). Simulated environments also encourage learners to address their mistakes constructively, fostering resilience and continuous improvement.

Enhancing Interprofessional Collaboration

Interdisciplinary collaboration is a cornerstone of effective healthcare. Simulation promotes teamwork by replicating real-world interprofessional challenges, such as handovers, surgical procedures, or crisis responses. Frameworks like TeamSTEPPS integrate simulation to improve communication, clarify roles, and strengthen collaborative practices within healthcare teams (TeamSTEPPS, 2024).

Addressing Psychosocial Aspects of Care

Simulation also prepares learners for the emotional and psychosocial dimensions of patient care. Scenarios involving end-of-life discussions, cultural sensitivities, or delivering bad news enable learners to build empathy and refine their communication skills. AI-based tools like SimConverse offer unique advantages by simulating diverse patient interactions, helping learners navigate complex emotional contexts effectively (HealthySimulation, 2023).

Supporting Lifelong Learning and Adaptability

The rapid pace of innovation in healthcare necessitates lifelong learning. Simulation lets healthcare professionals stay updated on new technologies, medical devices, and evolving treatment protocols. Simulation ensures practitioners remain agile and prepared for future challenges, whether training for new surgical techniques or responding to emerging diseases.

By integrating technical, non-technical, and psychosocial aspects of care, simulation achieves a holistic approach to healthcare education. It bridges the gap between theory and practice, creating a safer and more effective learning environment while addressing the complexities of modern medicine.

1.4 Defining Simulation Operations

Simulation operations are the backbone of effective simulation-based education in healthcare, encompassing the planning, execution, and sustainment of all elements required to deliver high-quality training programs. While simulation technology and curriculum design often receive the spotlight, operational strategies ensure the seamless integration of these components, providing learners with impactful and efficient educational experiences. Simulation operations are multidisciplinary, requiring technology, education, logistics, and program management expertise.

Key Components of Simulation Operations

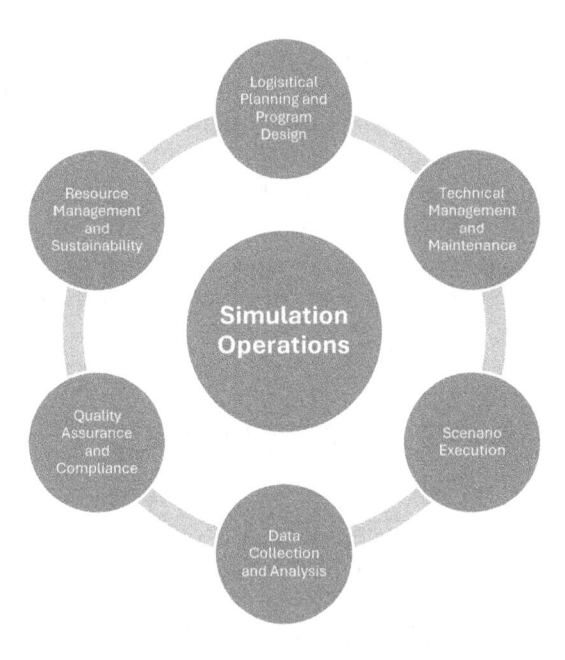

Figure 1 Key Components of Simulation Operations

1. <u>Logistical Planning and Program Design</u>
   The first step in simulation operations is the detailed planning and design of simulation programs. This involves:

   - *Scenario Development*: Collaborating with clinical educators and subject matter experts to create scenarios that replicate real-world medical situations. These scenarios must align with specific learning objectives, accreditation standards, and institutional goals.
   - *Resource Allocation*: Identifying and organizing the physical and digital resources required, such as simulation labs, high-fidelity mannequins, task trainers, virtual reality platforms, and consumables like syringes or medical dressings.
   - *Scheduling*: Coordinating with faculty, learners, and technical staff to develop schedules that optimize resource utilization and participant availability.
   - *Space Management*: Preparing and maintaining dedicated simulation spaces, including control rooms, debriefing areas, and multi-purpose labs, to accommodate different training needs.

2. <u>Technical Management and Maintenance</u>
   Simulation operators are responsible for ensuring that all technical aspects of the simulation environment function correctly. This includes:

- *Equipment Setup and Calibration*: Configuring mannequins, medical devices, and other hardware to reflect the clinical scenarios accurately. For example, mannequins might need programmed vital signs or preloaded clinical pathologies.
- *Software Integration*: Installing and updating software for virtual simulations, data tracking, and audiovisual recording systems. Virtual platforms often require custom configurations to simulate patient responses or clinical workflows.
- *Preventative Maintenance*: Regularly inspecting, repairing, and upgrading simulation equipment to prevent breakdowns and ensure longevity.
- *Troubleshooting*: Quickly diagnosing and resolving technical issues during live sessions, such as software glitches, hardware malfunctions, or connectivity problems.

3. Scenario Execution

   During simulation sessions, operators play a central role in executing scenarios by:

   - *Controlling Scenarios*: Using control room software to adjust mannequin responses, such as heart rates, breathing patterns, or verbal prompts, to reflect learner actions.
   - *Facilitating Realism*: Managing props, moulage (injury simulation makeup), and other enhancements to create immersive environments.
   - *Monitoring and Adjusting*: Observing learner interactions in real-time and modifying scenarios dynamically to challenge participants or accommodate unexpected actions.

4. Data Collection and Analysis

   Simulation operations also involve capturing and analyzing data to assess learner performance and improve program quality. Key tasks include:

   - *Recording and Documentation*: Operating audiovisual systems to record debriefing, reflection, and evaluation sessions.
   - *Performance Metrics*: Collecting data on key performance indicators (e.g., response times, decision-making accuracy) using simulation software.
   - *Feedback Delivery*: Preparing detailed reports and facilitating debriefing sessions where learners can reflect on their performance. This iterative feedback process enhances knowledge retention and skill development.

5. Quality Assurance and Compliance

   Simulation programs must meet industry standards and continuously improve to remain effective and relevant. Simulation operations include:

   - *Standards Alignment*: Ensuring compliance with guidelines from organizations such as the *Society for Simulation in Healthcare* (SSH) or the International Nursing Association for Clinical Simulation and Learning (INACSL).

- *Regular Audits*: Conducting internal and external evaluations to assess program effectiveness and identify areas for improvement.
- *Innovation and Adoption*: Staying abreast of technological advancements, such as integrating augmented reality (AR), virtual reality (VR), and artificial intelligence (AI) into training programs.

6. <u>Resource Management and Sustainability</u>

Simulation operations teams manage financial, physical, and human resources to ensure sustainable program delivery. Key considerations include:

- *Budgeting*: Allocating funds for equipment procurement, software licenses, maintenance, and staffing.
- *Human Resource Development*: Recruiting and training simulation operators, educators, and support staff to maintain high operational standards.
- *Sustainability Initiatives*: Implementing cost-effective practices, such as using reusable training supplies or shared simulation resources across departments.

Role of Simulation Operations in Enhancing Education

Operational excellence is crucial to the effectiveness of simulation-based education. By integrating technical expertise, logistical precision, and continuous improvement, simulation operations create an environment where learners can engage in realistic, stress-controlled, and reflective training experiences. Simulation centers also foster interprofessional collaboration, helping healthcare teams develop communication, decision-making, and technical skills in a safe setting.

Ultimately, simulation operations bridge the gap between innovative educational technologies and practical applications, ensuring that learners are well-prepared to meet the challenges of modern healthcare.

Core Functions of Simulation Operations

1. <u>Strategic Planning and Program Alignment</u>

Effective simulation operations begin with aligning educational programs with institutional goals. This involves identifying training needs, defining objectives, and establishing metrics to measure success. For example, a hospital-based simulation center may focus on improving staff response to sepsis alerts. At the same time, an academic nursing program may aim to prepare students for clinical placements through competency-based assessments.

- Strategic Planning and Program Alignment
- Scenario Design and Development
- Resource and Technology Management
- Session Logisitics and Scheduling
- Facilitation and Support
- Debrief Support and Data Management
- Administration and Reporting

Figure 2 Core Functions of Simulation Operations

2. <u>Scenario Design and Development</u>

Scenario creation is a collaborative effort involving subject matter experts (SMEs), educators, and simulation technicians. The process includes scripting clinical cases, defining expected learner actions, and integrating objectives such as skill mastery or critical thinking. Advanced scenarios often incorporate branching pathways, where learner decisions influence the course of the simulation, adding complexity and realism.

3. Resource and Technology Management
Simulation centers rely on various resources, including mannequins, task trainers, virtual reality platforms, and consumables like syringes and wound dressings. Maintaining these resources requires a robust inventory system and technical expertise. Regularly maintaining high-fidelity simulators and software updates is essential to ensure reliability and realism during sessions.

4. Session Logistics and Scheduling
Simulation sessions require careful coordination to accommodate learners, faculty, and facilitators while optimizing the use of facilities and equipment. Scheduling software is often employed to manage bookings, reduce conflicts, and ensure equitable program access.

5. Facilitation and Support
During simulation sessions, operations teams play a critical role in setting up scenarios, operating simulators, and assisting facilitators. This includes adjusting simulator settings in real-time to respond to learner actions, such as simulating a drop in blood pressure if a medication is administered incorrectly.

6. Debriefing Support and Data Management
Much of the learning occurs during debriefing. Simulation operations teams assist facilitators by ensuring audiovisual recordings and performance data are available for review. Learner feedback and performance metrics are then analyzed to guide improvements in individual skills and program effectiveness.

7. Administration and Reporting
Administration and reporting are integral to simulation operations, ensuring programs are well-coordinated, transparent, and aligned with institutional goals. Core responsibilities include:

- **Policy Development**: Establishing policies and procedures for simulation operations, including safety protocols, data management practices, and staff roles.
- **Documentation**: Maintaining detailed records of simulation activities, such as session schedules, attendance, equipment usage logs, and incident reports.
- **Compliance Reporting**: Submitting reports to accrediting bodies, institutional stakeholders, and external partners to demonstrate adherence to standards and highlight program achievements.
- **Performance Tracking**: Using data analytics to monitor program effectiveness, learner outcomes, and return on investment (ROI). These insights guide decision-making for future program improvements.
- **Stakeholder Communication**: Serving as a liaison between simulation centers, educators, administrators, and external partners, ensuring clear and consistent communication about goals, progress, and needs.
- **Grant and Funding Management**: Managing budgets, pursuing grants, and

reporting on fund utilization to sustain and expand simulation programs.

Challenges in Simulation Operations

While pivotal to healthcare education, simulation operations face various challenges that can impede their effectiveness and growth. Resource limitations are one of the most significant hurdles. Funding constraints often force simulation centers to prioritize certain aspects of their programs over others, such as choosing between acquiring new technology or maintaining existing equipment. Staffing shortages compound the issue, as skilled simulation technicians and educators are critical for ensuring that sessions run smoothly. The lack of sufficient space further complicates matters, with many institutions struggling to accommodate growing class sizes or expanding program offerings within limited physical facilities.

The rapid pace of technological advancements in healthcare simulation presents another pressing challenge. Staying abreast of innovations in virtual reality (VR), augmented reality (AR), artificial intelligence (AI), and high-fidelity simulation tools requires continual investment in both equipment and training. Simulation centers must procure cutting-edge technology and ensure that their staff is proficient. This dual demand often stretches budgets and resources to their limits. Furthermore, integrating new technologies into established workflows can be time-consuming, requiring updates to scenarios, recalibration of equipment, and adaptation by educators and learners alike.

Maintaining realism in simulations is a delicate balancing act. On the one hand, creating lifelike scenarios is essential for immersing learners in experiences that closely mimic real-world healthcare situations. On the other hand, the drive for authenticity must not compromise accessibility or safety. For example, advanced mannequins or VR systems can simulate complex clinical situations, but they might also intimidate novice learners or overwhelm those with limited technical skills. Simulation operators and educators must carefully tailor scenarios to match the learners' experience levels while providing meaningful challenges. This requires a nuanced understanding of pedagogy, technical capabilities, and learner needs.

Additionally, ensuring that simulations are inclusive and equitable poses its challenges. Learners come from diverse backgrounds, with varying prior experience, technical aptitude, and confidence. Simulation operations must accommodate these differences, designing scenarios and environments that are adaptable and accessible to all participants. For example, operators may need to adjust the difficulty of a simulation or provide additional guidance for learners who are less familiar with the technology.

Administrative demands also weigh heavily on simulation operations. Coordinating schedules, managing resources, and documenting activities require significant time and effort, often stretching administrative staff thin. Reporting to accrediting bodies, tracking learner outcomes, and justifying program costs to stakeholders add further complexity.

Despite these challenges, simulation operations remain a cornerstone of healthcare education. Simulation teams provide invaluable training opportunities by creatively addressing resource constraints, investing in professional development, and fostering adaptability in their programs. The commitment to overcoming these obstacles reflects simulation's critical role in preparing healthcare professionals to navigate the complexities of modern clinical practice.

The Role of Simulation Operations Specialists

Simulation operations specialists (SOSs) are professionals dedicated to simulation management's technical and logistical aspects. Their expertise spans a wide range of areas, including:

- <u>Technology Proficiency:</u> Expertise in using and maintaining simulators, audiovisual systems, and software platforms.
- <u>Educational Support</u>: Collaborating with faculty to develop and refine simulation scenarios.
- <u>Process Optimization</u>: Streamlining workflows to improve efficiency and reduce downtime between sessions.

The *Society for Simulation in Healthcare* (SSH) offers the Certified Healthcare Simulation Operations Specialists (CHSOS) certification, which recognizes the vital contributions of SOSs and sets standards for their training and professional development (SSH, 2020).

The importance of robust simulation operations cannot be overstated. Operations teams contribute to improving healthcare education by ensuring that simulations run efficiently and effectively. Their work supports the development of competent, confident healthcare professionals who are prepared to meet the challenges of real-world practice.

By embedding simulation operations into the strategic framework of healthcare education, institutions can create sustainable, impactful programs that drive learner success and patient safety.

1.5 Types of Medical and Nursing Simulations

Simulation methods in healthcare education encompass a range of tools and techniques, each tailored to meet specific learning objectives. These methods can be broadly categorized into four main types: mannequin-based simulations, task trainers, standardized patients, and virtual/augmented reality platforms. Together, they create diverse opportunities for learners to develop technical skills, decision-making abilities, and interpersonal competencies.

Mannequin-Based Simulations

High-fidelity mannequins are central to many simulation programs, providing realistic models that replicate physiological functions such as breathing, heart sounds, and pupil reactions. These advanced simulators, like Laerdal's SimMan and Gaumard's HAL, enable learners to practice life-saving procedures, including intubation, defibrillation, and trauma management. Scenarios involving these mannequins are particularly effective for training in high-stakes situations, such as cardiac arrests or obstetric emergencies (Lindeman, 2021).

One key advantage of mannequin-based simulations is their capacity to provide real-time feedback. Learners can observe the physiological effects of their interventions, such as changes in blood pressure or oxygen saturation, reinforcing the connection between their actions and patient outcomes.

Task Trainers

Task trainers are low-fidelity simulation tools designed for learners to practice specific technical skills repeatedly in a focused manner. Examples include arm models for intravenous (IV) insertion, laparoscopic trainers for surgical techniques, and suture boards for stitching practice. These tools are particularly valuable in early skill acquisition, as they allow learners to master the mechanics of a procedure before progressing to more complex, integrated scenarios (Bradley, 2006).

Task trainers are cost-effective and highly portable, making them accessible in various settings. Their simplicity does not detract from their effectiveness; research shows that repeated practice with task trainers enhances muscle memory and procedural confidence (Advances in Simulation, 2023).

Standardized Patients

Standardized Patients (SPs) are a critical component of healthcare simulation, providing an interactive and human-centered approach to training. SPs are individuals trained to portray specific medical conditions, behaviors, or emotional states consistently and realistically, enabling learners to practice essential clinical and communication skills in a safe and controlled environment. This method is widely used by medical, nursing, and allied health students to develop a holistic understanding of patient care.

Enhancing Communication and Empathy
One of SPs' primary benefits is their ability to simulate the complexities of patient-provider interactions. Learners practice conducting thorough patient histories, performing physical examinations, and delivering diagnoses or treatment plans. SPs are particularly effective for developing empathy and cultural competence by simulating diverse patient backgrounds, preferences, and values. For example, scenarios involving end-of-life discussions, sensitive diagnoses, or cross-cultural care allow learners to explore the psychosocial dimensions of patient interactions.

AI-enhanced tools, such as SimConverse, now complement traditional SP methods by simulating realistic conversations and providing immediate feedback on tone, phrasing, and non-verbal communication. This integration expands the potential for standardized, reproducible training in areas where live SPs may be unavailable or cost-prohibitive.

Objective Structured Clinical Examinations (OSCEs)
SPs play a pivotal role in Objective Structured Clinical Examinations (OSCEs), where learners are evaluated on their clinical skills in a series of timed, standardized scenarios. In these settings, SPs are often trained to provide structured feedback, both verbal and written, on the learner's performance. This approach is particularly effective for assessing competencies in communication, professionalism, and clinical reasoning, which are challenging to evaluate using traditional written tests.

Developing Diagnostic and Critical Thinking Skills
Through SP encounters, learners gain exposure to various medical conditions, some of which may be rare in real clinical settings. These scenarios challenge trainees to synthesize information, refine diagnostic skills, and prioritize interventions under realistic conditions. Additionally, SPs allow for iterative learning; the controlled environment enables learners to receive feedback, reflect on their performance, and improve through repeated practice.

Psychosocial and Ethical Training
Standardized patients excel in preparing learners for healthcare's human and ethical challenges. Scenarios involving delivering bad news, handling family dynamics, or addressing mental health concerns provide opportunities to navigate sensitive situations with compassion and professionalism. For example, SPs may simulate a grieving family member during a critical care scenario, helping learners manage emotional conversations while maintaining clinical focus.

Limitations of Standardized Patients
Despite their many advantages, SPs come with certain limitations. Training and employing SPs can be resource-intensive, requiring careful recruitment, scenario development, and ongoing training to ensure learner consistency. Additionally, SPs cannot fully replicate certain physiological conditions or responses, such as changes in vital signs, which might require integration with other simulation modalities like mannequins or task trainers.

Integration with Other Modalities
Combining SPs with other simulation techniques enhances the learning experience. For example, a scenario involving an SP portraying a patient in distress might incorporate a high-fidelity mannequin to simulate physiological deterioration. This hybrid approach gives learners a more comprehensive understanding of care's clinical, technical, and interpersonal aspects.

By offering a human element to simulation, SPs remain a cornerstone of healthcare education, bridging the gap between technical expertise and the interpersonal skills necessary for effective and compassionate care.

Virtual and Augmented Reality

Virtual reality (VR) and augmented reality (AR) have introduced immersive, interactive environments into simulation-based education. VR platforms like SimX and Body Interact allow learners to navigate complex clinical scenarios, ranging from emergency room trauma cases to surgical procedures. AR applications overlay digital information onto the physical world, providing real-time guidance during anatomy exploration or ultrasound interpretation (Lindeman, 2021; HealthySimulation, 2023).

One of VR and AR's greatest strengths is their scalability. These tools can replicate rare and high-risk scenarios, ensuring learners gain exposure to conditions they might not encounter frequently in clinical practice. Additionally, VR systems' adaptive capabilities allow for personalized learning experiences, enabling learners to progress at their own pace.

Despite their many benefits, VR and AR technologies also present limitations that educators must consider:

> High Cost of Implementation: Developing and maintaining VR/AR platforms requires significant financial investments, particularly for high-fidelity systems. The cost of hardware, software licenses, and ongoing updates can strain budgets, especially for smaller institutions or programs in resource-limited settings (Advances in Simulation, 2023).
>
> Technical Challenges: Effective use of VR and AR often depends on reliable technology infrastructure, including high-speed internet and compatible hardware. Technical glitches or system failures can disrupt training sessions, reducing effectiveness and learner engagement (Lindeman, 2021).
>
> Limited Haptic Feedback: While VR offers visual and auditory realism, it often lacks the tactile feedback necessary for mastering procedures requiring fine motor skills. Although some AR systems incorporate haptic devices, these are typically expensive and not universally available (HealthySimulation, 2023).
>
> Accessibility and Equity Issues: The high cost and technological requirements of VR/AR tools can create disparities in access, potentially excluding learners from underserved regions or institutions with limited resources. This raises concerns about equity in healthcare education (Bradley, 2006).
>
> Steep Learning Curve: Learners and educators may require significant training to use VR and AR systems effectively. Time spent mastering the technology could detract from actual skill development, particularly during early adoption phases (Advances in Simulation, 2023).
>
> Potential for Simulator Sickness: Prolonged use of VR systems can cause simulator sickness, with symptoms such as dizziness, nausea, and visual discomfort. This side effect can reduce learner participation and limit the duration of effective training sessions (HealthySimulation, 2023).

While these limitations do not negate the value of VR and AR in healthcare simulation, they highlight the importance of careful planning and implementation. Combining VR and AR with other simulation modalities can help educators balance their strengths and weaknesses, ensuring effective and equitable training experiences.

Integration and Hybrid Approaches

While these categories are distinct, many simulation programs integrate multiple methods to create comprehensive learning experiences. For instance, a cardiac arrest scenario might combine a high-fidelity mannequin for procedural practice, standardized patients to simulate distressed family members, and VR tools for post-scenario debriefing. Such hybrid approaches capitalize on the strengths of each method, offering learners a holistic view of patient care.

1.6 The Role of Simulation in Nursing Education

Simulation has become a cornerstone of nursing education, addressing many challenges modern healthcare training programs face. With clinical placements becoming increasingly scarce—affecting as many as 50% of nursing programs in the United States, according to the *American Association of Colleges of Nursing* (AACN, 2022)—simulation provides an essential alternative for skill development.

The complexity of patient care is also on the rise, with chronic conditions now affecting 60% of the adult population worldwide (WHO, 2023), requiring nurses to master advanced technical and decision-making skills. Simulation enables students to practice and refine technical and non-technical skills, such as teamwork and communication, in a controlled, reproducible environment, ensuring competency without risking patients (Hayden et al., 2014). Research supports this approach, with studies showing that replacing up to 50% of traditional clinical hours with simulation leads to equivalent or better learning outcomes in nursing education (Hayden et al., 2014). As of 2022, 23 nursing regulatory bodies in the United States permit substituting up to 50% of traditional clinical hours with simulation in prelicensure nursing programs (Journal of Nursing Regulation, 2022).

> As of 2022, **23** nursing regulatory bodies in the United States permit substituting up to 50% of traditional clinical hours with simulation in prelicensure nursing programs.

This represents a significant increase from 2014 when only one state allowed such substitution. The change reflects growing evidence supporting simulation's effectiveness in nursing education (Hayden et al., 2014). However, regulations vary widely across states. For instance, Colorado permits up to 50% replacement if the nursing program is accredited but only 25% if it is not (HealthySimulation, 2023). These variations highlight the importance of nursing programs consulting their state boards to ensure compliance with local policies.

Replacing Traditional Clinical Hours

Nursing education has increasingly relied on simulation to supplement and sometimes replace traditional clinical hours. Research by Hayden et al. (2014) demonstrated that high-quality simulation experiences could substitute up to 50% of traditional clinical training without compromising learning outcomes. This finding has been significant as clinical placement opportunities become more constrained due to growing student cohorts and limited availability of hospital spaces.

Simulation provides consistent exposure to clinical scenarios, ensuring all students encounter comparable learning opportunities. Unlike traditional clinical rotations, where experiences depend heavily on patient availability and case variety, simulation ensures comprehensive and equitable training for all learners (Lindeman, 2021).

Addressing Core Nursing Competencies

Simulation has become a cornerstone of nursing education, addressing key challenges modern healthcare training programs face. The increasing scarcity of clinical placements—reported as a significant barrier by nearly 50% of nursing programs in the U.S. (AACN, 2022)—has led to simulation becoming an essential alternative for meeting educational needs. Additionally, the complexity of patient care continues to rise, with chronic conditions affecting approximately 60% of adults globally (WHO, 2023). Simulation allows nursing students to develop and refine technical and non-technical skills in a safe, controlled, and reproducible environment.

The integration of simulation aligns closely with the *American Association of Colleges of Nursing* (AACN) Essentials Core Competencies, emphasizing competency-based education for nursing graduates. For instance, simulation supports the development of clinical judgment, a critical element of the "Scholarship for Nursing Practice" domain (AACN, 2021). It also strengthens interprofessional collaboration skills outlined in the "Interprofessional Partnerships" domain by enabling learners to engage in team-based scenarios that mimic real healthcare settings. Furthermore, simulation facilitates ethical decision-making and cultural humility as students encounter diverse patient cases in controlled settings, addressing competencies within the "Personal, Professional, and Leadership Development" domain (AACN, 2021).

Research confirms simulation's effectiveness, with studies demonstrating that replacing up to 50% of traditional clinical hours with simulation results in equivalent or superior learning outcomes in nursing education (Hayden et al., 2014).

Decision-Making and Critical Thinking

Simulated scenarios often mimic the complexities of real-world clinical settings, requiring students to assess situations, make decisions, and execute interventions under time pressure. Scenarios can be designed to reflect the dynamic nature of healthcare, presenting learners with evolving conditions and unexpected challenges. This fosters critical thinking, decision-making, and adaptability, essential skills for effective nursing practice (Advances in Simulation, 2023).

Interprofessional Collaboration

Simulation also promotes interdisciplinary learning by integrating nursing students with peers from other healthcare disciplines, such as medicine, pharmacy, and respiratory therapy. Collaborative scenarios, such as trauma resuscitations or patient handovers, help nursing students understand their roles within a team, enhance communication, and improve teamwork skills. These experiences align with real-world healthcare practices, where interprofessional collaboration is crucial for patient safety and outcomes (TeamSTEPPS, 2024).

Psychosocial and Cultural Competence

Simulation supports training in the psychosocial aspects of nursing care, including communication with patients from diverse cultural and linguistic backgrounds, delivering bad news, and managing family dynamics. Scenarios involving standardized patients or virtual simulations allow nursing students to practice empathy, cultural sensitivity, and patient advocacy. These skills are increasingly critical in addressing healthcare disparities and promoting equitable care (HealthySimulation, 2023).

Supporting Transition to Practice

Simulation has become a cornerstone of nursing education, effectively bridging the gap between academic preparation and real-world practice. Transition-to-practice programs, including simulation-based "boot camps," have been instrumental in preparing nursing graduates for professional roles.

As of 2022, approximately 20.7% of registered nurses in the United States participated in residency or transition-to-practice programs, with 93.3% being assigned a preceptor during their training (HRSA, 2022). Among nurses who obtained their initial nursing degrees between 2016 and 2020, 46.4% reported participating in such programs, reflecting a growing emphasis on structured transition experiences for new graduates (HRSA, 2022). This upward trend underscores the healthcare sector's recognition of the value of these programs in enhancing clinical competence, improving confidence, and reducing turnover among newly licensed nurses (HRSA, 2022).

These programs have demonstrated value in high-intensity specialties like critical care or emergency nursing by providing realistic, high-fidelity scenarios that replicate the demands of clinical practice. Studies report that simulation boot camps significantly improve new nurses' confidence, clinical decision-making, and readiness for the fast-paced healthcare environment (Lindeman, 2021; LWW, 2021). The growing prevalence of such programs highlights their effectiveness in facilitating smoother transitions for nursing graduates into the workforce.

1.7 The 12 Pillars of Success for Simulation Operations

The pillars of success for simulation operations provide a foundation for effective planning, execution, and continuous improvement in simulation-based activities. These pillars ensure that simulation programs achieve their goals, maximize impact, and deliver value to stakeholders. Below are the key pillars of success for simulation operations:

1. Clear Objectives and Goals

- **What It Is**: Defining specific, measurable, achievable, relevant, and time-bound (SMART) objectives for simulation activities.
- **Why It Matters**: Clear goals guide the design, execution, and evaluation of simulations, ensuring alignment with organizational priorities.
- **Key Practices**:
    - Align objectives with institutional goals, such as improving patient safety, optimizing workflows, or enhancing learner outcomes.

o Regularly review and update goals to reflect evolving needs.

2. Effective Scenario Design

- **What It Is**: Developing realistic, evidence-based scenarios tailored to the intended audience and objectives.
- **Why It Matters**: Well-designed scenarios improve engagement, relevance, and learning outcomes.
- **Key Practices**:
  o Use subject matter experts (SMEs) input to ensure accuracy and realism.
  o Include variability to address common, rare, and worst-case scenarios.
  o Integrate cultural and contextual factors to enhance applicability.

3. Skilled Facilitation and Leadership

- **What It Is**: Using trained facilitators and leaders to guide simulation activities effectively.
- **Why It Matters**: Skilled facilitators create a psychologically safe environment, promote engagement, and drive reflective learning.
- **Key Practices**:
  o Provide training and certification for facilitators, such as Certified Healthcare Simulation Educator (CHSE).
  o Foster a culture of continuous professional development for simulation leaders.

4. Advanced Technology and Tools

- **What It Is**: Leveraging high-quality simulation equipment, software, and environments to replicate real-world conditions.
- **Why It Matters**: Advanced tools enhance realism, engagement, and the ability to simulate complex scenarios.
- **Key Practices**:
  o Regularly update technology to meet industry standards and organizational needs.
  o Use simulation modalities appropriate to the objectives, such as high-fidelity manikins, virtual reality (VR), or augmented reality (AR).

5. Robust Feedback and Debriefing Processes

- **What It Is**: Conducting structured debriefing sessions to reflect on performance, extract insights, and drive improvement.

- **Why It Matters**: Effective debriefing transforms simulation experiences into actionable learning.
- **Key Practices**:
  - Use structured models like PEARLS, Plus-Delta, or Advocacy-Inquiry to guide discussions.
  - Incorporate bi-directional feedback loops to ensure insights from participants and stakeholders are captured and applied.

6. Stakeholder Engagement

- **What It Is**: Actively involving all relevant stakeholders in the design, execution, and evaluation of simulations.
- **Why It Matters**: Engagement fosters collaboration, relevance, and support for simulation initiatives.
- **Key Practices**:
  - Include input from learners, facilitators, administrators, and industry partners.
  - Maintain open communication channels to ensure alignment and transparency.

7. Comprehensive Evaluation and Metrics

- **What It Is**: Measuring the effectiveness of simulation activities using data-driven approaches.
- **Why It Matters**: Evaluation ensures continuous improvement and demonstrates the value of simulation programs.
- **Key Practices**:
  - Use metrics like participant satisfaction, skill improvement, and system-level outcomes.
  - Conduct after-action reviews to identify strengths, weaknesses, and opportunities for refinement.

8. Resource Optimization

- **What It Is**: Efficiently managing time, budget, personnel, and equipment to support simulation operations.
- **Why It Matters**: Optimized resources ensure the sustainability and scalability of simulation programs.
- **Key Practices**:
  - Regularly assess resource allocation to identify gaps or inefficiencies.

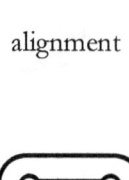

o Prioritize investments in areas with the highest impact on objectives.

9. Collaboration and Interdisciplinary Focus

- **What It Is**: Promoting teamwork across disciplines to reflect the complexity of real-world environments.
- **Why It Matters**: Interdisciplinary simulations prepare participants for collaborative practice in diverse fields.
- **Key Practices**:
    o Design team-based scenarios that mimic interdisciplinary workflows.
    o Foster collaboration between departments, such as nursing, medicine, IT, and administration.

10. Continuous Improvement and Innovation

- **What It Is**: Adopting a mindset of ongoing learning and adaptation to refine simulation practices.
- **Why It Matters**: Staying current with emerging trends and best practices ensures long-term relevance and effectiveness.
- **Key Practices**:
    o Incorporate lessons learned from evaluations and stakeholder feedback.
    o Explore new technologies, methodologies, and accreditation standards to enhance operations.

11. Alignment with Accreditation Standards

- **What It Is**: Following professional guidelines, such as those from SSH and INACSL, to ensure quality and accountability.
- **Why It Matters**: Accreditation aligns simulation operations with recognized best practices, boosting credibility and outcomes.
- **Key Practices**:
    o Regularly review and implement standards from accrediting bodies.
    o Use accreditation as a framework for continuous improvement.

12. Psychological Safety

- **What It Is**: Creating an environment where participants feel safe to make mistakes, ask questions, and provide honest feedback.
- **Why It Matters**: Psychological safety fosters learning, confidence, and collaboration during simulations.
- **Key Practices**:
    o Set clear expectations for a nonjudgmental and supportive environment.

o   Address participant concerns and anxieties proactively.

By building simulation operations around these pillars, organizations can ensure that their programs are effective, engaging, and aligned with strategic objectives. These principles enhance learning outcomes and contribute to organizational success in achieving system improvements, teamwork, and innovation.

1.8 The Future of Simulation in Healthcare

As technology continues to evolve, the scope and impact of simulation in healthcare are expected to expand. Emerging trends include the integration of artificial intelligence (AI) to create adaptive simulations, increased use of virtual and augmented reality, and remote simulation for distance learning. These advancements promise to make simulation more accessible, personalized, and effective (Lateef, 2010).

Moreover, as healthcare systems face mounting pressures from workforce shortages and aging populations, simulation will play an increasingly vital role in training competent, confident professionals capable of delivering high-quality care in diverse settings.

1.9 Summary

Simulation has revolutionized healthcare education by providing a safe, controlled, and immersive environment where learners can develop critical skills and competencies. Chapter 1 explores the evolution of medical and nursing simulation operations, tracing their journey from basic anatomical models to sophisticated technologies like virtual reality (VR), augmented reality (AR), and artificial intelligence (AI). Simulation has evolved into a cornerstone of healthcare education, addressing the growing complexity of patient care and the increasing demand for high-quality training in limited clinical environments.

Simulation addresses challenges such as constrained clinical placements, increasing patient complexity, and a growing need for interdisciplinary collaboration. Simulation ensures comprehensive and equitable training opportunities by enabling learners to engage with high-risk, rare, or complex scenarios that might not occur during clinical rotations. For example, research shows that replacing up to 50% of clinical hours with simulation leads to equivalent or superior learning outcomes, highlighting its effectiveness as a teaching tool (Hayden et al., 2014).

Key pioneers like Dr. Michael Gordon, who developed the Harvey cardiology simulator, and Dr. David Gaba, who introduced Crisis Resource Management (CRM) principles from aviation into healthcare, have significantly influenced simulation's trajectory. These early innovators recognized simulation's potential to improve technical skills and non-technical competencies, such as communication, teamwork, and decision-making—critical for patient safety and outcomes.

Today, simulation transcends technical training by fostering critical thinking, leadership, and collaboration. Interdisciplinary simulations mirror real-world healthcare challenges, preparing learners for team-based patient care. Tools like SimConverse and TeamSTEPPS enhance communication training, while high-fidelity simulations improve team efficiency and reduce errors by 25% to 30% (Weaver et al., 2010).

Technological advancements have propelled simulation into new realms of interactivity and accessibility. AI-powered platforms and VR/AR systems create adaptive, highly realistic learning experiences that respond to learner needs in real-time. These technologies have made simulation more immersive and scalable, enabling global access to quality training—even in resource-limited settings (Advances in Simulation, 2023).

Simulation operations are integral to the successful implementation of these educational tools. From logistical planning and scenario execution to technology management and data analysis, operations specialists ensure that simulation programs are efficient, effective, and aligned with institutional goals. Compliance with standards from the Society for Simulation in Healthcare (SSH) and the International Nursing Association for Clinical Simulation and Learning (INACSL) underscores the importance of maintaining quality and accountability in simulation practices.

As the healthcare landscape evolves, simulation remains vital to modern education. It bridges gaps in traditional training and prepares learners for the complexities of clinical practice. Integrating emerging technologies and innovative educational strategies ensures that simulation will continue to advance, shaping the future of healthcare by fostering competent, confident professionals and improving patient outcomes.

1.10 Chapter Review

Review Questions

1. **Evolution and History**
   a. Describe how simulation has evolved in healthcare education from its early origins to the modern era.
   b. Identify key milestones in the development of high-fidelity simulation tools.
2. **Pioneers and Theories**
   a. Who was Dr. Michael Gordon, and what was his contribution to healthcare simulation?
   b. Explain how the aviation industry's CRM influenced healthcare simulation practices.
3. **Applications and Benefits**
   a. What are the primary advantages of using simulation in healthcare training over traditional methods?
   b. Discuss how simulation improves technical and non-technical skills.
4. **Simulation Operations**
   a. List and describe the core functions of simulation operations.
   b. What role do simulation operators play in ensuring successful training sessions?
5. **Challenges and Future Trends**
   a. What are the key challenges simulation programs face in healthcare education today?

    b. Predict how emerging technologies like AI and VR will shape the future of simulation.

Critical Thinking and Application

1. **Scenario Design**
   Imagine you are tasked with designing a simulation scenario for a nursing student learning to manage a cardiac arrest. What key elements would you include to ensure the scenario is realistic and educational?
2. **Interdisciplinary Collaboration**
   Reflect on a time when teamwork played a critical role in solving a problem. How could simulation scenarios be used to enhance team-based decision-making in healthcare?
3. **Addressing Challenges**
   Propose solutions to overcome financial and technological barriers to implementing simulation in resource-limited settings.

Hands-On Activity

- **Simulation Observation Exercise**
  Attend or review a recorded simulation session. Take notes on the scenario's design, learner engagement, and debriefing process. Identify areas for improvement based on the concepts covered in Chapter 1.

Summary Reflection

Reflect on how simulation has transformed healthcare education. Consider its impact on patient safety, learner confidence, and interdisciplinary collaboration. How do you envision its role in shaping the future of healthcare practice?

Chapter 2

Shaping Healthcare Competencies through Simulation

The integration of simulation into healthcare education has transformed how clinical competencies are developed among medical and nursing professionals. Simulation offers a unique opportunity to bridge the gap between theory and practice, creating safe yet realistic environments for learners to build critical skills. It is vital to understand its transformative role to examine the core principles of healthcare simulation, the operational strategies that support it, and the ethical frameworks ensuring its effectiveness. This chapter delves into these aspects, focusing on how simulation shapes healthcare competencies and prepares professionals for real-world challenges.

2.1 Simulations Operations and Their Role in Simulation

Effective simulation operations management underpins the success of simulation-based education. Simulation operations encompass supply chain management, workflow optimization, staffing, and patient safety—all critical for ensuring that simulation environments function seamlessly. These operations ensure that high-fidelity mannequins, task trainers, virtual simulation platforms, and standardized patients are available when needed and properly maintained.

Simulation centers rely on robust operations to manage resources, schedule sessions, and provide learners with a structured and effective educational experience. For example, streamlined processes for scheduling simulations and ensuring equipment functionality are essential for avoiding disruptions in training programs. Moreover, well-trained faculty and supportive infrastructure enhance the learning experience by enabling high-quality simulation guidance and feedback.

2.2 Key Performance Metrics for Simulation Effectiveness

Measuring the effectiveness of simulation-based education is critical for ensuring its impact on learner performance, patient outcomes, and operational efficiency. Below is a detailed exploration of the key performance metrics used to evaluate healthcare simulation programs, supported by statistics and evidence from academic research.

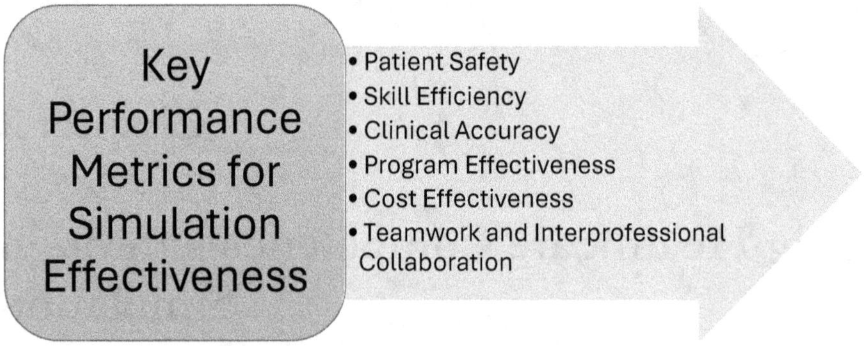

Key Performance Metrics for Simulation Effectiveness

- Patient Safety
- Skill Efficiency
- Clinical Accuracy
- Program Effectiveness
- Cost Effectiveness
- Teamwork and Interprofessional Collaboration

Figure 3 Key Performance Metrics for Simulation Effectiveness

Patient Safety

Patient safety is the cornerstone of healthcare training, and simulation allows the refining of critical skills in a controlled environment where errors do not result in harm. Metrics related to patient safety assess how well learners can:

- Perform high-risk procedures, such as intubation or defibrillation, without errors.
- Recognize and manage clinical emergencies, such as sepsis or cardiac arrest.
- Follow protocols designed to prevent harm, such as infection control practices.

For example, studies have shown that simulation training in cardiopulmonary resuscitation (CPR) improves adherence to compression depth and rate guidelines by up to 22% compared to traditional methods (Anderson et al., 2019). Similarly, a meta-analysis revealed that healthcare professionals trained in patient safety-focused simulations reduced medical errors by 37% in clinical practice (Weaver et al., 2010).

High-fidelity simulation scenarios also improve performance in high-stakes situations. For instance, a simulated cardiac arrest may involve adhering to Advanced Cardiovascular Life Support (ACLS) guidelines, and learners often demonstrate a 25-30% improvement in protocol compliance after repeated practice (American Heart Association, 2020).

Skill Proficiency

Skill proficiency metrics evaluate a learner's ability to perform technical tasks required for safe and effective patient care. Proficiency is assessed through:

- <u>Repetition:</u> Repeated practice of procedures such as suturing, catheterization, or laparoscopic surgery.
- <u>Precision:</u> How accurately learners execute procedures, such as maintaining sterile technique during central line insertion.

- Speed and Efficiency: The time it takes to complete a task without compromising quality.

A randomized controlled trial found that learners practicing intravenous (IV) line placement through simulation demonstrated an 18% higher success rate in their first attempt on patients than those trained traditionally (Krogh et al., 2015). Similarly, surgical residents trained using task trainers achieved 35% faster completion times for laparoscopic procedures while maintaining accuracy (Gurusamy et al., 2014).

These improvements directly impact clinical safety, as proficiency reduces complications and improves patient trust in providers.

Clinical Accuracy

Clinical accuracy measures a learner's ability to assess, diagnose, and treat patients correctly based on clinical data. This metric evaluates:

- Diagnostic Accuracy: Correct interpretation of symptoms, vital signs, and diagnostic tests.
- Decision-Making: Timeliness and appropriateness of treatment plans.
- Adherence to Guidelines: Following evidence-based protocols during patient management.

For example, a high-fidelity simulation might involve diagnosing and treating a simulated stroke patient. Research indicates that learners exposed to stroke management simulations were 28% more likely to recognize symptoms and initiate time-sensitive treatments, such as thrombolysis, than those who only received classroom instruction (Liyanagunawardena et al., 2017).

A study on emergency department training showed that simulation improved diagnostic accuracy in trauma scenarios by 32%, reducing the time to correct diagnoses by several minutes—critical in life-threatening conditions (Rosen et al., 2012).

Educational Program Effectiveness

Simulation programs are not just about individual skills—they must also be evaluated for their effectiveness as teaching tools. Metrics include:

- Learner Satisfaction and Engagement
  Engaged learners are more likely to retain information and build confidence. A survey of nursing students reported that 87% found simulation more engaging and beneficial for skill acquisition than traditional clinical placements (Hayden et al., 2014).
- Competency Mastery
  Competency assessments often show that learners who engage in simulations reach predefined skill benchmarks faster. For example, a study of medical residents found that simulation training reduced the time to competency in performing lumbar punctures by 40% compared to on-the-job training (Barsuk et al., 2010).

- Behavioral Changes
Beyond technical skills, simulations foster behaviors that improve patient care. A study focusing on interprofessional communication training through simulation found a 27% improvement in teamwork and collaboration in real clinical environments (Weaver et al., 2010).
- Learning Outcomes
Pre- and post-simulation assessments consistently show significant gains. For example, a study assessing pre- and post-simulation knowledge of sepsis management found an 18% improvement in knowledge retention scores after a single simulation session (Pottle, 2019).

Cost-Effectiveness

Simulation-based education requires substantial investment in technology, equipment, infrastructure, and faculty training. However, its long-term benefits often justify these costs by improving patient outcomes, reducing medical errors, and optimizing resource use. Below is a detailed exploration of how simulation enhances cost-effectiveness in healthcare education.

Return on Investment (ROI)
Simulation programs generate a high return on investment by reducing the financial burden of medical errors and adverse events. For instance, central line-associated bloodstream infections (CLABSIs) are a costly and preventable complication. Hospitals that implemented simulation-based central line insertion training reported a 45% reduction in CLABSIs, translating into annual savings of approximately $2 million per facility (Lindeman, 2021).

Similarly, simulation training for surgical residents has been shown to reduce the incidence of complications such as surgical site infections, which can cost hospitals thousands of dollars per patient. By preventing errors through practice in a risk-free environment, simulation reduces the hidden costs associated with litigation, prolonged hospital stays, and patient dissatisfaction.

Beyond direct savings, simulation contributes to financial stability by fostering confidence and competence in healthcare providers, which can improve institutional reputation and patient retention. For example, healthcare organizations with robust simulation programs are often seen as leaders in quality care, attracting more patients and skilled professionals.

Resource Utilization
Another key advantage of simulation is another key advantage of resources. Virtual simulation programs offer significant cost savings by reducing the need for physical infrastructure and equipment while accommodating larger numbers of learners. For instance, virtual reality (VR) platforms can host 20% more learners per session than traditional in-person simulations, reducing the costs of maintaining physical simulation centers (Lapkin et al., 2010).

Moreover, proper scheduling and maintenance of simulation facilities can minimize downtime and optimize resource use. Simulation centers that adopt efficient scheduling systems ensure that mannequins, task trainers, and other equipment are utilized to their full potential. This maximizes learner throughput and reduces operational waste.

For example, by combining virtual simulations with mannequin-based training, a nursing school can expand its student intake without requiring additional lab space, resulting in lower per-student training costs. These efficiencies make simulation programs a scalable solution for institutions looking to grow their capacity without proportional increases in overhead expenses.

Reduced Training Time
Simulation significantly accelerates the acquisition of clinical skills, reducing the overall time required for training. This efficiency translates into cost savings by shortening the duration of educational programs and reducing reliance on expensive clinical placements.

A study on neonatal resuscitation training found that learners achieved competency 50% faster with simulation than with traditional apprenticeship models (Niles et al., 2017). Faster skill acquisition not only lowers the cost of training but also enables learners to enter the workforce more quickly, addressing shortages in critical healthcare roles.

Furthermore, faster mastery of skills reduces the need for repeat training or remediation, which can be costly in time and resources. For example, surgical residents trained in laparoscopic procedures using VR simulations required 30% fewer attempts to reach proficiency than those trained with traditional methods (Gurusamy et al., 2014). This efficiency minimizes faculty time and the wear-and-tear on physical equipment, further reducing costs.

Reduction in Faculty Time and Workload
Simulation programs can also alleviate clinical educators' workloads by allowing learners to practice independently or in small groups. For example, virtual simulations and self-directed modules enable learners to develop foundational skills without constant instructor supervision. Faculty time is reserved for higher-level interventions, such as debriefing and advanced skill evaluations, optimizing their contribution to the training process.

Some institutions have reported that adopting blended simulation models—combining virtual platforms, task trainers, and in-person sessions—has reduced faculty teaching hours by 15-20% without compromising learner outcomes. These efficiencies free up faculty for research, curriculum development, or patient care duties, further enhancing institutional productivity.

Preventative Savings in Patient Care
The financial impact of simulation extends beyond the educational setting into patient care. By producing highly competent healthcare providers, simulation helps prevent costly errors in clinical practice. For example:

- A simulation program focusing on medication administration reduced dosing errors by 38%, saving hospitals significant costs associated with adverse drug events (Hayden et al., 2014).
- Team-based simulation training improved communication during emergencies,

reducing response times and improving outcomes for critically ill patients. This translates to shorter hospital stays and lower healthcare costs (Weaver et al., 2010).

Additionally, high-quality simulation training reduces staff turnover by increasing job satisfaction and confidence, key drivers of workforce retention. Lower turnover rates reduce the expenses of recruiting and onboarding new employees, further contributing to cost-effectiveness.

Futureproofing through Technology
Investing in simulation prepares institutions to adapt to future challenges in healthcare education. For example, the COVID-19 pandemic highlighted the importance of scalable and remote learning solutions. Simulation programs incorporating virtual and augmented reality technologies were better equipped to continue training during lockdowns, avoiding costly disruptions.

Integrating artificial intelligence (AI) into simulation can save even more cost. AI-driven platforms can provide real-time feedback, track learner progress, and adapt scenarios to individual needs, reducing the need for human facilitators in some settings.

Teamwork and Interprofessional Collaboration

Simulation often involves team-based scenarios designed to improve collaboration and communication among healthcare professionals. Metrics include:

- **Team Dynamics:**
  Simulation enhances team efficiency and role clarity. For example, in trauma team training simulations, structured debriefing improved team performance by 30%, with fewer errors in real clinical settings (Salas et al., 2008).

- **Interprofessional Skills:**
  Interprofessional simulations focusing on communication and collaboration showed a 40% improvement in learners' ability to work effectively across disciplines (Reeves et al., 2013). Such training fosters a culture of teamwork essential for patient-centered care.

Simulation programs can refine their approaches by systematically evaluating these metrics to ensure they deliver high-value education. These evaluations improve learner performance and enhance patient safety and care quality, underscoring the critical role of simulation in modern healthcare education.

2.3 Simulation Modalities in Healthcare Education

Healthcare simulation employs various modalities to achieve diverse educational goals, from technical skill acquisition to enhancing critical thinking and communication. Each modality offers unique strengths and is often used in combination to provide a well-rounded learning experience tailored to specific objectives. Below, we explore the key modalities in greater detail, highlighting their applications, benefits, and contributions to healthcare education.

Mannequin-Based Simulations

Mannequin-based simulations are among the most commonly used tools in healthcare education, particularly for high-fidelity simulations. These advanced mannequins are designed to mimic human physiology and responses to medical interventions, providing learners with realistic training scenarios. Mannequins such as Laerdal's *SimMan* or *Resusci Anne* can simulate various conditions, including changes in vital signs, respiratory distress, cardiac arrest, and more.

For example, a mannequin may be programmed to simulate an acute myocardial infarction, allowing learners to practice interpreting clinical signs like an irregular ECG, administering appropriate medications, and performing cardiopulmonary resuscitation (CPR) or defibrillation. These scenarios help students refine their technical skills and improve their decision-making and teamwork under pressure.

Mannequin-based simulations are particularly valuable for practicing rare or high-risk scenarios that learners may not frequently encounter in clinical settings. Research shows that exposure to these simulations significantly improves procedural competence and confidence. For instance, a study found that medical residents who trained with high-fidelity mannequins performed 25% better in managing acute trauma cases compared to those who underwent traditional instruction (Bradley, 2006).

Task Trainers

Task trainers focus on building proficiency in specific technical skills by allowing learners to practice repetitive tasks in a controlled environment. These low-fidelity models are designed to replicate specific anatomical features or procedural contexts, making them ideal for skill acquisition and refinement.
Common examples include:

- **IV Insertion Models:** Replicating veins for learners to practice starting intravenous lines.
- **Suturing Models:** Providing skin-like surfaces for practicing incision closure techniques.
- **Pelvic Examination Trainers:** Allowing learners to gain competency in gynecological procedures.

The simplicity of task trainers enables learners to focus on mastering a single skill without the complexity of a full scenario. For instance, nursing students using an IV trainer can repeatedly practice inserting a catheter until they achieve accuracy and efficiency. Studies show that repetitive practice on task trainers results in 40% fewer errors when transitioning to real patient care (Gurusamy et al., 2014).

Additionally, task trainers are cost-effective and durable, making them accessible in various educational settings, from classrooms to simulation centers.

Virtual Simulations

Virtual simulations use advanced technologies such as virtual reality (VR) and augmented reality (AR) to create immersive learning experiences. These modalities allow learners to navigate complex clinical scenarios in lifelike digital environments. VR and AR simulations are particularly useful for training in specialized or high-stakes areas, such as surgical procedures, emergency response, or anatomy exploration.

For example, VR-based surgical simulations enable learners to practice techniques like laparoscopic procedures in a virtual operating room. These platforms often include haptic feedback, allowing learners to "feel" the resistance of tissues or the pressure required for suturing. Similarly, AR simulations might overlay digital images onto a mannequin or physical space, enhancing realism and interactivity.

Virtual simulations offer several distinct advantages:

- **Accessibility:** Learners can access training remotely, breaking down geographical barriers.
- **Customization:** Scenarios can be tailored to specific learning objectives or repeated with varying difficulty levels.
- **Safety:** Mistakes in a virtual environment carry no risk to patients, fostering a safe space for experimentation and learning.

Research indicates that learners using VR and AR simulations acquire skills 30% faster and retain knowledge longer than those using traditional methods (Liyanagunawardena et al., 2017).

Standardized Patient Programs

Standardized patient (SP) programs involve trained actors portraying patients in realistic clinical scenarios. These programs are particularly effective for developing interpersonal and communication skills, practicing diagnostic reasoning, and providing patient-centered care. SPs simulate various conditions, from routine checkups to complex emotional or ethical scenarios, such as delivering bad news or handling a patient with cultural sensitivities.

A typical SP session might involve a medical student taking a detailed patient history, performing a physical exam, and formulating a diagnosis. Feedback from SPs and instructor evaluation provide learners valuable insights into their communication style, bedside manner, and clinical reasoning.

Standardized patients also play a crucial role in high-stakes assessments, such as Objective Structured Clinical Examinations (OSCEs), where learners are evaluated on their ability to perform clinical tasks and interact professionally. Studies show that SP programs improve learners' patient communication skills by 25-35% compared to traditional training methods (Hayden et al., 2014).

Integrating Modalities for Comprehensive Learning

While each simulation modality has unique strengths, their combined use provides a more holistic educational experience. For instance:

- A nursing program might begin with task trainers for IV insertions, progress to

mannequin-based simulations for responding to complications, and culminate in standardized patient encounters to refine communication skills.
- Similarly, medical students could use VR for surgical practice, then transition to mannequin simulations for practicing procedural workflows, followed by SP interactions to address patient concerns.

This integrative approach ensures that learners develop the technical and non-technical skills necessary for comprehensive patient care. For example, a trauma team training exercise might involve mannequin-based simulations for resuscitation procedures, coupled with SPs portraying family members to simulate real-world emotional dynamics.

2.4 Principles of Effective Simulation

The success of simulation-based education hinges on core principles that enhance its realism, engagement, and educational value:

Effective Simulation:
- Realism
- Interactivity
- Feedback and Debriefing

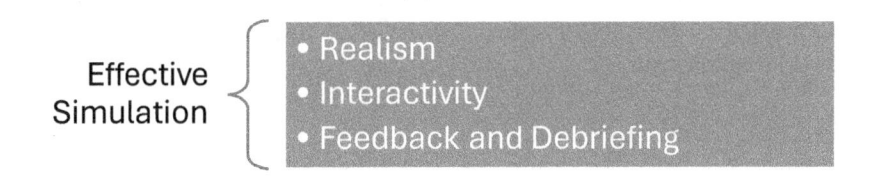

Figure 4 Principles of Effective Simulation

1. **Realism**
   Simulations aim to replicate real-world conditions as closely as possible, using high-fidelity mannequins, realistic environments, and immersive VR systems. For example, a simulated operating room setup helps learners acclimate to high-pressure scenarios.

2. **Interactivity**
   Interactive simulations encourage active participation, such as performing a procedure or making clinical decisions. Interprofessional simulations, which require collaboration across disciplines, enhance teamwork and communication skills.

3. **Feedback and Debriefing**
   Constructive feedback is vital for learning. Real-time feedback during simulations helps learners correct mistakes, while debriefing sessions encourage reflection and reinforce lessons learned.

2.5 Ethical Considerations in Simulation

Ethical considerations are a cornerstone of simulation-based education, ensuring that training environments uphold the principles of respect, fairness, and professionalism. By adhering to these standards, simulation programs create a safe space for learners to practice and grow while maintaining the dignity of all participants, including learners, educators, and standardized patients. Below, we explore the key ethical considerations in simulation education, focusing on privacy, fairness, and feedback.

Privacy and Confidentiality

Maintaining privacy and confidentiality is paramount in simulation-based education, particularly when scenarios involve sensitive information or learner performance assessments. Just as healthcare professionals are bound by confidentiality in real patient care, simulation programs must uphold similar standards to protect simulated patients and learners.

Confidentiality of Patient Records

In simulations that replicate patient scenarios using actual patient data, it is critical to ensure that all identifiable information is de-identified or anonymized. Adhering to privacy laws, such as the Health Insurance Portability and Accountability Act (HIPAA) in the United States, is non-negotiable. For instance, if a simulation involves analyzing real patient lab results, those results must be stripped of any identifying information before use. This practice protects patient privacy and models ethical standards that learners must uphold in clinical practice.

Confidentiality of Learner Performance

Confidentiality also extends to learners whose simulation performance should be treated with the same sensitivity. Publicly criticizing or sharing a learner's performance without consent can create a hostile learning environment, undermining trust and stifling growth. Simulation centers often adopt strict policies to ensure that performance evaluations remain confidential between the learner and instructor unless explicitly required for certification purposes. This confidentiality fosters a safe space where learners feel comfortable taking risks and learning from their mistakes without fear of judgment or repercussion.

For example, video recordings of simulation sessions used for debriefing should only be accessible to authorized personnel. Unless learners provide explicit consent for further educational or research purposes, they should be deleted after their intended use. A study by Bradley (2006) emphasizes that confidentiality in simulation creates a psychologically safe environment that enhances learning outcomes.

Fair and Inclusive Training

Simulation-based education must reflect the diversity and complexity of real-world clinical environments, ensuring that all learners are treated equitably and are exposed to a broad range of clinical scenarios. Fair and inclusive training practices are essential to preparing healthcare professionals to provide equitable care and foster cultural competence.

Avoiding Bias in Scenarios

Clinical scenarios in simulations should be designed to include diverse patient populations, representing variations in age, gender, ethnicity, socioeconomic status, and health conditions. For example, a scenario involving a patient with a heart attack might also incorporate considerations of how cultural beliefs could affect treatment decisions, such as the use of alternative therapies. Please include diverse scenarios to avoid inadvertently perpetuating biases and leaving learners unprepared to address the needs of underrepresented populations in clinical practice.

Equity in Learning Opportunities
Instructors should ensure all learners receive equal opportunities to practice and demonstrate their skills. This includes providing equitable access to simulation resources, such as scheduling sufficient time with mannequins or task trainers for all participants. Additionally, instructors should avoid favoritism during evaluations and offer constructive guidance tailored to each learner's needs. Research by Lindeman (2021) underscores the importance of equitable training environments in fostering confidence and competence among diverse learner groups.

Promoting Cultural Competence
Inclusive simulations should also address cultural nuances that influence patient care. For example, a standardized patient scenario might involve a non-English-speaking patient requiring the learner to navigate language barriers effectively while demonstrating empathy and respect. Exposure to such scenarios prepares learners to deliver patient-centered care in diverse settings, ultimately improving health equity.

Non-judgmental Feedback

Feedback is a critical component of simulation-based education, serving as the bridge between practice and improvement. To be effective, feedback must be delivered non-judgmentally and constructively, ensuring learners view mistakes as opportunities for growth rather than personal failures.

Constructive Feedback in Real Time
During simulations, instructors may provide immediate feedback to guide learners' actions. For instance, if a learner incorrectly positions a patient during a procedure, an instructor might offer gentle, corrective feedback to prevent the error from escalating. This real-time feedback helps learners adjust their approach without feeling criticized, reinforcing positive behaviors and correcting mistakes in a supportive environment.

Debriefing with Psychological Safety
Debriefing sessions occur after a simulation and are pivotal for reflective learning. These sessions should be structured to promote psychological safety, encouraging learners to openly discuss their experiences, challenges, and emotions without fear of blame or judgment. A facilitator might ask open-ended questions like, "What went well during the scenario?" or "What would you do differently next time?" to guide the discussion and allow learners to identify areas for improvement themselves.

Research shows that debriefing is most effective when it fosters an environment of trust and mutual respect. For example, Weaver et al. (2010) found that learners who participated in supportive debriefing sessions were 35% more likely to retain critical skills and report improved confidence levels than those who received evaluative or punitive feedback.

Framing Mistakes as Learning Opportunities
Mistakes in simulation are inevitable and should be embraced as a natural part of the

learning process. Rather than focusing on errors as failures, instructors should frame them as opportunities for growth. For example, suppose a learner administers an incorrect dose of medication during a simulation. In that case, the facilitator might guide a discussion about the potential consequences and strategies to prevent similar errors in clinical practice. This approach not only reinforces learning but also encourages resilience and adaptability.

2.6 Summary

This chapter highlights how simulation shapes healthcare competencies by integrating operational excellence, diverse modalities, and ethical principles. Simulation empowers learners to develop technical skills, clinical accuracy, and critical thinking by providing safe, realistic environments. Furthermore, by adhering to ethical standards and leveraging feedback, simulation-based education fosters trust and professionalism, ensuring future healthcare providers are well-equipped to meet real-world challenges.

2.7 Chapter Review

Review Questions

1. **Simulation Operations**
   a. What are the key functions of simulation operations in healthcare education?
   b. How does operational excellence impact the effectiveness of simulation programs?
2. **Key Metrics and Effectiveness**
   a. What metrics are used to measure simulation effectiveness? Provide examples.
   b. How does simulation contribute to cost savings in healthcare education?
3. **Simulation Modalities**
   a. Compare and contrast mannequin-based simulations and standardized patient programs.
   b. What are the benefits of using virtual simulations in healthcare training?
4. **Principles of Effective Simulation**
   a. How do realism and interactivity enhance the effectiveness of simulations?
   b. Describe the role of feedback and debriefing in simulation-based education.
5. **Ethical Considerations**
   a. Why is confidentiality important in simulation-based education?
   b. How can simulation programs ensure fair and inclusive training?

Critical Thinking and Application

1. **Simulation Metrics**
   Propose a method to evaluate the effectiveness of a new simulation program in improving communication skills among healthcare teams.
2. **Integration of Modalities**
   Design a comprehensive training session for managing a cardiac arrest, integrating at least two simulation modalities. Explain your choices.

3. **Addressing Ethical Issues**
   How would you handle a scenario where learners feel uncomfortable discussing their simulation performance during a debriefing session?

Hands-On Activity

- **Simulation Scenario Design**
  Develop a simulation scenario for a nursing student practicing infection control protocols. Include key objectives, required resources, and metrics for evaluating performance.

Summary Reflection

Reflect on how simulation fosters technical expertise, critical thinking, and teamwork in healthcare education. Consider its ethical implications and operational strategies. How can these principles be applied to enhance future healthcare training programs?

Chapter 3

Simulation Design and Implementation

3.1 Introduction to Simulation Design

Effective simulation design for healthcare education requires a meticulous approach that aligns with learning objectives, integrates core simulation principles, and meets the needs of diverse learners. Simulation design involves creating realistic scenarios and ensuring they reflect current best practices, ethical standards, and relevant clinical challenges. Effective simulation design includes:

- Establishing the need.
- Clearly defined learning objectives.
- Selection of appropriate simulation modalities.
- Development of realistic, engaging scenarios.
- Consideration for learner evaluation and feedback.

The following sections provide a detailed breakdown of the elements contributing to designing and implementing impactful healthcare simulations.

3.2 Establishing a Standardized Model for Simulation Design

Simulation-based education in healthcare has evolved into a cornerstone of medical and nursing training, providing learners with an environment to practice clinical and interpersonal skills without jeopardizing patient safety. However, the successful implementation of simulation activities relies heavily on a structured and standardized approach to design and execution. To address the growing complexity of healthcare education, educators and simulation specialists have embraced established frameworks such as the ADDIE model and the six-step approach to curriculum development. These frameworks offer systematic methodologies for ensuring that simulation programs are pedagogically sound, scalable, and aligned with institutional goals.

The ADDIE Model of Instructional Design

The ADDIE model is a systematic framework used in instructional design to create effective and learner-centered educational programs. The acronym represents the five key phases of the process: Analyze, Design, Develop, Implement, and Evaluate. Each phase builds upon the previous one, ensuring a structured approach to creating instructional materials or programs.

1. Analyze

This phase involves gathering information to understand the learning problem, audience, and desired outcomes. Key activities include:
- Identifying learning goals and objectives.
- Understanding learner characteristics, such as prior knowledge, skills, and needs.
- Assessing environmental and contextual factors that may impact learning.
- Determining performance gaps and the feasibility of simulation as a solution.

For example, this phase might include a needs analysis in healthcare simulation to identify whether a team requires training in managing pediatric emergencies or advanced cardiac life support.

2. Design

In the design phase, the learning experience is planned in detail. Key elements include:
- Crafting specific learning objectives using frameworks like Bloom's Taxonomy.
- Choosing the appropriate instructional strategies and delivery methods (e.g., simulation modality).
- Developing assessment tools to measure learning outcomes.
- Outlining the structure of the content, scenarios, and activities.

This phase emphasizes blueprinting. For instance, a healthcare simulation designer might map out a scenario for managing sepsis and defining learner roles, decision points, and expected actions.

3. Develop

During the development phase, the planned content and materials are created. Key activities include:

- Developing simulation scenarios, including scripts, technical equipment setup, and environmental details.
- Creating multimedia elements, such as instructional videos or virtual reality modules.
- Build and test task trainers or software for technical skill practice.
- Conducting a pilot test to refine materials and ensure usability.

In healthcare, this phase might involve programming a high-fidelity mannequin to simulate specific patient symptoms or creating a checklist for evaluating clinical performance during the scenario.

4. Implement

This phase focuses on delivering the developed learning experiences to the target audience. Key activities include:

- Scheduling and facilitating simulation sessions.
- Training instructors or facilitators on scenario delivery and debriefing techniques.
- Ensuring learners have access to required materials, tools, and environments.
- Monitoring the simulation process to ensure smooth execution.

Implementing healthcare education might involve a multidisciplinary simulation, such as an interprofessional team practicing a code blue scenario in a simulated hospital room.

5. Evaluate

Evaluation occurs throughout and after the learning experience. It ensures the simulation achieves its objectives and identifies areas for improvement. This phase involves:

- Formative evaluation: Conducted during the design and development phases to make iterative improvements.
- Summative evaluation: Conducted after implementation to assess the overall effectiveness.
- Measuring outcomes, such as skill acquisition, knowledge retention, and learner satisfaction.
- Gathering feedback from learners and facilitators.

For instance, evaluation might include pre- and post-simulation assessments of proficiency and learner reflections during debriefing in a simulation on surgical skills.

Key Features of the ADDIE Model

- *Iterative Process*: Although the phases are linear, they often overlap, and feedback loops can prompt revisiting earlier phases.
- *Learner-Centered Approach*: Focuses on tailoring instruction to meet the needs of learners.
- *Flexibility*: Can be adapted for different learning contexts, including classroom, online, and simulation-based environments.

Key Features of ADDIE Model

- Iterative Process
- Learner-centered
- Flexible

The ADDIE model ensures that instructional programs are well-planned, effectively implemented, and continuously improved to maximize their impact on learning outcomes.

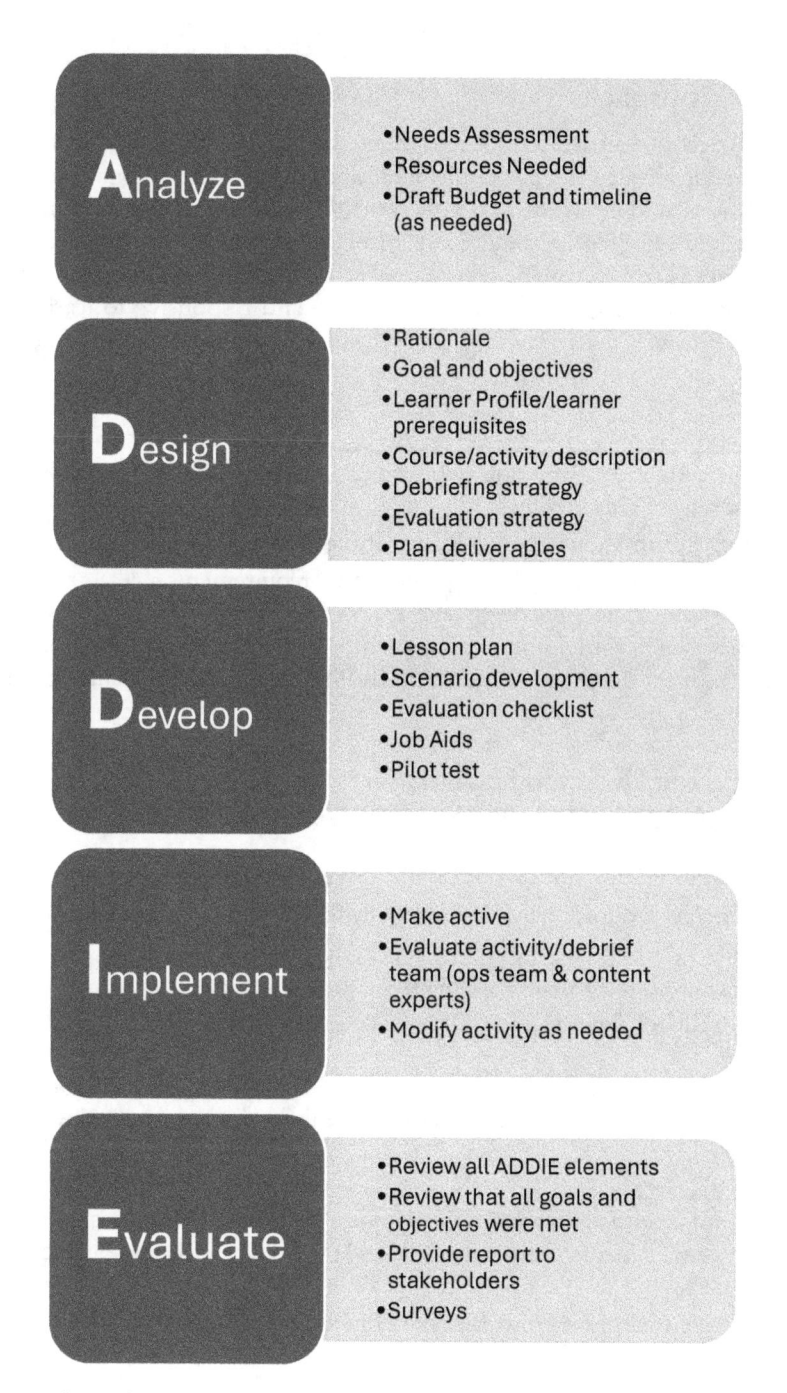

Analyze
- Needs Assessment
- Resources Needed
- Draft Budget and timeline (as needed)

Design
- Rationale
- Goal and objectives
- Learner Profile/learner prerequisites
- Course/activity description
- Debriefing strategy
- Evaluation strategy
- Plan deliverables

Develop
- Lesson plan
- Scenario development
- Evaluation checklist
- Job Aids
- Pilot test

Implement
- Make active
- Evaluate activity/debrief team (ops team & content experts)
- Modify activity as needed

Evaluate
- Review all ADDIE elements
- Review that all goals and objectives were met
- Provide report to stakeholders
- Surveys

Figure 5 ADDIE model specific to simulation design.

Kern's Six-Step Approach

The Six-Step Approach to Curriculum Development is a structured framework widely utilized in medical education to design, implement, and evaluate educational programs. Initially proposed by David E. Kern and colleagues in Curriculum Development for Medical Education: A Six-Step Approach, it offers a systematic methodology for addressing learning needs and enhancing educational effectiveness. Each step builds upon the previous, ensuring that programs are comprehensive and responsive to learner and institutional needs. Below is a narrative of the six steps, enriched with examples and references.

Step 1: Problem Identification and General Needs Assessment

The process begins with identifying the educational problem and understanding the broader needs it addresses. This involves:

- Recognizing gaps in knowledge, skills, or attitudes among learners.
- Assessing societal, institutional, and professional requirements.

For example, a program addressing diagnostic errors in primary care might begin by examining their prevalence and impact on patient safety. National trends, such as recommendations from the Institute of Medicine (IOM), can guide the identification of gaps.

Step 2: Needs Assessment for Targeted Learners

After defining the general problem, the next step focuses on assessing the target audience's needs. This includes:

- Surveys, focus groups, or interviews with learners to understand their perspectives.
- Observing clinical performance to identify competency gaps.
- Gathering feedback from faculty, patients, or stakeholders.

For instance, if a medical school identifies deficiencies in end-of-life care communication, they might survey students and faculty to pinpoint weaknesses in their curriculum.

Step 3: Goals and Objectives

In this phase, clear, measurable goals and objectives are developed. Goals describe broad outcomes, while objectives focus on specific skills or knowledge. Effective objectives:

- Use action-oriented verbs from Bloom's Taxonomy (e.g., analyze, demonstrate, evaluate).
- Align with the identified needs of the learners.

For example, a goal might be to improve residents' competency in pediatric resuscitation. Objectives could include:

- Demonstrating proper technique for endotracheal intubation.

- Applying evidence-based protocols for pediatric cardiac arrest.

Step 4: Educational Strategies
Here, instructional methods and materials are selected to achieve the objectives. Strategies should:

- Cater to different learning styles (e.g., auditory, visual, kinesthetic).
- Incorporate active learning techniques like case-based discussions, simulations, or flipped classrooms.

In the resuscitation example, simulation-based training using high-fidelity mannequins might be chosen to replicate real-life scenarios. This provides hands-on experience in a safe, controlled environment.

Step 5: Implementation
This phase involves rolling out the educational program. Key considerations include:

- Training faculty to effectively deliver the curriculum.
- Ensuring access to required resources, such as simulation labs or online platforms.
- Scheduling sessions to fit within learners' existing responsibilities.

For instance, introducing a new communication skills workshop for medical students might require faculty development sessions and coordination with clinical rotations to minimize scheduling conflicts.

Step 6: Evaluation and Feedback
The final step assesses the program's effectiveness and identifies areas for improvement. Evaluation methods include:

- *Formative evaluation*: Ongoing assessments during implementation to adjust.
- *Summative evaluation*: Outcomes assessment, such as learner performance or patient care improvements.

For the pediatric resuscitation curriculum, evaluation might include pre-and post-training assessments of knowledge and skills and feedback from learners on the session's effectiveness.

The Six-Step Approach provides a robust, iterative framework for designing and refining medical education programs. Its focus on alignment between needs, objectives, and strategies ensures that programs are learner-centered and outcome-driven. Educators can address healthcare training gaps and improve learner and patient outcomes by applying this approach.

Step 1   Problem Identification

- How is it currently being addressed?
- How should it be addressed?
- Whom does it affect?
- What does it affect?
- How are they affected?
- What is currently being done?
- What are the environmental factors?
- What Ideally should be done?
- General needs assessment

Step 2   Needs Assessment

- Identify differences from current and ideal for learners
- Identify differences from current and ideal for learners environment
- Tageted needs assessment

Step 3   Goals & Objectives

- Broad goals that communicate purpose
- Specific objectives that are measurable

Step 4   Educational Strategies

- Content
- Learning styles
- Methods

Step 5   Implementation

- Identify resources
- Obtain support for curriculum - training faculty
- Administer curriculum

Step 6   Evaluation & Feedback

- Closing the loop
- Evaluation methods
- Satisfy internal/external requirements

Figure 6 Kern's Six-Step Approach

3.3 Establishing the Need and Performing a Needs Assessment

In simulation-based education (SBE), establishing the need and conducting a needs assessment are crucial initial steps to ensure the program's effectiveness and relevance. These processes help identify knowledge, skills, or behavior gaps within a target audience and align the simulation activities with specific educational goals.

Establishing the Need
Establishing the need involves understanding the context and rationale for implementing simulation training. This process typically begins with identifying key challenges or deficiencies in current practices. For example:

- *Performance gaps*: Are there critical areas where learners struggle or fail to meet expected competencies?

- *Healthcare outcomes*: Is there evidence linking educational gaps to adverse patient care or safety outcomes?

- *Stakeholder requirements*: What are the expectations or demands from regulatory bodies, institutions, or clinical leaders?

This step may also include reviewing existing literature, analyzing incident reports, or conducting stakeholder surveys to pinpoint improvement areas.

Conducting a Needs Assessment
A needs assessment is a systematic process for gathering data to define and prioritize the educational needs of the learners. The steps often include:

- *Defining the objectives*: What competencies (knowledge, skills, attitudes) should the learners develop?
- *Identifying the target audience*: Who are the learners (e.g., students, healthcare professionals)? What are their roles, levels of expertise, and learning preferences?
- *Gathering data*: Collect information through various methods, such as:
- *Surveys or questionnaires*
- *Focus groups or interviews with learners and stakeholders*
- *Direct observation of clinical practice*
- *Analysis of patient care metrics or clinical outcomes*
- *Analyzing the data*: Determine the gap between current performance and desired outcomes.
- *Prioritizing needs*: Rank the identified gaps based on factors such as impact on patient care, frequency, and feasibility of addressing them through simulation.

Linking Needs to Simulation Design
The results of the needs assessment guide the design of simulation-based interventions, ensuring that they are:

- *Targeted*: Focused on addressing identified gaps.
- *Relevant*: Aligned with learners' roles and institutional priorities.
- *Measurable*: Incorporating specific objectives and evaluation metrics.

By systematically establishing the need and conducting a needs assessment, SBE programs can maximize their educational value and impact, fostering meaningful improvements in learner performance and patient outcomes.

3.4. Establishing Learning Objectives

Effective healthcare simulation hinges on the clarity and precision of its learning objectives. These objectives provide a roadmap for designing meaningful simulations and assessing learner performance. A well-crafted objective sets the stage for what learners will achieve regarding skills, knowledge, and behaviors, guiding both instructors and participants in their educational journey. This chapter explores establishing clear, measurable learning objectives for healthcare simulation using Bloom's Taxonomy, a widely recognized framework for categorizing cognitive, affective, and psychomotor learning outcomes (Bloom, 1956; Anderson & Krathwohl, 2001).

The Role of Learning Objectives in Simulation Design

Learning objectives define the specific outcomes learners should achieve by the end of a simulation. These objectives serve several key purposes:

- Guidance for Scenario Development: Well-defined objectives help instructors design focused and effective simulation scenarios.
- Evaluation Criteria: Objectives provide a basis for assessing learners' progress and success.
- Alignment with Educational Goals: Objectives ensure that simulations are designed to meet institutional and accrediting body standards.

For instance, a simulation focusing on "demonstrating proper sterile technique during a central line insertion" addresses specific technical skills (e.g., aseptic procedures). Similarly, objectives such as "practicing effective team communication during a cardiac arrest" target non-technical skills, such as communication and teamwork. When using Bloom's Taxonomy to establish these objectives, we can align each goal with one of the cognitive levels of learning, ensuring a well-rounded educational experience.

Using Bloom's Taxonomy to Structure Learning Objectives

Bloom's Taxonomy classifies learning into six hierarchical categories: Remembering, Understanding, Applying, Analyzing, Evaluating, and Creating. These categories offer a structured way to develop learning objectives that address various levels of cognitive processing, ensuring that learners engage in deep and meaningful learning. Additionally, the taxonomy can be extended to include the affective and psychomotor domains, which are essential in healthcare training (Krathwohl, 2002).

Each level of Bloom's Taxonomy provides a framework for specifying the expected outcome of the simulation and can guide both scenario development and learner assessment. Explain how Bloom's Taxonomy can be applied to healthcare simulation learning objectives.

Cognitive Domain: Developing Clinical Reasoning and Decision-Making Skills
The cognitive domain focuses on intellectual skills, such as knowledge recall, analysis, and application. Effective simulation-based objectives in this domain often emphasize clinical reasoning, diagnostic acumen, and adaptability.

- *Remembering*: The first level involves recalling facts or basic concepts. Example: "List the steps involved in performing a sterile central line insertion."
- *Understanding*: At this level, learners demonstrate comprehension of the material. Example: "Explain why proper sterile technique is critical in preventing infections during central line insertion."
- *Applying*: Learners use knowledge in new situations. An example is "Apply sterile technique during the central line insertion in a simulated environment."
- *Analyzing*: This level encourages learners to break down complex information into components. Example: "Analyze a cardiac arrest scenario to identify breakdowns in team communication."
- *Evaluating*: involves making judgments based on criteria. An example is "Evaluate the effectiveness of communication in the team during a simulated cardiac arrest."
- *Creating*: This highest level involves synthesizing information to create something new. Example: "Develop a checklist for optimal team communication during a cardiac arrest response."

These cognitive objectives aim to improve learners' clinical reasoning, adaptability, and ability to manage complex medical situations (Anderson & Krathwohl, 2001). They also enable healthcare professionals to enhance their decision-making abilities under pressure, a critical skill in high-stakes environments.

Affective Domain: Enhancing Non-Technical Skills
In addition to cognitive skills, non-technical skills such as communication, teamwork, and empathy are essential for effective healthcare delivery. Bloom's Taxonomy's affective domain addresses attitudes, feelings, and values, vital components of healthcare simulations.

- *Receiving*: The learner is passively involved in the learning process. Example: "Listen to feedback regarding your communication with the patient during a simulated clinical encounter."
- *Responding*: The learner actively participates in learning. Example: "Demonstrate active listening when responding to feedback from team members."
- *Valuing*: The learner begins recognizing the worth of certain behaviors or practices. For example, "Value the importance of team coordination during a cardiac arrest scenario."
- *Organizing*: The learner integrates values and behaviors into a coherent structure. An example is to "Organize team roles and responsibilities based on individual skills and strengths in a simulated trauma scenario."

- *Characterizing:* The learner consistently demonstrates desired values and behaviors. Example: "Consistently demonstrate calm, clear, and decisive communication during high-stress medical emergencies."

By addressing these levels of the affective domain, simulation scenarios help build the non-technical competencies essential for healthcare professionals, such as leadership, interpersonal communication, and emotional resilience.

Psychomotor Domain: Mastery of Clinical Procedures

The psychomotor domain focuses on physical skills and the ability to perform clinical procedures. In healthcare simulations, these objectives often center on mastering technical skills such as suturing, catheter placement, or intubation.

- *Perception:* The learner uses sensory cues to guide actions. Example: "Identify the correct anatomical landmarks for catheter placement using tactile feedback."
- *Set:* The learner is ready to perform a skill. Example: "Prepare the sterile field for a central line insertion."
- *Guided Response:* The learner performs the skill with guidance. Example: "Perform the first few steps of the suturing procedure under instructor supervision."
- *Mechanism:* The learner can perform the skill independently, with some effort. Example: "Suture a wound with minimal supervision."
- *Complex Overt Response:* The learner performs the skill fluently and without hesitation. Example: "Perform an emergency intubation in a high-stakes simulation scenario."
- *Adaptation:* The learner modifies the technique to suit new conditions. Example: "Adapt the standard suturing technique for use in a difficult-to-reach area."
- *Origination:* The learner can create a new technique. Example: "Develop a modified approach to catheter placement in patients with unusual anatomy."

Through these objectives, healthcare professionals develop the psychomotor skills necessary to perform clinical procedures efficiently and effectively, ensuring high-quality patient care (Hassan et al., 2017).

SMART Objectives: Enhancing Clarity and Measurement

To ensure that learning objectives are effective, they should follow the SMART criteria:
- ✓ **Specific**: Clear and unambiguous goals.
- ✓ **Measurable**: Outcomes that can be assessed.
- ✓ **Achievable**: Realistic objectives based on learner capabilities.
- ✓ **Relevant**: Aligned with healthcare goals and institutional needs.
- ✓ **Time-bound**: Defined timelines for completion.

For example, a SMART objective for a simulation scenario might be: "*Demonstrate proper sterile technique during a central line insertion within 10 minutes of starting the procedure.*" This objective is specific (sterile technique), measurable (completion of the procedure), achievable (based on prior skill level), relevant (direct impact on patient safety), and time-bound (completion within a defined period).

Bloom's Taxonomy	Verbs
Remember or Know	list, outline, define, name, match, quote, recall, identify, label, recognize
Understand or comprehend	describe, explain, paraphrase, restate, give examples of, summarize, contrast, interpret, discuss
Apply	calculate, predict, apply, solve, illustrate, use, demonstrate, determine, model, perform, present
Analyze	classify, categorize, analyze, diagram, illustrate, criticize, simplify, associate.
Evaluate or Synthesize	relate, determine, defend, judge, compare, contrast, argue, justify, support, convince
Create	design, formulate, build, create, compose, generate, derive, modify, develop

Table 1 Measurable verbs based on Bloom's Taxonomy

Establishing clear learning objectives based on Bloom's Taxonomy ensures that healthcare simulations are structured, purposeful, and impactful. Healthcare educators can design simulations that improve clinical competence and foster essential non-technical skills like communication and teamwork by addressing cognitive, affective, and psychomotor domains. Using Bloom's Taxonomy as a guide allows educators to develop well-rounded, comprehensive objectives that cater to the diverse learning needs of healthcare professionals, ultimately enhancing patient care and safety.

3.5. Selecting the Appropriate Modality

The choice of simulation modality significantly impacts the success of the learning experience. Selection depends on factors like the complexity of the objectives, the available resources, and the learners' needs. Common modalities include:

- *Mannequin-based simulations* are useful for high-stakes procedural training or teamwork, such as advanced cardiac life support (ACLS) or trauma resuscitation.
- *Task Trainers*: Focus on IV insertion, suturing, or lumbar puncture skills.
- *Standardized Patients (SPs)* are ideal for enhancing communication and diagnostic skills and practicing patient-centered care.
- *Virtual and Augmented Reality (VR/AR)*: These technologies provide immersive experiences for procedures, anatomy exploration, and rare clinical scenarios.

Case Example: If the goal is to train surgical residents on laparoscopic techniques, task trainers or VR systems may be the optimal choice due to their focus on hand-eye coordination and precision.

3.6 Scenario Development

The heart of simulation design is creating realistic, engaging scenarios. Scenarios should reflect clinical situations learners will likely encounter while progressively increasing complexity to challenge their skill levels.

Key Components of Scenario Design:

- *Clinical Relevance*: Scenarios must align with real-world challenges in healthcare. For example, nursing students might practice responding to a deteriorating patient due to hypoglycemia.
- *Level of Difficulty*: Tailor scenarios to match the learners' experience levels. Novices may require guided experiences, while advanced learners benefit from independent problem-solving.
- *Contextual Details*: To enhance realism, incorporate accurate clinical settings, equipment, and patient histories. For instance, use a hospital ward setup for nursing simulations or an operating room for surgical training.
- *Unfolding Scenarios*: Gradually introduce complications to mimic dynamic clinical environments, such as a patient developing arrhythmias during a routine procedure.

Types of Healthcare Scenario Design

Healthcare simulation scenarios are structured learning activities that mimic clinical situations to help learners practice and develop knowledge, skills, and behaviors in a safe environment. Scenario design varies depending on the educational objectives, the learners' level, and the practice context. The main types of scenario design in healthcare simulation include:

1. Skill-Based Scenarios
   - *Purpose*: Focused on teaching or practicing specific procedural or technical skills.
   - *Design Features*:
     - Typically use task trainers (e.g., suturing arms, intubation heads).
     - Emphasize repetitive practice of psychomotor skills.
     - Feedback is immediate and targeted at skill improvement.
   - Examples: Central venous catheter placement, endotracheal intubation, or suturing.

2. Case-Based Scenarios
   - *Purpose*: Develop clinical reasoning, decision-making, and diagnostic skills.
   - *Design Features*:
     - Simulates patient cases requiring learners to gather information, make diagnoses, and plan treatments.
     - Includes realistic patient histories, vital signs, and lab results.
     - Facilitates integration of knowledge across disciplines.
   - Examples: Managing a patient presenting with chest pain or a sepsis workup.

3. Crisis Resource Management (CRM) Scenarios
   - *Purpose*: Enhance teamwork, leadership, communication, and other non-technical skills critical during high-pressure situations.
   - *Design Features*:
     - Focus on team dynamics and effective resource utilization.

- Often involve high-fidelity manikins and complex clinical emergencies.
- Debriefing emphasizes human factors and interprofessional collaboration.
- Examples: Code blue (cardiac arrest), massive hemorrhage in the operating room.

4. Communication-Focused Scenarios
   - *Purpose*: Train learners in interpersonal and communication skills, including sensitive conversations and patient-centered care.
   - *Design Features*:
     - Often use standardized patients (actors) to mimic realistic interactions.
     - Scenarios address challenges like breaking bad news, delivering discharge instructions, or conflict resolution.
     - Emphasizes empathy, clarity, and professionalism.
   - Examples: Discussing end-of-life care with a family and obtaining informed consent.

5. Hybrid Scenarios
   - *Purpose*: Integrate technical and non-technical skills within a single simulation activity.
   - *Design Features*:
     - Combine task trainers, manikins, and/or standardized patients.
     - Allow learners to practice clinical procedures and communication in a cohesive context.
   - Examples: managing a patient who requires CPR (technical skill) while communicating with a distressed family member (non-technical skill).

6. High-Stakes Assessment Scenarios
   - *Purpose*: Evaluate learner competencies in a controlled and standardized setting.
   - *Design Features*:
     - Scenarios are consistent and reproducible for fair assessment.
     - Criteria for evaluation are predefined and objective.
     - Feedback focuses on specific performance metrics.
   - Examples: OSCEs (Objective Structured Clinical Examinations) or high-fidelity simulations for certification exams.

7. Longitudinal or Sequential Scenarios
   - *Purpose*: Simulate the progression of a patient's condition over time or across care settings.
   - *Design Features*:
     - It involves multiple phases of patient care (e.g., from the emergency department to the ICU).
     - Helps learners understand the continuity of care and systems-based practice.
   - Examples: Managing a patient through initial trauma assessment, stabilization, and post-operative care.

By tailoring scenario designs to specific learning objectives and contexts, educators can maximize the effectiveness of healthcare simulation in fostering both technical proficiency and holistic clinical competence.

3.7 Standardized Simulation Scenario/curriculum Templates

The success of healthcare simulation relies not only on advanced technology and skilled facilitators but also on the foundation of well-designed scenarios and curricula. Standardized templates for simulation scenarios and curricula provide a framework that ensures consistency, quality, and alignment with educational goals. By offering a structured approach, these templates save time, enhance collaboration, and improve the effectiveness of simulation-based learning programs. This narrative, supported by evidence and real-world examples, explores the importance and advantages of using standardized templates in healthcare simulation.

The Importance of Standardized Templates

Standardized simulation templates are essential for ensuring uniformity and quality across training programs. They provide a consistent structure that guides educators in developing scenarios and curricula, ensuring alignment with institutional goals, learner objectives, and accreditation standards. This consistency is particularly critical in healthcare education, where variability can lead to unequal learning experiences and affect skill acquisition.

> Ensuring Alignment with Learning Objectives: Standardized templates ensure every scenario is tied to clear, measurable learning objectives. For example, a template may specify that learners will "demonstrate proper sterile technique during central line placement," ensuring all instructors focus on this skill across sessions (Kardong-Edgren et al., 2020).

> Improving Quality Control: Standardized templates help maintain high quality across simulations, especially in programs with multiple facilitators. A survey of nursing programs found that standardized templates reduced inconsistencies in scenario delivery by 40%, leading to more predictable and effective learning outcomes (INACSL, 2021).

Facilitating Accreditation Compliance: Accrediting bodies, such as the Accreditation Commission for Education in Nursing (ACEN) and the Liaison Committee on Medical Education (LCME), increasingly require simulation programs to document their alignment with competency-based standards. Templates simplify this process by ensuring scenarios consistently address required competencies.

Advantages of Using Standardized Templates

Standardized templates offer benefits beyond consistency, offering practical advantages that improve the efficiency and effectiveness of simulation programs.

> **Advantages of using standardized templates:**
> - Time efficiency
> - Promotes collaboration
> - Adaptable and reuseable
> - Enhances learner outcomes
> - Simplifies documentation
> - Consistent

Time Efficiency:
Designing simulation scenarios from scratch is time-intensive. Standardized templates streamline the development process by providing pre-structured outlines for facilitators to fill in specific details. A study found that using templates reduced scenario preparation time by 35%, freeing educators to focus on other critical aspects of simulation, such as facilitation and debriefing (Fey et al., 2020).

Promoting Collaboration:
Templates foster collaboration among interdisciplinary teams by offering a common language and structure. For instance, standardized fields for scenario objectives, roles, and equipment requirements make it easier for teams of educators, technicians, and administrators to coordinate effectively. Template programs reported a 25% increase in team productivity and fewer logistical errors during simulation setup (Rosen et al., 2018).

Supporting Adaptability and Reuse:
Standardized templates make adapting scenarios for different contexts or learner levels easy. For example, a cardiovascular emergency scenario can be modified for nursing students, medical students, or paramedics by adjusting objectives and complexity without starting from scratch. This adaptability increases the utility and longevity of simulation scenarios.

Enhancing Learner Outcomes:
Templates help ensure scenarios are consistently well-structured and pedagogically sound, positively impacting learner performance. A randomized trial found that learners exposed to simulations designed with standardized templates performed 20% better on post-simulation assessments than those trained with non-standardized scenarios (Cook et al., 2011).

Simplifying Documentation and Evaluation:
Templates provide built-in fields for documenting scenario execution and learner performance. This documentation is invaluable for program evaluation and accreditation reviews. Programs using standardized templates reported a 30% reduction in documentation errors and faster audit preparation (INACSL, 2021).

Standardized templates for healthcare simulation scenarios and curricula are more than a convenience—they are vital for **ensuring consistency, efficiency, and effectiveness** in simulation-based education. Templates support educators and learners in achieving meaningful outcomes by aligning with learning objectives, improving quality, and offering practical advantages such as time savings and adaptability. As simulation plays a pivotal role in healthcare education, adopting standardized templates will remain a best practice for advancing training programs and improving patient care.

3.8 Integrating Feedback and Debriefing

Feedback and debriefing play distinct yet complementary roles in maximizing simulations' learning potential. Both are essential components that serve different purposes in the educational process, ensuring learners derive the full benefit from their simulation experiences.

Immediate Feedback: Delivered in real-time during the simulation, immediate feedback provides learners with actionable insights as they perform tasks. It reinforces learning through direct, in-the-moment adjustments, allowing learners to modify their approach and improve performance.

For example, alerts about procedural errors or changes in a simulator's physiological responses help learners recognize and correct mistakes instantly.

Debriefing Sessions: Conducted after the simulation concludes, debriefing encourages deeper reflection on the experience. These sessions are designed to help learners analyze their actions, understand their reasoning, and identify areas for improvement. A well-structured debriefing session provides a space for discussing key takeaways, addressing knowledge gaps, and consolidating lessons learned. Unlike immediate feedback, which focuses on specific tasks or decisions, debriefing offers a broader perspective on the overall performance and emphasizes critical thinking and long-term learning.

The synergy between immediate feedback and debriefing ensures that learners not only receive feedback in real time but also have the time and reflective skills needed to apply their learning to future scenarios. Thus, both elements are integral to successful simulation-based education.

Aspect	Feedback	Debriefing
Timing	Delivered in real-time	Conducted after the simulation ends
Focus	Task-specific and immediate actions	Broad analysis of performance and decision-making
Purpose	To correct mistakes or reinforce correct actions instantly	To encourage reflection, identify knowledge gaps, and consolidate learning
Scope	Narrow, focusing on specific tasks or behaviors	Holistic, addressing overall performance and teamwork
Interaction level	Primarily one-way	Interactive, involving dialogue and self-reflection
Impact on learning	Reinforces immediate behavioral changes	Promotes critical thinking and long-term skill development
Key Objective	Immediate performance impact	Comprehensive understanding and future application of lessons learned

Table 2 The differences in feedback and debriefing

Debriefing Models

Debriefing is a critical component of healthcare simulation, providing a structured opportunity for learners to reflect on their performance, consolidate learning, and connect simulation experiences to clinical practice. Various debriefing models are used, each with distinct frameworks and approaches to achieving learning objectives. Below are some commonly used debriefing models in healthcare simulation:

1. Plus-Delta Model
The Plus-Delta Model is a simple, learner-centered approach that focuses on self-reflection and feedback. Learners identify what went well during the simulation (Plus) and areas for improvement (Delta) (Sawyer et al., 2016). It is easy to use and promotes active learner participation, but it may lack depth without effective facilitation.

2. The Three-Phase Model
The Three-Phase Model includes a logical progression through the Reaction, Analysis, and Summary phases (Fanning & Gaba, 2007). During Reaction, learners express emotional responses to the simulation. The analysis explores performance and decision-making, while the Summary reinforces key learning points. This model is adaptable but requires skilled facilitators to maintain focus.

3. PEARLS (Promoting Excellence and Reflective Learning in Simulation)
PEARLS combines structured feedback, focused facilitation, and learner self-assessment. It includes phases such as Reactions, Description, Analysis, and Application (Sawyer et al., 2016). This flexible blended approach supports diverse learner needs but demands experienced facilitators to balance guidance and learner-driven discussion.

4. Debriefing for Meaningful Learning (DML)
DML emphasizes connecting simulation experiences with clinical practice through reflective and evidence-based discussions. It involves phases like Engage, Explore, Explain, Elaborate, and Evaluate (Arafeh et al., 2010). This model encourages critical thinking and application of learning but can be time-intensive.

5. Advocacy-Inquiry Model
The Advocacy-Inquiry Model is a nonjudgmental framework in which facilitators combine observations (Advocacy) with open-ended questions (Inquiry) to explore learners' perspectives and reasoning (Rudolph et al., 2007). It fosters psychological safety and reflective learning but relies heavily on facilitator skills.

6. Gibbs' Reflective Cycle
Gibbs' Reflective Cycle provides a structured approach to debriefing through six stages: Description, Feelings, Evaluation, Analysis, Conclusion, and Action Plan (Gibbs, 1988). It encourages deep reflection and action planning, though it can be time-consuming for complex scenarios.

7. The 3D Model (Defusing, Discovering, Deepening)
The 3D model focuses on emotional and cognitive engagement through three phases:

Defusing emotions, discovering performance insights, and Deepening understanding by connecting lessons to clinical practice (Fanning & Gaba, 2007). It balances emotional and cognitive aspects but may require more time and skilled facilitation.

8. <u>TeamSTEPPS Debriefing Model</u>
The TeamSTEPPS framework emphasizes communication, teamwork, and collaboration. It includes reviewing team performance using structured tools, discussing aspects like leadership and mutual support, and identifying areas for team improvement (TeamSTEPPS National Implementation Team, 2014). This model is ideal for interprofessional simulations but focuses more on team dynamics than individual learning.

Choosing a Debriefing Model

Debriefing is the cornerstone of healthcare simulation, transforming a simulation experience into a powerful learning opportunity. The choice of debriefing model is critical to achieving the intended educational outcomes and ensuring that learners can translate insights from the simulation into real-world clinical practice. A well-chosen debriefing model aligns with the simulation's learning objectives, accommodates the context and participants, and leverages the facilitator's expertise to foster a productive and reflective discussion.

<u>Key Factors to Consider When Selecting a Debriefing Model</u>

1. **Learning Objectives**
    - The debriefing model must align with the primary goals of the simulation. For instance:
        - If the focus is on **technical skills**, such as airway management or chest compressions, a structured debriefing model emphasizing performance metrics and clinical accuracy may be most effective.
        - For **teamwork or communication** training, a model that prioritizes behavioral dynamics, decision-making processes, and interpersonal interactions will yield better results.
        - Understanding the specific outcomes you want to achieve—whether clinical proficiency, situational awareness, or interprofessional collaboration—guides the choice of model.
2. **Simulation Context**
    - Different simulation scenarios require tailored approaches:
        - <u>Individual Scenarios</u>: When debriefing a single learner, the facilitator can focus on individual performance, decision-making, and personal reflections.
        - <u>Team-Based Scenarios</u>: In team simulations, the debriefing should highlight group dynamics, communication patterns, and collective problem-solving strategies, ensuring all voices are heard and shared learning is prioritized.
3. **Learner Level and Experience**
    - The learners' experience level influences how debriefing is structured:

- Novice Learners: May benefit from a supportive, scaffolded approach that emphasizes building confidence, providing constructive feedback, and encouraging self-assessment.
- Experienced Learners: Often prefer advanced debriefing methods that delve into complex clinical reasoning, peer feedback, and nuanced discussions of system-based practices.

4. **Facilitator Expertise and Comfort**
   - The facilitator's familiarity with a specific debriefing model plays a significant role in its effectiveness. A confident and well-prepared facilitator can adapt the model dynamically to meet the needs of the learners and the situation.
   - Facilitators should consider their strengths, such as their ability to guide reflective discussions, analyze clinical performance, or manage group dynamics. Training in specific debriefing models, such as PEARLS (Promoting Excellence and Reflective Learning in Simulation) or the Plus-Delta approach, ensures they can effectively lead sessions.

Using Debriefing Models Effectively

When applied thoughtfully, debriefing models transform a passive post-simulation discussion into an active, learner-centered process. Effective debriefing is not about assigning blame or merely critiquing performance—it is about fostering critical reflection, promoting emotional safety, and driving continuous improvement. Here are some guiding principles for using debriefing models effectively:

1. **Create a Safe Learning Environment**
   - Begin by establishing a supportive atmosphere where learners feel comfortable sharing their thoughts and insights. Psychological safety is crucial for open, honest discussions.
2. **Encourage Reflective Learning**
   - Use open-ended questions to guide learners in analyzing their actions, identifying strengths, and recognizing areas for improvement. For example:
     - "What were you aiming to achieve in this scenario?"
     - "How did you feel about your communication with the team?"
     - "What might you do differently in a similar situation?"
3. **Balance Facilitation and Learner Input**
   - While the facilitator guides the session, the focus should remain on the learners' experiences. Encourage them to lead the reflection and provide peer feedback, fostering active engagement and collaborative learning.
4. **Adapt to Real-Time Needs**
   - Be flexible in applying the debriefing model. If unexpected emotions or insights arise during the discussion, adjust the structure to address these effectively while staying aligned with learning objectives.

Impact of the Right Debriefing Model

When the debriefing model is carefully chosen and skillfully applied, its impact can be profound. Learners leave the session with:

- A deeper understanding of their clinical performance and thought processes.
- Enhanced awareness of teamwork dynamics and communication strategies.
- Increased confidence and readiness to apply their skills in real-world settings.

For facilitators, an effective debriefing session reinforces the value of simulation as an educational tool and builds trust and collaboration with learners. Over time, consistent and impactful debriefing fosters a culture of reflection and continuous improvement within the institution, leading to better outcomes for learners and patients.

Selecting the appropriate debriefing model is more than a procedural choice—it is a deliberate step toward maximizing the educational impact of simulation. By considering the learning objectives, context, learner experience, and facilitator readiness, healthcare simulation programs can ensure that debriefing sessions drive meaningful growth, individually and collectively.

3.9 Addressing Common Challenges in Simulation Design

Simulation-based education is a powerful and transformative tool for healthcare training, but it also presents challenges that must be addressed to ensure the effectiveness of training programs. These challenges include resource limitations, time constraints, and learner engagement issues, all of which can impact the overall success of simulation initiatives. Addressing these challenges requires careful planning, innovative solutions, and ongoing evaluation.

Resource Limitations

High-fidelity simulation programs often require substantial financial and logistical investments. Advanced mannequins, virtual reality platforms, and dedicated simulation labs are expensive to procure and maintain. For example, high-fidelity mannequins such as *SimMan* can cost between $50,000 and $100,000 each, not including software updates, maintenance, or faculty training. Additionally, trained personnel are required to design, facilitate, and debrief simulations, adding to the operational costs.

To address these resource limitations, many institutions are turning to creative solutions:

- *Hybrid Scenarios*: Combining low-fidelity trainers with high-fidelity components to balance costs. For instance, using a basic task trainer for IV insertion while integrating it into a larger, high-fidelity scenario involving a mannequin.
- *Low-Cost Alternatives*: Virtual simulations, which require lower infrastructure investment, be cost-effective. A study found that using virtual reality for surgical training reduced costs by 30% compared to physical training setups while maintaining comparable learning outcomes (Gurusamy et al., 2014).

- *Collaborative Models*: Sharing simulation resources across institutions or creating regional simulation centers can help reduce individual institutional costs while expanding access.

Time Constraints

Scheduling simulations within busy academic curricula or clinical schedules is another significant challenge. Healthcare education programs are already constrained by packed schedules, making it difficult to allocate time for lengthy or complex simulations. Similarly, clinical staff may need help finding time for simulation training alongside their patient care responsibilities.

Strategies to overcome time constraints include:
- *Short, Focused Simulations*: Designing "micro-simulations" that target specific skills or competencies in 10–15 minutes. Studies show that brief, targeted simulations can achieve 70-80% of the learning objectives of longer sessions (Pottle, 2019).

- *Integrated Learning*: Embedding simulation into existing coursework or clinical rotations. For example, a brief simulation session on sepsis management could be incorporated into a broader clinical workshop on critical care.

- *Flexible Scheduling*: Offering evening or weekend sessions or using virtual simulations that learners can access on-demand provides more flexibility for busy schedules.

Learner Engagement

One of the primary benefits of simulation is its ability to immerse learners in realistic, hands-on scenarios. However, poorly designed or overly artificial simulations can fail to capture participants' attention, reducing their educational value.

For example, scenarios that lack realism, are misaligned with learning objectives, or feel irrelevant to the learner's professional context can lead to disengagement.

Strategies to enhance engagement include:

- *Enhancing Realism*: Incorporating realistic details, such as lifelike patient monitors, realistic clinical environments, and accurate physiological responses, increases immersion. High-fidelity simulations have been shown to improve learner engagement by 30% compared to low-fidelity simulations (Weaver et al., 2010).

- *Aligning Scenarios with Objectives*: Ensuring simulations are closely tied to specific, measurable learning outcomes. For example, designing a scenario to practice trauma resuscitation should include appropriate complexity and relevant clinical protocols.

- *Interactive Scenarios*: Interactive scenarios actively foster deeper engagement by allowing learners to participate in problem-solving and decision-making. A study found that interactive simulations resulted in 25% higher knowledge retention than passive learning methods like lectures (Lapkin et al., 2010).

> ↑25%
> Interactive simulations result in higher knowledge retention over passive learning methods.

Learner-Centered Design: Incorporating feedback from learners when designing scenarios ensures that the content feels relevant and impactful.

3.10 Evaluation of Simulation Effectiveness

Evaluating the success of a simulation program is a multifaceted process that involves assessing both the participants' immediate learning outcomes and the program's broader impact on professional practice and patient care. A comprehensive evaluation strategy ensures that simulation-based education achieves its intended goals, identifies areas for improvement, and justifies the investment in this training method. Below, we explore the various methods used to measure the effectiveness of simulation.

Pre- and Post-Simulation Testing

One of the most straightforward ways to evaluate simulation outcomes is through pre- and post-simulation testing, which measures knowledge acquisition and skill improvement. These assessments often involve written exams, practical skill evaluations, or simulated patient encounters conducted before and after a simulation session.

For instance, a pre-simulation test might assess learners' baseline knowledge of Advanced Cardiovascular Life Support (ACLS) protocols. After participating in a high-fidelity simulation of a cardiac arrest scenario, a post-simulation test could measure their retention and application of this knowledge. Studies have shown that learners often demonstrate a 20-30% increase in knowledge retention and skill accuracy following simulation-based training (Pottle, 2019).

Pre- and post-testing also allows educators to identify specific areas where learners struggle, enabling targeted remediation and curriculum adjustments.

Objective Structured Clinical Examinations (OSCEs)

Objective Structured Clinical Examinations (OSCEs) are widely used to assess performance systematically. They consist of multiple stations where learners perform specific tasks or interact with standardized patients under the observation of trained evaluators. Each station focuses on a particular competency, such as physical examination skills, diagnostic reasoning, or communication.

Simulations integrated into OSCEs allow for evaluating complex scenarios, such as managing a patient with sepsis or delivering bad news to a family. These assessments use structured rubrics that provide clear criteria for evaluating performance, ensuring consistency and objectivity. For example, a rubric for a sepsis management scenario might include categories like timely recognition of symptoms, appropriate treatment initiation, and effective communication with team members.

Research shows that incorporating simulation into OSCEs improves learners' performance in real-world settings by 25%, as it mirrors the pressures and complexities of clinical practice (Hayden et al., 2014).

Feedback from Learners

Collecting qualitative feedback from learners is an invaluable part of evaluating simulation programs. Learners provide insights into the realism, relevance, and overall impact of the simulation experience, which can guide future improvements. Feedback mechanisms include surveys, focus groups, and post-simulation interviews.

For example, learners might rate the effectiveness of the debriefing process, comment on the realism of the simulated environment, or suggest areas where the scenario could be more aligned with their learning needs. In one study, 85% of learners reported that simulations helped them feel more prepared for real clinical situations, highlighting the importance of aligning simulation design with learner expectations (Lindeman, 2021).

> 85% of learners reported that simulations helped them feel more prepared for real clinical situations

Analyzing learner feedback allows educators to refine scenarios, improve facilitation techniques, and ensure that simulations remain engaging and impactful.

Long-Term Outcomes

While immediate performance improvements are important, the ultimate measure of a simulation program's success is its long-term impact on clinical practice and patient outcomes. Tracking these outcomes involves evaluating how simulation training translates into real-world skills and behaviors.

Examples of Long-Term Metrics:

- *Clinical Error Rates*: Institutions that implement simulation-based training in high-risk areas, such as medication administration or central line insertion, often see significant reductions in clinical errors. For example, hospitals using simulation to train for central line placement reported a 45% decrease in bloodstream infections(Lindeman, 2021).

- *Retention of Knowledge and Skills*: Long-term assessments, such as follow-up testing months after training, measure how well learners retain critical competencies over time.

- *Patient Care Improvements*: Improved patient outcomes, such as shorter hospital stays or fewer complications, are often linked to enhanced clinical skills gained through simulation. A meta-analysis found that simulation-based team training improved patient survival rates during cardiac arrests by 10-15% (Weaver et al., 2010).

- *Professional Confidence and Competency*: Simulation training often boosts healthcare providers' confidence in handling complex situations, leading to better decision-making and teamwork in clinical settings.

Tracking these metrics requires collaboration with healthcare organizations to monitor outcomes and collect data on graduates' performance in their professional roles.

3.11 Ethical Considerations in Simulation Design

Ethics are foundational in designing and implementing healthcare simulations, ensuring fairness, respect, and psychological safety for all participants. Thoughtful adherence to ethical principles protects learners and reinforces professional values they will carry into their clinical practice. Below, we expand on key ethical considerations in simulation design, addressing potential challenges and strategies for maintaining ethical integrity.

Avoiding Scenarios That Cause Undue Stress or Emotional Harm

While simulations are designed to replicate the pressures of real-world clinical environments, scenarios that may cause unnecessary stress or emotional harm to participants must be avoided. Ethical simulation design requires a balance between challenging learners and ensuring their psychological well-being.

Trauma-Informed Design: Scenarios involving emotionally charged topics, such as pediatric deaths or critical medical errors, must be carefully crafted. For instance, a scenario addressing neonatal resuscitation could include appropriate preparatory discussions and a debriefing session that provides emotional support. Research shows that debriefing significantly reduces post-simulation stress and enhances learning retention by 30% (Weaver et al., 2010).

Gradual Complexity: Introducing learners to simulations with progressively increasing complexity allows them to build confidence before facing high-stakes scenarios. For example, nursing students might first practice basic patient communication before engaging in simulations involving end-of-life discussions with grieving family members.

Monitoring Emotional Responses: Facilitators should be trained to recognize signs of distress during simulations. If a participant becomes overwhelmed, facilitators must be prepared to pause the session, provide support, and offer resources if needed. This approach fosters a culture of care and respect.

Ensuring Inclusivity in Simulation Design

Ethical simulation design must reflect the diversity of real-world patient populations and conditions. Failing to include diverse scenarios risks perpetuating biases and leaving learners unprepared to deliver equitable care.

- *Representation in Scenarios*: Simulations should include patients from racial, ethnic, cultural, socioeconomic, and gender backgrounds.

- For example, a scenario involving a diabetic patient could consider cultural factors influencing diet and treatment adherence. Inclusive scenarios promote cultural competence and prepare learners to address disparities in healthcare.

- *Addressing Health Inequities*: Simulations can highlight systemic healthcare inequities and train learners to navigate these challenges.

For instance, a scenario might involve a patient who delays seeking care due to financial barriers, prompting learners to explore solutions like social work referrals or community health resources.

Accessibility for Learners: Inclusivity also applies to the learners themselves. Simulation design should consider accommodations for participants with disabilities, such as providing alternative ways to engage with VR tools or ensuring physical accessibility in simulation labs. Research by Lindeman (2021) emphasizes the importance of inclusivity in fostering a supportive learning environment.

Protecting Confidentiality of Learner Performance and Simulation Data

Confidentiality is a cornerstone of ethical simulation practice. Protecting learner performance data fosters trust and ensures a safe environment for participants to learn from mistakes without fear of judgment or repercussions.

- *Anonymity in Assessment*: Simulation performance data should be anonymized for research, program evaluation, or institutional reporting. For example, video recordings of simulations should be stored securely and used only with the participant's consent.

- *Non-Punitive Feedback*: Ethical principles dictate that simulation be a space for learning rather than punitive evaluation. For instance, if a learner fails to recognize a deteriorating patient in a simulated scenario, the focus should be constructive feedback rather than penalizing the error. This approach aligns with the core purpose of simulation, which is to create a safe environment for growth.

- *Transparency in Data Use*: Participants should be informed about how their simulation data will be used. For example, if performance metrics will contribute to their course grades or be shared with clinical instructors, this should be communicated at the outset.

Balancing Ethical Challenges

Ethical dilemmas can arise during simulation design, such as deciding how much realism to incorporate without harming people or how to prioritize inclusivity without reinforcing stereotypes. Addressing these challenges requires collaboration among educators, ethicists, and stakeholders to ensure that simulations are impactful and respectful.

For example, designing a scenario about a patient experiencing intimate partner violence might involve consulting with experts in trauma care to strike a balance between realism and sensitivity. Similarly, addressing conditions disproportionately affecting certain groups, such as sickle cell anemia, requires avoiding stereotypes while educating learners about cultural competence.

3.12 Summary

Chapter 3 delves into the essential principles and processes of creating and implementing effective simulation-based education in healthcare. It emphasizes a structured and thoughtful approach to ensure simulations are engaging, pedagogically sound, and aligned with institutional goals. The chapter also explores strategies to overcome practical challenges and ethical concerns, ensuring the educational experience is impactful and equitable.

The chapter begins by highlighting the foundational importance of simulation design. Effective simulations rely on clearly defined learning objectives established through frameworks like Bloom's Taxonomy. These objectives ensure simulations address the cognitive, affective, and psychomotor domains of learning, fostering both technical competence and interpersonal skills. A systematic needs assessment forms the basis for simulation activities, identifying gaps in knowledge and aligning scenarios with learners' specific requirements and institutional priorities.

Frameworks such as the ADDIE model and the Six-Step Approach to Curriculum Development provide structured methodologies for simulation design. These frameworks guide educators through the analysis, design, development, implementation, and evaluation phases. For instance, the ADDIE model emphasizes iterative improvement, while the Six-Step Approach ensures alignment between educational objectives and instructional strategies. Together, they offer scalable solutions for building effective, learner-centered simulations.

The choice of simulation modality is critical to achieving desired outcomes. Mannequin-based simulations are ideal for high-stakes clinical training, task trainers focus on procedural skills, standardized patients enhance communication and diagnostic abilities, and VR/AR technologies provide immersive environments for complex scenarios. The appropriate modality depends on the objectives, resources, and learner needs.

Feedback and debriefing are integral to the simulation's success. Immediate feedback during scenarios helps learners correct mistakes in real-time, reinforcing task-specific learning. Debriefing sessions, conducted after the simulation, encourage deeper reflection and critical thinking. PEARLS and the Advocacy-Inquiry Model provide structured approaches to debriefing, fostering psychological safety, and promoting long-term skill development.

Ethical considerations underpin every aspect of simulation design. Scenarios must avoid causing undue stress while ensuring inclusivity and representing diverse patient populations. Protecting the confidentiality of learner performance is vital to maintaining trust and creating a supportive learning environment. Balancing realism with sensitivity is critical to designing impactful scenarios without reinforcing stereotypes or causing emotional harm.

The chapter also addresses challenges in simulation, such as resource limitations, time constraints, and learner engagement. Hybrid models and virtual simulations can mitigate the high equipment and training costs, while short, focused scenarios and flexible scheduling help integrate simulations into busy academic and clinical programs. Realistic, interactive, and learner-centered scenarios are key to maintaining engagement and ensuring educational value.

Finally, evaluating the effectiveness of simulation is essential. Methods such as pre-and post-simulation testing, OSCEs, and learner feedback assess immediate outcomes, while long-term metrics track the impact on clinical practice and patient care. For example, simulation programs have been shown to reduce clinical errors and improve patient outcomes, demonstrating their value as a transformative tool in healthcare education. Chapter 3 provides a comprehensive guide to designing and implementing simulation-based education. By addressing both the practical and ethical dimensions of simulation, educators can create programs that enhance learner performance, build confidence, and ultimately improve patient care.

3.13 Chapter Review

Review Questions

1. **Simulation Design**
   a. What are the key steps of the ADDIE Model and the Six-Step Approach to curriculum development?
   b. How do these frameworks contribute to effective simulation design?
2. **Learning Objectives**
   a. How does Bloom's Taxonomy aid in establishing learning objectives for healthcare simulations?
   b. Provide an example of an objective for each domain (cognitive, affective, psychomotor).
3. **Simulation Modalities**
   a. What factors should be considered when selecting a simulation modality?
   b. Compare and contrast mannequin-based simulations and standardized patient programs.
4. **Scenario Development**
   a. What are the characteristics of an effective simulation scenario?
   b. Describe the purpose and design features of crisis resource management (CRM) scenarios.
5. **Feedback and Debriefing**
   a. Differentiate between feedback and debriefing in simulation education.
   b. How do debriefing models like PEARLS or Advocacy-Inquiry enhance learning?
6. **Ethical Considerations**
   a. Why is inclusivity important in simulation design, and how can it be achieved?
   b. Discuss the importance of confidentiality in simulation-based education.

7. **Evaluation of Effectiveness**
   a. What methods can be used to evaluate the success of a simulation program?
   b. How do long-term outcomes, such as improved patient care, demonstrate simulation effectiveness?

Critical Thinking and Application

1. **Scenario Design**
   Design a simulation scenario for managing a sepsis case. Include objectives, selected modality, and debriefing approach.
2. **Feedback Integration**
   Propose a method for combining immediate feedback with structured debriefing to maximize learning outcomes.
3. **Overcoming Challenges**
   Suggest strategies to address resource limitations in implementing high-fidelity simulations in a resource-constrained institution.

Hands-On Activity

- **Simulation Scenario Template**
  Develop a standardized simulation scenario template. Include fields for objectives, modality, required resources, learner roles, and evaluation criteria.

Summary Reflection

Reflect on the critical components of simulation design, including learning objectives, modality selection, and feedback mechanisms. How do these elements collectively ensure simulations are impactful, ethical, and aligned with real-world healthcare challenges?

Chapter 4

Operational Management in Medical and Nursing Simulation Centers

The increasing emphasis on simulation-based training in healthcare has driven the rapid expansion of dedicated simulation centers, particularly within medical and nursing schools. Beginning in the early 2000s, these centers became a cornerstone of healthcare education worldwide, providing learners with a safe and controlled environment to hone their clinical skills, practice critical procedures, and experience high-pressure scenarios—all without posing any risk to patients. However, to ensure the effective delivery of simulation education, the operation of these centers must be carefully managed. This chapter explores the key elements of operational management in medical and nursing simulation centers, focusing on facility design and workflow optimization, resource and inventory management, and scheduling and capacity planning.

4.1 Justification for a Simulation Center and Crafting a Business Plan

Simulation centers are transformative spaces that blend cutting-edge technology with innovative teaching methodologies, creating immersive environments for learners. They have become essential in education and professional training, particularly in high-stakes fields like healthcare, aviation, and engineering. This section explores the rationale for establishing a simulation center and guides you through crafting a compelling business plan to turn this vision into reality.

The Case for a Simulation Center

Simulation centers address a growing need for experiential learning by offering controlled environments where individuals can develop and refine skills without real-world consequences. This approach bridges the gap between theoretical knowledge and practical application, providing learners with opportunities to practice, fail safely, and ultimately succeed. For example, in healthcare, simulation-based training has been shown to improve clinical competencies and enhance patient safety (Gaba, 2004).

From an organizational perspective, simulation centers align closely with institutional goals. Many accreditation bodies emphasize the importance of practical training and assessment, making these centers invaluable. Beyond fulfilling accreditation requirements, they enable continuous professional development, supporting professionals in maintaining and advancing their skills over time (Ziv et al., 2003).

The evidence further reinforces the value of simulation centers. Studies demonstrate that simulation-based education leads to better skill retention, reduced error rates, and improved learner confidence (Issenberg et al., 2005). These benefits enhance individual performance and improve organizational outcomes, particularly in fields where errors have significant consequences, such as medicine and aviation.

Moreover, simulation centers offer organizations a competitive advantage. They signal a commitment to innovation, quality, and safety, attracting students, employees, and collaborators. For instance, institutions investing in state-of-the-art simulation technology often distinguish themselves as leaders in their field, enhancing recruitment and reputation (Lateef, 2010).

Crafting a Business Plan

A successful simulation center requires more than a compelling justification; it needs a robust business plan to ensure its establishment and sustainability. A well-crafted plan serves as a roadmap, guiding decision-making and demonstrating the center's value to stakeholders.

Executive Summary
The business plan should begin with an executive summary clearly articulating the simulation center's mission, vision, and objectives. This section sets the tone for the document, highlighting the center's potential to address critical needs and deliver measurable outcomes.

Market Analysis
Understanding the market is essential. A thorough analysis identifies the primary audience—whether medical students, healthcare professionals, or corporate clients—and assesses the demand for simulation-based training. It also examines competitors, pinpointing unique selling points that distinguish the proposed center from others. For example, a simulation center focused on interdisciplinary training might cater to a niche not addressed by traditional facilities.

Strategic Goals and Objectives
Defining clear goals is critical for aligning the simulation center's development with organizational priorities. Short-term objectives might include securing funding and acquiring equipment, while long-term goals could focus on expanding services and achieving financial sustainability.

Infrastructure and Technology Requirements
Another vital component is a detailed inventory of infrastructure and technology needs. This includes identifying the types of simulators, software, and physical spaces required for operations. Estimating costs for initial setup and ongoing maintenance ensures the plan is grounded in financial reality.

Financial Planning

Financial sustainability is a cornerstone of any business plan. Budgeting should account for development, operations, marketing expenses, and projected revenues from training programs, partnerships, and grants. Identifying funding sources—such as internal allocations, external sponsorships, or governmental grants—adds credibility to the plan (Medley & Horne, 2005).

Organizational Structure and Staffing

A well-defined organizational structure ensures the center's effective management and operation. This section should outline the roles and responsibilities of staff, including instructors, technicians, and administrative personnel. Clear delineation of responsibilities helps maintain operational efficiency.

Marketing and Outreach Strategies

A strong marketing strategy is required to attract users and stakeholders. Tactics might include hosting open house events, conducting live demonstrations, and sharing success stories from simulation-based training. Demonstrating the center's value through testimonials and data-driven outcomes can build trust and enthusiasm among potential clients.

Risk Assessment and Contingency Planning

No venture is without risks. It is crucial to identify potential challenges—such as financial shortfalls, operational inefficiencies, or technology obsolescence—and develop strategies to address them. A contingency plan ensures that the center remains resilient despite unforeseen circumstances.

Integrating Justification with the Business Plan

The justification for a simulation center forms the backbone of the business plan, linking its purpose to the proposed structure and operations. For instance, data demonstrating the effectiveness of simulation-based training can be incorporated into the executive summary and market analysis, reinforcing the center's value proposition. Similarly, aligning the center's goals with organizational priorities ensures buy-in from leadership and stakeholders.

A simulation center is more than a training facility—it is a catalyst for innovation, safety, and excellence. Justifying its establishment requires a clear understanding of its benefits, supported by evidence and aligned with organizational goals. However, turning the vision into reality depends on a comprehensive business plan that integrates justification with actionable strategies. By investing in both, institutions can create impactful simulation centers that serve learners, professionals, and communities for years.

> A simulation center is a catalyst for innovation, safety, and excellence.

4.2 Simulation Center Design and Workflow Optimization

The design of a simulation center plays a critical role in the effectiveness of simulation-based training, as it must replicate real healthcare environments as authentically as possible. Achieving this involves careful planning and the inclusion of diverse, specialized spaces that mirror the settings healthcare professionals encounter in their practice (Gaba, 2004).

Core Areas of a Simulation Center

Simulation centers typically feature a variety of spaces designed to replicate different clinical environments. These include:

Patient Rooms: Modeled after hospital or clinic rooms, patient rooms are essential for simulating routine care, bedside procedures, and patient-provider interactions. They are equipped with beds, monitoring equipment, and other standard medical tools to provide a realistic setting (Gaba, 2004).

Treatment Bays: These areas are designed for outpatient or ambulatory care scenarios, focusing on short-term treatments and minor procedures (Bradley, 2006).

Emergency Care Areas: These spaces simulate high-acuity settings such as emergency departments and include features like crash carts, defibrillators, and triage stations to prepare learners for urgent care situations (Issenberg et al., 1999).

Operating Rooms: Operating rooms replicate surgical environments and are equipped with operating tables, surgical lights, anesthesia machines, and sterilization areas. These spaces allow learners to practice surgical procedures, teamwork, and sterile techniques (Gaba, 2004).

Trauma Bays: Dedicated trauma areas provide learners with an opportunity to experience high-stakes scenarios requiring rapid assessment and intervention, such as multi-system trauma or resuscitation (Kneebone et al., 2004).

Each of these spaces should be meticulously designed to mirror real-world environments, enabling learners to seamlessly transfer skills from simulation to clinical practice (Bradley, 2006).

Average Square Footage for Healthcare Simulation Spaces

Simulation Space	Average Size (Square Feet)	Purpose/Notes
Patient Rooms	120–150 sq. ft.	Simulate standard inpatient or clinic care; includes space for bed, monitors, and seating.
Treatment Rooms	100–120 sq. ft.	Outpatient care or minor procedures; smaller than inpatient rooms.
Emergency Care Areas	150–200 sq. ft. per bay	Open layout with dividers; supports team-based urgent care scenarios.
Operating Rooms (ORs)	400–600 sq. ft.	High-fidelity surgical training includes space for tables, anesthesia machines, and AV systems.

Simulation Space	Average Size (Square Feet)	Purpose/Notes
Trauma Bays	200–250 sq. ft. per bay	Team-based critical care scenarios; accommodates resuscitation tools and multiple participants.
Debriefing Rooms	200–300 sq. ft.	Space for post-simulation discussions; accommodates 10–15 participants.
Control Rooms	50–75 sq. ft. per simulation space	Houses AV equipment and simulator controls; located adjacent to simulation rooms.
Storage Areas	150–200 sq. ft.	Secures simulators, props, and consumables; accessible from simulation areas. More storage the better.
Classrooms	300–500 sq. ft.	Used for pre- and post-simulation didactic instruction; accommodates up to 20 learners.

Flexibility in Layout

One of the defining features of a modern simulation center is its adaptability. Healthcare training encompasses a broad spectrum of scenarios, from primary care to critical emergencies, and the facility layout must support this diversity. Flexibility in design allows the simulation center to accommodate evolving curricula, new technologies, and interdisciplinary training (Gaba, 2004).

Modular Walls: Incorporating modular walls enables simulation centers to reconfigure spaces quickly, transforming a patient room into a trauma bay or an operating suite as needed. This adaptability is particularly valuable for training programs with a wide range of specialties (Issenberg et al., 1999).

Movable Furniture and Equipment: Utilizing furniture and medical equipment that can be easily repositioned ensures that spaces can be tailored to specific scenarios. For example, an outpatient clinic setup can be swiftly converted into an inpatient ward for a different training module (Kneebone et al., 2004).

Convertible Zones: Open-plan areas with movable partitions can serve multiple purposes, such as hosting large group debriefings, team-based simulations, or individual skill assessments (Bradley, 2006).

This level of customization allows simulation centers to provide diverse learning opportunities while maximizing the use of available space (Gaba, 2004).

Incorporating Specialized Features

To enhance realism and support complex training scenarios, simulation centers may include advanced features and specialized areas:

Virtual Reality (VR) and Augmented Reality (AR) Labs: Dedicated VR/AR spaces allow learners to engage in immersive simulations that would be challenging to replicate physically, such as mass casualty incidents or rare clinical cases (Issenberg et al., 1999).

Control Rooms: Hidden control rooms equipped with audiovisual technology enable instructors to monitor and guide simulations in real-time without being visible to learners, maintaining the authenticity of the scenario (Gaba, 2004).

Debriefing Rooms: These spaces are crucial for post-simulation discussions, allowing learners to reflect on their performance and receive feedback. Equipped with screens for video playback, debriefing rooms help reinforce key lessons (Kneebone et al., 2004).

Skills Labs: Separate from full-scale simulation environments, skills labs are dedicated spaces for practicing specific tasks like suturing, IV insertion, or catheter placement using task trainers (Bradley, 2006).

Attention to Detail

Attention to detail ensures learners feel fully immersed in the simulated environment. Elements such as lighting, sound, and even smells can enhance the realism of the experience:

Realistic Lighting: Adjustable lighting allows for the simulation of various scenarios, such as dim lighting in operating rooms or natural daylight in patient rooms (Kneebone et al., 2004).

Sound Effects: Incorporating ambient noises, such as alarms, patient voices, or equipment sounds, can replicate the auditory challenges of real healthcare settings (Issenberg et al., 1999).

Medical Supplies: Stocking rooms with authentic medical supplies—bandages, syringes, medication labels—adds another layer of realism (Bradley, 2006).

Future-Proofing the Facility

As technology and educational methods evolve, simulation centers must be designed with the future in mind. Key considerations include:

Technological Infrastructure: Adequate wiring and network capabilities ensure compatibility with advanced simulation technologies, including high-fidelity mannequins, VR systems, and remote learning tools (Gaba, 2004).

Sustainability: Incorporating energy-efficient designs and materials can reduce the facility's environmental impact while lowering operating costs (Bradley, 2006).

Scalability: Building in the capacity for expansion allows the simulation center to grow alongside its program, accommodating increased student enrollment or additional training modules (Kneebone et al., 2004).

The design of a simulation center plays a critical role in the effectiveness of simulation-based training, as it must replicate real healthcare environments as authentically as possible. Achieving this involves careful planning and including diverse, specialized spaces that mirror the settings healthcare professionals encounter in their practice (Gaba, 2004).

Equipment and Infrastructure:

Simulation centers require significant infrastructure to support sophisticated simulation equipment, including high-fidelity mannequins, audiovisual recording systems, and monitoring equipment. A robust IT infrastructure is essential for running simulation software, managing virtual simulations, and analyzing learner performance. Proper storage and charging facilities are also needed for equipment maintenance and organization (Issenberg et al., 2005). Specialized rooms for equipment calibration and maintenance should be planned to prevent delays in simulation readiness.

Workflow Optimization:

Behind every successful simulation center lies a meticulously designed workflow that ensures seamless operations, minimizes downtime, and maximizes the educational impact of each session. While cutting-edge technology and realistic environments often take center stage, the unseen backbone of any simulation center is its workflow optimization. From preparation to execution and scenario turnover, an efficient workflow enhances the learning experience. It ensures that staff, instructors, and learners can focus on what matters most—education and skill development.

Building a Streamlined Process

The foundation of effective workflow optimization begins with understanding the specific needs of the simulation center and its users. Each stage of the simulation process, from setup to debriefing, should flow logically and minimize disruptions. Achieving this requires thoughtful planning, team coordination, and standardized protocols.

1. **Simulation Preparation**:
    - Setting up a simulation can be time-intensive, especially when scenarios involve complex equipment or specific patient cases. To streamline this phase, simulation centers should develop detailed checklists for each type of scenario. For example, a checklist for a trauma simulation might include setting up monitors, loading a scenario into a high-fidelity mannequin, and arranging necessary supplies like IV kits or blood transfusion equipment.
    - Efficient storage systems play a crucial role here. By organizing supplies and equipment systematically, staff can quickly locate and prepare materials without unnecessary delays. Labeling drawers, cabinets, and storage bins with scenario-specific tags ensures nothing is overlooked (Gaba, 2004).

2. **Scenario Execution**:
    - During the simulation, workflow optimization involves creating an environment where instructors can focus solely on facilitating the scenario and guiding learners. This means having a trained support team ready to handle technical issues, manage equipment, and monitor timing.

- Control room operators should be well-versed in the technical aspects of the simulation, such as adjusting mannequin responses or introducing new challenges mid-scenario. Seamless communication between the control room and the simulation floor is critical, often facilitated by headsets or real-time messaging systems (Issenberg et al., 1999).

3. **Scenario Turnover**:
    - One of the most challenging aspects of workflow optimization is the transition between scenarios. Whether moving from one patient case to another or resetting for the next group of learners, minimizing downtime is essential to maintain momentum and maximize learning opportunities.
    - To achieve this, simulation centers should establish clear protocols for scenario turnover. For example, one team might be responsible for cleaning and resetting equipment while another prepares the next scenario. This division of labor allows instructors to focus on teaching rather than administrative tasks (Kneebone et al., 2004).
    - Incorporating modular systems, such as plug-and-play components for mannequins or preloaded scenario software, further reduces setup times.

Incorporating Automation and Technology

Advancements in technology offer significant opportunities to optimize workflow in simulation centers. By automating routine tasks and leveraging digital tools, simulation centers can enhance efficiency and reduce the burden on staff.

Scenario Management Software:

Many simulation centers now use dedicated software platforms to manage scenarios, track equipment usage, and document learner progress. These systems allow instructors to pre-program scenarios, schedule sessions, and even automate mannequin responses, saving valuable time during setup and execution (Bradley, 2006).

Automated Maintenance Systems:

Routine maintenance of high-fidelity mannequins and other simulation equipment is essential to prevent technical issues and ensure smooth operation. Automated systems are critical in monitoring equipment performance, providing real-time alerts for required updates, repairs, or potential malfunctions. These systems can significantly reduce unexpected downtime by identifying issues early and streamlining maintenance tasks.

Many advanced simulator platforms integrate maintenance monitoring into their software packages, offering tools to track performance and notify staff when intervention is needed. However, automated systems are only a partial replacement for regular hands-on maintenance by staff. Routine cleaning and physical inspections often uncover maintenance needs that automated systems might need to be aware of. A combination of automated tools and diligent staff involvement ensures that equipment remains reliable, extending its lifespan and minimizing disruptions to training sessions.

RFID and Inventory Management:

Radio-frequency identification (RFID) tags efficiently track equipment and supplies in real-time, ensuring that materials are readily available and minimizing delays caused by missing or misplaced items (Issenberg et al., 1999). In recent years, advancements in location-tracking technology, such as Apple's Air Tag and other Bluetooth-enabled devices, have provided additional tools for inventory management. Many simulation centers now use these tagging systems to physically mark equipment, enabling precise real-time location tracking and streamlining the management of essential resources.

Team Coordination and Training

A well-optimized workflow is only as strong as the team behind it. Effective simulation centers invest in staff training and foster a culture of collaboration to ensure that every team member understands their role in the workflow.

Staff Training:
Simulation center staff should be cross-trained in multiple roles, from operating mannequins to managing equipment. This flexibility allows team members to step in wherever needed, ensuring smooth operations even during high-demand periods.

Role Clarity:
Clearly defined roles and responsibilities ensure clarity and redundancy. For example, one staff member might oversee equipment setup while another focuses on learner orientation. Regular team meetings and debriefings can help refine these roles over time.

Communication Protocols:
Effective communication is the backbone of workflow optimization. Teams should use standardized language and tools to convey critical information quickly and accurately. For instance, during scenario turnover, a checklist-based handoff system can ensure that all tasks are completed efficiently.

Balancing Efficiency and Flexibility

While optimizing workflow is critical for simulation centers, maintaining flexibility is equally important to accommodate unexpected changes. Simulations are dynamic, and unforeseen challenges such as scenarios running over time, technical malfunctions, or last-minute adjustments to participant schedules can arise. Staff must be prepared to adapt quickly, ensuring the training experience remains effective without compromising quality. By incorporating flexibility into the workflow, centers can maintain efficiency while prioritizing the learning outcomes of each session.

Buffer Time
A key strategy for managing unpredictability is to build buffer time into the schedule. This involves intentionally creating gaps between sessions to allow for overruns, equipment resets, or additional debriefing.

- *Importance in High-Stakes Scenarios:* In simulations focused on critical situations, such as trauma response or cardiac emergencies, the post-scenario debriefing is as important as the simulation itself. Buffer time ensures that instructors can thoroughly review performance, provide constructive feedback, and address questions without feeling rushed.

- *Equipment Maintenance and Reset*: Mannequins and equipment often require recalibration or restocking between sessions. Buffer time allows staff to perform these tasks without impacting the subsequent schedule.

- *Rest*: Ensure your staff has regular daily breaks, including sufficient meal time, to maintain energy and focus.

- *Real-World Example*: A center running back-to-back emergency response simulations might allocate 15-20 minutes between scenarios to reset the environment, restock supplies, and allow the next group to enter without delay. This would prevent staff from becoming overburdened and improve overall efficiency.

Adaptable Schedules

Adaptable scheduling systems are another vital component of flexibility in simulation center workflows. These systems enable staff to adjust real-time session timings, resource allocations, and participant rosters.

Dynamic Scheduling Tools
- **Digital Platforms**: Simulation management software like SimCapture or CAE LearningSpace provides tools for dynamic scheduling. These platforms allow administrators to modify schedules in real-time, ensuring that changes—such as extending a session or rescheduling a canceled one—are reflected immediately.

- **Automated Alerts**: These systems can notify instructors, staff, and participants of changes via email or text, reducing confusion and ensuring smooth transitions.

Rescheduling and Extending Sessions
- **Scenario Extensions**: If a session runs over due to an in-depth discussion or unexpected challenges during the simulation, adaptable schedules ensure that subsequent activities can be adjusted without derailing the entire day's plan.

- **Efficient Rescheduling**: In the event of a last-minute cancellation, simulation centers can quickly reallocate resources and reassign time slots, preventing downtime and maintaining productivity.

- **Prioritizing Sessions**
- Adaptable schedules also allow simulation centers to prioritize sessions based on urgency or complexity. For example, if a technical issue delays a lower-priority session, staff can reassign resources to ensure that a critical, high-stakes simulation is unaffected.

Integrated Flexibility Strategies

To maintain adaptability while minimizing disruption, simulation centers can implement a combination of strategies:

- **Team Preparedness**: Train staff to handle unexpected changes and empower them to make real-time decisions, such as reallocating resources or adjusting session durations.

- **Communication Systems**: Use clear communication channels, such as instant messaging apps or group emails, to promptly inform all stakeholders of schedule adjustments.

- **Predefined Contingency Plans**: Develop and document protocols for common disruptions, such as equipment failures or participant no-shows so that staff can respond quickly and effectively.

- **Resource Redundancy**: Maintain backups for critical equipment, such as additional mannequins or monitors, to ensure smooth operations even in a failure.

The Balance Between Structure and Flexibility

While maintaining a structured workflow is essential for efficiency, integrating flexibility into the system ensures that simulation centers can respond to the unexpected without compromising the quality of the training experience. Simulation centers can effectively manage disruptions while delivering high-quality, impactful training sessions by building in buffer time, leveraging dynamic scheduling tools, and fostering a culture of adaptability. This balance allows centers to meet operational demands and prioritize the goal of preparing learners for the complexities of real-world healthcare.

4.3 Resource and Inventory Management

Resource and inventory management are critical to a simulation center's operational efficiency. Given the high cost of equipment and consumables, effective management ensures that the center can operate sustainably while delivering quality training experiences.

Managing Consumables

Simulation centers use a variety of consumables, from medical supplies such as syringes, gauze, and medications to disposable parts for simulators, like airway components and blood bags. Establishing an inventory system that tracks consumable usage and reordering is essential to avoid shortages and ensure that simulation activities are not interrupted. Implementing barcode scanning or RFID technology can help streamline tracking and provide real-time updates on inventory status (Zendejas et al., 2013).

Maintaining Simulators

High-fidelity simulators, like mannequins and task trainers, require regular maintenance to ensure they function correctly. Simulators are expensive investments, and proper care is necessary for them to deteriorate quickly, affecting the quality of training and the longevity of the equipment. Routine calibration, cleaning, and part replacements are necessary to keep these devices operational. Scheduling regular maintenance checks and having a dedicated team for simulator upkeep can help prevent costly repairs or downtime

(Gaba, 2004).

Planning for Equipment Lifecycle

Managing the lifecycle of equipment is a critical responsibility for simulation center managers. High-fidelity simulators and other advanced technology have finite lifespans, requiring eventual replacement or upgrades. Planning for these transitions demands careful budget forecasting and long-term strategic planning to meet future needs while maintaining the center's current training capacity. Proactively budgeting for upgrades and building relationships with manufacturers for early access to new technologies can help mitigate the operational challenges of equipment obsolescence (Schwartz & Barnett, 2011).

In addition to simulators, managers must consider the lifecycle of all supporting technologies, such as computers, laptops, and other essential IT infrastructure. While some centers rely on their institution's IT department to monitor and manage replacement cycles, others must independently plan and execute these upgrades. Overlooking these items can disrupt operations if critical systems fail unexpectedly.

Another often-overlooked area of equipment lifecycle management is the audio-visual infrastructure, including video switchers, audio mixers, and other recording or display systems used for simulation sessions and debriefings. These components also have a finite end of life, and failing to plan for their replacement can lead to costly downtime and interruptions in training. By incorporating these items into the overall lifecycle strategy and budgeting for their replacement, centers can ensure operations continuity and maintain the simulation experience's quality.

Equipment Type	Typical Lifespan	Replacement Timing
High-Fidelity Manikins	5–7 years	Replace or upgrade at Year 5
Task Trainers	5–10 years	Replace selectively based on usage
AV and Recording Systems	5–7 years	Evaluate for refresh at Year 5
IT Hardware (e.g., computers)	3–5 years	Replace at Year 3–5
VR/AR Equipment	3–4 years	Replace or upgrade at Year 3
Medical Devices	5–7 years	Refresh based on condition and usage
Furniture and Fixtures	7–10 years	Replace as needed

Table 3 Key Timelines for Different Equipment Types

Budgeting for Resources

Effective budgeting is a cornerstone of resource management in simulation centers, where funding demands can be diverse and substantial. Simulation centers rely on a steady influx of financial resources to maintain high-fidelity equipment, stock consumable supplies, conduct regular maintenance, and implement technological upgrades. Beyond maintaining operations, securing adequate funding enables simulation centers to expand their offerings, improve training quality, and remain competitive in an evolving educational landscape.

SIMULATION OPERATIONS IN HEALTHCARE EDUCATION: A PRIMER INTO THE ROLE OF OPERATIONS IN MEDICAL AND NURSING TRAINING

The Challenges of Budgeting

One of the primary challenges simulation centers face is the pressure to justify their financial needs to stakeholders. Institutional administrators, grant providers, and external partners often require a clear demonstration of how funds are used and the value they bring to educational and patient outcomes. This emphasizes collecting and presenting data that illustrates the impact of simulation on learner performance, patient safety, and institutional goals.

For example, centers may need to show that simulation-based training reduces medical errors, enhances clinical competence, or shortens the learning curve for complex procedures. Combined with cost-benefit analyses, these data points can demonstrate that the simulation investment is justified and essential to achieving long-term healthcare objectives (Ziv et al., 2006).

Funding Sources

To secure the necessary resources, simulation centers often draw from multiple funding streams:

Institutional Support: Many centers receive funding from their parent organizations, such as universities or healthcare systems. This support may cover operational costs, staff salaries, and a baseline of equipment purchases.

Grants: National and regional grants, often from organizations like the National Institutes of Health (NIH) or private foundations, can provide significant funding for new technology or research-focused initiatives. Writing compelling, data-driven grant proposals is a critical skill for simulation center leaders.

Sample Allocation of Funding

- Revenue Generation 10%
- External Partnerships 13%
- Grants 22%
- Institutional Support 55%

External Partnerships: Collaborations with medical device manufacturers, pharmaceutical companies, or technology firms can lead to sponsorships or donations. These partnerships often offer access to cutting-edge technology.

Revenue Generation: Some simulation centers supplement their budgets by offering training programs to external organizations, such as hospitals, emergency services, or corporate clients.

Allocating Funds Strategically

Once funding is secured, careful resource allocation is essential to maximize its impact. Budget planning must account for predictable expenses, such as equipment maintenance and consumables, and unforeseen costs, such as emergency repairs or rapid technological advancements.

Capital Expenditures include major purchases such as high-fidelity mannequins, virtual reality (VR) systems, and audiovisual infrastructure. Given their high cost, these investments should be planned with a long-term perspective, considering the potential for upgrades or replacement in future budgets.

Operational Costs: Regular expenses, such as salaries for instructors and technicians, utilities, and routine maintenance, must be forecasted precisely. This ensures the center can operate smoothly without financial shortfalls.

Consumables: Items like syringes, IV bags, and bandages are often overlooked in initial budgets but are critical for creating realistic scenarios. Tracking usage patterns can help centers estimate and allocate funds effectively.

Research and Development: Setting aside funds for innovation allows centers to explore new methodologies, integrate emerging technologies, and pilot novel simulation techniques.

The Role of Data in Budgeting

Data collection and analysis are integral to effective budgeting. Simulation centers can use key performance indicators (KPIs) to track resource usage, measure learning outcomes, and evaluate return on investment (ROI). For example:

Tracking Utilization: Monitoring how often equipment is used helps identify high-value items versus those that may not justify their cost.

Outcome Metrics: Measuring learner performance pre- and post-simulation can provide compelling evidence of simulation's impact on clinical skills and patient safety.

Cost Analysis: Comparing the costs of simulation-based training to traditional methods, such as clinical rotations or didactic lectures, can highlight simulation's financial and educational benefits.

Long-Term Financial Planning

Successful simulation centers also focus on long-term financial sustainability. Leaders must anticipate future needs, such as equipment upgrades or expansion, to accommodate more learners and integrate these into multi-year budget plans. This forward-thinking approach reduces the risk of unexpected financial strain and ensures the center remains a state-of-the-art facility.

Proactive financial planning might include:

Establishing Reserve Funds: Allocating a portion of the budget to a reserve fund can cover unexpected expenses or provide seed money for new initiatives.

Building Endowments: Partnering with donors or alumni to create endowment funds can provide a steady source of income for years to come.

<u>Negotiating Bulk Purchases:</u> For consumables or equipment, purchasing in bulk or negotiating contracts with suppliers can yield significant cost savings.

Revenue Optimization

Optimizing a simulation center's budget is critical to balancing financial sustainability with delivering high-quality education and training. Simulation programs can maximize their impact by strategically managing revenues and expenses while ensuring efficient resource use. This requires thoughtful planning, innovative revenue generation, and careful cost control.

Revenue Optimization
- Enhancing Revenue Streams
- Reducing Expenses
- Streamlining Operations
- Leveraging Innovation
- Demonstrating Value

<u>Enhancing Revenue Streams</u>
Diversifying funding sources is one of the most effective ways to strengthen a simulation center's financial base. Both local and national grants provide significant opportunities, particularly those tailored to healthcare education or technological innovation. Collaborations with external partners, such as medical device manufacturers or pharmaceutical companies, can bring additional funding and access to advanced equipment through sponsorships or donations.

Offering fee-based training programs for external organizations is another lucrative strategy. Hospitals, emergency medical teams, and corporate clients often seek specialized training, which simulation centers can provide. By hosting workshops, certification courses, or professional development sessions, centers can generate revenue while expanding their reach and reputation. Renting out the facility to other institutions for training needs or conferences is another option to use underutilized resources.

Simulation centers should actively demonstrate their value to secure ongoing institutional funding. Reports and dashboards showcasing key outcomes, such as reduced clinical errors or improved accreditation readiness, provide compelling evidence to stakeholders. These tools also help build trust and justify budget increases.

<u>Reducing Expenses</u>
Careful management of expenses is equally important in optimizing a simulation center's budget. Maintenance plays a crucial role in prolonging the lifespan of high-cost equipment. Preventive maintenance schedules and automated tracking systems can prevent unexpected breakdowns and reduce costly repairs. Purchasing extended warranties or service agreements ensures that equipment remains operational with minimal disruptions.

Consumable supplies, such as syringes or IV kits, are another significant expense. Regular inventory checks can minimize waste while adopting reusable tools and virtual simulations can reduce reliance on physical materials. Investing in digital platforms like virtual reality (VR) or augmented reality (AR) might seem costly initially. Still, these reusable scenarios often lead to long-term savings by minimizing the need for consumables.

Prioritizing spending ensures that funds are directed toward high-impact areas. For example, scenarios aligned with accreditation requirements or institutional priorities should precede non-essential upgrades. Partnerships with nearby institutions or departments can also facilitate shared resources, reducing duplication of equipment or facilities.

Streamlining Operations
Operational efficiency is a key component of budget optimization. Advanced scheduling software can ensure maximum utilization of simulation spaces and equipment while batching similar sessions together can reduce setup and reset times. Hybrid training models that combine online simulations with in-person practice offer additional savings by reducing the need for physical space and consumables.

Staffing optimization also plays a critical role. Cross-training staff to handle multiple roles can reduce the need for highly specialized personnel while leveraging graduate students or faculty as facilitators can lower labor costs without sacrificing quality.

Another way to enhance efficiency is data-driven decision-making. Simulation centers can analyze usage data to identify underutilized programs or equipment and adjust resource allocation accordingly. Evaluating the cost-effectiveness of specific scenarios allows for better prioritization of activities.

Leveraging Innovation
Investing in new technologies can provide significant returns when done strategically. Hybrid training models, for instance, enable centers to offer flexibility while retaining hands-on components. Remote simulations and virtual patient platforms expand access to training, particularly for learners in underserved areas. Testing new technologies on a smaller scale through pilot programs ensures that only cost-effective innovations are implemented more broadly.

Simulation centers can also reduce operating costs through energy-efficient practices. Simple measures, such as scheduling sessions during off-peak hours or investing in energy-efficient lighting, can lead to noticeable savings over time.

Demonstrating Value
Ultimately, showcasing the simulation center's value is key to securing institutional and external support. By tracking outcomes, such as improved learner competence or reduced patient safety incidents, centers can demonstrate their role in achieving organizational goals. Highlighting financial benefits, such as reduced staff turnover or malpractice claims, strengthens the case for continued funding.

Regularly publishing reports and case studies that illustrate successes helps maintain transparency and trust with stakeholders. Visual tools like dashboards or infographics make complex data accessible, allowing decision-makers to see the center's impact.

4.4 Scheduling and Capacity Planning

One of the most challenging aspects of managing a simulation center is balancing the demand for simulation training with the institution's available resources, such as space, equipment, and instructor availability.

Managing Schedules for Students, Instructors, and Simulation Sessions

Simulation centers must coordinate schedules for students, instructors, and equipment. Given the limited number of simulation rooms and the high demand for hands-on training, developing an efficient scheduling system is essential. Scheduling software can automate bookings, minimize conflicts, and ensure all stakeholders are aligned during simulations. Additionally, managing the availability of instructors is crucial, as these trained professionals are often in high demand for clinical teaching and other educational roles (Issenberg et al., 2005).

Balancing Demand and Capacity:

Simulation centers often need help to balance institutional capacity with the growing demand for simulation-based training. With limited space, equipment, and instructor availability, optimizing the use of available resources becomes critical. Prioritizing simulation sessions based on course objectives, student learning needs, and clinical requirements can help ensure that high-priority programs receive the necessary resources. Every simulation center should have a definite prioritization hierarchy in place, preferably in their policies and procedures, that help guide operations to balance the demand and capacity. Additionally, expanding virtual simulations or mobile simulation units can help increase capacity without investing in additional physical space (Cook et al., 2011).

Sample 1 Academic Setting	Sample 2 Hospital Setting
• Degree Program Requirements/core competency [School Internal] • Experiential Training [Health System Internal] • Simulation-based Reseach • Experiential Training [External] • Outreach • Tours	• Emergency and High-priority Training • Faculty and Staff Development Activities • Routine and Practice Simulation • Research • External Partnerships and Outreach

Figure 7 Sample Simulation Center Prioritization Hierarchy

Capacity Planning for Future Growth:

To accommodate increasing demand, simulation centers must anticipate future needs for resources and space. Capacity planning involves forecasting the growth of student numbers, the evolution of training requirements, and the integration of new technologies. As medical and nursing education continues to embrace simulation, the demand for more diverse and specialized simulations will likely grow, necessitating a forward-thinking approach to resource allocation. Integrating future trends, such as the rise of virtual reality

(VR) and augmented reality (AR), into capacity planning can help ensure that simulation centers remain at the forefront of healthcare education (Bradley, 2006).

4.5 Policies and Procedures

Healthcare simulation centers are complex environments that combine advanced technology, multidisciplinary collaboration, and high-stakes learning. To ensure their effective operation, robust policies and procedures are essential. These frameworks provide the structure needed to maintain consistency, uphold quality standards, and address operational challenges. Policies and procedures form the backbone of a well-managed healthcare simulation center. They define roles, establish expectations, and provide guidance on everything from scenario execution to equipment maintenance. With them, consistency in training delivery, communication among staff, and operational inefficiencies can ensure the effectiveness of the simulation program is maintained. A 2020 survey of simulation center administrators revealed that centers with comprehensive policies and procedures experienced 25% fewer operational disruptions than those without standardized guidelines (Fey et al., 2020).

Ensuring Consistency and Quality

One of the most significant benefits of having formalized policies is the ability to deliver consistent, high-quality educational experiences across all simulation activities.

Standardizing Scenario Delivery: Policies ensure that scenarios are executed uniformly, regardless of which staff member facilitates them. For example, guidelines on debriefing techniques help maintain a consistent approach to post-simulation discussions, enhancing learner outcomes (INACSL, 2021).

Maintaining Accreditation Standards: Simulation centers must adhere to standards set by organizations like the *Society for Simulation in Healthcare* (SSH) and the International Nursing Association for Clinical Simulation and Learning (INACSL). Policies align operational practices with these standards, ensuring compliance and supporting accreditation processes.

Improving Learner Outcomes: Research indicates that centers with standardized scenario design and delivery procedures report a 15% improvement in learner satisfaction and knowledge retention (Cook et al., 2011).

Enhancing Operational Efficiency

Policies and procedures streamline operations, minimizing disruptions and optimizing resource utilization.

Guiding Daily Operations: Detailed procedures for equipment setup, simulator programming, and room turnover ensure smooth transitions between sessions, saving valuable time. Simulation centers with standardized turnover protocols have reported a 20% increase in session throughput.

Resource Management: Policies on inventory control and equipment maintenance help prevent resource shortages and technical failures. For instance, guidelines requiring routine simulator checks can reduce downtime by up to 30%, ensuring simulations proceed without interruptions (Rosen et al., 2018).

Promoting Safety and Risk Management

Healthcare simulation involves complex scenarios that mimic real clinical environments, sometimes incorporating invasive procedures or high-tech equipment. Policies are critical in managing risks and ensuring a safe environment for learners and staff.

- *Learner Safety*: Clear guidelines on physical safety, such as the proper use of equipment or infection control protocols, protect learners from harm.

- *Data Security*: Policies governing the storage and handling of learner data, including video recordings and performance metrics, ensure compliance with privacy regulations like HIPAA.

- *Crisis Management*: Emergency procedures, such as protocols for responding to equipment malfunctions or medical emergencies during simulations, help staff effectively handle unexpected events.

Supporting Staff Training and Development

Policies and procedures are valuable tools for onboarding and training simulation center staff.

- *Standardized Training Programs*: New staff benefit from clear, written guidelines that outline their roles and responsibilities. This starts with a standardized, position-specific orientation. For example, a policy might include a procedural checklist for simulation technicians to follow when setting up high-fidelity mannequins.

- *Professional Growth*: Policies encouraging ongoing education and certification, such as obtaining CHSOS or CHSE credentials, contribute to staff development and retention. Simulation centers with such policies report a 25% higher staff satisfaction rate (SSH, 2022).

Facilitating Continuous Improvement

Policies and procedures create a culture of accountability and feedback, which is essential for continuous improvement.

- *Performance Metrics*: Policies that mandate regular evaluations of simulations, such as learner feedback surveys and staff performance reviews, provide actionable data to improve program quality.

- *Adaptability*: Well-documented policies make it easier to implement changes when new technologies or best practices emerge, ensuring the center stays at the forefront of innovation.

Healthcare simulation centers thrive on precision, organization, and adaptability, all supported by well-crafted policies and procedures. These frameworks ensure consistency, enhance efficiency, promote safety, and support continuous improvement, essential for maintaining the high standards expected in healthcare education. As simulation grows as a critical component of medical and nursing training, investing in robust policies and procedures will remain key to achieving operational excellence and impactful learning outcomes.

4.6 Committees in Simulation Center Operations

Effective operations management in simulation centers often requires a collaborative, structured decision-making and strategy development approach. Committees are a proven mechanism for ensuring that diverse perspectives are considered while aligning the center's operations with its strategic goals. By creating dedicated committees, such as a Steering Committee, Business Committee, and Education Committee, simulation centers can streamline decision-making, foster accountability, and ensure that all aspects of the center's mission are addressed.

Each committee serves a distinct purpose, with clearly defined roles and responsibilities contributing to the center's overall success. This section outlines their structure and function, emphasizing their interdependence and contributions to operational excellence.

1. Steering Committee

The Steering Committee acts as the simulation center's strategic leadership body, providing oversight and direction. Comprised of senior leaders, stakeholders, and key decision-makers, this committee ensures that the center's goals align with institutional priorities and broader educational or healthcare objectives.

Responsibilities
- **Strategic Planning**: The Steering Committee develops and reviews long-term strategies for the simulation center, such as expanding services, integrating new technologies, or forming partnerships.
- **Policy Development**: It establishes high-level policies to guide operations, including policies on resource allocation, interdepartmental collaborations, and compliance with accreditation standards.
- **Stakeholder Engagement**: Members liaise with institutional leadership, donors, and external partners to secure funding and promote the center's mission (Nestel et al., 2017).

Typical Composition
The Steering Committee typically includes:
- The simulation center director.
- Senior institutional leadership (e.g., deans, department heads).
- Representatives from key user groups (e.g., nursing, medical, and allied health faculty).
- External stakeholders, such as industry partners or community leaders.

Meetings and Deliverables
The Steering Committee meets quarterly to review progress, address challenges, and

approve strategic initiatives. Deliverables include annual reports, strategic plans, and funding proposals.

2. Business Committee

The Business Committee focuses on the financial and operational aspects of the simulation center. This committee ensures the center's fiscal health while optimizing operational efficiency and resource utilization.

Responsibilities
- **Budget Management**: The committee reviews and monitors the center's budget, ensuring funds are allocated effectively to support operations, staff, and equipment maintenance.
- **Revenue Generation**: It identifies opportunities for additional revenue, such as fee-based external training, grants, or partnerships with industry.
- **Operational Efficiency**: The committee evaluates resource usage, such as scheduling software, facility utilization, and staffing needs, to maximize efficiency (Society for Simulation in Healthcare, 2022).
- **Risk Management**: It assesses financial and operational risks, implementing measures to mitigate them.

Typical Composition
The Business Committee includes:
- The operations manager or administrator.
- Financial officers or accountants from the institution.
- Representatives from the technical and administrative teams.
- Faculty members involved in simulation program development.

Meetings and Deliverables
This committee meets monthly to track budgetary performance, review operational metrics, and prepare financial reports. Deliverables may include cost-benefit analyses for new equipment, grant applications, and detailed annual budgets.

3. Education Committee

The Education Committee is responsible for maintaining the educational quality and relevance of the simulation center's offerings. It ensures that the center's programs align with institutional curricula and meet the needs of diverse learners.

Responsibilities
- **Curriculum Integration**: The committee collaborates with academic departments to integrate simulation activities into curricula, aligning scenarios with learning objectives and accreditation requirements (Dieckmann et al., 2007).
- **Program Development**: It oversees the design, implementation, and evaluation of new simulation programs, ensuring they meet evidence-based standards and learner needs.
- **Faculty Development**: The committee coordinates training for faculty and staff, emphasizing simulation pedagogy, debriefing techniques, and scenario design.
- **Assessment and Evaluation**: It develops methods to assess learner

performance and evaluate the educational impact of simulations.

Typical Composition
The Education Committee typically includes:
- Faculty representatives from nursing, medicine, and allied health programs.
- Simulation educators and content experts.
- The simulation center's educational director or equivalent role.
- Learner representatives, when appropriate, to provide end-user feedback.

Meetings and Deliverables
The Education Committee meets bi-monthly to review educational initiatives and ensure alignment with institutional goals. Deliverables include scenario libraries, program evaluations, and faculty development schedules.

Interdependence of Committees

Although each committee has distinct responsibilities, their work is interconnected. For example:

- The Steering Committee sets strategic goals, which the Business Committee translates into operational plans and budgets.
- The Education Committee ensures that programs align with the Steering Committee's strategic vision and the Business Committee's resource allocations.
- Cross-committee collaboration ensures that initiatives like adopting new simulation technologies are financially feasible, strategically aligned, and educationally effective.

Establishing a robust committee structure enhances governance and operational efficiency in simulation centers. The Steering Committee, Business Committee, and Education Committee each play a vital role in ensuring the center achieves its mission of advancing healthcare education and improving patient outcomes. By fostering collaboration, leveraging expertise, and maintaining clear lines of accountability, these committees create a strong foundation for sustained success.

4.7 Day-to-Day Management and Decision-Making

Running a simulation center requires a dynamic and responsive approach to day-to-day management. With numerous moving parts—staff schedules, equipment preparation, scenario execution, and unforeseen challenges—simulation center managers must balance immediate priorities with long-term goals. Effective management ensures not only operational efficiency but also high-quality educational experiences. This balance often hinges on structured decision-making processes, such as task prioritization using frameworks like the Eisenhower Matrix, resource allocation, and fostering team coordination.

The Importance of Task Prioritization

Simulation centers thrive on precision and preparation, but not all tasks carry equal weight. From addressing urgent technical malfunctions to planning staff training sessions, managers must prioritize effectively to keep the center running smoothly. Mismanagement of priorities can lead to inefficiencies, burnout, and compromised educational outcomes.

A valuable tool for prioritizing tasks is the **Eisenhower Matrix**, which categorizes activities based on urgency and importance (Eisenhower, 1954). This matrix provides a structured approach to decision-making, enabling managers to allocate their time and resources effectively. The matrix divides tasks into four quadrants:

- Urgent and Important (Quadrant I): Tasks requiring immediate attention, such as troubleshooting a manikin malfunction during a live session.

- Not Urgent but Important (Quadrant II): Strategic tasks like planning faculty development or updating simulation protocols contribute to long-term success.

- Urgent but Not Important (Quadrant III): Distractions that can be delegated, such as responding to routine inquiries or resolving minor scheduling conflicts.

- Not Urgent and Not Important (Quadrant IV): Tasks that should be minimized or avoided, like excessive email checking or redundant documentation (Covey, 1989).

For example, if a high-fidelity manikin malfunctions during a scenario, addressing the issue immediately falls under Quadrant I. Meanwhile, updating the center's equipment maintenance schedule belongs in Quadrant II and can be scheduled for later. This structured approach ensures that critical needs are met without neglecting strategic objectives.

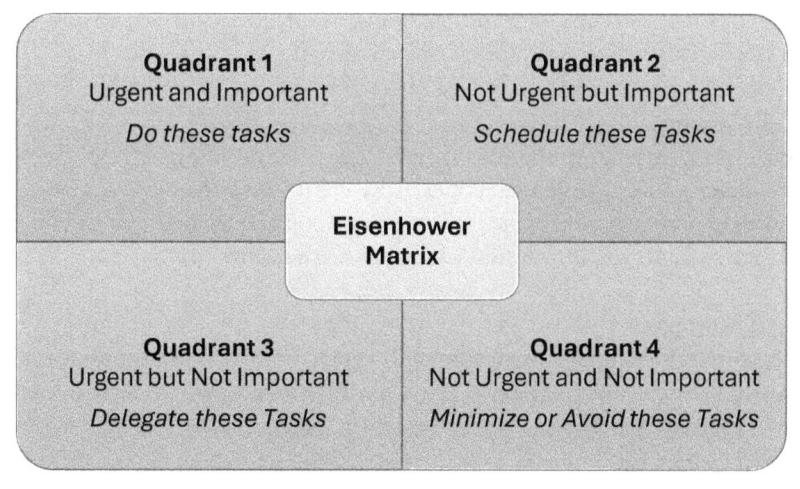

Figure 8 The Eisenhower Matrix

Resource Allocation and Utilization

Resource allocation is another critical aspect of daily management in simulation centers. Managers must balance the availability of staff, equipment, and physical space to ensure seamless operations.

- Staff Scheduling
  Coordinating faculty, technicians, and standardized patients can be challenging, especially during peak periods like clinical exams or interprofessional training sessions. Flexible schedules and cross-training help mitigate potential bottlenecks. For instance, faculty trained in basic manikin troubleshooting can step in temporarily if a technician is unavailable, ensuring minimal disruption (Nestel et al., 2017).

- Equipment Management
  Simulation centers rely heavily on sophisticated technology, from high-fidelity manikins to audiovisual systems. Ensuring the optimal use of these resources requires careful planning and proactive maintenance. Scheduling software, such as SimCapture or Skedda, can automate resource allocation, reducing administrative workloads and minimizing scheduling conflicts (Society for Simulation in Healthcare, 2022).

- Budget Oversight
  Daily financial decisions often involve tracking consumable supplies like syringes and moulage materials or justifying investments in equipment upgrades. Managers must weigh immediate costs against the potential for long-term efficiency gains, such as purchasing task trainers to supplement high-demand manikins during busy weeks.

Communication and Coordination

Effective communication is the backbone of daily operations in simulation centers. Regular briefings, clear communication channels, and feedback loops ensure the team is aligned on priorities and prepared to address challenges.

- Daily Briefings
  Short team huddles at the start of each day provide an opportunity to review the schedule, address potential issues, and clarify responsibilities. For example, a morning briefing might include updates on equipment availability, session objectives, and any last-minute changes to scenarios.

- Staff Meetings
  Regular staff meetings, typically held weekly or bi-weekly, allow for a more in-depth discussion of ongoing operations, challenges, and strategic initiatives.

- Project Meetings
  Project meetings are dedicated to coordinating efforts on specific simulation initiatives, such as developing new scenarios, implementing new technology, or planning large-scale training events.

- Other Mediums
  Diverse communication mediums support day-to-day coordination, especially for teams with varying schedules or remote contributors.

- *Email*: Ideal for formal updates, documentation, and sharing resources such as policies or detailed schedules.
- *Messaging Apps*: Tools like Slack, Microsoft Teams, or WhatsApp can facilitate real-time communication and quick updates.
- *Shared Calendars*: Centralized scheduling tools help avoid conflicts and ensure visibility into simulation activities.
- *Simulation Software Platforms*: Many simulation centers use integrated platforms for managing scenarios, scheduling, and communication.
- *Digital Dashboards*: Displaying key metrics, such as daily schedules or equipment status, keeps everyone informed.

- Feedback Mechanisms
Encouraging real-time feedback from staff fosters a culture of continuous improvement. For instance, technicians might report recurring issues with a particular manikin model, prompting the manager to schedule additional training or maintenance.

Monitoring and Problem-Solving

Unexpected challenges are inevitable in simulation centers, but a proactive approach to monitoring and problem-solving can mitigate their impact.

Real-Time Decision-Making
Managers must be prepared to make quick decisions without compromising quality. For example, if a network outage disrupts a scheduled session, managers might use a low-tech alternative, such as task trainers for manual skill practice, while IT resolves the issue.

Performance Tracking
Tracking daily performance metrics, such as session completion rates or equipment usage, helps identify patterns and areas for improvement. Software dashboards and session feedback forms can provide valuable insights into operational efficiency and learner satisfaction (FEMA, 2021).

Continuous Improvement

Day-to-day management is not just about maintaining operations but also about creating opportunities for continuous improvement.

End-of-Day Evaluations
After sessions conclude, managers can review the day's successes and challenges. For instance, if staff report delays due to a lack of pre-assembled supplies, the manager can implement a preparation checklist to streamline future setups.

Documentation
Detailed records of decisions, completed tasks, and unresolved issues provide a foundation for better planning and decision-making. For example, documenting peak equipment usage times can inform future budget proposals for additional resources.

The daily operations of a simulation center are complex but manageable, with structured decision-making and effective prioritization. Tools like the Eisenhower Matrix provide a framework for distinguishing between urgent and important tasks, while clear communication and proactive problem-solving ensure smooth operations. By balancing immediate needs with strategic goals, simulation center managers can create an environment where staff thrive, learners succeed, and the center delivers high-quality educational experiences.

4.8 Best Practice in Handling Tours in Your Simulation Center

Simulation centers are increasingly recognized as innovation hubs, blending advanced technology with education to improve healthcare outcomes. Hosting tours of your simulation center provides a unique opportunity to showcase your resources, highlight your mission, and engage stakeholders ranging from institutional leaders to prospective students and external partners. However, a successful tour requires careful planning and execution to ensure visitors leave with a positive impression and a clear understanding of the center's value.

This section outlines best practices for preparing and conducting tours of a simulation center, focusing on professionalism, engagement, and alignment with the center's goals.

Preparation: Setting the Stage for Success

Effective tours begin with thorough preparation. From understanding the audience to ensuring the center is ready for visitors, planning is key to creating an impactful experience.

Know Your Audience
Tailoring the tour to the interests and expertise of your visitors is essential. For example:
- A group of nursing students may be most interested in hands-on demonstration areas and debriefing rooms.
- Institutional leaders might focus on the center's alignment with strategic goals, such as interprofessional education or accreditation standards.
- External partners may want to see how the center's capabilities align with their business or training needs (Nestel et al., 2017).

Prepare Your Space
Ensure that all areas of the simulation center are clean, organized, and visually appealing. Key preparation steps include:
- Checking that manikins and equipment are functional and properly displayed.
- Organizing supplies and ensuring storerooms are tidy if they are part of the tour route.
- Testing audiovisual systems and simulation software to avoid technical issues during demonstrations.

Develop a Structured Itinerary
A well-organized tour itinerary keeps the experience focused and professional. Include time for introductions, guided exploration of key areas, and opportunities for questions

and interaction. For example:
- **Welcome and Introduction**: Provide an overview of the center's mission, vision, and capabilities.
- **Tour Stops**: Highlight essential areas, such as high-fidelity simulation rooms, task trainer labs, and debriefing spaces.
- **Demonstrations**: Include live or recorded scenarios to illustrate how the center operates.
- **Closing Discussion**: Allow visitors to ask questions and share their impressions.

Engagement: Bringing the Tour to Life

Once the tour begins, engagement is the key to making the experience memorable and informative. Tours should emphasize interactivity, storytelling, and adaptability to the audience's interests.

Create an Interactive Experience
Encourage visitors to engage directly with the environment. For example:
- Allow visitors to handle basic task trainers, such as suturing kits or airway management devices.
- Demonstrate a manikin's capabilities, such as simulating a cardiac arrest or childbirth.
- Allow visitors to observe or participate in debriefing (Dieckmann et al., 2007).

Use Storytelling to Highlight Impact
Share real-world examples of how the simulation center has impacted education or patient care. For instance:
- "Recently, our simulations helped a cohort of nursing students improve their teamwork skills, leading to better outcomes during their clinical rotations."
- "One of our scenarios on managing sepsis led to significant improvements in knowledge and confidence among learners, as demonstrated by post-simulation evaluations."

Adapt to On-the-Spot Interests
Be prepared to adjust the tour to focus on topics or technologies that resonate with visitors. For example, if a group is interested in virtual reality (VR) applications, spend additional time demonstrating VR-based simulations and discussing their potential.

Professionalism: Leaving a Lasting Impression

Professionalism throughout the tour reinforces the center's reputation as a simulation-based education and training leader.

Designate Knowledgeable Tour Guides
Select staff members who are both knowledgeable and enthusiastic about the center's work. Effective guides should be able to:
- Answer questions confidently and accurately.
- Connect the center's capabilities to visitors' interests or needs.
- Share insights into the educational and operational aspects of the center.

Focus on Clear Communication
Avoid overwhelming visitors with excessive technical jargon. Instead, provide concise explanations and relatable examples to make complex concepts accessible to diverse audiences (Society for Simulation in Healthcare, 2022).

Prepare Materials for Follow-Up
Provide visitors with handouts or digital materials summarizing key points from the tour. Include contact information, links to the center's website or social media, and information about upcoming events or opportunities for collaboration.

Reflection and Continuous Improvement

After the tour, gather feedback and reflect on what worked well and what could be improved.

Request Feedback
Use a brief survey or informal conversations to gather visitors' impressions. Questions might include:
- "What did you find most engaging about the tour?"
- "Were there areas where you would have liked more information?"
- "Do you see opportunities to collaborate with our center in the future?"

Debrief with Staff
Meet with tour guides and support staff to discuss the experience. Document lessons learned and suggestions for enhancing future tours.

Refine Your Approach
Incorporate feedback into future tour planning. For example:
- If visitors frequently ask about a specific technology, ensure it is highlighted prominently in the next tour.
- If time management is a challenge, adjust the itinerary to allocate more time to high-interest areas.

Tours of a simulation center are powerful opportunities to showcase its mission, engage stakeholders, and build partnerships. Simulation center staff can ensure that every tour leaves a lasting impression by preparing thoughtfully, engaging visitors interactively, and maintaining a professional demeanor. Reflection and continuous improvement further enhance the center's ability to communicate its value effectively, making it a cornerstone of education, innovation, and collaboration.

4.9 Advocating for Program Growth

Advocating for program growth is a critical component of simulation center operations management. As healthcare education and training evolve, simulation centers must expand their capabilities to meet rising demands, incorporate new technologies, and address emerging educational priorities. Successfully advocating for growth requires a strategic approach that aligns the center's goals with institutional priorities, leverages data-driven evidence, and effectively engages stakeholders.

This section explores best practices for advocating program growth, including defining needs, building a compelling case, and fostering stakeholder support.

Identifying and Defining Growth Needs → Building a Data-driven Case for Growth → Engageing Stakeholders and Building Support → Developing Growth Proposal → Overcoming Challenges

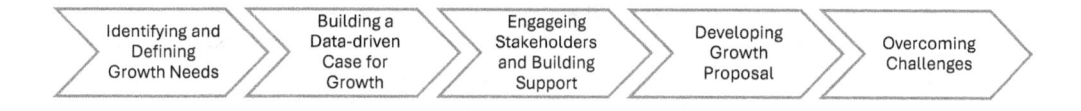

Figure 9 Advocating for Program Growth

Identifying and Defining Growth Needs

The first step in advocating program growth is identifying specific needs and opportunities. Growth may be driven by various factors, including increased learner enrollment, advancements in simulation technology, or expanding training programs to new audiences.

Assessing Current Capacity
Begin by evaluating the center's current resources and identifying areas of limitation. For example:
- Are existing simulation rooms and equipment sufficient to meet current and projected demand?
- Are staff adequately trained and resourced to handle increasing workloads?
- Are there new educational objectives or competencies that the center is unable to address with its current setup?

Example: A simulation center supporting a growing nursing program might find that the current number of high-fidelity manikins is insufficient to accommodate additional cohorts, leading to scheduling conflicts and reduced access for learners (Nestel et al., 2017).

Identifying Opportunities for Expansion
Growth opportunities may include:
- Integrating cutting-edge technologies, such as virtual reality (VR) or augmented reality (AR).
- Expanding services to include continuing education programs for practicing professionals.
- Offering interprofessional education (IPE) simulations fosters teamwork and collaboration across healthcare disciplines.

Building a Data-Driven Case for Growth

A strong advocacy effort relies on clear, evidence-based arguments demonstrating the need for and benefits of program expansion.

Collecting and Analyzing Data

Quantitative and qualitative data can illustrate the center's impact and justify the need for additional resources. Key metrics to gather include:

- **Utilization Rates**: Measure the frequency of simulation room and equipment usage, highlighting periods of peak demand.
- **Learner Outcomes**: Data on performance improvements, satisfaction scores, and competency achievements should be collected to demonstrate the educational value of simulations (Dieckmann et al., 2007).
- **Return on Investment (ROI)**: Calculate current programs' financial and operational benefits, such as reduced training costs or improved learner preparedness.

Framing the Benefits
Present the potential benefits of program growth in terms that resonate with stakeholders:
- **For Institutional Leadership**: Emphasize alignment with strategic goals, such as enhancing accreditation readiness, increasing enrollment, or fostering partnerships.
- **For Faculty and Learners**: Highlight improved access to simulation resources, expanded learning opportunities, and innovative training modalities.
- **For External Stakeholders**: Showcase potential collaborations with industry partners or opportunities for community impact through workforce development programs.

Example: Data showing a 20% increase in learner performance after introducing advanced simulation technology can underscore the educational benefits of further investment (Society for Simulation in Healthcare, 2022).

Engaging Stakeholders and Building Support

Advocating for growth requires engaging stakeholders at multiple levels to build consensus and secure necessary support.

Institutional Leadership
Engage decision-makers by aligning the proposal with institutional priorities. Strategies include:

- **Strategic Alignment**: The proposed expansion should be linked to the institution's mission, such as improving healthcare education or addressing regional workforce shortages.
- **Financial Planning**: Provide detailed cost estimates and funding strategies, including grant opportunities, revenue from external training programs, or philanthropic support.

Example: A proposal to add a dedicated IPE simulation lab could be framed to enhance accreditation compliance and improve healthcare teamwork outcomes, addressing institutional and societal goals.

Faculty and Staff

Involve faculty and staff in the advocacy process to foster a sense of ownership and collaboration. Encourage them to:

- Share their insights on how growth will benefit their teaching or operational roles.
- Provide testimonials or case studies showcasing the center's current impact and potential.

<u>External Stakeholders</u>
Engage industry partners, alumni, and community organizations to build external support. Opportunities include:

- Highlighting potential collaborations, such as offering customized training programs or conducting joint research.
- Showcasing the center's role in addressing community healthcare challenges, such as training first responders or supporting public health initiatives.

Developing a Growth Proposal

A comprehensive growth proposal serves as the cornerstone of advocacy efforts. It should be clear, concise, and visually appealing, addressing key concerns and showcasing the center's vision for the future.

Key Components of the Proposal
1. <u>Executive Summary</u>: Provide a high-level overview of the proposal, including its purpose, scope, and expected outcomes.
2. <u>Current State Assessment</u>: Present data and evidence illustrating the center's capabilities and limitations.
3. <u>Proposed Expansion</u>: Outline the specific growth initiatives, such as adding new facilities, upgrading equipment, or hiring additional staff.
4. <u>Budget and Funding Plan</u>: Include detailed cost estimates and potential funding sources.
5. <u>Expected Outcomes</u>: Highlight anticipated benefits, such as improved learner outcomes, increased enrollment capacity, or enhanced institutional reputation.

<u>Visual Aids</u>
Use charts, graphs, and images to support key points and make the proposal engaging and easy to understand. For example:

- A graph showing trends in learner enrollment alongside simulation utilization rates can illustrate the need for additional capacity.

Overcoming Challenges

Advocating for growth often involves addressing potential challenges, such as budget constraints or competing institutional priorities.

<u>Proactive Problem-Solving</u>
Anticipate potential objections and prepare solutions, such as:
- Identifying cost-saving measures, such as shared resource models or phased

- implementation.
- Demonstrating the alignment of growth initiatives with long-term institutional benefits, such as attracting high-quality faculty or improving accreditation outcomes.

Leveraging Success Stories
Highlight successful expansion efforts from other institutions or prior initiatives within the center to build credibility and inspire confidence.

Advocating for program growth is essential for ensuring that simulation centers remain at the forefront of healthcare education. By identifying specific needs, building a data-driven case, and effectively engaging stakeholders, managers can secure the support needed to expand the center's impact. With thoughtful planning and strategic advocacy, simulation centers can continue to innovate, educate, and transform healthcare training.

4.10. Summary

Simulation centers have become integral to healthcare education, offering safe environments for learners to practice clinical skills, enhance procedural proficiency, and manage high-pressure scenarios. Chapter 4 delves into the operational management strategies that underpin the successful functioning of these centers, emphasizing their pivotal role in improving learner outcomes, fostering innovation, and ensuring sustainability.

The chapter begins by establishing the necessity of simulation centers in bridging the gap between theoretical knowledge and practical application. These centers address critical educational needs, improve patient safety, and enhance institutional competitiveness. A robust business plan—encompassing market analysis, financial planning, and strategic goals—is crucial for establishing and sustaining a simulation center. By aligning the center's objectives with organizational priorities and leveraging evidence-based outcomes, leaders can effectively advocate for institutional and external support.

The design of a simulation center significantly impacts its educational effectiveness. The chapter highlights the importance of creating realistic environments, such as patient rooms, trauma bays, and operating rooms, while incorporating modular and flexible layouts to accommodate evolving educational needs. Advanced features like VR/AR labs, control rooms, and debriefing spaces enhance training capabilities. Workflow optimization is a cornerstone of operational efficiency, with strategies including scenario preparation checklists, streamlined transitions, and automation and technology for scheduling and equipment management.

Sustainable operation requires meticulous resource management, from maintaining high-fidelity manikins to tracking consumable supplies. The chapter emphasizes planning for equipment lifecycles, adopting preventative maintenance practices, and leveraging data-driven approaches to optimize resource allocation. Diversifying funding sources—such as grants, partnerships, and revenue-generating programs—is critical to financial sustainability. Simulation centers can secure ongoing support by effectively managing costs and demonstrating value through outcomes.

Balancing demand with capacity is a recurring challenge for simulation centers. The chapter outlines the importance of efficient scheduling systems to coordinate learners, instructors, and equipment, alongside strategies for prioritizing sessions based on educational objectives. Capacity planning involves anticipating future growth needs, integrating technological advancements, and expanding virtual and mobile simulation options to enhance accessibility and scalability.

Robust policies and procedures form the backbone of a well-managed simulation center, ensuring consistency, quality, and compliance with accreditation standards. These frameworks streamline operations, promote safety, and provide clear guidelines for staff training, scenario execution, and risk management. Centers with comprehensive policies experience fewer disruptions and demonstrate improved learner outcomes and operational efficiency.

Structured committees—such as Steering, Business, and Education Committees—play vital roles in simulation center governance. The chapter explores how these groups facilitate strategic planning, financial oversight, and curriculum alignment. By fostering collaboration and leveraging diverse expertise, committees ensure simulation centers remain responsive to institutional goals and stakeholder needs.

Daily operations in simulation centers require balancing immediate needs with long-term objectives. The chapter introduces the Eisenhower Matrix as a tool for prioritizing tasks and underscores the importance of resource allocation, communication, and adaptability. Proactive problem-solving, performance monitoring, and continuous improvement are essential practices for maintaining high-quality operations.

Tours provide an opportunity to showcase a simulation center's capabilities to stakeholders, prospective students, and external partners. The chapter outlines strategies for preparing impactful tours, emphasizing tailored itineraries, interactive demonstrations, and professional communication. Gathering feedback and refining the approach ensures continuous improvement in presenting the center's value.

Advocacy ensures simulation centers meet rising demands and integrate emerging technologies. The chapter emphasizes the importance of data-driven arguments to justify growth, engaging stakeholders, and crafting comprehensive proposals. Aligning expansion efforts with institutional priorities and addressing potential challenges proactively can secure the support necessary for program success.

Chapter 4 underscores the multifaceted nature of operational management in simulation centers, from strategic planning and resource optimization to daily decision-making and advocacy for growth. By adopting evidence-based practices, fostering collaboration, and embracing innovation, simulation centers can continue to drive excellence in healthcare education and improve outcomes for learners, institutions, and communities.

4.11 Chapter Review

Review Questions

1. **Business Planning**
   a. What are the essential components of a simulation center business plan?
   b. How can data demonstrating the effectiveness of simulation-based education support the justification for a new center?
2. **Center Design**
   a. Why is flexibility important in the layout of simulation centers?
   b. Describe the role of advanced features like VR/AR labs and control rooms in enhancing training capabilities.
3. **Resource Management**
   a. What strategies can simulation centers use to effectively manage consumables and simulator maintenance?
   b. How can centers plan for equipment lifecycle replacements?
4. **Scheduling and Capacity**
   a. What are the challenges of balancing demand and capacity in simulation centers?
   b. Discuss strategies for prioritizing simulation sessions and expanding capacity.
5. **Policies and Committees**
   a. How do comprehensive policies improve operational efficiency and learner outcomes in simulation centers?
   b. Explain the roles and responsibilities of the Steering, Business, and Education Committees.
6. **Daily Operations**
   a. How does the Eisenhower Matrix help prioritize tasks in simulation center management?
   b. What are key considerations for effective communication and coordination in daily operations?
7. **Tours and Advocacy**
   a. What best practices ensure a successful simulation center tour?
   b. How can simulation centers advocate for growth and secure funding for expansion?

Critical Thinking and Application

1. **Design a Simulation Center**
   Develop a new simulation center layout that accommodates diverse healthcare training needs. Consider modular design and specialized features.
2. **Resource Optimization**
   Propose a strategy for managing the lifecycle of high-fidelity manikins and other key equipment.
3. **Advocacy Case**
   Create a data-driven proposal for expanding a simulation center, addressing stakeholder concerns and highlighting anticipated benefits.

Hands-On Activity

- **Simulation Workflow Analysis**
  Map out the workflow of a typical simulation session, identifying potential bottlenecks and proposing optimization solutions.

Summary Reflection

Reflect on the role of simulation centers in bridging the gap between theory and practice in healthcare education. How do operational management strategies ensure that these centers meet current demands while planning for future growth and innovation?

Chapter 5

Staff Management in Medical and Nursing Simulation Centers

The hum of a high-fidelity simulator, the flicker of a monitor displaying real-time vitals, and the focused murmurs of learners practicing critical skills are the sights and sounds of a well-run simulation center. Behind this orchestrated environment lies a diverse team of professionals whose roles are as interconnected as the systems they operate. Staff management in a simulation center is about filling positions and cultivating a team that embodies technical expertise, educational vision, and collaborative spirit.

In many ways, the staff is the backbone of a simulation center. Whether it's the simulation technician ensuring that a manikin functions seamlessly, the educator guiding participants through debriefing, or the administrator managing schedules and budgets, each role contributes to the center's success. Yet managing such a team comes with unique challenges. Unlike traditional educational or healthcare settings, simulation centers operate at the intersection of multiple disciplines, requiring staff with a wide range of skills, from medical knowledge to technical aptitude and pedagogical insight (Lateef, 2010).

Effective staff management begins with recognizing the complexity of the roles within a simulation center. For example, the simulation technician's expertise spans troubleshooting high-tech equipment to creating realistic moulage for trauma scenarios, while faculty members must balance clinical accuracy with educational outcomes. This diversity is both a strength and a challenge, requiring leaders to adopt tailored strategies for recruitment, training, and retention (Nestel et al., 2017).

Recruiting the right people is only the beginning. Once on board, staff members must be supported through comprehensive training and professional development opportunities. Simulation is a field that evolves rapidly with advancements in technology and educational methodologies, making continuous learning essential. Certifications such as Certified Healthcare Simulation Educator (CHSE) and Certified Healthcare Simulation Operations Specialist (CHSOS) are increasingly valued, not only as markers of individual expertise but as contributors to the center's credibility and success (Society for Simulation in Healthcare, 2022).

Beyond technical skills, fostering a culture of collaboration and mutual respect is critical. The multidisciplinary nature of simulation requires clear communication and a shared understanding of goals. For instance, a cardiac arrest simulation scenario might require seamless coordination between technical staff managing the manikin, faculty guiding the learners, and standardized patients playing distressed family members. When managed effectively, this teamwork enhances the learners' experience and the staff's engagement and job satisfaction (Dieckmann et al., 2007).

However, even the best teams face challenges. Staff burnout, resource constraints, and conflicting priorities can disrupt operations and morale. Leaders must proactively address these issues, balance workloads, resolve conflicts, and create opportunities for recognition and career growth. By doing so, they not only retain talented staff but also build a resilient team capable of adapting to the dynamic demands of a simulation center.

This chapter explores the multifaceted aspects of staff management in a simulation center, from defining roles and responsibilities to fostering professional growth and maintaining team cohesion. It draws on best practices, real-world examples, and evidence-based strategies to provide a comprehensive guide for simulation center leaders. By investing in effective staff management, simulation centers can ensure that their teams remain a cornerstone of excellence, innovation, and impactful learning.

5.1 Staffing Roles and Responsibilities

Simulation centers are complex operations that rely on a multidisciplinary team to function effectively. From administrative leadership to support staff, each team member plays a critical role in ensuring smooth operations, delivering high-quality educational experiences, and fostering a culture of innovation. This section provides an in-depth exploration of the primary roles and responsibilities within a simulation center, highlighting the interconnected nature of these positions and their contributions to the center's success.

Administrative Leadership

Administrative staff are the architects of the simulation center's vision and the custodians of its daily operations. They provide strategic oversight, enforce policies, and manage logistics to align resources with the center's goals.

Simulation Center Director
The director is the strategic leader of the simulation center and is responsible for aligning its operations with institutional objectives. This role demands a balance of educational, technical, and administrative expertise. The director sets the tone for the center, ensuring it fosters a culture of collaboration, excellence, and innovation.

- **Strategic Oversight**: The director oversees the center's strategic direction, including integrating simulation into curricula, promoting interprofessional education, and expanding the center's reach through partnerships. For example, they might spearhead initiatives to integrate virtual reality or artificial intelligence

into the center's offerings to remain at the forefront of simulation-based education.
- **Budget Management**: Effective budget management is central to the director's responsibilities. This includes allocating funds for equipment, staff salaries, and professional development while identifying opportunities for additional revenue, such as fee-based training for external partners or grant-funded research.
- **Stakeholder Engagement**: The director is the liaison between the simulation center and its stakeholders, including institutional leadership, faculty, donors, and external organizations. They advocate for the center's needs and highlight its successes, fostering long-term support.

Administrative Staff (e.g., Operations Manager, Administrative Assistants)
The administrative staff ensures the simulation center runs smoothly by managing its logistical and operational needs. Their responsibilities include:

- **Scheduling**: Coordinating simulation sessions to optimize rooms, equipment, and personnel use. In high-demand centers, scheduling software such as SimCapture or Skedda can streamline this process and prevent conflicts.
- **Record-Keeping**: Maintaining accurate session attendance records, performance data, and equipment usage. These records are critical for tracking progress, identifying areas for improvement, and preparing for accreditation reviews.
- **Policy Enforcement**: Ensuring all participants adhere to institutional policies, such as confidentiality agreements, safety protocols, and equipment handling guidelines.

Administrative staff acts as the connective tissue between faculty, technical teams, and learners, facilitating seamless communication and workflow.

Technical Staff

Technical staff are the backbone of the simulation center's technological operations, ensuring that all equipment and systems function reliably. Their expertise is essential for creating realistic and immersive learning environments.

Simulation Technicians
Simulation technicians are the operational experts who bring scenarios to life. Their responsibilities include:

- **Equipment Setup**: Preparing manikins, task trainers, and other equipment to meet the specific needs of each scenario. This might involve programming high-fidelity manikins to simulate cardiac arrest or applying moulage to replicate wounds or burns.
- **Maintenance and Troubleshooting**: Conducting regular maintenance to prevent equipment failures and troubleshooting technical issues during sessions. For instance, if a manikin suddenly loses connectivity mid-simulation, the technician must quickly resolve the issue to minimize disruption.

- **Scenario Programming**: Using software to customize scenarios based on faculty requirements. This might include adjusting manikin vitals, integrating patient monitors, or triggering pre-recorded verbal responses.
- **Collaboration**: Working closely with faculty to align technical operations with educational objectives, ensuring the technology enhances the learning experience rather than overshadowing it.

Simulation technicians must possess a blend of technical understanding and problem-solving skills, enabling them to adapt to the dynamic needs of the simulation center.

IT Support

IT support staff manage the digital infrastructure that underpins modern simulation centers. Their responsibilities include:

- **Software and Network Management**: Ensuring that simulation software, learning management systems (LMS), and other digital tools operate seamlessly. They also maintain network connectivity for integrated systems, such as AV equipment and real-time data streaming.
- **Data Security**: Protecting sensitive learner data and session recordings through robust cybersecurity measures and compliance with privacy regulations (e.g., HIPAA in healthcare settings).
- **AV Systems**: Overseeing the operation of audiovisual systems used for recording and debriefing. For example, IT staff might configure multi-camera setups to capture critical angles during a simulation or troubleshoot playback issues in a debriefing room.

Educational Staff

Educational staff are responsible for designing and delivering simulation-based learning experiences. Their work bridges technical operations and pedagogical objectives, ensuring that simulations align with educational goals.

Faculty and Instructors

Faculty and instructors design scenarios, facilitate sessions, and guide learners through debriefings. Their responsibilities include:

- **Scenario Development**: Collaborating with content experts to create realistic, curriculum-aligned scenarios. This might involve drafting detailed patient histories, setting learning objectives, and planning anticipated learner actions.
- **Facilitation**: Guiding learners through simulations, ensuring that sessions unfold as intended while adapting to unexpected learner decisions. For example, an instructor might provide subtle cues to redirect a team if they overlook a critical step.
- **Debriefing**: Leading reflective discussions to help learners analyze their performance, identify strengths and weaknesses, and apply lessons to real-world practice. Debriefing frameworks such as PEARLS or GAS (Gather-Analyze-Summarize) structure these conversations (Dieckmann et al., 2007).

Effective instructors must balance clinical expertise with strong communication and coaching skills to foster a supportive and engaging learning environment.

Content Experts
Content experts ensure that simulations are clinically accurate and relevant. Their role involves:

- **Providing Expertise**: Advising on the clinical details of scenarios, such as patient presentations, diagnostic cues, and appropriate interventions. For example, an emergency medicine expert might design a trauma scenario involving a patient with a pneumothorax.
- **Training Faculty**: Supporting faculty members by sharing the latest evidence-based practices and updates in clinical guidelines.

Content experts play a critical role in maintaining the educational integrity of simulation activities.

Support Staff

Support staff contribute to simulations' realism and operational efficiency, often working behind the scenes to enhance the learner experience.

Standardized Patients (SPs)
Standardized patients are individuals trained to portray patients, family members, or other roles in simulations. Their contributions include:

- **Role-Playing**: Delivering consistent and realistic portrayals to challenge learners in communication, empathy, and clinical reasoning. For example, an SP might play a grieving family member during an end-of-life care scenario, testing a learner's ability to deliver bad news compassionately.
- **Feedback**: Providing direct feedback to learners on their interpersonal skills and professionalism, offering unique insights that complement clinical evaluations.

Facilities and Maintenance
Facilities staff ensure that the physical environment of the simulation center is safe, clean, and well-organized. Their responsibilities include:
- **Preparing Spaces**: Reconfiguring rooms to suit different scenarios, from emergency departments to operating theaters.
- **Stocking Supplies**: Managing inventory of consumables, such as syringes, bandages, and medications, to ensure readiness for every session.

Facilities staff ensure the simulation center remains a functional and welcoming space for learners and educators alike.

A simulation center's success depends on the collective efforts of a diverse and skilled team. Each role, from administrative leadership to support staff, uniquely creates impactful learning experiences. By understanding and valuing these roles, leaders can build cohesive teams that drive innovation, support learners, and elevate the center's mission.

Through effective management and collaboration, simulation centers can continue to thrive as hubs of education and excellence.

5.2 Recruitment Strategies

Recruiting the right team for a simulation center is a strategic and multifaceted process that ensures that its operations align with its mission and objectives. Simulation centers require professionals who can navigate the intersection of healthcare, education, and technology and thrive in a dynamic, collaborative environment. By focusing on crafting detailed job descriptions, employing diverse recruitment channels, and implementing structured evaluation processes, simulation center leaders can build a team that excels in both technical competence and cultural fit.

Defining Job Descriptions

A comprehensive job description is the cornerstone of effective recruitment. It is a roadmap for potential candidates, outlining the role's skills, responsibilities, and expectations. Additionally, well-crafted job descriptions reduce the risk of mismatched expectations, ensuring long-term job satisfaction and productivity.

Components of an Effective Job Description

1. **Role Overview**: Provide a concise summary of the role and its significance within the simulation center. For example:
   - *"The Simulation Technician supports the center's mission by ensuring the seamless operation of simulation equipment and environments, contributing to high-quality learning experiences for healthcare trainees."*

2. **Key Responsibilities**: Use action-oriented language to describe specific duties. For example:
   - *"Prepare and configure simulation manikins, task trainers, and associated equipment for scheduled scenarios."*
   - *"Collaborate with faculty to implement and troubleshoot simulation scenarios."*

3. **Required Qualifications**: Clearly state the educational background, certifications, and experience needed. For instance:
   - *"Bachelor's degree in healthcare, education, or a related field; CHSOS certification preferred."*
   - *"Minimum of three years' experience in simulation technology or a clinical setting."*

4. **Preferred Qualifications**: Highlight additional skills or experience that would make candidates more competitive. For example:
   - *"Experience with Laerdal or CAE simulation systems."*
   - *"Knowledge of audiovisual systems and software."*

5. **Work Environment and Expectations**: Provide insights into the role's working conditions and expectations, such as flexibility, physical demands, or availability during evenings or weekends.

6. **Growth Opportunities**: Emphasize professional development, such as opportunities to attend conferences, gain certifications, or advance within the organization.

Benefits of Clear Job Descriptions
- Attracts candidates who align with the role and organization's needs.
- Reduces ambiguity during onboarding and performance evaluations.
- Enhances transparency, fostering trust between the organization and potential hires.

Attracting Talent
Simulation centers must use various channels and strategies to recruit top-tier professionals. These approaches ensure a broad reach and increase the likelihood of finding candidates who meet technical and cultural criteria.

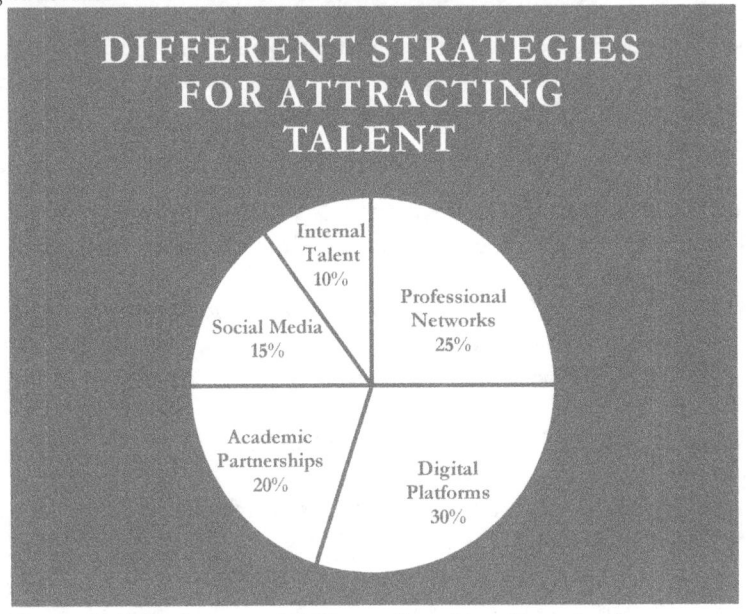

Figure 10 Effectiveness of Different Recruiting Strategies for Attracting Talent

Professional Networks and Associations
Professional organizations such as the *Society for Simulation in Healthcare* (SSH) are excellent platforms for recruiting qualified candidates. These networks offer:

- Job boards tailored to simulation-related positions.
- Access to conferences and events like the International Meeting on Simulation in Healthcare (IMSH), where recruiters can meet potential candidates.
- Certification programs (e.g., CHSE, CHSOS) that highlight credentialed professionals with relevant expertise (Society for Simulation in Healthcare, 2022).

Academic and Clinical Partnerships

Collaboration with academic and healthcare institutions is a strategic way to recruit faculty, technicians, and standardized patients. Examples include:

- Partnering with nursing and medical schools to identify candidates with a blend of clinical and educational experience.
- Offering internships or fellowships to students or residents interested in simulation education.
- Hosting open house events for local healthcare professionals to introduce them to the center's operations and opportunities.

Digital Job Market Platforms

General platforms such as LinkedIn, Indeed, and Glassdoor are essential for reaching diverse audiences. Strategies include:

- Crafting job postings with specific keywords like "simulation operations specialist," "manikin programming," or "simulation-based education."
- Highlighting the center's mission and unique features to attract candidates motivated by innovation and education.
- Using LinkedIn's talent search tools to identify and engage with qualified candidates actively.

Social Media and Online Communities

Social media platforms provide a cost-effective way to reach candidates, particularly those in niche communities. For example:

- Joining LinkedIn or Facebook groups dedicated to healthcare simulation.
- Sharing job postings on social media with relevant hashtags, such as #SimulationJobs or #HealthcareEducation.
- Posting videos or images showcasing the center's facilities and staff to attract candidates interested in joining a cutting-edge team.

Internal Talent Development

Promoting from within the organization can streamline recruitment for leadership roles. For example:

- Identifying high-performing staff and providing opportunities for certification or training to prepare them for advanced roles.
- Encouraging technicians or faculty to pursue leadership certifications, such as CHSE or CHSOS, as part of a structured career development plan.

Standardized Patient Recruitment

For standardized patients, outreach efforts may include:

- Posting roles on local theater community boards, given the overlap in performance skills.
- Partnering with drama schools or community centers to recruit individuals interested in acting or healthcare education.

- Conducting open casting calls with clear instructions and expectations for SP roles.

Evaluating Candidates

A structured evaluation process ensures that recruitment decisions are fair, consistent, and aligned with the center's needs. Simulation center roles often require a mix of technical, clinical, and interpersonal skills, so evaluation methods must be tailored to each position.

Structured Interviews

Interviews should include technical, situational, and behavioral questions to assess the candidate's capabilities and cultural fit. Examples include:

- **Technical**: *"Describe when you had to troubleshoot a high-fidelity manikin. How did you resolve the issue?"*
- **Situational**: *"If a faculty member requests last-minute changes to a simulation scenario, how would you handle it?"*
- **Behavioral**: *"Tell us about a time you worked in a team under pressure. How did you contribute to its success?"*

Practical Assessments

For technical and operational roles, hands-on assessments are invaluable. For example:

- Asking a simulation technician candidate to set up and operate a manikin for a scenario.
- Evaluating faculty candidates by having them lead a mock debriefing session or develop a scenario outline.

Panel Interviews

Panel interviews involving staff from different roles provide a well-rounded perspective on the candidate's suitability. For example, a faculty interview panel might include a simulation technician, an instructor, and an administrator to assess technical knowledge, educational alignment, and teamwork.

Cultural Fit

Assessing cultural fit is critical in ensuring the candidate aligns with the center's values and work environment. Role-playing exercises or informal conversations can provide insights into the candidate's adaptability, collaboration, and communication style.

References and Certifications

Verifying references and certifications is essential for roles that require specific credentials. For example:

- Confirming that a candidate has earned CHSE or CHSOS certification.
- Contacting previous employers to gather insights into the candidate's work ethic and ability to handle the demands of simulation-based education.

Ensuring Diversity and Inclusion

Simulation centers benefit from diverse teams that bring various perspectives to scenario development and operational challenges. Recruitment efforts should:

- Use inclusive language in job postings to attract candidates from diverse backgrounds.
- Actively seek candidates from underrepresented groups through targeted outreach.
- Standardize evaluation criteria to reduce unconscious bias and ensure fairness.

Recruitment is more than filling vacancies—building a team that embodies the simulation center's mission and values. Simulation center leaders can attract and hire professionals who excel by investing in clear job descriptions, leveraging diverse recruitment channels, and implementing rigorous evaluation processes. Thoughtful recruitment strategies ensure that the center remains a dynamic, innovative environment where staff collaborate effectively to advance education and improve outcomes.

5.3 Training and Onboarding

Effective training and onboarding are critical to integrating new staff into a simulation center's operations. The unique demands of simulation-based education—blending technology, pedagogy, and clinical expertise—require a robust and structured approach to preparing staff for their roles. Comprehensive training and onboarding enhance staff performance and improve job satisfaction and retention by fostering confidence, competence, and a sense of belonging.

Comprehensive Orientation

A well-designed orientation program introduces new hires to the simulation center's mission, culture, and operations. This initial phase provides the foundation for their understanding of the center's workflows and sets expectations for their roles.

Key Components of Orientation

1. **Mission and Vision**
   - Begin with an overview of the simulation center's mission and alignment with the broader institutional goals.
   - Example: *"Our mission is to advance healthcare education through innovative simulation experiences that improve patient outcomes."*

2. **Organizational Structure**
   - Introduce staff and key personnel to the center's hierarchy, including administrators, educators, and technicians.
   - Provide a clear understanding of reporting lines and collaboration points.

3. **Policies and Procedures**
   - Cover essential policies like confidentiality agreements, data security protocols, and equipment handling guidelines.
   - Provide a staff handbook for reference.

4. **Facility Tour**

- o Familiarize new hires with simulation spaces, equipment storage, debriefing rooms, and administrative offices.
- o Highlight safety measures, such as fire exits and first aid locations.

Orientation Tools

- **Welcome Kits**: Include a staff handbook, contact lists, and access credentials for systems and spaces.
- **Digital Resources**: Provide access to online orientation modules or video tours for review at their own pace.
- **Shadowing Opportunities**: Pair new hires with experienced staff to observe workflows in real-time.

Role-Specific Training

Beyond general orientation, staff require tailored training programs to develop the skills necessary for their roles. These programs should focus on technical and interpersonal competencies, ensuring each team member can contribute effectively to the center's operations.

Simulation Technicians

Technicians require hands-on training to master simulation equipment's operation, maintenance, and troubleshooting. Training topics include:

- **Manikin Operations**: Programming scenarios, calibrating manikins, and managing technical failures.
- **Scenario Execution**: Running scenarios in collaboration with educators, including managing real-time scenario changes.
- **Equipment Maintenance**: Conducting routine checks and preventative maintenance to ensure system reliability.

Example Activity: Technicians practice programming a high-fidelity manikin to simulate respiratory distress, adjusting parameters such as oxygen saturation and heart rate based on learner actions.

Faculty and Instructors

Faculty training focuses on simulation pedagogy, scenario facilitation, and debriefing techniques. Key training areas include:

- **Scenario Development**: Designing cases that align with curriculum objectives and competency frameworks.
- **Facilitation Skills**: Guiding learners through scenarios while balancing realism with educational goals.
- **Debriefing Frameworks**: Using structured debriefing methods, such as PEARLS or the Advocacy-Inquiry approach, to foster reflective learning (Dieckmann et al., 2007).

Example Activity: Faculty participate in mock scenarios that alternate between facilitator and learner roles to understand both perspectives.

Standardized Patients (SPs)
SPs require specialized training to deliver consistent, realistic portrayals while providing constructive feedback to learners. Training components include:

- **Role Preparation**: Learning case details, emotional cues, and scripted responses.
- **Feedback Delivery**: Teaching SPs how to provide objective, actionable feedback on communication and professionalism.

Example: SPs rehearse a case where they play a patient experiencing severe anxiety, focusing on non-verbal behaviors and scripted dialogue.

Ongoing Development
Simulation centers must invest in continuous learning to keep staff updated on emerging technologies, best practices, and evolving educational methods. Ongoing development ensures that all team members remain engaged and capable of meeting the center's changing needs.

Certifications and Advanced Training
Encourage staff to pursue industry-recognized certifications, such as:

- Certified Healthcare Simulation Educator (CHSE) for faculty and instructors.
- Certified Healthcare Simulation Operations Specialist (CHSOS) for technicians.

These certifications validate expertise and demonstrate the center's commitment to professional excellence (Society for Simulation in Healthcare, 2022).

Workshops and Conferences
Sponsor staff attendance at conferences like the International Meeting on Simulation in Healthcare (IMSH) to network with peers and learn about the latest advancements. Organize internal workshops to share new knowledge with the broader team.

Cross-Training Opportunities
Promote cross-training to enhance flexibility and collaboration. For example, technicians might learn basic debriefing skills while faculty gain a working knowledge of simulation equipment. Cross-training improves resilience during staff shortages and peak demand periods.

Example: A technician attends a workshop on debriefing techniques to support faculty during post-scenario discussions better.

Feedback and Evaluation During Onboarding
Continuous feedback during the onboarding process helps staff adjust to their roles and identify areas for improvement. Regular check-ins with supervisors and mentors provide opportunities for reflection and growth.

Onboarding Checkpoints
1. **30-Day Review**

- Assess initial adjustment, addressing any challenges or knowledge gaps.
- Example: *"How confident do you feel programming manikins for different scenarios?"*

2. **60-Day Review**
   - Evaluate role-specific competencies and provide additional training if needed.
   - Example: *"Have you encountered any equipment issues, and how did you resolve them?"*

3. **90-Day Review**
   - Conduct a formal performance evaluation, focusing on both technical and interpersonal skills.
   - Example: *"How effectively are you collaborating with faculty and learners?"*

Mentorship Programs
Pairing new hires with experienced staff fosters collaboration and provides a support system during onboarding. Mentors can offer practical advice, share institutional knowledge, and serve as role models.

Benefits of Mentorship
- Accelerates learning by providing real-time guidance.
- Builds trust and camaraderie within the team.
- Enhances retention by creating a sense of belonging.

Conclusion
Training and onboarding are not one-size-fits-all processes but tailored journeys that equip simulation center staff to excel. A strong onboarding program, with role-specific training and continuous development opportunities, ensures that new hires are confident, capable, and fully integrated into the team. By investing in comprehensive training, simulation centers enhance operational efficiency and foster a culture of lifelong learning and professional growth.

5.4 Retention and Engagement

Retention and engagement are critical to building a cohesive and high-performing team in a simulation center. Retaining skilled staff reduces turnover costs, minimizes operations disruptions, and fosters institutional knowledge. Additionally, an engaged workforce is more productive, innovative, and satisfied with their roles, contributing to the simulation center's overall success.

Despite these benefits, retention can be challenging in high-pressure environments like simulation centers, where roles often demand a blend of technical, clinical, and educational expertise. This section outlines strategies for retention and engagement, supported by data and best practices.

Retention Challenges in Simulation Centers

The complex nature of simulation center roles, combined with the rapid evolution of technology and pedagogy, presents unique retention challenges:

- **Burnout**: High workloads and the pressure to deliver seamless simulations can lead to fatigue and stress, particularly for technical staff and educators (Maslach & Leiter, 2016).
- **Limited Advancement Opportunities**: Talented staff may seek opportunities elsewhere without clear career progression pathways.
- **Competitive Market**: Simulation professionals with specialized skills are in high demand, making it difficult to retain top talent.

According to the *Society for Human Resource Management (SHRM)*, the average annual turnover rate across industries is approximately 19%, while turnover in healthcare settings can exceed 25% (SHRM, 2022). Simulation centers, as specialized healthcare-education hybrids, face similar or higher turnover rates if proactive retention strategies are not implemented.

Retention Strategies

1. Career Development Opportunities

Providing pathways for growth is one of the most effective ways to retain talented staff. Employees who perceive opportunities for advancement are significantly more likely to stay with their organizations.

- **Certifications and Training**: Encourage staff to pursue certifications like Certified Healthcare Simulation Educator (CHSE) or Certified Healthcare Simulation Operations Specialist (CHSOS). These credentials enhance skills and demonstrate the organization's investment in staff development (Society for Simulation in Healthcare, 2022).

> **94%** of employees said they would stay at a company longer if it invested in their career development.

- **Leadership Development**: Offer mentorship programs, cross-training opportunities, and leadership workshops to prepare staff for advanced roles. For example, a technician might transition to an operations manager role through targeted development.
- **Tuition Reimbursement**: Subsidize further education in related fields, such as instructional design or healthcare technology.

Statistics: According to LinkedIn's *Workforce Learning Report (2022)*, 94% of employees said they would stay at a company longer if it invested in their career development.

2. Recognition and Rewards

Acknowledging and rewarding staff contributions fosters a sense of appreciation and motivation.

- **Formal Recognition Programs**: Establish awards for exceptional performance, such as "Simulation Innovator of the Month" or team-based recognitions for successful large-scale simulations.

> Employees are **63%** more likely to stay with their current employer if they feel recognized.

- **Informal Acknowledgements:** During team meetings, provide verbal praise, handwritten notes, or shout-outs to highlight individual and team achievements.

- **Incentives**: Offer financial bonuses, gift cards, or extra time off to meet significant milestones or deliver high-quality work.

Statistics: According to Gallup, employees who feel recognized are 63% more likely to stay with their current employer (Gallup, 2021).

3. Competitive Compensation and Benefits
Competitive pay and comprehensive benefits are fundamental to retaining skilled professionals.

- **Salary Benchmarking**: Regularly review and adjust salaries to remain competitive with industry standards. Data from organizations like the Society for Simulation in Healthcare or regional salary surveys can be used.

> **45%** of employees cited competitive pay as the top reason for staying with their employer.

- **Flexible Work Options**: Offer hybrid schedules or flexible hours where feasible, particularly for roles that involve data analysis, scenario development, or administrative tasks.

- **Wellness Programs**: Provide access to wellness initiatives, such as gym memberships, mental health resources, and stress management workshops.

Statistics: A 2022 survey by Mercer found that 45% of employees cited competitive pay as the top reason for staying with their employer.

Engagement Strategies
While retention focuses on keeping staff, engagement ensures that employees remain committed and enthusiastic about their work. Engaged employees are not only more productive but also act as advocates for the organization.

1. Cultivating a Positive Work Environment
- **Team Collaboration**: Foster an inclusive and collaborative culture by encouraging interdisciplinary teamwork. For example, host cross-departmental meetings where faculty, technicians, and administrative staff share feedback and ideas.

- **Open Communication**: Create channels for staff to voice concerns and suggestions. Regular one-on-one meetings and anonymous surveys can provide valuable insights into engagement levels.

Statistics: Gallup reports that highly engaged teams show a 21% increase in productivity compared to less engaged teams (Gallup, 2021).

2. Providing Meaningful Work
Employees are more engaged when they see the impact of their work.
- **Connecting to the Mission**: Remind staff how their roles contribute to improving healthcare education and patient outcomes. For instance, highlight success stories where simulation training directly influenced clinical decision-making.

- **Involvement in Innovation**: Encourage staff to participate in pilot programs, research projects, or the development of new simulation techniques.

3. Social and Team-Building Activities
Strengthening interpersonal relationships among staff boosts morale and engagement.
- **Team Events**: Organize social gatherings, such as potlucks, team lunches, or outings, to build camaraderie.
- **Recognition Celebrations**: Host annual events to celebrate staff achievements and milestones.
- **Wellness Challenges**: Create friendly competitions, like step challenges or mindfulness programs, to promote health and team bonding.

Statistics: A survey by McKinsey & Company found that employees who feel a strong sense of belonging are 50% more likely to report high engagement (McKinsey, 2021).

Evaluating Retention and Engagement
Regularly assess retention and engagement levels to identify areas for improvement.

Retention Metrics
- **Turnover Rate**: Calculate the percentage of staff leaving annually and analyze trends by role or department.

- **Exit Interviews**: Conduct interviews with departing staff to identify factors contributing to turnover.

Engagement Metrics
- **Pulse Surveys**: Use short, frequent surveys to gauge staff satisfaction and engagement.

- **Stay Interviews**: Meet with current staff to discuss their experiences and identify what motivates them to stay.

Retention and engagement are two sides of the same coin. Keeping staff requires creating an environment where they feel valued, supported, and connected to the mission. By investing in career development, recognizing contributions, and fostering a positive workplace culture, simulation centers can build stable teams that are highly motivated to excel. These strategies ensure the center thrives as a hub for innovation, collaboration, and transformative learning experiences.

5.5 Performance Evaluation

Performance evaluation is a cornerstone of effective staff management in simulation centers. It provides a structured approach to assessing individual contributions, identifying areas for improvement, and aligning staff efforts with the center's goals. A well-designed evaluation process fosters professional growth, enhances team dynamics, and ensures the simulation center operates efficiently.

The Importance of Performance Evaluation

Performance evaluations serve multiple purposes in a simulation center:
- **Accountability**: Clarify expectations and ensure that staff are meeting their responsibilities.
- **Professional Development**: Identify skill gaps and provide opportunities for growth through targeted training.
- **Operational Excellence**: Assess how individual performance impacts the center's overall success.
- **Retention and Engagement**: Demonstrate to staff that their work is valued and their contributions are recognized.

Studies show that employees who receive regular feedback are 3.6 times more likely to feel engaged in their roles and are significantly less likely to leave their organizations (Gallup, 2021).

Components of a Comprehensive Evaluation Process

An effective performance evaluation includes clearly defined criteria, regular feedback opportunities, and actionable outcomes.

1. Establishing Performance Metrics
Metrics should reflect the unique responsibilities of each role in the simulation center. These metrics provide a fair and objective basis for evaluation.

Examples of Role-Specific Metrics:
- **Simulation Technicians**:
    - Percentage of scenarios executed without technical disruptions.
    - Responsiveness to equipment troubleshooting and repairs.
    - Proficiency in programming and maintaining simulation equipment.

- **Faculty and Instructors**:
    - Quality and alignment of simulation scenarios with curriculum objectives.
    - Effectiveness of debriefing sessions as measured by learner feedback.

- o   Contribution to research or program development initiatives.

- **Administrative Staff**:
    - o   Accuracy and timeliness of scheduling and record-keeping.
    - o   Compliance with policy enforcement.
    - o   Communication effectiveness with staff, learners, and stakeholders.

- **Standardized Patients (SPs)**:
    - o   Consistency in role portrayal across multiple scenarios.
    - o   Feedback quality provided to learners.
    - o   Responsiveness to scenario adjustments during sessions.

2. Feedback Frequency

While annual reviews are a standard practice, incorporating regular feedback sessions can enhance the effectiveness of the evaluation process.

Types of Feedback Opportunities:
- **Real-Time Feedback**: Provide immediate, constructive input during or after scenarios. For example, a technician might receive feedback on how efficiently they resolved a mid-scenario technical issue.

- **Quarterly Check-Ins**: Schedule formal meetings to discuss progress, challenges, and short-term goals.

- **Annual Reviews**: Conduct comprehensive evaluations, including performance over the year, professional development milestones, and future plans.

Research shows that 96% of employees prefer frequent feedback over traditional annual reviews alone (PwC, 2022).

3. Tools for Evaluation

Implementing structured tools can streamline the evaluation process and ensure consistency across roles.

Examples of Evaluation Tools:
- **Performance Rubrics**: Use detailed rubrics tailored to each role to assess specific skills and outcomes. For instance, a rubric for instructors might evaluate their ability to facilitate discussions, adapt to learner needs, and incorporate simulation best practices.

- **Self-Assessments**: Encourage staff to reflect on their strengths and areas for improvement, fostering accountability and self-awareness.

- **360-Degree Feedback**: Collect input from peers, supervisors, and learners to provide a well-rounded perspective on performance.

Best Practices for Effective Evaluations

1. Set Clear Expectations
Performance expectations should be defined during onboarding and revisited periodically. Provide staff with documentation outlining their responsibilities, metrics, and evaluation criteria.

Example: During onboarding, a simulation technician might be informed that they will be assessed on equipment uptime, scenario setup accuracy, and responsiveness to troubleshooting requests.

2. Foster Open Communication
Performance evaluations should be a two-way conversation. Encourage staff to share their perspectives on their roles, challenges, and career aspirations.

Example: During an evaluation, an instructor might express interest in pursuing a CHSE certification, prompting the manager to discuss opportunities for professional development funding.

3. Focus on Growth
Rather than solely identifying weaknesses, emphasize opportunities for improvement and provide actionable recommendations. Pair constructive feedback with resources, such as training programs, mentorship opportunities, or shadowing experienced staff.

Example: If a technician struggles with scenario programming, the manager might arrange for them to attend a workshop on simulation software.

4. Recognize Achievements
Acknowledging accomplishments builds morale and motivates staff to maintain high performance. Recognize milestones during evaluations and in public forums, such as team meetings or newsletters.

Statistics: Employees who feel recognized are 63% more likely to stay with their organizations (Gallup, 2021).

Addressing Underperformance

Maintaining a high-performance standard within a team is crucial to achieving organizational goals. However, when a team member's performance falls short of expectations, it is vital to address the issue with care, clarity, and a focus on improvement. A proactive and supportive approach helps the individual get back on track and fosters a positive work environment where challenges are seen as opportunities for growth.

Steps for Managing Underperformance

1. **Identify the Root Cause**

Begin by understanding the underlying reasons for the underperformance. Is it due to skill gaps that require additional training? Are resource constraints or unclear expectations creating barriers? Or could personal challenges outside of work be impacting their focus and productivity? Identifying the root cause is the foundation of effective problem-solving.

2. **Develop an Action Plan**

Once the cause is clear, collaborate with the individual to create a tailored improvement plan. This plan should include specific, measurable goals, a realistic timeline, and clear expectations. Involving the team member in this process ensures accountability and demonstrates mutual commitment to their success.

3. **Provide Support**

Offer the necessary tools and resources to help the individual achieve the goals outlined in the action plan. This might include training sessions, mentorship programs, or access to additional materials. Ensuring they feel supported can significantly boost their confidence and motivation.

4. **Monitor Progress**

Improvement takes time and effort. Schedule regular check-ins to review progress, celebrate small wins, and provide constructive feedback. Maintaining open communication during this phase helps identify lingering challenges and reinforces the manager's dedication to their growth.

Example in Practice

Consider a situation where a Standardized Patient (SP) struggles to maintain consistency in role portrayal. This inconsistency could undermine the effectiveness of simulations. To address this, the manager could first determine whether the issue stems from a lack of preparation, difficulty memorizing scenarios, or inadequate understanding of the expectations. Together, they might devise an action plan that includes attending additional training sessions, practicing role scenarios with peers, and using memory aids to improve performance. Regular check-ins would help track progress, adjust strategies as needed, and ensure the SP feels supported.

By approaching underperformance as an opportunity for development rather than a point of criticism, managers can inspire confidence, nurture talent, and strengthen the team dynamic.

Evaluating the Evaluation Process

Just as staff performance is assessed, the evaluation process should be reviewed periodically to ensure its effectiveness.

Metrics for Evaluation Effectiveness:

- <u>Retention Rates</u>: High retention rates often indicate that staff feel supported and valued.
- <u>Engagement Levels</u>: Measure engagement through surveys or informal feedback to determine whether staff feel motivated and aligned with the center's mission.
- <u>Goal Achievement</u>: Track whether performance evaluation outcomes, such as professional development goals, are being met.

Performance evaluations are more than a formal process; they are an opportunity to nurture talent, foster engagement, and drive the simulation center's success. By setting clear expectations, providing regular and actionable feedback, and emphasizing growth and recognition, simulation center leaders can create an environment where staff feel valued and empowered to excel. This commitment to continuous improvement benefits the individual staff members and the learners, stakeholders, and institutions the center serves.

5.6 Conflict Resolution and Team Dynamics

Conflict is inevitable in any workplace, including simulation centers, where diverse roles, responsibilities, and perspectives converge. Effectively managing conflict and fostering positive team dynamics are essential for ensuring operational efficiency, enhancing staff satisfaction, and achieving the center's goals. When conflicts are resolved constructively, they can strengthen collaboration, innovation, and trust within the team.

This section outlines common sources of conflict, resolution strategies, and methods for building a cohesive and high-performing team.

Common Sources of Conflict in Simulation Centers

Simulation centers bring together professionals with varying expertise, including technicians, faculty, standardized patients, and administrators. While these differences can be beneficial, they can lead to misunderstandings or disagreements.

1. Role Misunderstandings
- *Example*: Faculty members may not fully understand the technical constraints of manikin operations, leading to unrealistic expectations of simulation technicians.

- **Impact**: This can result in frustration, miscommunication, and inefficiencies in scenario execution.

2. Resource Allocation
- *Example*: Competing demands for equipment or simulation spaces can create tension between departments or programs.

- **Impact**: Staff may feel that their needs are deprioritized, leading to dissatisfaction and strained relationships.

3. Communication Breakdowns

- *Example*: Failure to communicate last-minute scenario changes can confuse a session.

- **Impact**: Misaligned expectations and errors in execution can undermine trust and team morale.

4. Workload Imbalances
- *Example*: A technician may feel overburdened if they are frequently called upon to assist with scenarios beyond their scheduled duties.

- **Impact**: Perceived inequities can lead to resentment and burnout.

Strategies for Conflict Resolution

Conflict resolution in simulation centers requires a proactive, structured approach that prioritizes understanding, fairness, and collaboration.

1. Address Conflicts Early
Unresolved conflicts tend to escalate, making them more challenging to resolve. Managers should encourage staff to raise concerns promptly and provide opportunities for open dialogue.
- *Example*: A simulation director notices growing tension between a technician and a faculty member over scenario setup delays. They arrange a meeting to address the issue before it disrupts operations.

2. Foster Active Listening
Active listening ensures that all parties feel heard and understood, which is critical for de-escalating tensions.
- **Technique**: During conflict discussions, summarize what the other person has said to confirm understanding.
  - *"So, you're concerned that last-minute changes to the scenario make it difficult to set up the manikin correctly. Is that accurate?"*

3. Focus on Interests, Not Positions
Encourage team members to articulate their underlying interests rather than rigidly defending their positions.
- *Example*: Instead of arguing over who should have access to a high-fidelity simulator, staff could discuss their shared interest in ensuring equitable access for all programs.

4. Mediation and Neutral Facilitation
When conflicts cannot be resolved independently, involve a neutral third party, such as a manager or HR representative, to facilitate discussions.
- *Example*: During a mediated session, the facilitator helps a faculty member and technician identify common ground, such as their shared commitment to providing high-quality simulation experiences.

5. Develop Action Plans
Create actionable steps to resolve conflicts and prevent future issues.
- *Example*: After addressing a scheduling conflict, the team agrees to implement a shared calendar system to improve visibility and coordination.

Statistics: Research shows that 76% of employees who experience workplace conflict cite lack of effective management as a key factor in escalation (CPP Global, 2021).

Building Positive Team Dynamics

Strong team dynamics reduce the likelihood of conflict and create an environment where collaboration and innovation can thrive. Simulation centers can enhance team cohesion through intentional practices.

1. Establish Clear Roles and Responsibilities
Defining roles reduces misunderstandings and ensures that each team member understands their contributions to the center's goals.
- *Example*: A detailed onboarding process includes a discussion of how each role (e.g., technician, faculty, SP) supports the overall mission of the center.

2. Encourage Interdisciplinary Collaboration
Simulation centers thrive on the interplay of clinical, technical, and educational expertise. Creating opportunities for collaboration fosters mutual respect and understanding.
- *Example*: Host cross-departmental meetings where technicians, faculty, and administrators share insights and jointly solve operational challenges.

Statistics: Teams collaborating effectively are 25% more productive and 50% more likely to report high job satisfaction (McKinsey, 2021).

3. Promote Team-Building Activities
Regular team-building activities help build trust and camaraderie.
- **Ideas for Team-Building Activities**:
    - Scenario Walkthroughs: Engage the team in designing and testing new simulation scenarios.
    - Social Events: Organize informal gatherings to strengthen relationships, such as potlucks or team lunches.
    - Workshops: Conduct communication skills or conflict resolution workshops to improve team dynamics.

4. Celebrate Successes
Recognizing individual and team achievements fosters a positive and supportive culture.
- *Example:* After a successful multi-departmental simulation event, the director hosts a celebration to thank the team and highlight specific contributions.

Leadership's Role in Conflict Resolution and Team Dynamics

Effective leadership is critical for resolving conflicts and fostering positive dynamics. Through their actions and attitudes, leaders set the tone for the team.

1. Lead by Example
Leaders who model respectful communication and collaboration inspire similar behavior in their teams.

2. Provide Ongoing Training
Offer professional development opportunities focused on teamwork, emotional intelligence, and conflict resolution.
- *Example*: Arrange a workshop on managing difficult conversations equipping staff with strategies to navigate challenging interactions.

3. Create Safe Spaces for Feedback
Encourage staff to share concerns and ideas without fear of retaliation. Use anonymous surveys or regular one-on-one meetings to gather honest feedback.

Evaluating and Monitoring Team Dynamics

Regular assessments of team dynamics can help identify potential issues before they escalate.

Evaluation Methods:

- Team Surveys: Gauge satisfaction and collaboration levels through anonymous surveys.
- Observation: Monitor interactions during meetings and scenarios to identify areas for improvement.
- Debriefing Feedback: Use debriefing sessions to evaluate teamwork and communication during simulations.

Statistics: A 2021 report by Deloitte found that organizations with strong team dynamics see 41% lower absenteeism and 59% higher employee engagement compared to those with weak dynamics.

Conflict resolution and team dynamics are interconnected aspects of effective simulation center management. By addressing conflicts early, fostering open communication, and building a culture of collaboration, leaders can create an environment where staff work together effectively toward shared goals. Investing in these strategies minimizes disruptions and enhances job satisfaction, retention, and the overall success of the simulation center.

5.7 Managing Workloads

At the heart of this intricate ecosystem are the staff—simulation technicians, faculty, standardized patients, and administrators—who ensure the center's seamless operation. However, the same complexity that drives a simulation center's innovation can lead to workload imbalances, burnout, and inefficiencies if not carefully managed.

Effective workload management is not just about assigning tasks; it's about fostering a culture where staff feel supported, valued, and equipped to handle their responsibilities.

This section explores strategies to balance workload distribution, optimize resources, and promote staff well-being, ensuring individual and organizational success.

Recognizing the Challenges of Workload Management

Simulation centers operate at the intersection of healthcare, education, and technology, each with its demands. This dynamic environment often leads to unique workload challenges:

1. Peak Demand Periods
Simulation centers experience fluctuations in demand, with peak periods often coinciding with academic exams, clinical competency assessments, or institutional events. For example, a center may need to run back-to-back simulations for nursing students preparing for Objective Structured Clinical Examinations (OSCEs).

2. Role Overlap
Staff often wear multiple hats. A simulation technician might set up equipment, troubleshoot technical issues, and assist during scenario execution while faculty balance teaching, scenario design, and debriefing responsibilities. This multitasking can lead to fatigue and reduced efficiency.

3. Resource Constraints
Limited equipment, space, or staff can exacerbate workload pressures, forcing teams to stretch their capabilities to meet demands. For instance, a single high-fidelity manikin shared among multiple programs can create scheduling bottlenecks and added stress for technicians.

Strategies for Effective Workload Management

1. Assessing Workload Distribution
The first step in managing workload is understanding how tasks are distributed across the team. Conducting regular workload assessments helps identify imbalances and ensures fairness.
- *Example*: During a biannual review, the simulation center director notices that technicians spend disproportionate time troubleshooting equipment, leaving little bandwidth for proactive maintenance. The team reallocates responsibilities to give technicians more time for preventative tasks.

2. Prioritizing Tasks
Not all tasks are created equal. Identifying high-priority activities ensures that critical needs are addressed without overwhelming the team.
- **Categorization Framework**:
    - **High Priority**: Certification training (e.g., ACLS, BLS), high-stakes assessments, and emergency preparedness drills.
    - **Moderate Priority**: Routine practice simulations and open lab sessions.
    - **Low Priority**: Administrative tasks that can be automated or postponed.

- *Example*: During a busy week, the team defers optional workshops to focus on an upcoming accreditation audit.

3. Leveraging Technology
Technology can streamline processes, reduce manual workloads, and free up staff for higher-value tasks.
- **Scheduling Software**: Tools like SimCapture or Skedda automate resource allocation and prevent double booking of spaces or equipment.
- **Inventory Management**: Systems like Asset Panda track equipment usage and maintenance schedules, ensuring readiness without overburdening staff.

- *Example*: The center implements scheduling software that automatically adjusts room assignments based on session duration and resource requirements, reducing administrative staff workload by 30%.

4. Cross-Training Staff
Cross-training ensures that team members can step into multiple roles, increasing flexibility and resilience during peak periods.
- *Example*: A faculty member is trained in basic manikin programming, allowing them to handle simple adjustments during scenarios without relying on a technician.

- **Benefit**: Cross-training lightens individual workloads and fosters teamwork and mutual understanding among staff.

Fostering a Culture of Support
Beyond task management, creating a supportive work environment is essential for preventing burnout and promoting long-term engagement.

1. Encouraging Open Communication
Staff should feel comfortable discussing workload challenges with their managers without fear of judgment. Regular check-ins provide a forum for addressing concerns and adjusting expectations.
- *Example*: During a team meeting, a technician says they've been staying late to complete scenario setups. The director reallocates some administrative tasks to lighten their load.

2. Promoting Work-Life Balance
Simulation centers can implement policies prioritizing staff well-being, such as flexible scheduling or compensatory time for after-hours work.
- *Example*: After a demanding week of evening sessions, the center offers technicians a half-day to recharge.

3. Recognizing and Rewarding Effort
Acknowledging formally and informally staff contributions can boost morale and motivate the team.
- *Example*: A faculty member who designed an innovative scenario for interprofessional collaboration receives a public shout-out during the weekly team huddle.

Optimizing Resources

Efficient resource management reduces workload pressure and ensures that the center operates smoothly.

1. Streamlining Processes
Evaluate workflows regularly to identify inefficiencies and implement improvements.
- *Example*: The center transitions to a digital documentation system, cutting the time spent on manual data entry by 40%.

2. Scaling Resources
As demand grows, simulation centers should advocate for additional resources, including staff, equipment, or funding.
- *Example*: The director presents a data-driven proposal to institutional leadership, securing funding for a second high-fidelity manikin to alleviate scheduling conflicts.

3. Managing Peak Periods
Anticipate busy times and plan accordingly by adjusting staffing levels or redistributing tasks.
- *Example*: During finals week, the center hires temporary assistants to help with session setups and logistics.

Monitoring Workload Over Time

Workload management is not a one-time effort but an ongoing process. Regular monitoring helps maintain balance and adapt to changing demands.

Metrics to Track:
- Task Completion Rates: Are deadlines consistently met without staff feeling rushed?
- Overtime Hours: High overtime rates may indicate workload imbalances.
- Employee Feedback: Use surveys or one-on-one meetings to gather insights into workload perceptions.

Managing workload in a simulation center is about more than assigning tasks—creating a system where staff feel empowered, supported, and engaged. Simulation center leaders can ensure that workloads are manageable and aligned with the center's goals by prioritizing tasks, leveraging technology, fostering open communication, and optimizing resources. In doing so, they enhance operational efficiency and build a resilient, motivated team ready to meet the dynamic challenges of simulation-based education.

5.8 Contingency Planning

Simulation centers operate in complex environments where disruptions—whether due to equipment failures, staffing shortages, or unforeseen emergencies—can have cascading effects on operations. Contingency planning is essential for maintaining operational continuity, ensuring learner outcomes are met, and protecting the center's resources and reputation. This section explores the importance of contingency planning, strategies for mitigating risks, and actionable steps to create a robust plan tailored to a simulation center's unique needs.

The Importance of Contingency Planning

Contingency planning is about readiness and resilience. It prepares the simulation center to address disruptions effectively, minimizing downtime and ensuring that sessions proceed as smoothly as possible.

Key Benefits of Contingency Planning:
1. **Operational Continuity**: Ensures critical activities, such as certification simulations or high-stakes assessments, are completed on schedule.
2. **Risk Mitigation**: Reduces the impact of potential risks, such as equipment malfunctions or staffing gaps.
3. **Stakeholder Confidence**: Demonstrates to learners, faculty, and institutional leadership that the center can handle challenges professionally.
4. **Resource Protection**: Safeguard the center's physical and digital assets during emergencies.

Statistics: According to the Federal Emergency Management Agency (FEMA), organizations with contingency plans recover from disruptions 40% faster than those without (FEMA, 2021).

Common Scenarios Requiring Contingency Plans

Simulation centers face a range of potential disruptions, including:

- **Equipment Failures**: High-fidelity manikins, audiovisual systems, or simulation software malfunctions can disrupt planned sessions.
- **Staffing Shortages**: Sudden absences due to illness, turnover, or personal emergencies can leave critical roles unfilled.
- **Environmental Issues**: Power outages, water leaks, or HVAC failures can render simulation spaces unusable.
- **Technology Outages**: Network disruptions or software crashes can hinder scenario execution and data access.
- **External Emergencies**: Natural disasters, pandemics, or campus-wide emergencies can disrupt operations entirely.

Developing a Contingency Plan

A well-rounded contingency plan should address the most likely risks and provide clear, actionable steps for mitigating their impact.

1. Risk Assessment
Identify and prioritize potential risks based on their likelihood and impact.
- *Example*: A risk assessment identifies aging audiovisual equipment as a high-priority risk due to frequent malfunctions during sessions.
- **Action**: Implement preventative maintenance schedules and secure funding for equipment upgrades.

2. Establishing Response Protocols
For each identified risk, outline detailed response steps, including roles, responsibilities, and timelines.

- **Example – Equipment Failure**:
    - **Step 1**: Notify the simulation technician on duty.
    - **Step 2**: Transition to backup equipment, such as a task trainer or alternate manikin.
    - **Step 3**: Log the issue and notify the operations manager for follow-up repair.
- **Example – Staffing Shortage**:
    - **Step 1**: Activate a cross-trained staff member to fill the role temporarily.
    - **Step 2**: Notify faculty and adjust the session plan as needed.
    - **Step 3**: Document the incident and review workload distribution to prevent recurrence.

3. Creating Backup Resources
Ensure that backup resources are readily available to minimize disruptions.
- **Equipment Backups**: Maintain a pool of task trainers or portable manikins to substitute for high-fidelity simulators.
- **Digital Redundancy**: Store scenario files and session data in cloud-based storage to ensure accessibility even during local network outages.
- **Staffing Alternatives**: Develop a list of on-call staff, including part-time or adjunct faculty, who can step in during emergencies.

4. Training Staff on Contingency Protocols
Provide regular training to ensure all team members understand their roles in executing contingency plans.
- *Example*: Conduct quarterly drills simulating common disruptions, such as a network failure during a scenario. Staff practice transitioning to manual operations while maintaining session quality.

5. Documenting and Updating the Plan
Maintain a clear, accessible document outlining the contingency plan. Update it regularly to reflect new risks, technologies, or organizational changes.

Technology and Equipment Contingencies

1. Preventative Maintenance
Schedule routine maintenance for all equipment to reduce the likelihood of failures.
- *Example*: Technicians perform monthly checks on manikins to proactively identify wear and replace components.

2. Rapid Troubleshooting
Develop quick-reference guides for troubleshooting common technical issues.
- *Example*: If connectivity is lost, a laminated guide near the control station details steps for reconnecting a manikin to the simulation software.

3. Vendor Support Agreements
Establish service agreements with vendors for expedited repairs or replacements.
- *Example*: A vendor agreement includes a 24-hour turnaround for critical parts and remote technical support.

Staffing and Scheduling Contingencies

1. Cross-Training Staff
Ensure that all staff members are equipped to perform basic tasks outside their primary roles.
- *Example*: Faculty are trained to perform minor manikin adjustments, reducing reliance on technicians during unexpected absences.

2. Flexible Scheduling
Adopt scheduling practices that allow for rapid adjustments in staffing.
- *Example*: Use software to create flexible schedules with built-in buffers for peak demand periods, ensuring adequate coverage.

3. Emergency Contact Lists
Maintain up-to-date contact lists for all staff, including on-call personnel, to quickly address shortages.

Environmental and External Contingencies

1. Facility Preparedness
Equip the simulation center to handle environmental challenges.
- Backup Power: Install generators to maintain power during outages.
- Flood Protection: Elevate critical equipment in areas prone to water leaks or flooding.
- HVAC Monitoring: Use temperature sensors to ensure optimal conditions for equipment and sessions.

2. Emergency Communication Plans
Establish protocols for communicating with staff, learners, and stakeholders during emergencies.
- *Example*: A mass notification system sends real-time updates to all stakeholders and clearly instructs them on session cancellations or relocations.

3. Remote Learning Options
Prepare contingency plans for remote learning in case the center becomes inaccessible.
- *Example*: Faculty transition to virtual simulations using platforms like SimX or virtual reality scenarios during campus closures.

Evaluating the Effectiveness of Contingency Plans

Conduct post-incident reviews to assess contingency plans' effectiveness and identify areas for improvement.
- **Debriefing Sessions**: Gather feedback from staff and faculty in implementing the plan.

- **Incident Logs**: Maintain detailed records of disruptions, including response times and outcomes.
- **Periodic Drills**: Test contingency plans through simulations of potential scenarios to ensure readiness.

Contingency planning is essential for the resilience and success of simulation centers. By anticipating potential risks, developing clear response protocols, and equipping staff with the necessary tools and training, centers can navigate disruptions confidently and professionally. These efforts protect the center's operations and reputation as a reliable hub for education and innovation.

5.9 Summary

Chapter 5 explores the essential role of a well-managed, cohesive team in successfully operating simulation centers. These centers rely on a diverse array of professionals—administrators, technicians, educators, and standardized patients—working together to create immersive, high-quality educational experiences. The chapter emphasizes that effective staff management is more than simply filling positions; it involves fostering collaboration, supporting professional growth, and building a resilient team capable of navigating the unique demands of simulation-based education.

The chapter begins by outlining the roles and responsibilities of simulation center staff, from directors who set the strategic vision to technicians ensuring seamless technology operations, faculty designing, and leading scenarios, as well as administrative staff managing schedules and policies. Each role is critical, and their interdependence underpins the center's success. A recurring theme is the importance of clear role definitions and communication to ensure smooth workflows and mutual respect among team members.

Recruiting the right individuals is pivotal. The chapter discusses the importance of crafting detailed job descriptions and utilizing diverse recruitment channels, including professional networks, academic partnerships, and digital platforms. Structured interviews, practical assessments, and panel evaluations are highlighted as effective tools for selecting candidates with the technical expertise, interpersonal skills, and cultural alignment needed for simulation center roles.

Once staff are on board, training and onboarding are critical to their success. Comprehensive orientation programs introduce new hires to the center's mission, policies, and operations. Tailored role-specific training ensures that each team member can perform their duties effectively, whether programming high-fidelity manikins, facilitating debriefing sessions, or providing constructive feedback as standardized patients. Continuous professional development, such as certifications and conference participation, is emphasized to keep staff updated on emerging trends and best practices.

Retention and engagement strategies are explored in depth. The chapter identifies common challenges, including burnout, limited career progression opportunities, and the competitive job market for skilled simulation professionals. Solutions include offering career development opportunities, recognizing staff achievements, and providing competitive compensation and benefits. Engaging employees through meaningful work, team-building activities, and open communication fosters a positive work environment and strengthens their connection to the center's mission.

Performance evaluation is a cornerstone of staff management, providing a structured approach to assessing contributions and identifying growth opportunities. The chapter underscores the value of role-specific metrics, regular feedback, and actionable recommendations. Constructive feedback is paired with strategies for underperformance, such as collaborative action plans and targeted training.

Conflict resolution and team dynamics are also critical to simulation center success. The chapter acknowledges that conflicts can arise from role misunderstandings, resource allocation disputes, or communication breakdowns. It provides strategies for addressing these issues constructively, fostering collaboration, and building a culture of mutual respect. Interdisciplinary collaboration, team-building activities, and celebrating successes further support positive team dynamics.

Workload management is another significant focus, as the complex operations of a simulation center often lead to peak demand periods, resource constraints, and role overlap. Strategies such as task prioritization, leveraging technology, and cross-training staff are presented as effective ways to balance workloads and prevent burnout. Creating a supportive culture with open communication and recognizing staff efforts is essential for maintaining morale and efficiency.

Finally, the chapter delves into contingency planning, underscoring the importance of readiness and resilience in disruptions. Simulation centers must have robust plans to maintain operational continuity from equipment failures and staffing shortages to external emergencies. Key strategies include conducting risk assessments, establishing response protocols, maintaining backup resources, and regularly training staff on contingency measures.

Overall, Chapter 5 presents a comprehensive guide to managing the human element of simulation centers. It highlights the importance of investing in recruitment, training, retention, evaluation, and contingency planning to build a motivated and skilled team. By prioritizing effective staff management, simulation centers can foster a culture of excellence, adaptability, and collaboration, ensuring they continue to deliver impactful learning experiences.

5.10 Chapter Review

Review Questions

1. **Roles and Responsibilities:**
    - How do the roles of simulation technicians differ from faculty in simulation centers?
    - Why is having a dedicated administrative staff in a simulation center critical?

2. **Recruitment:**
    - What are the benefits of partnering with academic institutions for recruitment?
    - Describe how panel interviews and practical assessments ensure a candidate's fit for the role.
3. **Retention and Engagement:**
    - What strategies can simulation centers use to reduce staff burnout?
    - How do recognition programs contribute to staff engagement and retention?
4. **Performance Evaluation:**
    - Why are role-specific metrics essential in performance evaluations?
    - How does providing regular feedback benefit staff and the simulation center?
5. **Contingency Planning:**
    - Identify three potential risks for simulation centers and outline corresponding contingency measures.
    - How can staff training improve the effectiveness of contingency plans?

Critical Thinking and Application

1. **Staffing Models:**
    - Design a staffing model for a mid-sized simulation center, detailing roles, responsibilities, and recruitment strategies.
2. **Training Programs:**
    - Develop a role-specific training module for simulation technicians, including onboarding and ongoing development activities.
3. **Conflict Resolution:**
    - Propose a step-by-step plan to resolve conflicts between faculty and technicians regarding last-minute scenario changes.
4. **Workload Management:**
    - Create a strategy to manage peak workload periods, ensuring equitable task distribution and staff well-being.

Hands-On Activities

- **Role Simulation:** Conduct mock interviews or training sessions to practice recruitment or onboarding processes.
- **Conflict Workshop:** Role-play common conflicts and apply resolution strategies in a team-building exercise.
- **Risk Scenario Drill:** Simulate an equipment failure or staffing shortage and test the effectiveness of your contingency plan.

Summary Reflection

Chapter 5 highlights that a simulation center's success is rooted in its staff—their expertise, collaboration, and resilience. Effective management requires strategic recruitment, tailored training, regular evaluation, and a supportive work environment. By investing in their team and addressing challenges proactively, simulation center leaders can cultivate a skilled and motivated workforce to advance healthcare education and innovation. How can your center implement these best practices to ensure operational excellence and staff satisfaction?

Chapter 6

Implementing Effective Simulation-Based Education Program Activities

Simulation-based education (SBE) has proven invaluable in medical and nursing training, fostering skill development, clinical reasoning, and teamwork in a controlled environment. However, to achieve their full potential, SBE programs must be implemented with attention to key components: facilitator training, debriefing techniques, and evaluating educational outcomes. This chapter explores these essential elements and provides evidence-based strategies for their successful application in healthcare education.

6.1 Facilitator Training and Assessment Preparation

Facilitators play a pivotal role in the effectiveness of simulation-based education. Their ability to guide, evaluate, and provide constructive feedback is integral to learning. While much emphasis is placed on the design and execution of simulations, the preparation and training of facilitators often receive less attention. Specific training for facilitators is critical to ensure they can fulfill their roles effectively, whether as educators, assessors, or both.

Core/Basic Facilitator Training

To ensure the success of simulation-based education, facilitators must be adequately prepared through comprehensive training programs that establish foundational skills and knowledge. Core or basic facilitator training provides the groundwork for effective facilitation, ensuring facilitators can confidently and competently guide learners through the simulation process. These programs should incorporate the following components:

<u>Initial Simulation Education</u>
Facilitators should begin their journey with a baseline training program that introduces them to the fundamental principles of simulation education. This initial training should be integral to their orientation to the simulation center.

Facilitators who assess learners should receive additional specific training in assessment practices. This includes familiarity with the tools and rubrics they use during evaluations to ensure accurate and consistent learner assessment.

Content Knowledge
Facilitators must have a strong understanding of the clinical concepts relevant to the simulations they will facilitate. This ensures they can provide contextually accurate guidance during the simulation and debriefing phases and confidently address learners' questions and knowledge gaps.

Simulation Technology Skills
Simulation-based education relies heavily on advanced technology, and facilitators must be proficient in operating the simulation tools and equipment. Training should cover:

- *Mannequins and Task Trainers*: Setting up, operating, and troubleshooting high-fidelity mannequins and task trainers.
- *Virtual and Augmented Reality Tools*: Using virtual and augmented reality platforms effectively.
- *Audio/Visual Systems*: Managing simulation capture software and recording systems for review and assessment.

Hands-on sessions should be included to allow facilitators to practice using simulation technologies in a controlled, supportive environment.

Pedagogical Skills

Facilitators must be trained in effective teaching and learning methodologies grounded in adult learning principles. These skills are essential for creating an inclusive and engaging learning environment that fosters active participation and critical thinking. Training should emphasize:

- Guiding learners through self-directed discovery.
- Tailoring facilitation styles to meet diverse learning needs.
- Ensuring psychological safety, encouraging learners to take risks, and learning from mistakes without fear of judgment.

The application of adult learning theories, as outlined by Jeffries (2012), should be a cornerstone of facilitator training to ensure sessions are learner-centered and outcomes-focused.

Specific Training for Facilitators Assessing Learners

Facilitators who take on the additional role of assessors require specialized training to perform their duties effectively. Specific training addresses the following key areas:

Standardization of Assessment Criteria
Facilitators must be trained to use standardized rubrics and assessment tools to ensure consistency and fairness in evaluating student performance. This training minimizes subjective biases and aligns assessments with the learning objectives of the simulation.

Observation and Documentation Skills
Facilitators must hone their ability to observe critical behaviors and outcomes during simulations. Training programs should focus on developing their capacity to identify key

performance indicators, document observations accurately, and differentiate between technical and non-technical skills.

Feedback Delivery Techniques
Assessors must provide constructive feedback that is specific, actionable, and aligned with the learner's level of experience. Training should include feedback delivery techniques that encourage improvement without discouraging the learner.

Ethical Considerations and Objectivity

Facilitators must be conscious of maintaining fairness and impartiality in assessments. Training programs should include discussions on ethical dilemmas that may arise during assessment and strategies for maintaining objectivity.

Cultural Sensitivity and Communication
Facilitators must be adept at delivering feedback and assessments culturally sensitively, ensuring clarity and respect across diverse learner backgrounds.

Implementing Comprehensive Training Programs

Institutions must prioritize developing comprehensive facilitator training programs tailored to simulation-based education. These programs should include:

- **Workshops and Seminars**: Focused sessions on assessment tools, debriefing techniques, and feedback delivery.
- **Observation and Practice**: Opportunities for facilitators to observe experienced assessors, followed by supervised practice with feedback.
- **Standardized Curriculum**: A structured training curriculum that aligns with accreditation standards and best practices in simulation-based education.
- **Continuous Professional Development**: Regular updates and advanced training sessions to keep facilitators abreast of new tools, methods, and research in simulation assessment.

The success of simulation-based education hinges on the quality of the scenarios and the expertise of facilitators. Comprehensive core training equips facilitators with essential knowledge and skills, while specific training for assessors ensures fair and effective learner evaluation. By investing in robust training programs, institutions can foster a generation of skilled facilitators who contribute to improved educational outcomes and enhanced patient care.

6.2 Debriefing and Feedback Techniques

Debriefing is often regarded as the most critical phase of a simulation. During this phase, learners reflect on their performance and internalize lessons learned. Effective debriefing facilitates deeper understanding, encourages self-assessment, and bridges the gap between simulation and real-world practice.

Structured Debriefing Models in Simulation Education

Debriefing is a cornerstone of simulation-based education, serving as a critical tool for reflection, learning, and performance improvement. Several structured debriefing models have been developed to provide frameworks for effectively guiding these discussions. Each model has its unique focus, approach, and application, allowing educators to choose one that best aligns with their objectives, curriculum, and learners' needs. Below are some widely used debriefing models and their core characteristics:

Plus-Delta Model

This straightforward model emphasizes identifying both positive aspects ("pluses") and areas for improvement ("deltas"). It is simple and appealing for quick debriefs or when working with novice facilitators.

>**Strengths**: Encourages balanced feedback and focuses on actionable improvements.

>**Example Use**: Participants discuss what went well during the simulation and what could be improved. (Sawyer, T., et al., 2016)

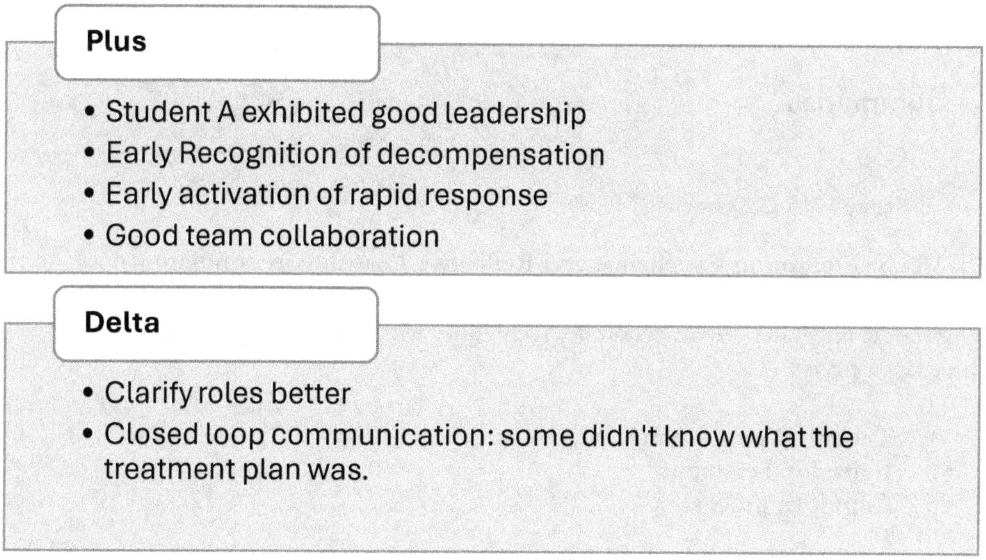

Plus
- Student A exhibited good leadership
- Early Recognition of decompensation
- Early activation of rapid response
- Good team collaboration

Delta
- Clarify roles better
- Closed loop communication: some didn't know what the treatment plan was.

Figure 11 Example of a Plus/Delta of a Rapid Response Simulation

GAS (Gather-Analyze-Summarize)

The GAS model guides facilitators through a structured conversation:

1. **Gather**: Collect initial learner impressions.
2. **Analyze**: Explore key actions, decisions, and thought processes.
3. **Summarize**: Highlight lessons learned and areas for improvement.

   Strengths: Provides a logical flow and ensures that key learning points are addressed without overwhelming learners. (Rudolph et al., 2007)

Gather
- Collect initial learner impression
- Team leader perspective
- Team members perspective

Analyze
- Explore key actions, decisions, and thought processes
- Facilitate student reflection and analysis

Summarize
- Highlight lessons learned and areas of improvement

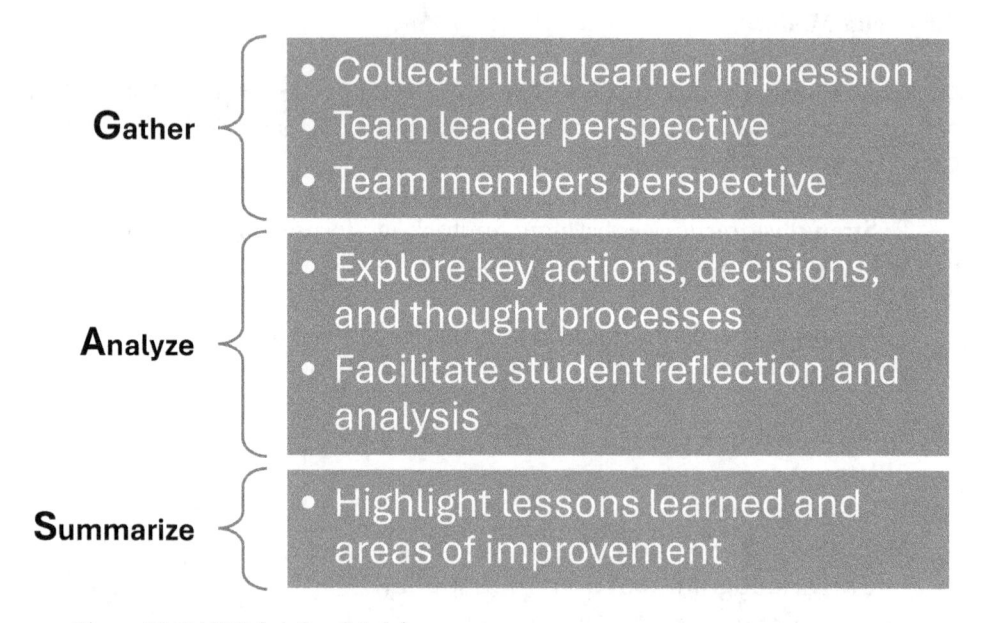

Figure 12 GAS Debriefing Model

PEARLS (Promoting Excellence and Reflective Learning in Simulation)

This model integrates advocacy-inquiry techniques with guided reflection, addressing three key aspects:

1. **Technical performance**
2. **Behavioral elements**
3. **Cognitive processes**

   Strengths: Combines a structured approach with the flexibility to adapt to learner needs, fostering deep reflection. (Eppich & Cheng, 2015)

Setting the Scene
- State the goal of debriefing

Reactions
- Solicit Initial Reactions & emotions

Description
- Develop shared understanding

Analysis
- Explore performance

Application/Summary
- Identify take-aways

The Three-Phase Model

A phased approach designed to build learners' understanding progressively:

1. **Reaction**: Address emotional responses to the simulation.
2. **Analysis**: Delve into performance details, exploring successes and errors.
3. **Summary**: Consolidate learning points and outline the next steps.

   Strengths: Provides an organized structure while addressing the emotional and analytical dimensions of learning. (Fanning, R. M., & Gaba, D. M., 2007)

Advocacy-Inquiry Model

Figure 13 PEARLS Debriefing

This reflective model integrates facilitator observations (Advocacy) with open-ended questions (Inquiry) to explore learners' thought processes and decision-making.

   Strengths: Encourages deeper insight into the reasoning behind actions, promoting critical thinking. (Rudolph, J. W., et al., 2007)

Phase	Process
Prebrief	• Provide information for simulation.
	• Ground rules.
	• Orientation to environment and simulator
	• Physical/Psychological Safety
Debrief: React	• Encourage participation.

	• Plus/Delta approach

Debrief: Understand	• Advocacy-Inquiry
	   o Uncover ideas, thought processes, and learner frames that lead to behavior.
	   o Facilitate the learner to find ways to improve performance

Wrap-up	• Invite reflection. • Takeaways

Figure 14 Advocacy-Inquiry Debriefing Tool

Debriefing for Meaningful Learning (DML)

This model links simulation experiences with clinical evidence using a three-phase structure:

1. **Engage**: Create a safe and interactive environment.
2. **Explore**: Discuss simulation events and their implications.
3. **Explain**: Relate experiences to clinical practice and evidence.

- **Strengths**: Focuses on bridging simulation scenarios with real-world clinical applications. (Arafeh, J. M., et al., 2010)

Gibbs' Reflective Cycle

A well-established six-stage iterative framework:

1. **Description**: What happened?
2. **Feelings**: What were your thoughts and emotions?
3. **Evaluation**: What went well and what didn't?
4. **Analysis**: Why did it happen?
5. **Conclusion**: What could you have done differently?
6. **Action Plan**: How will you apply this learning in the future?

- **Strengths**: Encourages comprehensive reflection and actionable outcomes. (Gibbs, G., 1988)

The 3D Model

This model takes a progressive approach to debriefing:

1. **Defusing**: Address emotional responses to the simulation.
2. **Discovering**: Explore key performance insights.

3. **Deepening**: Foster a deeper understanding of underlying concepts and behaviors.

- **Strengths**: Balances emotional processing with in-depth learning. (Fanning, R. M., & Gaba, D. M., 2007)

TeamSTEPPS Debriefing Model

Designed for team-based simulations, this model emphasizes communication, teamwork, and collaboration. It employs structured tools like the Team Performance Observation Tool to guide discussions.

Strengths: Ideal for simulations focusing on interprofessional teamwork and communication. (TeamSTEPPS® National Implementation Team, 2014)

Choosing the Right Model

Among these models, the Plus-Delta, PEARLS, and GAS are commonly used due to their simplicity and adaptability. However, the choice of model depends on the specific goals of the simulation, the learners' expertise, and the teaching methodology employed. Some programs may even combine elements from multiple models to create a hybrid approach that best suits their needs.

Providing Constructive Feedback

Effective feedback is specific, timely, and non-judgmental. Facilitators should balance positive reinforcement with constructive criticism, using frameworks such as the "feedback sandwich" (positive-constructive-positive). Engaging learners in dialogue about their performance encourages critical thinking and helps them identify areas for self-improvement (Archer, 2010).

6.3 Assessment and Evaluation of Simulation and Effectiveness

Assessment and evaluation are essential for measuring the success of SBE programs, ensuring they meet their objectives and provide value to learners and institutions alike.

Assessment tools should be tailored to evaluate both technical and non-technical skills. Common methods include:

- <u>Objective Structured Clinical Examinations (OSCEs)</u>: Standardized assessments testing procedural skills, diagnostic reasoning, and communication.

- <u>Checklists and Rating Scales</u>: Tools like the Simulation Effectiveness Tool (SET) or the SET-M evaluate learner confidence and scenario realism (Elfrink Cordi et al., 2012).

- <u>Self-Assessment and Peer Feedback</u>: Encourage learners to reflect on their performance and provide feedback to peers to promote collaborative learning.

Designing Assessment Tools

Assessment is a cornerstone of simulation-based education, enabling educators to evaluate learner performance, identify areas for improvement, and measure the achievement of learning objectives. Designing effective assessment tools for simulation requires careful consideration to ensure they are both reliable and valid, providing accurate and consistent results that are meaningful in clinical and educational contexts.

<u>Step 1</u>: Define the Purpose of Assessment
The first step in designing assessment tools is to define their purpose clearly. In simulation-based education, assessments can serve various goals:

- *Formative assessment*: Providing feedback during learning to improve performance.
- *Summative assessment*: Evaluating competence at the end of a training program.
- *Diagnostic assessment*: Identifying specific knowledge gaps or skill deficiencies.
- *Program evaluation*: Measuring the effectiveness of the simulation program itself (Cook et al., 2013).

Understanding the intended purpose helps shape the tool's design, ensuring it aligns with the simulation's learning objectives and outcomes.

<u>Step 2</u>: Choose an Assessment Framework
Selecting an appropriate framework for the assessment tool is critical. Common frameworks in simulation-based education include:

- *Objective Structured Clinical Examination (OSCE)*: A structured approach where learners perform specific tasks under observation (Harden & Gleeson, 1979).
- *Miller's Pyramid*: Evaluating learners across four levels—knows, knows how, shows how, and does (Miller, 1990).
- *Entrustable Professional Activities (EPAs)*: Assessing the ability to perform specific professional tasks independently (Ten Cate, 2005).
- *Core Competencies*: Assessing the ability to perform role-specific tasks independently.

These frameworks provide a structured foundation for developing reliable and valid assessment tools.

<u>Step 3</u>: Establish Criteria for Reliability
Reliability refers to the consistency of the assessment results. A reliable tool yields the same results under consistent conditions. To enhance reliability:
- *Standardize Scenarios*: Ensure all learners encounter similar conditions, tasks, and challenges in the simulation (McGaghie et al., 2010).
- *Develop Clear Rubrics*: Use objective, well-defined criteria to assess performance,

reducing subjectivity (De Villiers & Treadwell, 2021).
- *Train Assessors*: Provide thorough training to evaluators to ensure consistent interpretation and scoring (Cook & Hatala, 2015).
- *Pilot Testing*: Conduct trials of the assessment tool to identify variability and refine its components.

For instance, using a checklist with binary scoring (e.g., "performed" or "not performed") can reduce ambiguity compared to subjective rating scales (Ferguson et al., 2020).

Step 4: Ensure Validity
Validity refers to the degree to which the assessment tool measures what it is intended to measure. There are different types of validity to consider:

- *Content Validity*: Does the tool cover all relevant aspects of the assessed skill or knowledge? Engage subject matter experts to ensure comprehensive coverage (Polit & Beck, 2006).
- *Construct Validity*: Does the tool accurately measure the theoretical concept (e.g., clinical reasoning, teamwork)? Map items to specific competencies (Downing, 2003).
- *Criterion Validity*: Does the tool correlate with external measures of competence, such as clinical outcomes or standardized exams?
-

For example, a tool designed to assess teamwork in a code blue scenario should evaluate communication, leadership, and situational awareness, as these are integral components of team performance (Weaver et al., 2010).

Step 5: Integrate Technology to Enhance Objectivity
Technology can improve the objectivity and accuracy of assessment tools. Simulation platforms often include built-in data collection features that track learner actions, timing, and physiological responses. Video recording allows for detailed review and scoring, reducing biases associated with real-time evaluation (Dieckmann et al., 2009). Tools like eye-tracking software and wearable sensors can provide insights into situational awareness and task performance (Aggarwal et al., 2010).

Step 6: Conduct Validation Studies
Conduct validation studies with diverse learner groups and settings to confirm the assessment tool's reliability and validity. Analyze inter-rater reliability (consistency between different assessors) and test-retest reliability (consistency of results over time). Use statistical methods, such as Cronbach's alpha, to quantify reliability and ensure the tool meets acceptable thresholds (Tavakol & Dennick, 2011).

Step 7: Provide Learner Feedback
Assessment tools should not only measure performance but also facilitate learning. They should include mechanisms for providing detailed, actionable feedback to learners based on assessment results. For

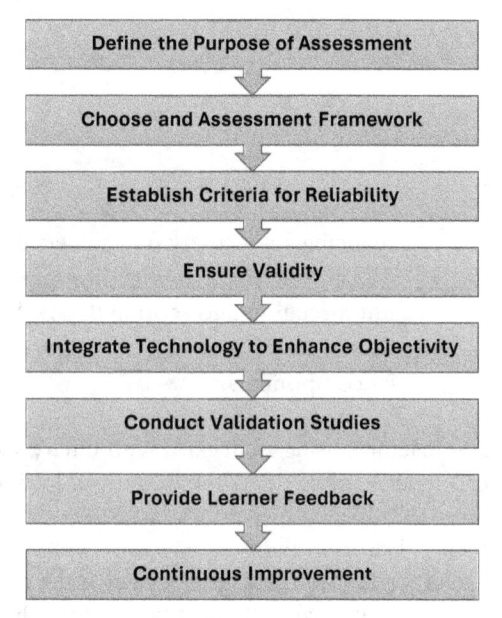

Figure 15 Designing Assessment Tools

example, debriefing sessions can highlight strengths and areas for improvement, linking assessment findings to clinical practice (Rudolph et al., 2007).

Step 8: Continuous Improvement
Assessment tools should be viewed as dynamic instruments that evolve. Based on feedback from learners, assessors, and validation studies, they should be regularly reviewed and revised. To keep them relevant and effective, advancements in simulation technology and educational research should be incorporated (McGaghie et al., 2011).

Evaluating Program Activities Outcomes
Program evaluation focuses on long-term outcomes, including knowledge retention, skill proficiency, and patient care improvements. The Kirkpatrick Model is frequently used to evaluate educational programs at four levels: reaction, learning, behavior, and results (Kirkpatrick & Kirkpatrick, 2006).

The Kirkpatrick's Four Levels of Training Evaluation:

- Reaction: Learner satisfaction and perceived relevance of the simulation activities.
- Learning: Knowledge, skills, and attitudes gained through simulation.
- Behavior: Application of learned skills in clinical practice.
- Results: Broader organizational outcomes, such as improved patient safety, team performance, and cost savings

Level 1	Reaction	The degree in which learners find the training favorable, engaging and relevant to their job.	*Did the learners enjoy the training?*

Level 2	Learning	The degree to which the learners acquire the intended knowledge, skills, attitudes, and confidence based on participation.	*Did the learners learn anything?*
Level 3	Behavior	The degree to which the learners apply what they learned during training when they are back on the job.	*Did the learners change their behavior in the workplace as a result of the training?*
Level 4	Results	The degree to which targeted organizational outcomes occur because of the training.	*Did the training make a significant impact on the organization?*

Figure 16 Kirkpatrick Model.

Aligning program goals with these levels helps ensure that the evaluation is comprehensive and measures outcomes that matter at multiple levels. Regular evaluations allow simulation centers to refine scenarios, update equipment, and adapt teaching methods to meet evolving healthcare needs.

Designing reliable and valid assessment tools for simulation-based education is a systematic process that requires aligning the tool with learning objectives, ensuring consistency, and rigorously validating its components. When thoughtfully designed, these tools not only evaluate learner competence but also drive meaningful improvements in clinical performance and patient safety. By embedding principles of reliability and validity into assessment design, educators can maximize the impact of simulation in healthcare education.

6.4 Summary

Chapter 5 explores the essential components of implementing effective simulation-based education (SBE) activities in healthcare training. It highlights the strategies needed to maximize the educational potential of SBE programs, focusing on three critical areas: facilitator training, debriefing techniques, and evaluation of educational outcomes. These elements ensure that simulation activities foster skill development, clinical reasoning, and teamwork, bridging the gap between simulation scenarios and real-world practice.

Facilitators are at the heart of successful simulation programs. Their role extends beyond managing technology to creating an engaging learning environment and guiding learners through reflective discussions. This chapter emphasizes the importance of comprehensive facilitator training that includes:

- **Simulation Pedagogy**: Training facilitators in scenario design, learner dynamics, and debriefing practices.
- **Technical Proficiency**: Ensuring facilitators can effectively operate simulation technologies, including high-fidelity mannequins and virtual reality tools.
- **Clinical Expertise**: Developing a strong knowledge base relevant to the taught scenarios.
- **Consistency**: Promoting standardized practices through operating procedures, checklists, and ongoing professional development to align facilitator approaches and enhance learning outcomes.

Debriefing and Feedback Techniques
Debriefing is identified as the most critical phase of SBE, allowing learners to reflect on their experiences and solidify lessons learned. The chapter outlines several structured debriefing models, including:

- **Plus-Delta Model**: Identifies strengths and areas for improvement.
- **PEARLS**: Combines advocacy-inquiry and reflective learning.
- **GAS**: Focuses on gathering impressions, analyzing actions, and summarizing improvements.

Effective debriefing encourages self-assessment, critical thinking, and collaborative learning. Constructive feedback is pivotal, emphasizing specificity, timeliness, and a balance of reinforcement and constructive critique.

Assessment and evaluation are essential for measuring the success of SBE programs and their impact on learners and organizations. This chapter discusses:

- **Assessment Tools**: Methods like Objective Structured Clinical Examinations (OSCEs), checklists, and self-assessments evaluate technical and non-technical skills.
- **Designing Valid Assessments**: Frameworks such as Miller's Pyramid and Entrustable Professional Activities (EPAs) ensure reliability and validity in assessments, providing actionable insights into learner performance.
- **Technology Integration**: Tools like video recording and data analytics enhance objectivity and precision in assessment.
- **Continuous Improvement**: Assessment tools must be regularly reviewed and updated based on feedback and advancements in simulation technology.
- Program evaluation focuses on long-term outcomes using frameworks like the **Kirkpatrick Model**, which measures reaction, learning, behavior, and results. This model evaluates the effectiveness of SBE activities at multiple levels, from learner satisfaction to improved patient safety and organizational impact.

Chapter 5 provides a comprehensive guide to implementing effective simulation-based education programs. Simulation centers can ensure their activities are impactful and aligned with educational and institutional goals by investing in facilitator development, adopting structured debriefing models, and designing robust assessment tools. These practices enable SBE programs to produce competent healthcare professionals with the skills and confidence to excel in real-world clinical environments.

6.5 Chapter Review

Review Questions

1. What are the essential components of facilitator training for simulation-based education (SBE)?

2. How does effective debriefing impact the learning outcomes of a simulation session?
3. Identify and describe three structured debriefing models and their key characteristics.
4. What steps should be taken to design reliable and valid assessment tools for simulation activities?
5. How does the Kirkpatrick Model evaluate the effectiveness of SBE programs at different levels?

Critical Thinking and Application

1. **Analyzing Facilitator Roles**:
   - Consider a scenario where a new facilitator struggles with operating simulation technology. What steps would you take to support their development, and how might this impact the quality of simulation sessions?
2. **Choosing a Debriefing Model**:
   - Imagine you are tasked with selecting a debriefing model for an interprofessional team simulation involving nurses and physicians. Which model would you choose (e.g., PEARLS, GAS, or Plus-Delta), and why? Provide justification based on the scenario's goals.
3. **Evaluating Outcomes**:
   - Discuss how you would use the Kirkpatrick Model to evaluate a new simulation program's success. Include examples of metrics or data you might collect at each level (reaction, learning, behavior, and results).

Hands-On Activities

1. **Facilitator Training Simulation**:
   - Design a mini-training session for new facilitators. Include exercises for operating simulation technology, practicing debriefing techniques, and providing constructive feedback.
   - Debrief with participants afterward to gather feedback on the training's effectiveness.
2. **Debriefing Practice**:
   - Conduct a simulation scenario with peers or learners and lead a debriefing session using two models (e.g., PEARLS and Plus-Delta). Compare the effectiveness of the models based on participant engagement and feedback.
3. **Assessment Tool Development**:
   - Create an assessment checklist for a simple simulation scenario (e.g., performing CPR or administering medication). Test the tool with a small group and refine it based on inter-rater reliability and participant feedback.
4. **Program Evaluation Workshop**:

- o Work with a team to evaluate a recent simulation program using the Kirkpatrick Model. Identify strengths, areas for improvement, and actionable changes for future programs.

Summary Reflection

Chapter 6 emphasizes the critical components of successful simulation-based education: **facilitator training**, **debriefing techniques**, and **assessment and evaluation**. Facilitators are central to SBE's success, requiring expertise in pedagogy, technology, and clinical content. Structured debriefing models, such as PEARLS and GAS, are pivotal in guiding reflective learning and bridging the gap between simulation and clinical practice. Reliable assessment tools and comprehensive program evaluations, including frameworks like the Kirkpatrick Model, ensure that SBE programs achieve their educational goals and improve learner performance.

Reflect on how you can apply these principles to your educational environment. How can investing in facilitator development and adopting structured debriefing and evaluation strategies enhance the outcomes of your simulation activities?

Chapter 7

Assessing Program Outcomes in Simulation Center Operations

Simulation centers are critical in healthcare education, providing a safe and controlled environment for learners to acquire and refine clinical skills, teamwork abilities, and decision-making competencies. Assessing the outcomes of an entire simulation program is crucial to determining its effectiveness, guiding quality improvement, and demonstrating value to stakeholders. This process requires evaluating the impact of the center's operations on educational, clinical, and organizational goals.

7.1 Key Metrics for Program Assessment

A comprehensive program assessment in simulation centers involves evaluating multiple dimensions to ensure that the simulation activities are effective, relevant, and impactful. These assessments provide valuable insights into the simulation programs' educational, clinical, operational, and experiential outcomes. Below is an expanded discussion of the key metrics for program assessment:

Educational Outcomes

Educational outcomes focus on the direct impact of simulation on learners' knowledge, skills, and attitudes.

- **Skill Improvement**: Use validated tools such as checklists, rubrics, and objective structured clinical examinations (OSCEs) to measure gains in clinical skills and procedural accuracy. For example, specific tools can evaluate learners' ability to perform CPR, manage a code, or execute surgical techniques effectively. (Cook & Hatala, 2015)

- **Knowledge Retention**: Post-training assessments should be conducted to determine how well learners retain knowledge and skills over time. Longitudinal

studies can help assess whether competencies are sustained and identify gaps requiring refresher training. (McGaghie et al., 2010)
- **Confidence**: Self-reported confidence levels often correlate with improved performance. Tracking these changes provides insight into learners' preparedness for real-world applications.

Clinical Outcomes

Simulation programs should be linked to tangible clinical improvements, demonstrating their value in enhancing patient care and safety.

- **Error Reduction**: Measure the incidence of medical errors in real clinical settings before and after implementing simulation-based training programs.
- **Procedural Success Rates**: Analyze success rates for high-stakes procedures, such as intubations, central line placements, or surgical interventions, to gauge the practical benefits of simulation training.
- **Patient Safety Indicators**: Use metrics like reduced infection rates, fewer adverse events, and improved emergency response times as benchmarks for success. Evidence suggests that simulation-based interventions improve team performance in crises like cardiac arrests or trauma resuscitations. (Weaver et al., 2010)

Operational Efficiency

Operational metrics examine how well the simulation center functions in terms of resource utilization and cost-effectiveness.

- **Utilization Rates**: Track the frequency and capacity of training sessions, including the number of participants and scenarios conducted. High utilization rates indicate efficient resource management. (LeFlore et al., 2007)
- **Cost-Effectiveness**: Compare the financial investment in simulation programs with measurable organizational benefits. For instance:
    - Reduced malpractice claims due to better-trained providers.
    - Decreased staff turnover because of enhanced confidence and preparedness.
    - Improved training outcomes compared to traditional methods, such as classroom-only instruction.

Learner and Faculty Feedback

Direct feedback from participants and faculty is vital for identifying strengths and areas requiring improvement in simulation programs.

- **Learner Experience**: Surveys, interviews, or focus groups can capture learners' perceptions of the realism, relevance, and overall quality of the simulation experience. Areas to evaluate include:
    - Psychological safety.
    - Clarity of objectives.

      o   The usefulness of debriefing sessions.
- **Faculty Evaluation**: Faculty feedback is crucial for refining scenarios and ensuring they align with clinical realities. Faculty can also provide insights into the adequacy of training resources and the effectiveness of simulation technology. (Dieckmann et al., 2009)

The Importance of Multi-Dimensional Assessment

Program assessment should not rely on a single metric or perspective but instead, adopt a holistic approach that captures the multifaceted impact of simulation. By combining educational, clinical, operational, and experiential metrics, simulation centers can achieve the following:

1. **Identify Areas for Growth**: Pinpoint inefficiencies or gaps in training that may hinder outcomes.
2. **Demonstrate ROI**: Provide tangible evidence of the benefits of simulation programs to stakeholders, including healthcare organizations and funding bodies.
3. **Enhance Program Quality**: Use assessment insights to refine and improve simulation curricula and delivery continually.
4. **Align with Strategic Goals**: Ensure simulation outcomes support broader organizational priorities, such as improved patient care, workforce development, and financial sustainability.

Simulation centers can meet and exceed their educational and operational goals through consistent evaluation and feedback integration, fostering a culture of excellence and continuous improvement.

Accreditation and Standards Compliance:

Academic-based Programs

Academic-based simulation programs will have college/university accreditation standards that the program must adhere to and requirements for degree programs that might address components the simulation program might address.

In the U.S., universities and colleges are primarily accredited regionally or nationally. Regional accreditation is considered more prestigious, widely recognized, and often associated with academic and non-profit institutions. National accreditation typically applies to for-profit schools and vocational or technical programs.

Approximately 85-90% of accredited institutions are regionally accredited, reflecting their focus on comprehensive academic standards and credit transferability. The remaining 10-15% are nationally accredited, primarily covering specialized or career-oriented institutions.

Examples of Regional Accreditation	**Examples of National Accreditation**
Southern Association of Colleges and Schools (SACS)	Accrediting Council for Continuing Education and Training (ACCET)
Western Association of Schools and Colleges (WASC)	Accrediting Commission of Career Schools and Colleges (ACCSC)

Academic-based programs will also have school-specific accreditation, such as the Liaison Committee on Medical Education (LCME), the Commission on Collegiate Nursing Education (CCNE) or the Accreditation Commission for Education in Nursing (ACEN)

Hospital-based simulation programs
Hospital-based simulation programs will likely be tied to an accrediting body such as The Joint Commission (TJC) or the Accreditation Association for Ambulatory Health Care (AAAHC). While this accreditation is directed toward hospital operations, the simulation program might have a component or establish a training program to rectify past recommendations.

Simulation-specific Accreditation and Endorsements
Simulation programs can be accredited or endorsed through various organizations, such as the *Society for Simulation in Healthcare* (SSH), the *American College of Surgeons* (ACS), and the *International Nursing Association for Clinical Simulation and Learning* (INACSL). These organizations have published standards for simulation programs.

7.2 Data Collection and Analysis

Data collection for program assessment should involve both quantitative and qualitative methods:

- *Quantitative Data*: Metrics such as learner performance scores, clinical error rates, and program utilization statistics provide measurable indicators of success. Common metrics captured in simulation programs:
    - Number of activities
    - Type of activities
    - Number of learners
    - Types of learners
    - Total contact hours

- Center/room utilization
- Staff utilization
- Equipment up/down time
- Number of tours
- Number of outreach activities
- Number of research activities

- *Qualitative Data*: Open-ended surveys, interviews, and observations offer insights into the experiences and perceptions of learners and faculty, uncovering factors that quantitative data may not capture.
  Common metrics captured in simulation programs:

  - Teaching Effectiveness
  - Learner Satisfaction Surveys
  - Facilitator/Faculty satisfaction surveys

- *Budgetary Data*: Metrics such as revenue or income, annual salaries and expenses in a particular category, expenses per activity, or for a particular program provide data that helps inform operational efficiencies and could provide data for a return-on-investment analysis.

Using mixed-methods analysis allows for a more comprehensive understanding of program outcomes and supports triangulation of results.

7.3 Reporting

Whether they are mandated to report activities, simulation programs should consider adopting regular reporting practices for their operations over a defined period. The reporting frequency may vary depending on the program's scope and workload, with some opting for quarterly updates and others providing annual summaries. Reporting is a valuable tool to highlight the program's activities and achievements to stakeholders. Moreover, collecting and analyzing data for these reports enables the program to benchmark its performance against previous periods and identify opportunities for quality improvement.

Moreover, reporting may be a requirement for the previously mentioned accrediting agencies.

7.4 Continuous Quality Improvement

The findings from program assessments should feed into a continuous quality improvement (CQI) cycle. Key steps include:
- *Analyzing Gaps*: Compare assessment data to program goals to identify areas for improvement.
- *Implementing Changes*: Revise simulation scenarios, teaching methods, or operational processes based on assessment findings.
- *Re-evaluating Outcomes*: Conduct follow-up assessments to evaluate the effectiveness of implemented changes.

For instance, if learner feedback highlights insufficient debriefing time, increasing debriefing duration and re-evaluating satisfaction scores can demonstrate CQI in action (Fanning & Gaba, 2007).

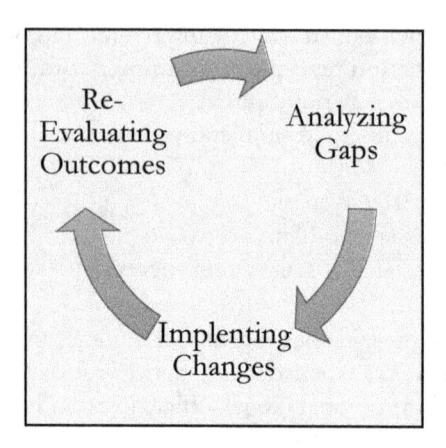

7.5 Demonstrating Value to Stakeholders

Communicating the value of a simulation center to institutional leaders and external stakeholders is vital for securing continued support, funding, and recognition. In a competitive environment where resources are limited, simulation centers must justify their contributions to organizational goals and demonstrate measurable benefits in outcomes, cost-effectiveness, and strategic alignment. Achieving this requires a thoughtful approach to presenting data and insights in ways that resonate with stakeholders and underscore the center's impact.

Presenting Evidence-Based Outcomes

One of the most compelling ways to demonstrate value is by showcasing evidence-based results that align with the organization's or institution's priorities. Simulation centers can use data to highlight their impact on critical areas such as:

Learner Competence: Reporting improvements in technical and non-technical skills, such as clinical reasoning, teamwork, and communication, demonstrates the center's role in preparing competent healthcare professionals. For example, post-simulation evaluations showing significant gains in procedural accuracy or diagnostic confidence can illustrate the effectiveness of training programs.

Examples:
- Skill Proficiency Gains
- Critical Thinking and Decision-making
- Teamwork and Communication

Patient Safety: Simulation programs that reduce medical errors or enhance crisis management skills directly contribute to better patient outcomes. Quantifiable data on reduced error rates or improved response times in clinical practice can make a powerful case.

> Examples:
> - Reduction in Medical Errors
> - Improved Emergency Response
> - Infection Control Compliance

Organizational Readiness: Simulation centers contribute to organizational resilience by preparing staff for high-risk, low-frequency events or accreditation processes. For instance, conducting mock drills for emergency preparedness or standardized patient encounters for accreditation assessments can directly support institutional goals.

> Examples:
> - Accreditation Readiness
> - Cost Avoidance from Errors

Highlighting Cost Savings

Cost-effectiveness is another critical area to emphasize. Simulation centers can highlight how their programs contribute to financial savings in several ways:

Reduced Training Costs: Traditional clinical training often requires extensive hospital resources, staff time, and patient interactions. Simulation provides a controlled, cost-efficient alternative that minimizes these demands while delivering high-quality education.

Avoiding Errors: Training staff to recognize and respond to potential errors reduces the likelihood of costly adverse events, including litigation and extended patient stays. Providing data on simulated scenarios that prevent these outcomes can strongly appeal to stakeholders.

Optimized Resource Utilization: By using simulation to assess and improve processes such as patient flow, equipment usage, or team coordination, centers can contribute to operational efficiency, indirectly impacting the bottom line.

Contributions to Strategic Goals

Simulation centers often align their programs with broader institutional priorities, such as:

Accreditation Readiness: Many accreditation bodies require or encourage simulation-based training for specific competencies. Demonstrating how the center fulfills these requirements—such as through Objective Structured Clinical Examinations (OSCEs) or interprofessional team simulations—can underscore its strategic importance.

Staff Retention and Satisfaction: By offering innovative training opportunities and professional development programs, simulation centers can enhance job satisfaction among healthcare workers, reducing turnover and recruitment costs. Surveys showing high satisfaction rates among staff who engage in simulation training can further illustrate this point.

Interdisciplinary Collaboration: Simulation fosters collaboration among departments and disciplines, breaking down silos and promoting teamwork. Documenting how simulation has enhanced interdepartmental communication or improved team dynamics adds another layer of value.

Making Data Accessible and Impactful

Simulation centers must present their data in inaccessible and impactful formats to ensure the message resonates with stakeholders. Complex statistics or detailed reports can overwhelm or disengage non-technical audiences, so clarity and visual appeal are essential:

Visual Dashboards: Creating user-friendly dashboards that display key metrics—such as the number of simulations conducted, learner outcomes, and cost savings—provides stakeholders with a quick and clear understanding of the center's impact.

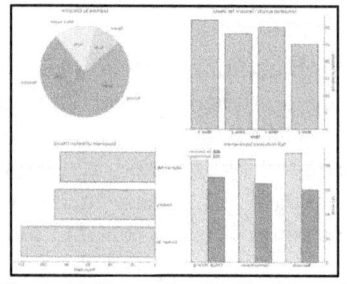

Figure 17 Example of a Dashboard

Case Studies: Sharing success stories, such as a team successfully applying simulation training to a real-world emergency, humanizes the data and creates a narrative that stakeholders can connect with emotionally.

Comparative Data: Improvements over time, such as increases in learner competence or decreases in error rates, demonstrate growth and sustained value.

Infographics and Reports: Summarizing findings in concise, visually appealing formats ensures busy decision-makers can quickly grasp the key takeaways.

Engaging Stakeholders Through Collaboration

Engagement goes beyond presenting data—it requires fostering a sense of partnership with stakeholders. Inviting institutional leaders to observe or participate in simulations, conducting tours of the center, or hosting regular briefings where stakeholders can provide input ensures they feel invested in the center's mission. Simulation centers can build long-term trust and support by maintaining open lines of communication and demonstrating responsiveness to institutional needs.

7.6 Summary

Chapter 6 emphasizes the importance of assessing program outcomes to evaluate simulation centers' effectiveness and alignment with educational, clinical, and organizational goals. This process is crucial for driving quality improvement, demonstrating value to stakeholders, and ensuring that simulation programs remain impactful and sustainable. The chapter explores key metrics for evaluation, data collection methods, reporting practices, and strategies for continuous quality improvement (CQI).

Program assessments encompass multiple dimensions:

Educational Outcomes: Measure learner improvements in clinical skills, knowledge, and confidence through validated tools like checklists and rubrics. Long-term retention assessments ensure sustained competency.

Clinical Outcomes: Link simulation training to real-world impacts, such as reduced medical errors, enhanced procedural success rates, and improved patient safety. Evidence-based examples include enhanced team performance and crisis management after simulation-based interventions.

Operational Efficiency: Assess the center's utilization rates, throughput, and cost-effectiveness by comparing training costs to benefits like reduced malpractice claims and improved staff retention.

Learner and Faculty Feedback: Use surveys and focus groups to capture insights on program strengths and areas for improvement, ensuring alignment with real-world clinical practices.

Simulation centers must align their programs with accrediting bodies to demonstrate adherence to institutional and professional standards. The chapter distinguishes between:

Academic-Based Accreditation: Programs adhere to university or college standards, such as those set by the Liaison Committee on Medical Education (LCME) or the Commission on Collegiate Nursing Education (CCNE).

Hospital-Based Accreditation: Programs linked to healthcare institutions may align with accrediting bodies like The Joint Commission (TJC).

Simulation-Specific Endorsements: Centers can seek accreditation from organizations like the *Society for Simulation in Healthcare* (SSH) or the International Nursing Association for Clinical Simulation and Learning (INACSL), demonstrating excellence in simulation-based training.

Effective program assessment requires collecting both quantitative and qualitative data:

Quantitative Data: Metrics such as learner performance scores, error reduction rates, and center utilization statistics offer measurable indicators of success. Examples include tracking the number of activities, types of learners, contact hours, and staff utilization.

Qualitative Data: Surveys, interviews, and observations provide insights into the experiences of learners and faculty, uncovering nuances that quantitative data may not capture. Metrics include teaching effectiveness and learner satisfaction surveys.

Budgetary Data: Financial metrics, such as expenses per activity and return on investment (ROI), inform operational efficiencies and demonstrate cost-effectiveness.

A mixed-methods approach ensures a comprehensive understanding of program outcomes, triangulating results for robust conclusions.

Simulation centers should adopt regular reporting practices to communicate their achievements and align activities with institutional goals. Quarterly or annual reports highlight metrics such as simulation volume, learner outcomes, and cost savings. They also serve as a benchmarking tool for tracking performance over time and identifying opportunities for improvement. Auditing agencies may mandate reporting requirements, underscoring their importance for compliance.

Program assessments feed directly into CQI processes, which involve:
- *Analyzing Gaps*: Compare assessment data against program goals to identify areas for improvement.
- *Implementing Changes*: Adjust scenarios, teaching methods, or operational processes based on identified gaps.
- *Reevaluating Outcomes*: Conduct follow-up assessments to measure the effectiveness of implemented changes.

For example, if feedback highlights insufficient debriefing time, centers can increase debriefing durations and monitor subsequent satisfaction scores to validate the improvement.

Simulation centers must effectively communicate their value to institutional leaders and external stakeholders to secure continued support and funding.

Strategies include:
- *Presenting Evidence-Based Outcomes*: Highlighting improvements in learner competence, patient safety, and organizational readiness through data-driven examples.

- *Emphasizing Cost Savings*: This section showcases the financial benefits of simulation, such as reduced training costs, minimized errors, and optimized resource utilization.

- *Aligning with Strategic Goals*: Demonstrating contributions to accreditation readiness, staff retention, and interdisciplinary collaboration.

The chapter underscores the importance of making data accessible through visual dashboards, case studies, and comparative reports. Engaging stakeholders through center tours, briefings, and collaborative discussions fosters trust and long-term support.

Chapter 6 outlines a comprehensive approach to assessing program outcomes in simulation centers, emphasizing the integration of data-driven evaluation, CQI, and stakeholder communication. Simulation centers can refine their programs, demonstrate their value, and ensure alignment with institutional priorities by measuring educational, clinical, and operational impacts. This ongoing process is vital for maintaining simulation-based education's relevance, effectiveness, and sustainability.

7.7 Chapter Review

Review Questions

1. What key metrics are used to assess simulation program outcomes, and how do they contribute to evaluating program success?
2. How do educational and clinical outcomes differ in the context of simulation-based education program assessment?
3. Why is stakeholder engagement important when demonstrating the value of simulation centers? Provide examples of strategies to achieve this.
4. What role does accreditation play in simulation center operations, and what are some examples of accrediting bodies relevant to simulation programs?
5. Explain the importance of both quantitative and qualitative data in assessing simulation center operations.

Critical Thinking and Application

1. **Analyzing Metrics for Program Success**:
    o Imagine you are leading a simulation center and notice a decline in learner confidence scores over several assessments. What steps would you take to investigate and address this issue? How would you adjust your metrics or evaluation tools?
2. **Connecting Outcomes to Stakeholder Goals**:
    o If a hospital administrator asked for evidence of your simulation center's impact on patient safety, how would you present the data? Include specific examples of metrics or case studies you would use to make your case.
3. **Balancing Quantitative and Qualitative Data**:
    o Discuss how qualitative feedback (e.g., learner or faculty surveys) might complement quantitative data (e.g., error reduction rates) when assessing the effectiveness of a new simulation program.

Hands-On Activities

1. **Data Collection and Analysis Exercise**:
    o Create a mock dataset of learner performance scores, utilization rates, and survey feedback from a simulation program. Analyze the data to identify trends, gaps, and areas for improvement. Present your findings to peers or colleagues.
2. **Accreditation Standards Alignment**:
    o Research accreditation requirements for a simulation-specific body, such as the Society for Simulation in Healthcare (SSH). Develop a checklist to ensure your simulation center's operations align with these standards.
3. **Stakeholder Presentation Practice**:
    o Prepare a five-minute presentation to demonstrate the value of your simulation center to institutional leadership. Include key metrics, cost-

effectiveness data, and success stories that align with organizational priorities.
4. **Continuous Quality Improvement (CQI) Project:**
   o Identify a hypothetical gap in a simulation program (e.g., low learner satisfaction with debriefing sessions). Develop a CQI plan that includes strategies for improvement, implementation steps, and methods for reevaluating outcomes.

Summary Reflection

Chapter 7 emphasizes assessing program outcomes in simulation center operations to ensure alignment with educational, clinical, and organizational goals. Effective program assessment involves evaluating multiple dimensions:

- **Educational Outcomes**: Measure improvements in learner skills, knowledge retention, and confidence through tools like OSCEs and rubrics.
- **Clinical Outcomes**: Link simulation training to tangible benefits, such as reduced medical errors, improved procedural success rates, and enhanced patient safety.
- **Operational Efficiency**: Monitor metrics like utilization rates, resource optimization, and cost-effectiveness to ensure the center operates sustainably.

The chapter also highlights the importance of accreditation, with examples of academic, hospital-based, and simulation-specific standards that guide operations. It underscores the value of collecting quantitative and qualitative data to better understand program impact.

Lastly, the chapter introduces strategies for engaging stakeholders, including presenting evidence-based outcomes, emphasizing cost savings, and aligning with institutional priorities. Simulation centers can achieve sustainable excellence by incorporating findings into continuous quality improvement cycles and effectively communicating their value.

Reflect on how your simulation center can integrate these strategies to enhance its operations. How can a data-driven approach and stakeholder collaboration support your center's mission and long-term success?

Chapter 8

Emerging Technologies in Healthcare Simulation

The evolution of technology has continuously reshaped healthcare education, enabling new opportunities for learning through advanced simulation techniques. Virtual reality (VR), augmented reality (AR), artificial intelligence (AI), and online platforms are transforming traditional simulation practices, offering immersive and adaptive experiences that cater to the complexities of modern medical training. This chapter explores these technologies and their implications for healthcare education.

8.1 Virtual Reality (VR) and Augmented Reality (AR)

Virtual reality (VR) and augmented reality (AR) are revolutionizing medical and nursing education by offering learners immersive environments that bridge the gap between theory and practice. These technologies are increasingly used to enhance spatial awareness, anatomy comprehension, and procedural training.

Applications in Healthcare Training

VR provides fully immersive simulations where learners can interact with virtual environments to practice skills such as surgical procedures, catheterization, and airway management (Farra et al., 2018). For example, VR platforms like *Osso VR* and *Touch Surgery* deliver realistic surgical experiences, allowing trainees to rehearse complex operations risk-free.

AR overlays digital elements in the real world, enriching hands-on training by enhancing visualization. Examples include tools like AccuVein, which uses AR to project a map of a patient's veins for accurate venipuncture, and HoloAnatomy, which allows learners to explore human anatomy in 3D (Sarfaty et al., 2020).

Educational Benefits

- *Spatial Awareness*: VR and AR help learners visualize anatomical structures in detail, improving their understanding of spatial relationships critical to procedural accuracy (Barsom et al., 2016).
- *Engagement and Retention*: These technologies promote active learning, leading to

better knowledge retention than traditional methods (Mantovani et al., 2011).
- *Scalability*: VR and AR simulations are accessible and reusable, making them cost-effective for large-scale implementation.

Educational Challenges

- *High Costs and Accessibility*: VR and AR hardware and high-quality content are often significant investments. Institutions in resource-limited settings may struggle to adopt these technologies, leading to inequities in training opportunities.
- *Technical Limitations*: VR/AR systems may suffer from issues such as latency, low resolution, or limited field of view, which can detract from the realism and educational value of simulations. Integrating VR/AR platforms with existing educational systems can be technically challenging, requiring ongoing support and upgrades.
- *Learner Adaptability*: When using VR/AR devices for extended periods, learners may experience motion sickness, eyestrain, or fatigue. Not all students may find immersive technologies equally beneficial, especially those who prefer traditional methods or hands-on interaction with real patients.
- *Training and Faculty Development*: Faculty may require additional training to effectively implement VR/AR into curricula, which can strain institutional resources. Educators accustomed to traditional methods may also resist adopting VR/AR technology, which can impact the integration process.

Addressing these challenges requires strategic planning, investment in faculty development, and a commitment to continuously evaluating and improving VR/AR applications in medical education.

8.2. Artificial Intelligence (AI) and Machine Learning

Artificial intelligence (AI) and machine learning (ML) are reshaping the landscape of simulation-based medical education, introducing adaptive, data-driven, and personalized approaches to training healthcare professionals. These technologies allow educators to bridge gaps in traditional methods, ensuring more effective learning and skill acquisition.

Adaptive Simulations

AI-powered simulations can dynamically adjust to the learner's proficiency level, presenting challenges that are neither too easy nor overwhelmingly complex. For example, AI-enhanced systems in high-fidelity mannequins can modify patient vital signs in real-time, simulating diverse clinical conditions based on learner actions (Topol, 2019). This adaptability ensures that each session remains relevant and challenging, accelerating skill development and fostering critical thinking.

Moreover, platforms like *SimX* integrate AI to create branching scenarios where clinical decisions lead to different outcomes, mimicking the variability of real-world patient care. These dynamic learning experiences help prepare trainees for unpredictable medical scenarios (Zhao et al., 2020).

Personalized Training

AI algorithms analyze learner interactions to identify specific strengths and weaknesses. This data is used to customize training plans, ensuring focused improvement in areas that require attention. For example, if a learner consistently struggles to recognize arrhythmias during a cardiac arrest simulation, the AI system can suggest targeted scenarios to build competency in this area.

Machine learning models can also predict learning curves, providing insights into how quickly an individual might master certain skills. This information helps instructors tailor their teaching approaches, making training more efficient and effective (Huang et al., 2020).

Real-Time Data Tracking and Analytics

AI-enabled systems can collect and analyze performance data during simulations, providing real-time feedback on technical and non-technical skills. Decision-making speed, procedural accuracy, and communication effectiveness are evaluated to offer actionable insights. This immediate feedback allows learners to understand their errors and improve before their next session.

Additionally, aggregated data across cohorts provides valuable information for program evaluation. Educators can identify trends, such as common errors or bottlenecks in learning, and adjust curricula accordingly to enhance overall training outcomes (Papanagnou et al., 2019).

Enhancing Team Training

AI also improves team-based simulations. AI systems can offer detailed feedback on team performance by analyzing communication patterns, leadership dynamics, and decision-making processes. For example, AI-powered tools can highlight instances where communication breakdowns occurred during a simulation, enabling teams to develop strategies to improve collaboration.

Challenges and Limitations

While AI and ML bring significant benefits, their integration into medical education comes with challenges:

- *High Development Costs*: Developing sophisticated AI-driven systems requires substantial investment, which may be prohibitive for smaller institutions (Topol, 2019).
- *Technical Expertise*: Implementing and maintaining AI systems necessitate skilled personnel, which may not always be available in educational settings (Zhao et al., 2020).
- *Ethical Considerations*: AI systems collect vast amounts of learner data, raising concerns about privacy and the ethical use of this information (Huang et al., 2020).

Despite these challenges, the benefits of AI and ML in simulation-based education continue to outweigh the barriers, positioning these technologies as critical components of future healthcare training.

Artificial intelligence and machine learning are revolutionizing medical education by providing adaptive simulations, personalized learning paths, and detailed analytics. These technologies enhance individual skill development and the collective performance of healthcare teams, ensuring preparedness for complex clinical scenarios. As AI continues to evolve, its role in simulation-based training will undoubtedly expand, fostering innovations that will shape the next generation of healthcare professionals.

8.3 Remote and Online Simulation

Remote and online simulation are emerging as pivotal solutions to expanding access to healthcare education, particularly in response to growing demands for flexible learning models and global disruptions like the COVID-19 pandemic. These technologies provide learners innovative ways to practice skills, engage in decision-making, and collaborate with peers regardless of physical location. However, they also present unique challenges that require careful consideration.

Expanding Access to Simulation

Remote simulation technologies enable learners in diverse locations to participate in otherwise inaccessible training. Virtual patient platforms, such as Shadow Health or Body Interact, simulate clinical scenarios where students interact with digital patients through structured question-and-answer interfaces (Kaufman et al., 2020). These tools allow learners to practice history-taking, diagnostic reasoning, and clinical decision-making from their homes or classrooms.

Additionally, live-streamed simulations can connect learners and facilitators in real-time. For example, a centralized simulation center can host scenarios using high-fidelity mannequins while participants engage remotely via videoconferencing tools. This approach minimizes the need for travel, reduces costs, and increases participation, especially for learners in remote or underserved areas (O'Regan et al., 2016).

Advantages of Remote and Online Simulations

- *Flexibility and Convenience*: Online simulations can fit into learners' schedules, making it easier for working professionals or those with family obligations to participate in advanced training programs (Nestel et al., 2021).
- *Scalability*: Institutions can simultaneously accommodate larger cohorts of students, addressing the growing demand for healthcare professionals (Cook et al., 2010).
- *Customization and Diversity*: Virtual patients can be designed to represent diverse demographics and medical conditions, ensuring a broad range of learning experiences (Kaufman et al., 2020).

Challenges of Remote Simulation

Remote simulation-based education offers many advantages but presents unique challenges that can impact its effectiveness. These challenges often fall into three main categories: technical barriers, reduced hands-on practice, and maintaining learner engagement.

Technical Barriers
One of the primary challenges in remote simulation is ensuring equitable access to the necessary technology. Reliable internet connections and access to compatible devices are critical prerequisites for participating in virtual simulations. However, learners in resource-constrained settings may face significant disparities in their ability to meet these requirements, creating unequal opportunities for learning (Bennett et al., 2020).

Additionally, the usability of simulation platforms can pose another technical hurdle. Complex or unintuitive platforms may frustrate both learners and instructors, hindering engagement and detracting from the overall learning experience. A steep learning curve for platform navigation can further exacerbate these issues, making it essential for simulation programs to prioritize user-friendly interfaces and comprehensive technical support.

Reduced Hands-On Practice
A significant limitation of remote simulation is the absence of tactile feedback, which is critical for developing psychomotor skills. Skills such as suturing, IV insertion, and other procedural techniques require hands-on practice to build muscle memory and precision. While virtual simulations can effectively teach cognitive and decision-making skills, they often fail to replicate the physical experience necessary for these tasks (Cook et al., 2010). This gap highlights the need for hybrid training models that combine online simulations with in-person practice sessions to ensure comprehensive skill development.

Maintaining Learner Engagement

Sustaining active participation in remote simulations can be a significant challenge. Virtual environments often lack the immersive quality of in-person simulations, leading to potential disengagement or difficulty maintaining focus. Learners may feel disconnected from the experience, impacting their ability to engage with the material and achieve desired learning outcomes fully (Nestel et al., 2021).

Strategies to address these challenges include incorporating interactive elements, such as real-time decision-making scenarios or team-based activities, to keep learners actively involved. Additionally, regular instructor check-ins and feedback can help foster a sense of connection and accountability, mitigating some of the engagement barriers posed by remote learning.

Hybrid Approaches: Bridging Remote and In-Person Training

Hybrid models that combine online simulation with periodic in-person training offer a balanced solution. For example, learners might complete virtual patient cases online and later attend simulation labs to practice procedural skills. This approach maximizes flexibility while retaining opportunities for hands-on experience (O'Regan et al., 2016).

Evaluating Effectiveness

Emerging research indicates that remote simulation can achieve comparable outcomes to traditional methods for cognitive and decision-making skills. However, studies emphasize the importance of robust instructional design and effective facilitation to ensure learners remain engaged and achieve desired competencies (Bennett et al., 2020).

Remote and online simulation represents a significant advancement in healthcare education, enabling broader access and fostering innovative learning models. By addressing technical limitations and engagement challenges, educators can leverage these tools to complement traditional training and prepare future healthcare professionals for complex, real-world scenarios.

8.4. Summary

Chapter 7 explores the transformative impact of emerging technologies on healthcare simulation, emphasizing their potential to revolutionize medical and nursing education. Virtual reality (VR), augmented reality (AR), artificial intelligence (AI), and remote simulation platforms are reshaping traditional approaches, offering innovative solutions to meet the demands of modern healthcare training. These technologies enhance immersion, adaptability, and accessibility but also introduce challenges requiring strategic planning and integration.

VR and AR technologies create immersive learning environments that bridge the gap between theoretical knowledge and practical skills. VR provides immersive experiences for practicing complex procedures like surgery and airway management. At the same time, AR enriches real-world training by overlaying digital elements, such as anatomical structures or procedural guides. Examples include platforms like Osso VR for surgical training and tools like AccuVein for venipuncture.

AI and ML introduce adaptive, personalized, and data-driven approaches to healthcare simulation. These technologies analyze learner performance, adjust scenarios dynamically, and provide real-time feedback to enhance individual and team training.

AI and ML are positioned as pivotal tools in future healthcare training, ensuring precision and adaptability in skill development while addressing evolving clinical complexities.

Remote simulation technologies, such as virtual patient platforms and live-streamed scenarios, expand access to education by enabling learners to engage in training from anywhere. These platforms are particularly valuable for overcoming geographic and resource barriers, offering flexibility for diverse learner needs.

Hybrid models that combine online simulations with in-person practice offer a balanced approach. They ensure comprehensive skill development while leveraging the convenience of remote learning.

Emerging technologies like VR, AR, AI, and remote simulation represent a paradigm shift in healthcare education, offering innovative ways to enhance learning outcomes. These tools enable immersive, personalized, and accessible training experiences, preparing learners for the complexities of real-world clinical practice. However, their successful integration requires addressing cost, accessibility, and faculty training challenges.

As research continues to validate the effectiveness of these technologies, simulation centers are positioned to adopt a blended approach, incorporating traditional and advanced methods to maximize impact. The chapter highlights the need for strategic planning, continuous evaluation, and a commitment to equity to realize the full potential of these groundbreaking tools.

8.5 Chapter Review

Review Questions

1. How do virtual reality (VR) and augmented reality (AR) enhance healthcare education? Please provide specific examples of their applications.
2. What are the primary advantages of using artificial intelligence (AI) in simulation-based education?
3. Discuss the benefits and challenges of remote and online simulation in healthcare training.
4. What strategies can educators implement to address technical and engagement challenges in remote simulation programs?
5. How can hybrid models balance the limitations of remote simulations with the benefits of in-person training?

Critical Thinking and Application

1. **Evaluating Technology Integration**:
    - Imagine your simulation center is considering adopting VR for surgical training. What factors would you evaluate to determine whether this technology aligns with your center's goals and resources?
2. **AI in Personalizing Training**:
    - Discuss how AI-driven adaptive simulations can address individual learner needs. How would you use data analytics to improve a learner's experience in your simulation program?
3. **Addressing Remote Simulation Challenges**:
    - Propose solutions to mitigate the lack of tactile feedback in remote simulations while maintaining high-quality training outcomes.
4. **Creating Equity in Simulation Access**:
    - What steps can be taken to ensure that resource-limited institutions benefit from advanced technologies like VR and AI in healthcare education?

Hands-On Activities

1. **Exploring VR and AR Tools**:
    - Organize a hands-on demonstration with VR and AR platforms like Osso VR or AccuVein. Evaluate their usability, educational value, and potential integration into your curriculum.
2. **Simulating AI-Driven Scenarios**:

- Develop a simple AI-powered branching simulation scenario using an online tool (e.g., Twine). Test the scenario with learners and gather feedback on its adaptability and educational value.
3. **Remote Simulation Design**:
    - Create a prototype remote simulation session using virtual patient platforms. Include interactive elements to enhance engagement and facilitate group discussion.
4. **Developing a Hybrid Training Model**:
    - Design a hybrid training module combining online simulations for theoretical learning and in-person practice sessions for skill development. Outline the logistics, learning objectives, and evaluation metrics.

Summary Reflection

Chapter 8 explores how emerging technologies like VR, AR, AI, and remote simulation transform healthcare education by creating immersive, adaptive, and accessible learning experiences. These innovations bridge the gap between traditional and modern training methods, enhancing outcomes for learners and institutions.

VR and AR offer unique advantages, such as spatial awareness and realistic procedural practice, but require strategic integration to overcome cost and technical challenges. AI and ML bring unprecedented personalization and analytics capabilities, fostering tailored learning paths and real-time feedback. Remote simulations expand access to education, enabling learners to engage from diverse locations, though challenges like limited hands-on practice and engagement barriers persist.

Hybrid models emerge as a balanced solution, combining the flexibility of remote learning with the tactile benefits of in-person training. Educators must adopt strategic approaches, including robust instructional design and faculty development, to ensure these technologies deliver their full potential.

Reflect on how emerging technologies could enhance your simulation programs. How can strategic planning and hybrid models help overcome challenges while maximizing impact? What steps will you take to ensure equitable access and effective implementation in your institution?

Chapter 9

Research and Continuous Improvement in Simulation Operations

Simulation-based education in healthcare is a dynamic field that demands constant evaluation, innovation, and improvement to meet the evolving needs of learners and healthcare systems. To remain effective and relevant, simulation programs must integrate rigorous research, systematic quality improvement, and dissemination of findings. This chapter delves into evaluating simulation effectiveness, implementing quality improvements, and contributing to the broader simulation community through collaboration and scholarship.

9.1 Evaluating Simulation Effectiveness and Return on Investment (ROI)

Simulation programs are designed to bridge the gap between theoretical knowledge and practical application, preparing learners to deliver safe, effective patient care. Their success lies in their measurable impact on clinical skills, decision-making, and patient outcomes. To assess these dimensions, simulation centers rely on various metrics and evaluation strategies that capture immediate and long-term benefits.

Skill Development

One of the most direct measures of simulation effectiveness is the improvement of learners' procedural and cognitive skills. Pre- and post-simulation assessments are routinely conducted to evaluate knowledge acquisition and skill mastery. These assessments often involve objective metrics, such as task completion time, procedure accuracy, and adherence to clinical protocols.

For example, learners practicing central line placement might be evaluated on sterile technique, anatomical precision, and success rate before and after simulation training. McGaghie et al. (2011) demonstrated that deliberate practice in simulation settings improves immediate performance and enhances long-term skill retention. This evidence underscores the value of repetitive, structured training for fostering competency in novice and experienced practitioners.

Additionally, simulation centers use structured frameworks such as Objective Structured Clinical Examinations (OSCEs) or standardized checklists to ensure consistency in evaluating skills across participants. These tools allow educators to pinpoint areas of weakness and provide targeted feedback, further reinforcing learning.

Impact on Patient Care

Beyond individual skill development, simulation programs aim to directly influence patient outcomes by reducing medical errors and improving care delivery. For instance, simulations designed to enhance communication during patient handovers have decreased the likelihood of information loss, a critical factor in preventing adverse events. Effective handover training may involve practicing structured communication techniques within a simulated environment, such as SBAR (Situation, Background, Assessment, Recommendation).

Research has consistently linked simulation training to improved clinical decision-making, faster response times, and better teamwork under pressure. These improvements are particularly evident in high-stakes scenarios, such as cardiac resuscitation or trauma management, where timely, coordinated actions are crucial. For example, studies have shown that teams trained in simulated cardiac arrest scenarios achieve earlier defibrillation and higher survival rates in real-world settings.

Simulation also supports patient safety by allowing learners to make and correct errors in a risk-free environment. For example, a medication administration simulation may expose common pitfalls, such as incorrect dosage calculations, and train participants to avoid these errors in clinical practice. Over time, the application of these lessons can significantly reduce the incidence of preventable harm.

Evaluating Team-Based Outcomes

Simulation programs often evaluate team performance in addition to individual competencies. Metrics such as communication effectiveness, role clarity, and conflict resolution are assessed during interprofessional simulations. For instance, AI-powered tools can analyze team interactions, identify communication breakdown patterns, and highlight improvement opportunities. These insights enable healthcare teams to function cohesively, translating into better patient care in complex clinical settings.

Tracking Long-Term Benefits

While immediate improvements in skills and decision-making are critical, simulation programs also track long-term benefits. Follow-up assessments may be conducted weeks or months after training to evaluate knowledge retention and the application of skills in clinical practice. For example, learners who completed advanced airway management simulations might be monitored during real patient encounters to measure their proficiency and confidence.

Simulation programs sometimes collaborate with healthcare organizations to gather data on patient outcomes, such as reduced hospital-acquired infections or shorter lengths of stay, after implementing simulation-based interventions. These longitudinal studies provide compelling evidence of simulation's role in advancing patient care quality.

Incorporating Learner Feedback

Finally, simulation centers consider qualitative feedback from participants to gauge the perceived impact of training on their clinical abilities. Learners often report increased confidence, enhanced problem-solving skills, and a better understanding of team dynamics following simulation sessions. This feedback validates the educational approach and highlights areas for program refinement.

Simulation programs can ensure that their training methods translate into tangible improvements in healthcare delivery by employing a comprehensive approach to measuring clinical and educational outcomes. This continuous evaluation and feedback cycle enhances individual and team performance and supports the broader goal of improving patient safety and care quality.

Financial and Operational Considerations

Justifying the investment in simulation centers involves demonstrating a positive ROI. Metrics include:

- *Cost Savings*: Simulation programs can decrease malpractice claims and improve operational efficiency by reducing training-related errors and mitigating risks.
- *Resource Optimization*: Efficient scheduling and utilization of simulation labs maximize throughput and reduce downtime, making every training dollar count (Zendejas et al., 2013).

Balancing Costs and Benefits

While high-fidelity simulation equipment and infrastructure are costly, the long-term benefits—including improved learner outcomes and enhanced patient safety—outweigh the initial investment when adequately managed.

Exploring Return on Investment and Return on Value in Healthcare Education

Understanding and justifying the resources invested in simulation-based learning programs is essential in healthcare simulation. Return on Investment (ROI) and Return on Value (ROV) provide frameworks to evaluate outcomes, but each emphasizes different value dimensions. Together, these metrics offer a comprehensive way to assess and communicate the impact of simulation education.

Return on Investment (ROI): Financial Impact

ROI is a widely recognized metric for evaluating the financial efficiency of investments. It evaluates whether the money spent on simulation programs leads to measurable financial benefits, such as cost reductions or revenue increases. This approach is critical for securing funding, justifying budgets, or demonstrating the economic value of simulation programs.

Key Components of ROI in Healthcare Simulation:

- *Cost Savings from Error Reduction*: Simulation training can significantly reduce medical errors, often associated with high legal and operational costs. For example, research has demonstrated that institutions using simulation to improve procedural training can experience fewer complications, saving millions in malpractice claims (AHRQ, 2020).
- *Resource Optimization*: Using simulation, organizations can identify inefficiencies in workflows or treatment protocols, ultimately saving costs associated with redundant efforts.
- *Revenue Generation*: Hospitals with robust simulation programs may attract high-caliber professionals or students, increasing revenue streams from tuition, certifications, or consulting opportunities.
-

Quantifying ROI: The ROI formula is straightforward:

$$ROI(\%) = \left(\frac{\text{Net Benefits}}{\text{Investment Costs}}\right) \times 100$$

For example, if a simulation program reduces errors by $500,000 annually, costing $100,000, the ROI would be 400%.

ROI in Action: A hospital that implemented simulation training to reduce sepsis mortality noted not only a decline in mortality rates but also financial savings from fewer intensive care days and reduced readmissions. These savings provided clear evidence of ROI to hospital administrators.

Return on Value (ROV): Holistic Benefits

While ROI focuses on direct financial outcomes, ROV provides a broader assessment of simulation programs' intangible and long-term benefits. These benefits are often qualitative yet critical to healthcare education's mission to improve patient safety and clinical quality.

Dimensions of ROV in Healthcare Simulation:

- *Educational Benefits:* Simulation enhances clinical competency, critical thinking, and confidence among learners. For instance, healthcare providers trained in high-fidelity simulations for emergency responses have demonstrated improved decision-making in real-world scenarios.
- *Patient Safety and Quality of Care*: Simulation has been directly linked to reduced adverse patient events, such as lower rates of hospital-acquired infections (Aggarwal et al., 2010). While these outcomes are harder to quantify financially, they reflect the intrinsic value of simulation in improving care.
- *Accreditation and Reputation*: Robust simulation programs contribute to meeting accreditation requirements, such as those outlined by organizations like the Joint Commission. Compliance enhances organizational credibility and boosts trust among patients and professionals.

Measuring ROV: ROV emphasizes qualitative metrics, such as:
- Learner and faculty satisfaction surveys.

- Patient outcomes linked to training programs.
- Stakeholder feedback and perceived value of simulation initiatives.

ROV in Practice: In a recent study, nursing schools using simulation-based training observed improved NCLEX pass rates and higher employment readiness among graduates. While these benefits were not directly tied to financial metrics, they significantly enhanced the school's reputation and student enrollment, showcasing ROV.

Return on Investment
- Measures financial gains
- Focus is on tangible gains
- Simple calculations

Return on Value
- Measures broader benefits of simulation
- Focus is on intangible gains
- Value of People

Figure 18 ROI vs. ROV

Integrating ROI and ROV for Comprehensive Evaluation

Healthcare simulation centers benefit from leveraging ROI and ROV to capture a full value spectrum. While ROI addresses the need for financial accountability, ROV highlights the broader mission of simulation education in advancing healthcare outcomes.

Stakeholder Communication:
- ROI is crucial for presenting financial gains to hospital administrators or university leaders.
- ROV resonates with educators, clinicians, and policymakers focused on quality improvement and learner outcomes.

Balancing Immediate and Long-term Impact:
- ROI often focuses on short-term, tangible gains.
- ROV emphasizes the long-term, sustainable benefits that contribute to systemic healthcare education and delivery improvements.

Case Example
Measuring ROI and ROV in a Simulation Program
A large hospital implemented a comprehensive simulation program designed to enhance clinical training, improve patient outcomes, and maximize operational efficiency. The program focused on two critical areas: **ROI** (Return on Investment), which measured tangible financial benefits, and **ROV** (Return on Value), which captured broader, qualitative outcomes.

<u>ROI-Focused Initiatives</u>
The simulation program streamlined training processes and reduced operational costs by consolidating multiple siloed training programs into an interdisciplinary simulation-based

curriculum. Key ROI metrics included:

Reduced Training Costs:
By transitioning from traditional in-service training to simulation-based programs, the hospital reduced the need for live patient cases and external training consultants.

Savings: The program saved $250,000 annually by eliminating venue rental costs, travel expenses for external trainers, and costs associated with patient risk during live training scenarios (Weaver et al., 2010).

Decreased Adverse Events:
Simulations targeted critical scenarios prone to errors, such as medication administration and surgical handovers. A post-implementation analysis showed a 30% reduction in medication errors and a 20% decrease in surgical site infections, which saved approximately $400,000 annually in malpractice claims and extended patient care costs (McGaghie et al., 2011).

Staff Retention Savings:
Simulation programs addressed high turnover rates among new nurses by providing comprehensive onboarding and skills-building simulations. The turnover rate dropped from 20% to 12%, saving the hospital approximately $150,000 annually in recruitment and training costs for replacing staff (Rosen et al., 2018).

ROV-Driven Efforts
While ROI metrics focused on financial returns, ROV efforts captured the broader value created by the program, emphasizing its impact on clinical care and institutional culture.

Interdisciplinary Collaboration:
The simulation program brought together teams from nursing, medicine, and allied health professions to train collaboratively on high-risk scenarios, such as cardiac arrests and trauma responses.

Outcome: Learners reported a 40% improvement in team communication skills, and simulations revealed a 25% faster response time during real-world code blue scenarios, directly contributing to improved survival rates (Rudolph et al., 2007).

Enhanced Accreditation Readiness:
The program aligned with standards from accrediting bodies such as The Joint Commission (TJC), meeting requirements for competency-based training in areas like infection control and emergency preparedness.

Outcome: The hospital achieved full accreditation during its next review, with simulation noted as a critical factor in compliance with safety and quality standards.

Patient Safety Culture:
By incorporating simulations into regular training, the program fostered a culture of safety and continuous improvement.

Outcome: Staff surveys showed a 25% increase in confidence when handling high-risk situations and a 50% reduction in the perception of blame culture, indicating a safer and more supportive work environment (Nestel et al., 2021).

Institutional Reputation:
The hospital's investment in innovative simulation practices attracted positive media coverage and

increased its reputation as a leader in healthcare education.

Outcome: This visibility led to partnerships with academic institutions and external organizations, generating an additional $100,000 annually in collaborative revenue streams.

Integrated ROI and ROV Analysis
By integrating ROI and ROV, the hospital demonstrated both tangible and intangible benefits of its simulation program:

Total ROI (Annual):
Training cost reductions, error prevention, and staff retention savings totaled $800,000 in annual financial benefits.

With an initial investment of $500,000, the program yielded a 60% ROI in its first year and was projected to deliver even higher returns as efficiencies improved.

Total ROV (Qualitative Gains):
Improved patient safety, enhanced staff collaboration, accreditation readiness, and strengthened institutional reputation created lasting organizational value beyond direct financial metrics.

Lessons Learned and Broader Implications
This case illustrates the importance of balancing ROI and ROV when evaluating simulation programs:

ROI ensures financial accountability and supports funding sustainability.
ROV highlights the program's alignment with the hospital's mission to deliver high-quality care and foster innovation.

By adopting a dual-focus approach, the hospital demonstrated fiscal responsibility and underscored the transformative potential of simulation-based training in healthcare.

In healthcare simulation education, ROI and ROV are complementary metrics. ROI provides a clear financial narrative, helping institutions justify investments, while ROV captures the qualitative and systemic benefits that are often more challenging to quantify but equally essential. Simulation centers can effectively communicate their impact to diverse stakeholders by integrating metrics into their evaluation strategies, ensuring sustainability and continued growth.

Return on Expectations (ROE) in Healthcare Simulation Operations

Return on Expectations (ROE) is a critical measure of success in healthcare simulation operations. Unlike Return on Investment (ROI), which focuses primarily on financial outcomes, ROE emphasizes the alignment of simulation outcomes with stakeholder goals and expectations. In a field as multifaceted as healthcare simulation, where education, safety, and competency are paramount, managing and achieving ROE ensures that the simulation program delivers value that meets or exceeds stakeholder expectations.

What is Return on Expectations (ROE)?
ROE evaluates whether a simulation program achieves the desired outcomes defined by its stakeholders. These outcomes are often tied to:

- **Educational Goals**: Improved clinical skills, critical thinking, and learner teamwork.
- **Operational Goals**: Efficient use of resources, smooth logistics, and effective delivery of scenarios.
- **Institutional Goals**: Reduced medical errors, enhanced patient safety, and compliance with accreditation standards.

ROE is qualitative but measurable through a structured approach to setting, managing, and evaluating expectations.

Key Stakeholders in Simulation Operations

Managing ROE begins with understanding the perspectives and expectations of all stakeholders, which may include:

- **Learners**: Expect realistic, immersive experiences that improve their clinical competencies and prepare them for real-world scenarios.
- **Faculty and Educators**: Seek seamless facilitation of simulation scenarios aligned with curriculum objectives.
- **Institutional Leaders**: Focus on cost-effectiveness, program outcomes, and alignment with broader organizational goals.
- **Accreditation Bodies**: Require compliance with specific training standards and documentation practices.
- **Simulation Team**: Value operational efficiency, resource management, and consistently delivering high-quality experiences.

Steps to Manage Return on Expectations

1. **Define Expectations Early**
   Engage Stakeholders: Meet with stakeholders to understand their goals. For example, faculty might prioritize learner competency in clinical decision-making. Institutional leaders may seek measurable reductions in medical errors after simulation integration.

   Set Clear Objectives: Define SMART (Specific, Measurable, Achievable, Relevant, Time-bound) objectives for each stakeholder group.

   Example: "Increase learner confidence in advanced cardiac life support (ACLS) protocols by 20% by the end of the semester."

2. **Align Simulation Design with Goals**
   Tailor scenarios, equipment, and learning objectives to meet stakeholder-defined outcomes.

   To measure progress, incorporate assessment tools such as pre- and post-simulation tests, learner evaluations, and scenario debriefing sessions. Use standardized rubrics to evaluate simulation performance and capture data on learner outcomes.

3. **Communicate Throughout the Process**
   Provide regular updates to stakeholders on program progress, challenges, and successes. Highlight how the simulation operations team addresses stakeholder needs (e.g., adjusting scenarios to align with new curriculum changes). Use transparent communication channels to manage expectations and foster trust.

4. **Measure and Analyze Outcomes**
   Use data-driven metrics to assess whether expectations were met:
   - Learner surveys to gauge confidence and skill acquisition.
   - Faculty feedback on scenario relevance and execution.
   - Institutional reports showing the impact of simulations on safety metrics (e.g., reduction in adverse events).
   - Compare outcomes to the original goals set during the planning phase.

5. **Address Gaps in Expectations**
   Identify and analyze gaps where expectations were not fully met.

   Example: If learners felt the simulation lacked realism, invest in better equipment or scenario scripting.

   Work collaboratively with stakeholders to revise goals or improve processes to close these gaps.

6. **Celebrate and Share Successes**
   Highlight successes to stakeholders by showcasing tangible outcomes.

   Example: "Learner performance on trauma care scenarios improved by 30%, exceeding our target of 20%."

   Use these achievements to advocate for continued support and funding.

Practical Tools for Managing ROE

Tool	Purpose
Stakeholder Surveys	Collect qualitative and quantitative data on satisfaction and perceived outcomes.
Pre- and Post-Simulation Assessments	Measure changes in learner skills, confidence, and knowledge.
Simulation Dashboard	Track and visualize key performance indicators (KPIs) related to simulation outcomes.
Regular Review Meetings	Align progress with stakeholder expectations and adjust goals as needed.

Case Study
Achieving ROE in a Healthcare Simulation Center

Scenario: A simulation center at a teaching hospital introduced a new sepsis protocol training simulation to reduce the average time to administer antibiotics to septic patients in the emergency department (ED).

Stakeholder Goals:
- **Learners**: Improve their ability to recognize and respond to sepsis.
- **Institutional Leaders**: Reduce average sepsis-related morbidity by 10%.
- **Educators**: Ensure the protocol training aligns with national guidelines.

Actions Taken:
- Designed realistic, high-fidelity sepsis scenarios with measurable learning objectives.
- Conducted pre- and post-simulation assessments to measure improvement in protocol adherence.
- Tracked real-world ED performance metrics before and after training implementation, such as time to antibiotics administration.

Outcomes:
- Learner performance improved by 35% in post-simulation assessments.
- Time to administer antibiotics in the ED decreased by 15%, exceeding the institution's goal.
- Stakeholder satisfaction surveys revealed an 85% alignment between simulation outcomes and expectations.
- This alignment of expectations with measurable outcomes demonstrated a strong ROE, securing continued funding and institutional support for the simulation program.

Return on Expectations is a vital measure of success in healthcare simulation operations. By engaging stakeholders, aligning goals, and rigorously evaluating outcomes, simulation centers can ensure their programs deliver meaningful, impactful results. ROE validates the value of simulation programs and strengthens relationships with stakeholders, paving the way for continued growth and innovation.

Return on Expectation vs. Return on Value

Return on Expectations (ROE) and Return on Value (ROV) are critical measures for evaluating the success of healthcare simulation operations, but they differ in focus and methodology. Understanding these distinctions allows simulation centers to employ each concept effectively, ensuring alignment with stakeholder goals and organizational objectives.

How ROE and ROV Work Together

While ROE ensures that simulation programs meet immediate, specific stakeholder expectations, ROV provides a more comprehensive picture of these programs' long-term value. For example:

- **ROE Example**: A simulation program aims to improve adherence to a new surgical protocol. Pre- and post-simulation assessments and stakeholder satisfaction measure success.
- **ROV Example**: The same program leads to fewer surgical complications over three years, enhances institutional reputation, and secures accreditation compliance.

ROE validates the program's short-term effectiveness in this scenario, while ROV captures its lasting value.

Comparison of ROE, ROV, and ROI

Aspect	Return on Expectations (ROE)	Return on Value (ROV)	Return on Investment (ROI)
Definition	Measures alignment with specific stakeholder-defined outcomes.	Measures the broader, often intangible, long-term value a program delivers.	Measures financial returns relative to the cost of the program.
Focus	Focuses on achieving predefined goals and expectations.	Focuses on holistic benefits, including cultural, operational, and community impact.	Focuses on cost-effectiveness and financial outcomes.
Stakeholders	Direct stakeholders, such as learners, educators, and faculty.	Institutional leadership, patients, and the broader community.	Organizational finance and budget stakeholders.
Measurement	Goal-driven and qualitative but measurable (e.g., surveys, assessments).	Context-driven may include intangible benefits (e.g., institutional reputation).	Quantitative, typically expressed as a percentage or ratio (e.g., cost savings vs. expenses).
Timeframe	Short to medium-term, tied to specific programs or projects.	Long-term, reflecting cumulative impact over years.	Short to medium-term, focused on financial results within budget cycles.
Examples	- Learner confidence improved by 25% post-simulation. - Stakeholder	- Reduction in medical errors across departments over three years.	- A $100,000 investment in a simulation program led to $150,000 in cost

Aspect	Return on Expectations (ROE)	Return on Value (ROV)	Return on Investment (ROI)
	satisfaction surveys show goals were met.	- Enhanced institutional reputation and trust.	savings from reduced training time.
Use Cases	- Evaluating immediate program outcomes. - Demonstrating alignment with stakeholder expectations.	- Articulating the simulation center's broader impact on institutional culture and patient outcomes.	- Justifying simulation program investments to financial stakeholders.

How ROE, ROV, and ROI Work Together

- **ROE**: Focuses on the short-term and specific goals, ensuring alignment with stakeholder expectations.
- **ROV**: Evaluates the broader, often intangible long-term benefits beyond individual programs.
- **ROI**: Provides a financial justification for simulation operations, demonstrating cost-efficiency and fiscal impact.

For example:

- **ROE** validates the success of a simulation-based sepsis protocol training by showing that learners' adherence to the protocol improved by 30%.
- **ROV** demonstrates that the same program reduced sepsis-related mortality in the hospital by 15% over three years.
- **ROI** quantifies that the program saved $500,000 annually by reducing ICU admissions and average patient length of stay.

Healthcare simulation centers must balance ROE, ROV, and ROI to evaluate and communicate their impact effectively. While ROI focuses on financial returns, ROE and ROV ensure the program delivers on expectations and long-term value, aligning with institutional goals. Simulation leaders can make a compelling case for ongoing support and investment by integrating these frameworks.

9.2 Quality Improvement in Simulation Programs

Continuous quality improvement (CQI) is a cornerstone of effective simulation programs, ensuring they remain aligned with educational goals, technological advancements, and evolving healthcare standards. Simulation programs can enhance learner outcomes, operational efficiency, and overall program impact by systematically identifying areas for improvement and implementing targeted interventions. This section explores the critical components of quality improvement, including feedback collection, performance metrics, benchmarking, and the integration of best practices.

Feedback Collection: The Foundation of Improvement

Feedback is an essential driver of quality improvement. Effective simulation programs employ diverse methods to gather insights from all stakeholders, ensuring that operational and educational aspects are addressed.

Learner Feedback: Learners provide valuable perspectives on their experiences, including the realism of scenarios, the effectiveness of debriefing sessions, and the clarity of learning objectives. Feedback is often collected through:
- *Post-simulation surveys*: Structured questionnaires that gauge learner satisfaction, perceived skill improvement, and overall experience.
- *Focus groups*: In-depth discussions that uncover specific challenges or areas for enhancement.

Facilitator Feedback: Instructors and facilitators offer critical insights into executing scenarios, resource adequacy, and operational hurdles. Their input helps identify logistical issues, such as insufficient prep time or technical glitches, that may affect the program's quality. If standardized patients were used for the activity, remember to include feedback from them.

Stakeholder Insights: Including program directors, administrators, and healthcare employers' input ensures that the program remains aligned with institutional goals and workforce needs.

Performance Metrics and Data Analysis

Data-driven decision-making is vital for quality improvement in simulation programs. By tracking and analyzing performance metrics, programs can objectively assess their effectiveness and identify trends or gaps.

Educational Metrics:
- *Knowledge Retention and Skill Acquisition*: Pre- and post-assessments evaluate the knowledge and skills gained through simulation sessions.
- *Competency Achievements*: Simulation outcomes tied to specific competencies, such as airway management or teamwork, provide measurable learner progress indicators.

Operational Metrics:
- *Session Throughput*: Monitoring the number of sessions and learners accommodated per week or month highlights operational efficiency.
- *Resource Utilization*: Metrics like simulator downtime, inventory usage, and staff-to-learner ratios reveal areas where resource allocation can be optimized.

Outcome Metrics: Linking simulation performance to real-world outcomes, such as reduced error rates or improved patient satisfaction, provides evidence of the program's broader impact.

Category	Description
Educational Metrics (Academic Programs)	
Learner Performance	Pre- and post-simulation scores; percentage achieving competency.
Knowledge Retention	Follow-up assessments for long-term retention.
Confidence and Self-Efficacy	Learner-reported confidence and preparedness.
Satisfaction	Learner and faculty satisfaction surveys.
Interprofessional Collaboration	Teamwork and communication evaluations during simulations.
Scenario Effectiveness	Alignment with learning objectives and scenario relevance.
Educational Metrics (Hospital-Based Programs)	
Competency Achievement	Competency percentages; time to mastery in procedures.
Error Reduction	Reduction in errors during simulations.
Simulation Impact on Clinical Practice	Application of simulation skills in clinical settings.
Team Training Outcomes	Team communication, leadership, and collaboration scores.
Accreditation Readiness	Alignment with requirements for accreditations.
Operational Metrics (Academic Programs)	
Utilization	Number of learners trained; simulation sessions conducted.
Program Reach	Number of courses/programs incorporating simulation.
Resource Allocation	Instructor-to-learner ratios; staff hours per session.
Research Contributions	Peer-reviewed publications; grants secured.
Technology Performance	Equipment uptime vs. downtime; maintenance adherence.
Operational Metrics (Hospital-Based Programs)	
Staff Training	Percentage of staff trained; training hours per staff.
Operational Efficiency	Setup and turnover times; cost savings from training.
Program Sustainability	Adherence to budget; external revenue generation.
Scalability	Growth in sessions or participants over time.
External Engagement	Number of partnerships or outreach activities.
Incident Mitigation	Reduction in adverse events or improved response times.
Common Metrics Across Both Settings	
Program Effectiveness	Achievement of learning objectives; stakeholder feedback.
Budget Metrics	Program costs, ROI, and ROV analysis.

Simulation Volume	Total simulations and scenarios executed.
Learner Demographics	Participant demographics: returning vs. new learners.
Technology Adoption	Adoption of VR, AR, and AI; feedback on usability.

Table 4 Common educational and operational metrics used in simulation programs

Benchmarking and Aligning with Standards

Benchmarking against established frameworks and industry standards ensures that simulation programs remain competitive and relevant. Key guidelines include:

- *Healthcare Simulation Standards of Best Practice*™: Published by INACSL, these standards offer detailed recommendations on scenario design, debriefing, and program evaluation (INACSL, 2021).
- *Society for Simulation in Healthcare Accreditation Standards*. Published by the Society for Simulation in Healthcare, it offers detailed standards on best practices for simulation programs best practice in teaching and education, assessment, research, systems integration, fellowship, and human simulation.
- *Kirkpatrick Model*: This widely used evaluation framework examines the effectiveness of training programs across four levels: reaction, learning, behavior, and results.

Simulation centers can identify gaps and prioritize improvements by comparing program performance to these benchmarks.

Integrating Best Practices

Simulation programs must adapt to changes in healthcare education, technology, and industry needs. Best practices serve as a roadmap for maintaining high-quality operations:

- *Scenario Updates*: Regularly revising scenarios to incorporate new clinical guidelines, emerging healthcare challenges, and learner feedback ensures relevance and engagement.
- *Technology Integration*: Upgrading to advanced tools, such as artificial intelligence-driven simulators or virtual reality platforms, enhances the realism and interactivity of training.
- *Interdisciplinary Collaboration*: Collaborating with other simulation centers and academic institutions fosters knowledge exchange and the adoption of innovative practices.

Implementing Changes

Turning insights and feedback into actionable improvements requires a structured approach:

- *Pilot Testing*: Before rolling out significant changes, pilot testing allows simulation teams to evaluate the feasibility and impact of modifications.
- *Stakeholder Engagement*: Involving all relevant parties in the planning and implementing changes ensures buy-in and smooth execution.

- *Ongoing Monitoring:* Continuous assessment of implemented changes helps determine their effectiveness and identify unintended consequences.

The Role of Leadership in Quality Improvement

Effective leadership is crucial for driving quality improvement in simulation programs. Program leaders must:

- Foster a culture of innovation and continuous learning.
- Allocate resources strategically to support improvement initiatives.
- Ensure transparent communication and collaboration across teams.

Quality improvement in simulation programs is a dynamic, ongoing process that integrates feedback, performance metrics, benchmarking, and best practices. By embracing these principles, simulation centers can continuously enhance their educational impact, operational efficiency, and alignment with evolving healthcare needs. This commitment to excellence improves learner outcomes and strengthens the program's role as a vital component of healthcare education.

9.3 Publishing and Sharing Findings

Research and dissemination are crucial elements of advancing the field of medical simulation. Publishing findings from simulation-based programs contributes to the collective knowledge base, establishes credibility, and fosters collaboration across institutions. This section explores the importance of contributing to research, collaborating with other institutions, and the broader benefits of sharing findings.

The Importance of Publishing in Medical Simulation

Medical simulation research provides critical insights into educational efficacy, operational strategies, and the integration of innovative technologies. By documenting and publishing outcomes, institutions help standardize best practices and drive improvements in healthcare education globally.

Contributions to Evidence-Based Practice:
- Published studies offer robust evidence to support the adoption of simulation methods in various healthcare domains. For instance, research highlighting the effectiveness of high-fidelity simulations in improving CPR skills has led to widespread implementation in training programs.
- Comparative studies between traditional and simulation-based learning methods inform educators about the most effective approaches for specific competencies.

Promoting Accountability:
- Publishing findings allows simulation programs to demonstrate their value to stakeholders, including institutional leadership, accrediting bodies, and funding organizations. Sharing metrics on learner performance, cost-efficiency, and patient safety outcomes highlights the program's ROI.

Collaboration and Networking Opportunities

Collaboration across institutions enhances the quality and impact of simulation research. Organizations can pool resources, share expertise, and work together to create synergies that advance the field.

Shared Research Projects:
- Collaborative studies allow for larger sample sizes, improving findings' statistical power and generalizability. For example, multi-center trials on debriefing techniques provide comprehensive insights that individual institutions may struggle to achieve alone.
- Partnerships also facilitate cross-disciplinary research, integrating perspectives from medicine, nursing, psychology, and technology.

Resource Sharing:
- Institutions can exchange scenario templates, instructional guides, and assessment tools, reducing duplication of effort and enhancing program quality.
- Access to shared databases, such as the Healthcare Simulation Dictionary provided by the *Society for Simulation in Healthcare* (SSH), ensures consistent terminology and methodologies.

Participation in Professional Organizations:
- Networks like the SSH and INACSL provide platforms for collaboration through conferences, webinars, and working groups. These forums enable practitioners to share innovations, discuss challenges, and align on standards (INACSL, 2021).

Benefits of Knowledge Dissemination

Publishing findings and participating in collaborative efforts extend beyond academic contributions; they create tangible benefits for simulation programs and the broader healthcare community.

Driving Innovation:
- Sharing research findings accelerates the adoption of emerging technologies, such as virtual reality (VR) and artificial intelligence (AI). Institutions that pioneer these technologies can guide others in implementing them effectively.

Improving Simulation Practices:
- Disseminating successful methodologies helps other institutions replicate proven practices. For example, publishing detailed protocols for interprofessional team simulations has enabled widespread adoption, improving team communication and patient safety.

Enhancing Professional Development:
- Engaging in research and publication activities promotes professional growth for simulation educators and leaders. These contributions build their reputations as thought leaders, opening doors for academic recognition and funding opportunities.

Expanding Access and Equity:
- Sharing cost-effective strategies for simulation implementation supports resource-limited institutions in developing robust programs. For instance, studies on low-cost task trainers have demonstrated their utility in settings with limited access to high-fidelity simulators.

Strategies for Effective Publishing in Simulation-Based Education

Effective publishing is vital to advancing the field of simulation-based education in healthcare. It contributes to the broader knowledge base and validates simulation's role as a transformative tool in modern healthcare training. A strategic and structured approach maximizes research impact and ensures meaningful contributions.

Selecting the Right Outlet
Choosing the appropriate journal is critical to reaching the intended audience and ensuring the research aligns with the publication's goals. Journals such as *Simulation in Healthcare*, *Advances in Simulation*, and *Clinical Simulation in Nursing* are well-regarded platforms for disseminating findings specific to healthcare simulation. By selecting outlets catering to healthcare education and simulation professionals, researchers can ensure their work reaches those who can most benefit from it.

The selection process should involve reviewing the journal's scope, recent articles, and submission guidelines. Targeting journals with audiences interested in specific topics—such as technology integration, patient safety, or interprofessional collaboration—further enhances the relevance and impact of the research.

Engaging Stakeholders
Involving key stakeholders throughout the research process strengthens the depth and applicability of the findings. Facilitators, learners, and institutional leadership bring diverse perspectives that enrich the study design and interpretation of results. For example, facilitators can provide insights into practical implementation challenges while learners offer feedback on the relevance and effectiveness of simulation scenarios. Engaging institutional leadership ensures alignment with organizational goals and enhances the potential for adopting findings in practice.

Collaboration with these groups improves the quality of the research and fosters support for the study's conclusions, making it more likely that the findings will influence educational practices or policies.

Ensuring Rigor and Transparency
Adherence to rigorous research methodologies is fundamental to producing credible and impactful work. This includes obtaining ethical approval when required, documenting the data collection and analysis processes thoroughly, and ensuring transparency in how results are derived. Clearly defined methodologies allow other researchers to replicate or build upon the work, contributing to the field's growth.

For instance, using validated assessment tools, clearly stating inclusion criteria for participants, and maintaining a transparent approach to data analysis bolster the credibility of the research. Thoughtful peer review and attention to ethical considerations further underscore the study's rigor.

Leveraging Dissemination Channels
While journal publications are a cornerstone of academic research, disseminating findings through additional channels broadens their reach and impact. Presenting at conferences, webinars, and professional society meetings allows researchers to engage directly with educators, practitioners, and policymakers. These platforms also provide opportunities for real-time feedback, networking, and collaboration, further amplifying the research's influence.

For instance, conferences like the *Society for Simulation in Healthcare* (SSH) Annual Meeting or the International Nursing Association for Clinical Simulation and Learning (INACSL) provide valuable venues for sharing innovative findings and exploring collaborative opportunities. Webinars and institutional presentations can also connect researchers with local or remote audiences, extending the reach of their work.

Fostering Growth and Sustainability
Publishing and disseminating research is about individual recognition and advancing the field of simulation-based education. By contributing to the collective knowledge base, researchers help improve educational practices, enhance patient care, and demonstrate the value of simulation in healthcare training. Collaborative efforts with other institutions and engagement with the academic community further strengthen the field and ensure its continued evolution.

These efforts highlight the transformative potential of simulation as a teaching and learning tool. Through thoughtful research, strategic publishing, and widespread dissemination, simulation programs continue to drive innovation, improve outcomes, and enhance the overall quality of healthcare education.

Best Practices for Publishing in Simulation-Based Education

Publishing in simulation-based education is a critical avenue for advancing the field, sharing innovations, and validating the role of simulation in healthcare training. Researchers must adopt a thoughtful and strategic approach to make a meaningful impact, focusing on rigor, relevance, and effective dissemination.

Identifying a Relevant and Impactful Research Topic
The foundation of a successful publication lies in selecting a topic that addresses an unmet need or emerging trend. Researchers should explore areas where simulation can significantly impact, such as improving patient safety, enhancing teamwork, or integrating new technologies like virtual reality (VR) and artificial intelligence (AI). Topics aligning with institutional priorities, such as accreditation readiness or workforce development, resonate strongly with stakeholders (Weaver et al., 2010).

Engaging stakeholders—including educators, learners, and institutional leaders—can provide valuable insights into practical challenges and ensure the research has real-world applicability. A review of recent literature helps identify knowledge gaps and ensures the topic contributes meaningfully to ongoing discussions in the field.

Designing a Rigorous and Transparent Study
A robust study design is essential for producing credible and impactful research. Researchers must clearly define objectives and select methodologies that align with their goals. For example, randomized controlled trials are ideal for measuring the effectiveness of interventions, while mixed-methods approaches can provide a deeper understanding of complex phenomena (McGaghie et al., 2011).

Validated tools such as Objective Structured Clinical Examination (OSCE) checklists or satisfaction surveys ensure data reliability. Ethical approval is another critical component, as it protects participants and upholds the integrity of the research process. Pilot studies are valuable for refining methodologies and troubleshooting potential issues before full-scale implementation.

Transparency in documenting data collection and analysis processes is equally important. By clearly outlining methodologies, researchers enable replication and contribute to the broader body of evidence in simulation-based education (Cook et al., 2013).

> **Examples of Impactful Research Topics:**
> - Comparing retention rates between simulation-trained and traditionally trained learners over time.
> - Exploring how game-based elements enhance learner engagement and knowledge retention.
> - Evaluating training programs that prepare facilitators for leading debriefings or managing simulations.
> - Aligning simulation activities with requirements from accrediting bodies like The Joint Commission or INACSL
> - Studying the impact of virtual simulation platforms in providing accessible training during events like the COVID-19 pandemic.

Selecting the Right Publication Outlet
Choosing the appropriate journal maximizes the reach and impact of research findings. Journals such as *Simulation in Healthcare*, *Advances in Simulation*, and *Clinical Simulation in Nursing* cater specifically to audiences interested in simulation-based education and healthcare training. Researchers should review submission guidelines, recent articles, and the journal's scope to ensure alignment with their study's focus.

Another important consideration is the decision to publish in open-access journals. Open-access platforms make research more accessible, particularly to educators and practitioners in resource-limited settings, broadening the study's potential impact (Ferguson et al., 2020).

Crafting a Clear and Compelling Manuscript
A well-structured manuscript is crucial for effective communication. Following the IMRAD format (Introduction, Methods, Results, and Discussion) ensures clarity and coherence:

- **Introduction**: Present the research problem, objectives, and significance, supported by a concise literature review.
- **Methods**: Detail the study design, participant demographics, and data collection tools, ensuring enough information for replication.
- **Results**: Clearly present findings using tables, charts, or graphs to enhance readability.
- **Discussion**: Interpret the results, connect them to existing literature, and highlight implications for practice, policy, or future research.

Attention to detail, such as adhering to journal-specific guidelines and proofreading meticulously, ensures professionalism. Engaging colleagues or professional editors for feedback can further refine the manuscript (Archer, 2010).

Disseminating Beyond Academic Journals
Publishing in journals is essential, but reaching a broader audience requires leveraging additional dissemination channels. Presenting findings at conferences such as the *Society for Simulation in Healthcare* (SSH) Annual Meeting or the *International Nursing Association for Clinical Simulation and Learning* (INACSL) Conference allows researchers to engage with practitioners and policymakers directly. These platforms also provide opportunities for feedback and networking (Rudolph et al., 2007).

Webinars, workshops, and digital platforms such as ResearchGate expand the reach of published work. Institutional presentations can also foster local engagement and promote the practical application of findings.

Engaging in Collaboration and Networking
Collaboration enriches research by incorporating diverse perspectives and expertise. Working with multidisciplinary teams—such as educators, clinicians, and technologists—broadens the scope and relevance of studies. Engaging with professional societies like SSH or INACSL provides access to resources, mentorship, and collaboration opportunities (Nestel et al., 2021).

Networking at conferences and through digital platforms also facilitates partnerships and cross-institutional studies, further enhancing the impact of research.

Responding Constructively to Peer Review
The peer review process is an opportunity to strengthen the manuscript. Researchers should approach feedback openly, addressing critiques thoroughly and providing evidence for any revisions made. If disagreements arise, a respectful and well-reasoned response is essential. A professional tone and clear revisions documentation demonstrate commitment to quality and collaboration (McGaghie et al., 2011).

Building a Sustainable Research Agenda
Publishing is not a one-time endeavor but part of a long-term commitment to advancing the field. Researchers should develop a research agenda that aligns with their interests and the community's needs. Diversifying outputs—such as journal articles, conference presentations, and book chapters—ensures sustained contributions. Tracking metrics such as citations and downloads helps assess the reach and influence of published work.

Embracing Open Science Principles
Transparency and accessibility are central to modern research practices. Sharing data, methods, and supplementary materials enhances trust and facilitates replication. Open-access publications and repositories make research available to a wider audience, including those in underserved areas (Topol, 2019).

The field of simulation-based education is dynamic, with emerging technologies and methodologies continually reshaping best practices. Staying informed about trends and adapting research to address new challenges ensures that studies remain relevant and impactful.

9.4 Summary

Simulation-based education in healthcare is an ever-evolving field that requires ongoing research, evaluation, and innovation to meet the demands of learners and healthcare systems. To maintain relevance and effectiveness, simulation programs must integrate rigorous research, continuous quality improvement (CQI), and proactive dissemination of findings. Chapter 8 explores these critical dimensions, emphasizing the importance of assessing effectiveness, implementing CQI initiatives, and contributing to the broader community through collaboration and scholarship.

Simulation programs bridge the gap between theoretical knowledge and practical application, enhancing clinical skills and decision-making while improving patient outcomes. Their effectiveness is often evaluated through skill development, impact on patient care, and team-based outcomes.

Skill Development: Pre- and post-simulation assessments measure learners' procedural and cognitive skills proficiency. Tools like Objective Structured Clinical Examinations (OSCEs) and standardized checklists ensure consistency and provide actionable feedback. Research has demonstrated that deliberate practice in simulation fosters immediate competency and long-term retention (McGaghie et al., 2011).

Impact on Patient Care: Simulation programs reduce medical errors and enhance care delivery by creating a risk-free environment for practicing high-stakes scenarios. For example, simulations focused on improving handovers using SBAR techniques have significantly reduced communication failures and associated adverse events.

Team-Based Outcomes: Metrics such as communication effectiveness and role clarity during interprofessional simulations highlight the importance of teamwork. Advanced tools, including AI analytics, can evaluate team dynamics and provide insights for improvement.

Long-Term Benefits: Follow-up assessments and collaboration with healthcare organizations allow simulation programs to track their influence on real-world outcomes, such as reduced hospital-acquired infections or improved survival rates.

Financially, simulation centers justify their investments by demonstrating ROI through cost savings, such as reduced malpractice claims and improved resource utilization

(Zendejas et al., 2013). Balancing ROI with Return on Value (ROV) highlights simulation's broader, qualitative benefits, such as enhanced patient safety, improved learner confidence, and institutional reputation.

CQI ensures simulation programs adapt to changing healthcare standards, learner needs, and technological advancements. Effective CQI strategies include:

- **Feedback Collection**: Input from learners, facilitators, and stakeholders provides valuable insights for program refinement. Learners' perceptions of realism, debriefing effectiveness, and learning outcomes are essential for improvement.
- **Performance Metrics**: Tracking data such as session throughput, resource utilization, and knowledge retention allows programs to identify trends and gaps. Linking these metrics to real-world outcomes, like reduced clinical errors, demonstrates a broader impact.
- **Benchmarking**: Aligning with industry standards, such as the Healthcare Simulation Standards of Best Practice™ (INACSL, 2021), ensures that programs remain competitive and effective.
- **Best Practices and Innovation**: Regular updates to scenarios, integrating emerging technologies like VR and AI, and fostering interdisciplinary collaboration keep programs at the forefront of healthcare education.

Publishing simulation research is essential for contributing to the broader knowledge base, establishing credibility, and fostering collaboration. Key strategies include:

- **Selecting Appropriate Journals**: Targeting outlets like *Simulation in Healthcare* and *Advances in Simulation* ensures that research reaches the right audience. Open-access options enhance accessibility and impact.
- **Crafting High-Quality Manuscripts**: Following the IMRAD structure (Introduction, Methods, Results, and Discussion) ensures clarity and professionalism. Incorporating feedback from peers and mentors strengthens the manuscript.
- **Leveraging Dissemination Channels**: Sharing findings at conferences, webinars, and institutional presentations broadens reach and encourages practical application.

Collaboration across institutions enhances research quality and impact. Shared projects, resource exchanges, and participation in professional organizations like the *Society for Simulation in Healthcare* (SSH) create opportunities for innovation and standardization. Collaborative efforts pool expertise and promote equity by supporting resource-limited programs.

Simulation programs benefit from evaluating both ROI and ROV to present a holistic picture of their value:

- **ROI**: Measures financial benefits, such as cost savings from error reduction and operational efficiency.
- **ROV**: Captures qualitative outcomes, including improved patient safety, learner confidence, and institutional reputation.

Simulation programs effectively communicate value to diverse stakeholders by combining ROI and ROV metrics, ensuring sustained funding and support.

Research and continuous improvement are the cornerstones of impactful simulation operations. Simulation programs advance healthcare education and practice by rigorously evaluating effectiveness, implementing CQI initiatives, and sharing findings with the broader community. This ongoing innovation cycle enhances learner outcomes and contributes to safer, more effective patient care.

9.5 Chapter Review

Review Questions

1. What are the key components for evaluating the effectiveness of a simulation program?
2. How can simulation programs measure Return on Investment (ROI) and Return on Value (ROV)? Provide examples for each.
3. What role does Continuous Quality Improvement (CQI) play in simulation program operations?
4. Describe the importance of publishing simulation research and its impact on healthcare education.
5. How can simulation centers effectively collaborate with other institutions to advance research and best practices?

Critical Thinking and Application

1. **Evaluating ROI and ROV**:
    - Your institution plans to invest in advanced high-fidelity mannequins for simulation training. How would you calculate ROI and assess ROV to justify this purchase?
2. **Implementing CQI**:
    - Imagine that learners have reported dissatisfaction with the realism of scenarios. How would you use feedback collection and benchmarking to address this issue?
3. **Research Design**:
    - Design a study to measure the long-term impact of simulation-based training on patient safety outcomes in your institution. What methodologies and tools would you use?
4. **Publishing Strategy**:

- Your team has developed an innovative debriefing technique. Outline a strategy for publishing your findings, including selecting a journal, designing the study, and presenting results.

Hands-On Activities

1. **Creating Evaluation Metrics**:
   - Develop a list of educational, operational, and outcome metrics for a simulation program in your institution. Include methods for data collection and analysis.
2. **CQI Implementation Exercise**:
   - Choose an aspect of your simulation program (e.g., debriefing sessions, technology use) and design a CQI plan to enhance its effectiveness. Include feedback mechanisms, pilot testing, and evaluation methods.
3. **Simulation Research Workshop**:
   - Conduct a workshop where team members collaboratively design a research project based on a current challenge in your simulation program. Identify the objectives, methodologies, and potential publication venues.
4. **Peer Review Simulation**:
   - Engage in a peer review exercise by exchanging draft research manuscripts with colleagues. Provide constructive feedback on methodology, clarity, and alignment with best practices.

Summary Reflection

Chapter 9 emphasizes the importance of continuous evaluation and innovation in simulation-based healthcare education. Programs must measure effectiveness, ensure quality, and share insights to advance local and global simulation practices.

Simulation programs are most impactful when they:

- Demonstrate measurable improvements in skills, decision-making, and patient outcomes.
- Balance financial justification (ROI) with broader educational and operational benefits (ROV).
- Integrate Continuous Quality Improvement (CQI) to stay aligned with evolving standards, learner needs, and technological advancements.

Publishing and sharing findings are critical to expanding knowledge and fostering collaboration. Institutions can maximize their impact by:

- Selecting relevant journals and engaging stakeholders in the research process.
- Ensuring rigorous study design and transparent methodologies.
- Leveraging conferences, webinars, and professional networks for dissemination.

Reflect on your institution's simulation program. How can you integrate research and CQI to enhance operations and demonstrate value to stakeholders? What steps will you take to contribute to the broader simulation community?

Chapter 10

Careers and Professional Development in Healthcare Simulation Operations

Healthcare simulation is an expanding field critical to modern medical and nursing education. As simulation becomes more integral to healthcare training, career opportunities in simulation operations have diversified and grown. This chapter explores the key roles, required qualifications, certifications, and career growth opportunities for professionals in this dynamic field.

10.1 Roles in Healthcare Simulation

Healthcare simulation programs rely on a diverse, multidisciplinary team to deliver impactful, realistic training that enhances clinical skills and decision-making. These programs incorporate technical, educational, administrative, and strategic roles, each contributing to creating and sustaining a simulation environment that meets educational and institutional goals. As the global simulation market grows—projected to reach $6.6 billion by 2027 with a compound annual growth rate (CAGR) of 14.7% (MarketsandMarkets, 2022)—the importance and scope of these roles continue to expand. There are many roles that a simulation program may have, as there are just as many job

Center Director/Medical Director	Simulation Specialist/Technician	Clinical Educator
SP Educator/Trainer	Operations Manager	Coordinator
Administrative Assistant	Research Director	Fellowship Director

Figure 19 Common Positions in Simulation Operations

titles out there for the same position. Regardless of the title, the simulation program will have a combination of faculty or staff in one of the following positions.

1. Simulation Specialist/Technician (Sim Tech)

Description
Simulation technicians are the backbone of simulation operations, ensuring the smooth execution of technological and logistical aspects of simulations. Their work directly supports the educational objectives of clinical scenarios.
Key Responsibilities
<ul><li>Operate high-fidelity simulators, manikins, and associated technologies.</li><li>Program and test simulation scenarios based on input from clinical educators.</li><li>Perform maintenance and troubleshooting of simulation equipment.</li><li>Manage the setup and breakdown of simulation spaces, including audiovisual tools.</li></ul>
Qualifications and Skills
<ul><li>An associate or bachelor's degree in healthcare, engineering, IT, or a related technical field is typical.</li><li>Certifications like the Certified Healthcare Simulation Operations Specialist (CHSOS) enhance career prospects.</li><li>Essential skills include technical proficiency, medical terminology understanding, and problem-solving abilities.</li></ul>
Job Outlook
<ul><li>Simulation technician roles are increasingly in demand as simulation-based training becomes standard in healthcare. The U.S. Bureau of Labor Statistics (BLS) estimates a 6% growth in medical equipment-related roles, including simulation technicians, through 2031.</li><li>The expansion of simulation centers globally aligns with predictions that simulation technology will be critical in 85% of healthcare training programs by 2030 (Frost & Sullivan, 2021).</li></ul>

2. Clinical Educator

Description
Clinical educators design and facilitate simulation-based training to bridge the gap between theoretical knowledge and practical application, ensuring learners are well-prepared for real-world challenges.
Key Responsibilities
<ul><li>Develop educational content, including simulation scenarios that reflect real-life clinical situations.</li><li>Facilitate simulation sessions, guide learners, and lead debriefings.</li><li>Collaborate with subject matter experts to align scenarios with clinical guidelines and institutional objectives.</li></ul>
Qualifications and Skills

- A bachelor's degree in a healthcare-related field is common, though many roles prefer a master's degree or higher.
- Clinical experience is essential, with many educators holding RN, MD, or allied health professional certifications.
- Strong communication and facilitation skills are critical for effective debriefing.

Job Outlook
- Over 90% of medical schools in the U.S. integrate simulation into their curriculum (AAMC, 2020), creating significant demand for clinical educators.
- Simulation-based education has been shown to reduce medical errors by up to 40%, further emphasizing the critical role of clinical educators (Aggarwal et al., 2010).

3. SP Educator/Trainer

Description

Standardized Patient (SP) Educators/Trainers play a pivotal role in healthcare simulation by recruiting, training, and managing SPs—individuals trained to portray patients in simulated clinical scenarios. These educators ensure that SPs deliver consistent, realistic, high-quality performances facilitating learner assessment and skill development.

Key Responsibilities
- Recruit and train standardized patients, ensuring they accurately portray medical conditions and respond to learners consistently.
- Develop case materials and role instructions in collaboration with clinical educators and subject matter experts.
- Monitor SP performances during simulations and provide feedback for improvement.
- Facilitate debriefing sessions, focusing on communication and interpersonal skills.
- Maintain SP rosters, schedules, and performance evaluation records.

Qualifications and Skills
- A bachelor's degree in healthcare, education, theater, or a related field is common, though experience in acting or role-playing training is highly valued.
- Strong communication and interpersonal skills, with an ability to guide SPs and learners.
- Familiarity with healthcare concepts and terminology to ensure realistic portrayals.

4. Operations Manager

Description

Simulation operations managers oversee simulation centers' daily operations, long-term strategy, and financial sustainability. They act as leaders, coordinating teams and managing resources effectively.

Key Responsibilities
• Develop and implement the strategic vision for simulation programs. • Manage budgets for equipment, maintenance, and operational costs. • Lead and support a multidisciplinary team of technicians, educators, and administrators. • Ensure compliance with accreditation standards and maintain quality benchmarks.
Qualifications and Skills
• A bachelor's or master's degree in healthcare, business, or a related field. • Certifications such as Project Management Professional (PMP) and CHSOS are highly regarded. • Strategic planning, financial management, and leadership skills are essential.
Job Outlook
• A 2020 SSH survey indicated that 70% of simulation centers plan to expand staffing within the next five years to meet increasing demand. • Simulation managers are at the forefront of adopting cutting-edge technologies like virtual reality (VR) and artificial intelligence (AI), both predicted to dominate the field by 2030 (Frost & Sullivan, 2021).

5. Center Director/Medical Director

Description
The Center Director or Medical Director provides overall leadership for the simulation program, ensuring alignment with institutional goals and clinical standards.
Key Responsibilities
• Develop strategic goals and vision for the simulation center. • Ensure alignment of educational and operational activities with organizational objectives. • Oversee quality assurance, program evaluation, and accreditation processes. • Represent the center to stakeholders, including leadership and external partners. •
Qualifications and Skills
• Advanced degrees in healthcare (e.g., MD, DO, DNP) or education are common. • Leadership experience with a focus on clinical quality and operational strategy. • Strong interpersonal and networking skills for stakeholder engagement.

6. Coordinator

Description
Coordinators manage simulation programs' logistical and operational aspects, ensuring seamless scheduling and team communication.

Key Responsibilities
• Schedule simulation sessions, manage participant rosters, and allocate resources. • Coordinate with educators, technicians, and facilitators to prepare scenarios. • Maintain detailed records of program activities, evaluations, and resource utilization. •
Qualifications and Skills
• A bachelor's degree in healthcare administration or a related field. • Strong organizational and communication skills. • Familiarity with simulation software and scheduling systems.

7. Administrative Assistant

Description
Administrative assistants provide essential clerical and organizational support to keep simulation centers running smoothly.
Key Responsibilities
• Manage day-to-day administrative tasks such as correspondence, invoicing, and meeting coordination. • Support event planning, including workshops, training sessions, and outreach activities. • Maintained records, assisted with budget tracking, and provided customer service to stakeholders. •
Qualifications and Skills
• A high school diploma or associate degree and office management experience is beneficial. • Proficiency in office software (e.g., Microsoft Office Suite). • Strong multitasking and communication skills.

8. Research Director

Description
The Research Director oversees research activities within the simulation program, ensuring scholarly contributions to the field.
Key Responsibilities
• Design and implement research studies aligned with the simulation program's goals. • Secure funding through grant writing and partnerships. • Mentor staff and faculty in research methods and publication strategies.

- Disseminate findings through journals, conferences, and professional networks.

Qualifications and Skills
- A terminal degree in healthcare, education, or research (e.g., PhD, EdD).
- Strong analytical skills and experience with research methodologies.
- Proven track record of scholarly publications.

9. Fellowship Director

Description

The Fellowship Director leads post-graduate training programs, nurturing the next generation of simulation educators and researchers.

Key Responsibilities
- Develop and oversee fellowship curricula in simulation education and operations.
- Mentor fellows in pedagogy, scenario development, and research.
- Facilitate networking opportunities for fellows within the simulation community.

Qualifications and Skills
- Advanced degrees and experience in simulation education.
- Leadership and mentorship abilities.
- Expertise in integrating simulation into clinical and academic training.

Other Roles that Programs may have

Healthcare simulation centers require a diverse range of professionals to ensure their smooth operation and the delivery of effective training programs. Here is a list of job positions typically found in such centers:

Leadership & Administrative Roles

1. **Program Coordinator**
   Handles scheduling, logistics, and coordination of training sessions and events.

Technical & Support Roles

2. **Simulation Technician/Technologist**
   Operates and maintains simulation equipment, sets up scenarios, and troubleshoots technical issues.
3. **IT Support Specialist**
   Ensures network, software, and hardware functionality for simulation and learning management systems.
4. **Biomedical Equipment Technician**
   Maintains and repairs specialized medical simulation equipment and manikins.

Educational & Training Roles

5. **Simulation Educator/Trainer**
   Designs, implements, and facilitates simulation-based education for learners.
6. **Clinical Educator**
   Provides clinical expertise and ensures simulation scenarios reflect real-world medical practice.
7. **Curriculum Developer**
   Designs educational content and integrates simulation-based learning into broader curricula.
8. **Standardized Patient Coordinator**
   Recruits, trains, and schedules standardized patients (actors portraying patients).

Clinical & Medical Roles

9. **Clinical Simulation Specialist**
   Assists with scenario development, conducts debriefings, and bridges clinical expertise with simulation training.

Research & Development Roles

10. **Simulation Researcher**
    Conducts studies to evaluate simulation effectiveness and contributes to academic publications.
11. **Data Analyst**
    Collects and analyzes data from simulation sessions to assess outcomes and improve training.
12. **Innovation Specialist**
    Develops new simulation technologies or methodologies.

Other Specialized Roles

13. **Human Factors Specialist**
    Analyzes workflows and designs simulations to improve team communication and patient safety.
14. **Quality Assurance Specialist**
    Ensures that simulation programs meet accreditation standards and continuously improve.
15. **Community Outreach Coordinator**
    Promotes the center's programs to external stakeholders, including healthcare organizations and educational institutions.
16. **Grant Writer**
    Secures funding through grant proposals and donor relations.

Simulation centers may customize roles based on their focus (e.g., academic training, clinical practice, or research), size, and the complexity of their programs.

Collaboration Among Roles

The success of healthcare simulation programs depends on seamless collaboration among team members. Each role, from the technical expertise of simulation technicians to the strategic leadership of directors, contributes to creating a comprehensive learning environment. Interdisciplinary teamwork ensures that programs are effective, innovative, and aligned with institutional objectives.

Future Outlook

With the simulation market projected to grow significantly in the coming years, roles in healthcare simulation will evolve, offering opportunities for greater specialization, professional development, and innovation. These roles collectively ensure simulation programs remain at the forefront of healthcare education and training.

10.2 Certification and Training

Certifications and specialized training are essential for professionals in healthcare simulation operations. They demonstrate competence, dedication, and expertise in this rapidly growing field. These credentials validate skills, enhance career opportunities, and ensure alignment with industry standards. This section explores key certifications, their requirements, and the benefits they offer simulation professionals.

Key Certifications in Healthcare Simulation

Certified Healthcare Simulation Educator (CHSE):
Purpose: The CHSE credential is designed for educators who use simulation as an instructional method to enhance healthcare training.

Eligibility Requirements:
- A bachelor's degree or higher in a healthcare-related field.
- At least two years of experience in simulation-based education.
- Document professional involvement in simulation, such as program design, facilitation, or research.

Certification Process:
- Candidates must pass a rigorous exam assessing knowledge in simulation principles, curriculum design, and evaluation strategies.

Impact on Careers:
- CHSE-certified educators report increased recognition within their institutions and improved opportunities for advancement (SSH, 2022).

Certified Healthcare Simulation Operations Specialist (CHSOS):
Purpose: Tailored for simulation technicians and operations personnel, the CHSOS certification focuses on the simulation's technical and logistical aspects.

Eligibility Requirements:

- A high school diploma (or equivalent) with significant experience in simulation or a related technical field.
- Experience with simulator maintenance, scenario execution, or audiovisual systems.

Certification Process:
- The CHSOS exam covers simulation technology, operational management, and troubleshooting.

Career Benefits:
- Due to their certified expertise, CHSOS professionals often secure higher salaries and leadership roles within simulation centers (SSH, 2022).

Benefits of Certification

Professional Credibility:
Certifications like CHSE and CHSOS serve as benchmarks of excellence. A Society for Simulation in Healthcare (SSH) survey found that 80% of certified professionals felt their credentials increased their credibility with peers and leadership.

Career Advancement:
Certification holders are more likely to secure promotions, leadership roles, and salary increases. For instance, on average, CHSE-certified educators earn 10–15% more than their uncertified counterparts (SSH, 2021).

Enhanced Skillsets:
Certification preparation involves mastering simulation principles, from scenario design to debriefing techniques, ensuring practitioners stay current with industry advancements.

Alignment with Standards:
Certified professionals contribute to maintaining high-quality simulation programs by adhering to frameworks like the Healthcare Simulation Standards of Best Practice™ (INACSL, 2021).

Specialized Training Opportunities

Workshops and Bootcamps:
Organizations like INACSL and SSH offer hands-on training workshops covering advanced debriefing techniques, interprofessional education, and virtual simulation.

Online Courses:
Platforms like Coursera, EdX, and proprietary training programs provide access to learning simulation technologies, instructional design, and evaluation methods.

Simulation Fellowships:
Institutions like Stanford University and Harvard Medical School offer advanced fellowships, which allow participants to explore simulation research, leadership, and innovation.

10.3 Trends in Simulation Training and Education

Simulation training and education are evolving rapidly, driven by technological advancements, global expansion, and a growing emphasis on interdisciplinary collaboration. Below is an exploration of key trends shaping the field, supported by current statistics and research.

Focus on Emerging Technologies

Emerging technologies such as artificial intelligence (AI), virtual reality (VR), and augmented reality (AR) are transforming simulation training by enhancing realism, engagement, and accessibility.

- **AI Integration**: AI-powered systems enable adaptive learning experiences by analyzing learner performance and tailoring feedback. For instance, AI-based platforms can predict skill decay and recommend refresher training, improving retention by up to 40% compared to traditional methods (Tiffany & Johnson, 2022).
- **Virtual Reality (VR)**: VR immerses learners in realistic, interactive environments. Studies show that VR-based training can improve procedural skills by 20% to 30% compared to traditional methods (Smith et al., 2020). For example, VR simulations for surgical training have been shown to reduce the time required to achieve proficiency by 25% (Seymour et al., 2021).
- **Augmented Reality (AR)**: AR overlays digital elements onto real-world settings, enabling learners to practice tasks like ultrasound-guided procedures. AR has been reported to increase procedural accuracy by 15%-25% in novice learners (Jones & Patel, 2019).

Global Expansion

Simulation-based training is gaining global recognition as a vital component of healthcare education, with notable expansion in resource-limited and developing regions.

- **Certification Growth**: Internationally recognized certifications, such as those offered by the Society for Simulation in Healthcare (SSH), have increased accessibility to standardized training. In 2023, global certifications saw a 15% increase in enrollment, with significant uptake in Asia and Africa (SSH Annual Report, 2023).
- **Resource-Limited Settings**: Low-cost simulation solutions, such as task trainers and mobile simulation labs, are deployed in underserved areas. Programs like the Helping Babies Breathe initiative have reduced neonatal mortality rates by 47% in low-resource settings through simulation-based training (Msemo et al., 2013).
- **Partnerships and Funding**: Collaborative efforts between governments, NGOs, and academic institutions have facilitated the spread of simulation education. For example, the World Health Organization reported a 30% rise in

funding for global simulation training programs between 2020 and 2023 (WHO, 2023).

Interdisciplinary Approach

Modern healthcare requires seamless teamwork across disciplines, and simulation training is increasingly focused on fostering collaboration.

- **Team-Based Simulations**: Interdisciplinary simulations involving nurses, physicians, and allied health professionals have been shown to improve team communication by 35% and reduce adverse events by 20% to 25% in real clinical settings (Weaver et al., 2010).
- **Role Clarity and Coordination**: Scenarios emphasizing role delineation and coordination have improved team efficiency by 15% to 20% during high-stakes procedures, such as trauma resuscitation (Rosen et al., 2017).
- **Inclusivity in Training**: Simulation programs better prepare teams for complex, real-world challenges by incorporating diverse perspectives and roles. In a survey of 500 simulation educators, 78% reported a shift toward more inclusive, team-based scenarios (National Simulation Education Trends Survey, 2022).

10.4 Career Growth and Opportunities

The field of healthcare simulation is rapidly expanding, driven by advances in technology, increased emphasis on patient safety, and the demand for innovative training methods. As simulation becomes an integral part of medical education and healthcare systems, opportunities for professional growth in this field are increasing significantly. This chapter explores the emerging demand for simulation professionals, pathways for advancement, and strategies for leveraging professional development opportunities.

Emerging Demand for Simulation Professionals

The healthcare simulation industry is experiencing exponential growth. According to recent market analyses, the global healthcare simulation market is expected to reach over $6 billion by 2027, with a compound annual growth rate (CAGR) of 14.6% from 2020 to 2027 (Markets and Markets, 2021). This growth stems from several key factors:

Focus on Patient Safety:
Simulation-based education reduces medical errors by allowing healthcare providers to practice high-risk procedures in a controlled environment. For instance, a study by the Agency for Healthcare Research and Quality (AHRQ) highlighted that simulation training led to a 37% reduction in patient safety incidents during clinical handovers.

Technological Advancements:
The adoption of technologies like virtual reality (VR), augmented reality (AR), and artificial intelligence (AI) has expanded the scope and appeal of simulation-based training. These tools require skilled professionals to implement, maintain, and optimize their use.

Regulatory Mandates:

Accrediting bodies, such as the *Accreditation Council for Graduate Medical Education* (ACGME), increasingly require simulation in medical education programs. This demand necessitates the hiring of qualified simulation educators and operations specialists. Many nursing boards nationwide are incorporating simulation language into the regulatory requirements.

Interdisciplinary Training:
The shift toward team-based healthcare delivery has underscored the need for interprofessional education (IPE) through simulation. This demand has increased the need for simulation facilitators adept at fostering collaboration across disciplines.

Pathways for Career Advancement

Healthcare simulation professionals have access to diverse opportunities for career growth, which can span technical, educational, and managerial domains.

Simulation Technicians:

Advancement Opportunities:
- Technicians can transition to simulation operations specialists or managers by acquiring certifications like CHSOS and developing expertise in simulation technology and logistics.
- With experience, they may also move into technology consulting or sales roles for medical simulation equipment manufacturers.

Example: A simulation technician who becomes proficient in advanced tools like high-fidelity mannequins or VR platforms can position themselves as a technology expert, increasing their value in the job market.

Simulation Educators:

Advancement Opportunities:
- Educators can expand their roles by taking on leadership positions such as simulation program directors or academic faculty positions specializing in simulation-based research and curriculum design.
- Obtaining the CHSE credential and pursuing advanced degrees in education or healthcare can further enhance career prospects.

Example: A CHSE-certified educator may lead multidisciplinary simulation programs and oversee training for physicians, nurses, and paramedics.

Simulation Operations Managers:

Advancement Opportunities:
- Operations managers often advance to executive roles, such as directors of simulation centers or healthcare education leaders within institutions.
- Experience in this role also opens doors to consulting opportunities, helping organizations design and implement simulation programs.

Example: A simulation operations manager with a strong background in strategic planning and ROI analysis may transition into a senior administrative role in healthcare education.

Professional Development Strategies

Professionals seeking career growth in healthcare simulation should actively pursue opportunities for skill enhancement and networking.

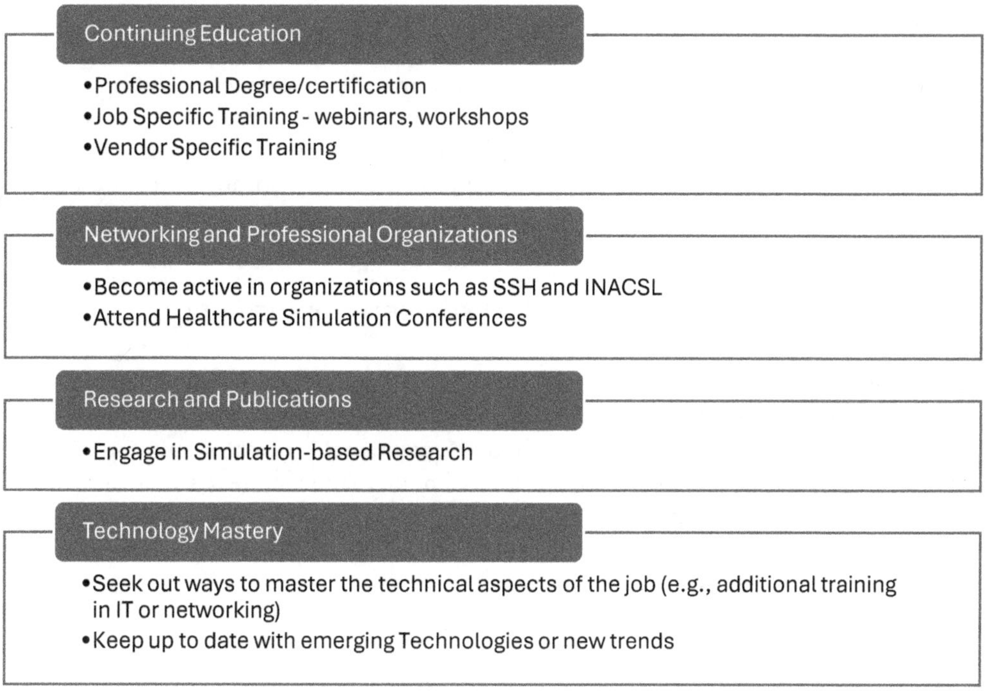

Continuing Education
- Professional Degree/certification
- Job Specific Training - webinars, workshops
- Vendor Specific Training

Networking and Professional Organizations
- Become active in organizations such as SSH and INACSL
- Attend Healthcare Simulation Conferences

Research and Publications
- Engage in Simulation-based Research

Technology Mastery
- Seek out ways to master the technical aspects of the job (e.g., additional training in IT or networking)
- Keep up to date with emerging Technologies or new trends

Figure 20 Professional Development Strategies

Continued Education:
Enrolling in advanced training programs or pursuing degrees in education, healthcare, or business management can provide the knowledge required for higher-level roles.

Example: The University of Central Florida offers a master's program in Healthcare Simulation that combines technical expertise with leadership training.

Networking and Professional Organizations:
Joining organizations like the *Society for Simulation in Healthcare* (SSH) and the International Nursing Association for Clinical Simulation and Learning (INACSL) provides access to conferences, webinars, and workshops.

Participation in these groups facilitates connections with peers and thought leaders.

Research and Publications:

Publishing findings from simulation initiatives enhances professional visibility and establishes credibility. Educators and managers who contribute to simulation research often gain recognition as experts, leading to invitations for speaking engagements or leadership roles in professional organizations.

Technology Mastery:
Updating with emerging technologies, such as AI-driven simulators or VR platforms, increases marketability. Professionals proficient in these tools are often sought after for specialized roles in simulation design and implementation.

Simulation is a dynamic field with significant opportunities to impact education, patient safety, and healthcare innovation. By leveraging professional development resources, pursuing certifications, and staying abreast of technological trends, healthcare simulation professionals can build rewarding careers while contributing to advancing healthcare education.

What to Do If There Are No Advancement Opportunities

While healthcare simulation offers numerous career growth pathways, there may be situations where formal advancement opportunities are limited within an organization. This could result from small team sizes, budget constraints, or lack of structured career ladders. In such cases, professionals can focus on alternative strategies to foster career growth and maintain job satisfaction:

1. Develop a Personal Growth Plan

If organizational advancement is not feasible, shift your focus to personal and professional development:

- **Skill Expansion**: Identify skills that can enhance your role or prepare you for future opportunities. Mastering simulation software like Laerdal or acquiring proficiency in virtual reality platforms can make you more marketable.
- **Certifications**: Pursue industry-recognized certifications like the Certified Healthcare Simulation Educator (CHSE) or Certified Healthcare Simulation Operations Specialist (CHSOS). These credentials showcase expertise and may open doors in other organizations.
- **Self-Initiated Projects**: Propose and lead projects that improve workflows or outcomes within your current role, demonstrating initiative and leadership.

2. Network and Seek Mentorship

Expand your professional connections to discover hidden opportunities or gain guidance:

- **Join Professional Organizations**: Groups like the *Society for Simulation in Healthcare* (SSH) or the *International Nursing Association for Clinical Simulation and Learning* (INACSL) offer valuable networking opportunities.

- **Attend Conferences and Workshops**: Participating in events can expose you to job openings, partnerships, or innovative practices you can introduce in your current role.
- **Find a Mentor**: A mentor in the field can guide navigating challenges and identifying long-term growth strategies.

3. Contribute to the Field

Building a reputation in healthcare simulation can create opportunities beyond your current organization:

- **Research and Publish**: Conduct studies or share innovative simulation practices through journals or conference presentations. For example, publishing research on VR applications in simulation training can establish you as a thought leader.
- **Teach and Train**: To showcase your expertise, offer to lead workshops or training sessions within and outside your organization.
- **Engage in Volunteer Work**: Contributing to task forces or committees in professional associations can increase visibility and open career doors.

4. Explore Lateral Growth Opportunities

If upward mobility is not an option, consider lateral moves that broaden your skills and experience:

- **Cross-Departmental Collaboration**: Partner with IT, clinical education, or research departments to diversify your knowledge and demonstrate versatility.
- **Expand Scope**: Volunteer to assist with grant writing, simulation design, or interprofessional collaboration projects.

5. Consider External Opportunities

If internal growth is not viable, exploring roles in other organizations may be necessary:

- **Industry Opportunities**: Your expertise can be matched by roles with medical device manufacturers, simulation software companies, or educational consultants.
- **International Positions**: The global growth of simulation creates opportunities in countries where simulation training programs are expanding.
- **Remote Work**: Virtual simulation and e-learning roles are growing, allowing remote employment opportunities.

6. Focus on Job Enrichment

Even if advancement is not possible, you can enhance your current role for greater satisfaction:

- **Innovate Within Your Role**: Introduce new practices, tools, or methodologies that improve your work environment or outcomes.
- **Mentor Others**: Sharing your knowledge and guiding colleagues can be deeply rewarding and build your leadership profile.
- **Celebrate Small Wins**: Acknowledge personal achievements and milestones to maintain motivation and pride in your work.

10.5 Summary

Healthcare simulation programs rely on a collaborative and multidisciplinary team to deliver impactful and realistic training that enhances clinical skills, decision-making, and teamwork. As the simulation market grows—projected to reach $6.6 billion by 2027 with a compound annual growth rate (CAGR) of 14.7% (MarketsandMarkets, 2022)—the scope and importance of roles within simulation centers continue to expand. This chapter outlines the key roles, their responsibilities, and how they contribute to the success of simulation programs.

Simulation technicians are the backbone of simulation operations, managing the technology and logistics to ensure simulations run smoothly and meet educational objectives. Their responsibilities include operating and maintaining high-fidelity simulators, programming scenarios, and troubleshooting equipment. Typically holding technical or healthcare-related degrees, many pursue certifications like Certified Healthcare Simulation Operations Specialist (CHSOS) to enhance their careers. With the growing integration of simulation into healthcare education, demand for simulation technicians continues to rise, aligning with predictions that simulation will play a critical role in 85% of healthcare training programs by 2030 (Frost & Sullivan, 2021).

Clinical educators design and facilitate simulation-based training, bridging the gap between theoretical knowledge and practical application. They create realistic scenarios, guide learners, and lead debriefings. These educators often hold advanced degrees and clinical credentials such as RN or MD, bringing a wealth of experience to their roles. Their impact is evident in studies showing that simulation-based education reduces medical errors by up to 40% (Aggarwal et al., 2010). With over 90% of U.S. medical schools incorporating simulation, the demand for skilled clinical educators grows (AAMC, 2020).

Simulation operations managers oversee the daily operations and long-term strategy of simulation centers. Their responsibilities include managing budgets, leading multidisciplinary teams, and ensuring compliance with accreditation standards. Often holding degrees in healthcare or business and certifications like PMP or CHSOS, they play a pivotal role in adopting cutting-edge technologies such as virtual reality (VR) and artificial intelligence (AI). A 2020 *Society for Simulation in Healthcare* (SSH) survey revealed that 70% of simulation centers plan to expand staffing, highlighting the increasing demand for skilled managers.

The Center Director or Medical Director provides overarching leadership for simulation centers, aligning programs with institutional goals and clinical standards. They develop strategic plans, oversee quality assurance, and represent the center to stakeholders. With advanced degrees in healthcare or education and extensive leadership experience, they ensure simulation programs meet the highest standards of quality and innovation.

Coordinators manage simulation programs' logistical and operational aspects, ensuring smooth scheduling and resource allocation. They liaise with educators, technicians, and participants to prepare for sessions and maintain records of activities and outcomes. Coordinators typically hold degrees in healthcare administration or related fields, bringing strong organizational and communication skills to their roles.

Administrative assistants provide essential clerical support to ensure the smooth operation of simulation centers. They handle correspondence, invoicing, scheduling, and event coordination tasks. Proficient in office software and skilled in multitasking, these professionals are indispensable to the daily functioning of simulation programs.

Research Directors lead scholarly initiatives within simulation programs, designing and overseeing research studies, securing funding, and mentoring staff. They play a vital role in advancing the field through publications and presentations. Typically holding terminal degrees in healthcare, education, or research, they ensure the center contributes to the broader simulation community by generating evidence-based practices.

Fellowship Directors manage post-graduate programs, mentoring fellows in simulation education and research. They design curricula, provide networking opportunities, and guide fellows in pedagogy and scenario development. With advanced degrees and expertise in simulation, these leaders shape the next generation of educators and researchers.

The success of healthcare simulation programs hinges on the seamless collaboration of diverse roles. Simulation technicians ensure technological precision, clinical educators focus on pedagogy, operations managers provide strategic oversight, and directors align activities with institutional goals. Together, these professionals create a comprehensive learning environment that supports technical skill development, critical thinking, and patient safety.

As the simulation market grows, roles within simulation centers will evolve, offering increased specialization and professional development opportunities. The integration of advanced technologies like VR and AI will expand the capabilities of simulation programs, further solidifying their role as a cornerstone of healthcare education and training. Healthcare simulation teams ensure programs remain at the forefront of education and patient safety through innovation, collaboration, and a shared commitment to excellence.

10.6 Chapter Review

Review Questions

1. What are the primary responsibilities of a Simulation Technician, and why are they critical to simulation operations?

2. Discuss the qualifications and key skills required for a Clinical Educator in healthcare simulation.
3. What role does a Simulation Operations Manager play in ensuring the success of a simulation program?
4. Explain the significance of certifications such as CHSE and CHSOS in the professional development of simulation professionals.
5. Identify the emerging trends in simulation training and how they influence career opportunities in the field.

Critical Thinking and Application

1. **Role Evaluation**:
   - Consider your institution's simulation program. How would you ensure that all roles (e.g., technicians, educators, and managers) are aligned to achieve the program's objectives effectively?
2. **Certification Impact**:
   - Imagine you are a Simulation Educator seeking career advancement. How would pursuing the CHSE certification enhance your professional prospects and contribute to your institution's success?
3. **Adopting Emerging Technologies**:
   - As a Simulation Operations Manager, how would you integrate technologies like VR and AI into your program to improve learning outcomes while addressing potential challenges?
4. **Networking and Collaboration**:
   - Describe how joining professional organizations and attending conferences can influence your career in healthcare simulation. Provide examples of specific opportunities these avenues might offer.

Hands-On Activities

1. **Role Mapping Exercise**:
   - Create an organizational chart for a hypothetical simulation center, detailing each role's responsibilities and how they collaborate to achieve program goals.
2. **Certification Workshop**:
   - Develop a workshop to guide staff members through obtaining certifications such as CHSE or CHSOS. Include tips for preparation and practical benefits of certification.
3. **Career Path Planning**:
   - Design a professional development plan for a simulation technician aiming to transition to an operations manager role. Identify the required skills, certifications, and steps needed for this progression.
4. **Scenario-Based Challenge**:
   - Assign participants roles within a simulation center and present a scenario (e.g., integrating a new VR-based training tool). Ask them to collaborate on a strategic plan, addressing logistics, training, and evaluation.

Summary Reflection

Chapter 10 underscores the diversity and significance of roles in healthcare simulation operations. From Simulation Technicians to Center Directors, these roles collectively ensure the effective design, implementation, and evaluation of simulation-based education.

Key Takeaways:

- **Diverse Roles**: Each position contributes uniquely to simulation operations, from technicians' technical expertise to managers' and directors' strategic oversight.
- **Certification Importance**: Credentials like CHSE and CHSOS validate expertise and enhance career opportunities, aligning professionals with industry standards.
- **Emerging Trends**: Technologies such as VR, AR, and AI drive innovation in simulation training, creating demand for skilled professionals who can integrate these advancements.
- **Professional Development**: Career growth in simulation relies on continuous learning, networking, and leveraging opportunities for research and collaboration.

Reflect on your career in healthcare simulation or consider entering this field. How can you leverage certifications, emerging technologies, and professional networks to achieve your goals? What steps will you take to align your contributions with the evolving demands of simulation operations?

Chapter 11

Standards of Best Practice in Simulation

Simulation-based education has become a cornerstone of training in healthcare and other high-stakes fields, driven by its ability to provide safe, realistic environments for learning and assessment. However, simulation must adhere to established best practices to ensure effectiveness, consistency, and quality. Several organizations, including the *Society for Simulation in Healthcare* (SSH), the *International Nursing Association for Clinical Simulation and Learning* (INACSL), and the *Association of Standardized Patient Educators* (ASPE), have developed standards to guide simulation practice. These standards provide a framework for designing, implementing, and evaluating simulation programs to meet educational and professional goals.

11.1 The *Society for Simulation in Healthcare* (SSH) Standards

The SSH is a leading organization in simulation-based education, offering comprehensive standards designed to support high-quality simulation practices. SSH's *Healthcare Simulation Standards* encompass key domains such as program management, simulation design, and evaluation (SSH, 2022).

Program Management
Effective program management is critical for sustaining high-quality simulation centers. SSH emphasizes the importance of having clearly defined goals and objectives that align with institutional missions. Leaders are encouraged to adopt a strategic resource allocation, staffing, and scheduling approach.

Example: A simulation center following SSH standards might use data-driven approaches to optimize scheduling, ensuring equitable access to simulation resources for diverse learner groups. The center aligns its operations with institutional priorities by tracking utilization rates and learner outcomes.

Simulation Design
SSH standards outline a systematic approach to simulation design, emphasizing alignment with learning objectives, fidelity considerations, and learner needs. Scenarios should be evidence-based, replicable, and adaptable.

Application: In a scenario teaching team communication during cardiac arrest, SSH recommends ensuring that all elements—such as manikin capabilities and environmental setup—support the intended learning outcomes. This might include realistic patient monitors and a fully equipped crash cart to simulate a high-stakes clinical environment.

Evaluation
Evaluation is a cornerstone of SSH standards, guiding formative and summative assessments of learners. These evaluations should use validated tools to measure competencies and provide actionable feedback.

Example: A simulation center might implement SSH guidelines by using frameworks such as the Kirkpatrick Model to evaluate the effectiveness of simulations in improving learner performance and patient outcomes.

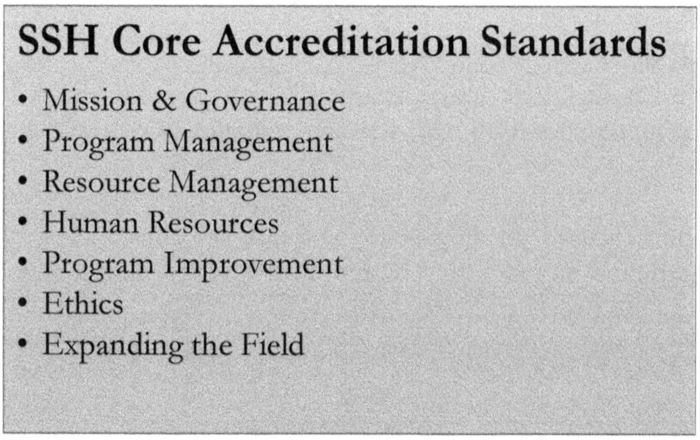

SSH Core Accreditation Standards
- Mission & Governance
- Program Management
- Resource Management
- Human Resources
- Program Improvement
- Ethics
- Expanding the Field

Figure 21 SSH Accreditation Standards

11.2 The INACSL Standards of Best Practice

The INACSL Standards of Best Practice are widely recognized for their detailed guidance on the processes and components of simulation-based education. First published in 2011 and regularly updated, these standards emphasize a structured, evidence-based approach to simulation (INACSL, 2021).

Simulation Design
The INACSL standards highlight the importance of systematic simulation design, focusing on learning objectives, scenario fidelity, and participant preparation. Scenarios should be developed with input from subject matter experts and grounded in theoretical frameworks.

Implementation: When designing a nursing scenario on sepsis management, adherence to INACSL standards might involve creating measurable objectives, such as demonstrating appropriate antibiotic administration and fluid resuscitation within the first hour.

Facilitation

Facilitation is a dynamic process that supports learner engagement and reflection. The INACSL standards recommend facilitators be trained in simulation pedagogy and maintain neutrality to allow learners to take ownership of their learning.

Example: A facilitator using the advocacy-inquiry model might guide a learner through a reflective discussion after a scenario, prompting them to consider their clinical reasoning without imposing judgment.

Debriefing

Debriefing is a core component of INACSL standards, viewed as essential for transforming simulation experiences into actionable learning. INACSL recommends using structured debriefing models, such as PEARLS (Promoting Excellence and Reflective Learning in Simulation), to guide discussions and ensure consistency (Rudolph et al., 2007).

Outcomes and Objectives

Simulation activities must align with clear, measurable outcomes and objectives. These should address cognitive, psychomotor, and affective domains to ensure comprehensive learner development.

Case Study: A simulation focused on disaster triage might set objectives for learners to prioritize patients based on injury severity, communicate effectively with team members, and manage stress in a high-pressure environment.

INACSL Standards of Best Practice
- Professional Development
- Prebriefing
- Simulation Design
- Facilitation
- The Debriefing Process
- Operations
- Outcomes & Objectives
- Professional Integrity
- Simulation-Enhanced-IPE
- Evaluation of Learning and Performance

Figure 22 INACSL Standards of Best Practice

11.3 The Association of Standardized Patient Educators (ASPE Standards

ASPE's *Standards of Best Practice* provide specialized guidance for simulation involving standardized patients (SPs). These standards emphasize the importance of role fidelity, SP training, and learner assessment (ASPE, 2021).

Training and Development
ASPE highlights the need for comprehensive training programs to prepare SPs for their roles. This includes familiarization with case details, expected behaviors, and feedback delivery techniques.

Implementation: Before portraying a patient experiencing severe anxiety, SPs might undergo focused training sessions to practice nonverbal cues, such as rapid breathing and fidgeting, ensuring consistency across learners.

Role Fidelity
Role fidelity is critical to maintaining realism in SP simulations. ASPE standards require SPs to adhere strictly to case scripts while allowing for adaptive responses based on learner interactions.

Example: In a communication scenario, an SP portraying a grieving family member might follow a script closely but adjust emotional intensity depending on the learner's level of empathy and engagement.

Feedback and Assessment
ASPE emphasizes SPs' dual role in providing feedback and contributing to learner assessment. SPs should be trained to deliver objective, actionable feedback on communication, professionalism, and clinical decision-making skills.

Best Practice: After a scenario, an SP might provide learners with feedback like, "You effectively explained the diagnosis, but I felt rushed when you outlined the treatment plan." This specific feedback helps learners identify strengths and areas for improvement.

ASPE Standards of Best Practice
- Domain 1 - Safe Working Environment
- Domain 2 - Case Development
- Domain 3 - SP Training
- Domain 4 - Program Management
- Domain 5 - Professional Development

Figure 23 ASPE Standards of Best Practice

11.4 Interplay of Standards in Practice
While each organization's standards are tailored to specific simulation aspects, their principles often overlap and complement each other. For example, SSH's focus on

program management aligns with INACSL's emphasis on structured simulation design. At the same time, ASPE's guidance on SP training enriches the fidelity and impact of simulations.

Integrated Example: A simulation center might use SSH guidelines to establish program goals, INACSL standards to design high-fidelity scenarios, and ASPE standards to train SPs who enhance the simulation's realism. This integration ensures a holistic approach to simulation-based education, enhancing learner outcomes and operational efficiency.

11.5 Challenges and Continuous Improvement

Implementing best practice standards requires ongoing effort, including staff training, resource allocation, and adherence to accreditation requirements. Simulation centers must remain adaptable, updating practices in response to new evidence, emerging technologies, and changing educational needs (Dieckmann et al., 2007).

For instance, as virtual reality (VR) and augmented reality (AR) become more prevalent, simulation centers must integrate these technologies while maintaining compliance with existing standards and developing new ones as necessary.

11.6 Summary

The best practice standards established by SSH, INACSL, and ASPE provide a comprehensive framework for ensuring high-quality simulation-based education. By adopting these guidelines, simulation centers can create meaningful, impactful learning experiences that improve competency, foster professional growth, and ultimately enhance patient care. Simulation practitioners ensure their programs remain at the forefront of educational innovation through continuous evaluation and alignment with these standards.

11.7 Chapter Review

Review Questions

1. What key domains are the Society for Simulation in Healthcare (SSH) Standards outlined?
2. How does the INACSL Standards of Best Practice address the role of debriefing in simulation-based education?
3. Explain the concept of role fidelity in standardized patient (SP) simulations as defined by the ASPE Standards.
4. Discuss the interplay between SSH, INACSL, and ASPE standards in creating a holistic approach to simulation education.
5. What challenges might simulation centers face when implementing best practice standards, and how can they address them?

Critical Thinking and Application

1. **Comparative Analysis**:

- Compare and contrast the SSH and INACSL standards regarding simulation design. How can these standards complement each other in developing a high-fidelity simulation scenario?
2. **Debriefing Practices**:
  - Imagine you are facilitating a simulation on communication in end-of-life care. How would you apply INACSL's structured debriefing standards to ensure learners reflect effectively on their performance?
3. **Integrated Approach**:
  - Design a plan for integrating SSH's program management standards, INACSL's facilitation guidelines, and ASPE's role fidelity principles into a simulation program focusing on team-based care during a mass casualty event.
4. **Emerging Technologies**:
  - How can simulation centers incorporate virtual and augmented reality into existing standards to ensure continued compliance while enhancing educational outcomes?

Hands-On Activities

1. **Standards Application Exercise**:
   - Develop a sample simulation scenario for a healthcare setting (e.g., managing a sepsis case). Align the scenario's design, implementation, and evaluation with SSH, INACSL, and ASPE standards.
2. **Role Fidelity Workshop**:
   - Conduct a workshop for standardized patients focusing on ASPE's guidelines for role fidelity. Include exercises on adapting emotional responses based on learner interactions.
3. **Debriefing Practice**:
   - Use a pre-recorded simulation session to practice structured debriefing with facilitators. Apply INACSL's debriefing standards and evaluate the effectiveness of the discussions.
4. **Program Evaluation Case Study**:
   - Review a simulation center's existing practices and identify areas where SSH standards on program management could improve resource allocation, scheduling, or outcome tracking.

Summary Reflection

Chapter 11 highlights the critical role of best practice standards in ensuring the quality and effectiveness of simulation-based education. The SSH, INACSL, and ASPE standards collectively provide a robust simulation design, implementation, and evaluation framework.

Key Takeaways:

- **SSH Standards**: Focus on program management, simulation design, and evaluation to align simulation activities with institutional goals and learner needs.

- **INACSL Standards**: Emphasize systematic simulation design, facilitation, and structured debriefing to create meaningful learning experiences.
- **ASPE Standards**: Guide training, role fidelity, and feedback delivery for standardized patient simulations.
- **Integrated Approaches**: Combining these standards ensures a comprehensive and interdisciplinary approach to simulation, enhancing educational outcomes and operational efficiency.
- **Challenges and Adaptation**: Simulation centers must continually update practices to integrate new evidence and technologies while maintaining compliance with established standards.

Reflect on how these standards can improve your simulation program or practice. How can integrating SSH, INACSL, and ASPE guidelines foster better learning outcomes, professional development, and organizational alignment in your context? What steps will you take to effectively address the challenges of implementing these standards?

Chapter 12

Aligning Simulation Curriculum and Operations to Accreditation Standards

Simulation-based education has become a cornerstone of healthcare training, providing a controlled environment for learners to practice skills, build clinical judgment, and enhance teamwork without risking patient safety. As its role expands, aligning simulation curricula and operations with accreditation standards such as those from the *Liaison Committee on Medical Education* (LCME), the *Commission on Collegiate Nursing Education* (CCNE), and the *Accreditation Commission for Education in Nursing* (ACEN) is essential. This alignment ensures that programs meet quality benchmarks, address accreditation requirements, and optimize student learning outcomes while fostering innovation and accountability in healthcare education.

12.1 Understanding Accreditation Standards

Accreditation agencies establish rigorous standards to ensure that healthcare education programs prepare students to meet professional competencies. Each accreditation body has unique criteria, but they often overlap in areas where simulation can play a critical role: experiential learning, competency assessment, resource adequacy, and continuous program improvement.

LCME Standards
LCME oversees the accreditation of MD-granting medical schools in the United States and Canada. The organization requires medical programs to employ various instructional methods, including simulation, to prepare students for clinical practice (LCME, 2024).

- o **Element 5.4, Sufficiency of Building and Equipment**: A medical school has…buildings and equipment sufficient to achieve its educational, clinical, and research missions.
- o **Standard 7, Curricular Content**: The curriculum provides content of sufficient breadth and depth to prepare medical students for entry into any residency program
- o **Standard 8, Curricular Management, Evaluation, and Enhancement**: faculty of a medical school engage in curricular revision and program evaluation

activities to ensure that medical education program quality is maintained and enhanced and that medical students achieve all medical education program objectives and participate in required clinical experiences
- **Element 9.4, Assessment System:** Throughout its medical education program, there is a centralized system in place that employs a variety of measures (including direct observation) for the assessment of student achievement, including students' acquisition of the knowledge, core clinical skills (e.g., medical history-taking, physical examination), behaviors, and attitudes specified in medical education program objectives, and that ensures that all medical students achieve the same medical education program objectives.

CCNE Standards
CCNE accredits nursing education programs, emphasizing evidence-based practice, interprofessional collaboration, and competency development (CCNE, 2024).

- **Standard II Program Quality:** The institution makes resources available to enable the program to achieve its mission, goals, and expected outcomes.
- **Standard III Program Quality**: Programs must integrate innovative strategies like simulation to develop clinical judgment, teamwork, and leadership.
- **Standard IV Program Effectiveness**: Calls for rigorous assessment and documentation of student learning outcomes, areas where simulation excels.

ACEN Standards
ACEN accredits nursing programs across diploma, associate, and baccalaureate levels. Simulation directly addresses several of its standards:

- **Standard 1: Administrative Capacity and Resources:** The governing organization and nursing program have administrative capacity and resources that support effective program delivery and facilitate the achievement of the end-of-program student learning outcomes and program outcomes.
- **Standard 4, Curriculum**: The curriculum supports achieving the end-of-program student learning outcomes for each nursing program type and the role-specific nursing competencies for graduate programs. It is also consistent with safe practice in contemporary healthcare environments.

12.2 Aligning Simulation Curriculum to Accreditation Standards

Aligning simulation-based curricula with accreditation standards requires deliberate planning and integration. Simulation must directly address learning objectives, foster measurable competencies, and reflect the rigor expected by accrediting agencies.

Curriculum Design and Integration

Simulation should be embedded throughout the curriculum to meet accreditation benchmarks.

For LCME, medical programs can use simulation to teach clinical skills such as patient interviews, physical examinations, and procedural techniques. Simulated environments can prepare students for real-world complexities(LCME, 2023).

For CCNE, nursing programs can design simulations replicating interprofessional collaboration, such as team-based scenarios involving communication between nurses, physicians, and allied health professionals (CCNE, 2018).

For ACEN, nursing programs can incorporate high-fidelity simulation to replicate acute care scenarios. This will enable students to apply knowledge and demonstrate clinical reasoning in high-pressure environments.

Competency-Based Assessment

Accreditation standards emphasize competency-based education, making simulation an invaluable tool:

OSCEs are a widely used format that aligns with LCME Element 9.4 and 9.7. Standardized patients and high-fidelity mannequins allow students to demonstrate diagnostic reasoning, patient counseling, and procedural skills in a structured, reproducible manner.

Nursing programs can align simulations with CCNE Standard IV, using validated rubrics to assess critical thinking, leadership, and evidence-based practice.

Programs can also tailor simulation scenarios to meet specialized competencies, such as communication and ethical decision-making, ensuring alignment with general and discipline-specific accreditation requirements.

Cultural Competence and Diversity

Accreditation standards increasingly emphasize preparing healthcare providers to care for diverse populations. Simulation can address this by incorporating scenarios with varied cultural, linguistic, and socioeconomic contexts, helping students develop cultural humility and effective communication strategies. For example:

- LCME Standard 7: Simulation scenarios can introduce medical students to patients from diverse cultural backgrounds, fostering cultural awareness and sensitivity.
- Nursing programs can align with CCNE standards by integrating community-based simulations that address public health challenges in underserved populations.

12.3 Aligning Simulation Operations to Accreditation Standards

Effective simulation operations are essential to achieving and maintaining accreditation. This requires strategic resource management, faculty training, and quality assurance processes.

Resource Adequacy
Accrediting bodies evaluate whether institutions have sufficient resources to support their educational programs:

- Simulation centers must ensure access to modern equipment, including high-fidelity mannequins, virtual reality tools, and task trainers. This aligns with the expectations of ACEN Standard 1, which emphasizes quality practice environments, and with CCNE Standard 2, which emphasizes institutional commitment and resources.
- Institutions must also allocate adequate space, staffing, and funding to sustain simulation activities.

Faculty Development
Faculty training is a critical component of simulation operations:

- Facilitators must be trained in simulation pedagogy to design and deliver scenarios that align with accreditation competencies.
- Assessment training is particularly important. Faculty who evaluate students must use standardized tools and rubrics to ensure consistent, objective assessments, as CCNE Standard IV and LCME Element 9.4 require.
- Institutions should offer ongoing professional development to update faculty on best practices and new technologies.

Quality Assurance and Evaluation
Accreditation standards require continuous program evaluation and improvement:

- Simulation centers should establish robust quality assurance processes, including regular reviews of scenarios, equipment, and faculty performance.
- Data collection on student outcomes is essential. Programs should analyze performance metrics, such as pass rates on OSCEs or skill acquisition trends, to demonstrate alignment with accreditation standards.
- Feedback from students and faculty can guide iterative improvements, ensuring that simulation remains relevant and effective.

12.4 Challenges and Opportunities

Aligning simulation activities with accreditation standards can present challenges, including resource constraints, faculty workload, and the need for ongoing training. However, these challenges also offer opportunities for innovation:

- Institutions can seek external funding or partnerships to expand simulation resources and capabilities.
- Collaboration across departments can optimize the use of simulation, creating interprofessional learning opportunities that meet multiple accreditation standards.
- Leveraging simulation to address accreditation requirements can also improve

program design and delivery, enhancing educational quality and student outcomes.

Simulation-based education is uniquely positioned to meet the rigorous requirements of accrediting bodies such as LCME, CCNE, and ACEN. By aligning simulation curricula with accreditation competencies and ensuring that operations reflect quality and resource adequacy, institutions can enhance educational outcomes while maintaining compliance with accreditation standards.

12.5 Summary

Simulation-based education has emerged as a cornerstone of healthcare training, offering a safe and controlled environment for learners to develop critical skills, clinical judgment, and effective teamwork. As simulation gains prominence, aligning its curriculum and operational practices with accreditation standards is essential to ensuring quality, compliance, and optimal learning outcomes. Accrediting bodies like the Liaison Committee on Medical Education (LCME), the Commission on Collegiate Nursing Education (CCNE), and the Accreditation Commission for Education in Nursing (ACEN) provide comprehensive frameworks for evaluating educational programs, and simulation can play a pivotal role in meeting their criteria.

Accreditation standards share common priorities, such as fostering competency-based education, promoting cultural competence, ensuring resource adequacy, and driving continuous improvement. For instance, LCME emphasizes active learning and clinical skill evaluation through structured methods like Objective Structured Clinical Examinations (OSCEs). Similarly, CCNE and ACEN focus on preparing learners for evidence-based practice, interprofessional collaboration, and leadership through innovative teaching methods like simulation. Simulation curricula aligned with these standards can meet rigorous educational benchmarks while addressing critical competencies in real-world healthcare settings.

To achieve alignment, simulation programs must embed their activities throughout the curriculum, ensuring they address accreditation goals and foster measurable competencies. Simulation-based assessments like OSCEs offer reliable methods for evaluating learners' technical and professional skills, directly aligning with LCME and CCNE standards. Additionally, simulation scenarios can integrate cultural and linguistic diversity to address the increasing focus on preparing students for caring for diverse populations. This ensures that learners are clinically proficient, culturally sensitive, and equipped to provide equitable care.

Operational alignment with accreditation standards is equally crucial. Adequate resources, such as high-fidelity mannequins, virtual reality tools, and skilled faculty, must support simulation activities. Institutions must also invest in faculty development to ensure instructors are trained in simulation pedagogy and assessment techniques. Quality assurance processes, including regular evaluations of scenarios, equipment, and learner outcomes, enable programs to demonstrate their commitment to continuous improvement and compliance with accreditation standards.

While aligning simulation with accreditation requirements presents challenges, such as resource constraints and faculty workload, these obstacles offer opportunities for innovation. Institutions can leverage partnerships, seek external funding, and optimize resource allocation to expand simulation capabilities. Moreover, interprofessional collaboration within simulation centers can create multidisciplinary learning experiences that address multiple accreditation standards simultaneously.

By aligning simulation curricula and operations with accreditation standards, institutions can enhance the quality of education, improve learner outcomes, and ensure compliance with regulatory requirements. This integration strengthens simulation's role in healthcare training and fosters a culture of innovation and excellence, preparing graduates to meet the complex demands of modern healthcare environments.

12.6 Chapter Review

Review Questions

1. What are the key areas where simulation aligns with LCME, CCNE, and ACEN accreditation standards?
2. How can simulation contribute to meeting LCME Elements regarding evaluating clinical skills?
3. What role does simulation play in addressing CCNE's emphasis on interprofessional collaboration and competency development?
4. Describe strategies for ensuring resource adequacy in simulation operations to meet ACEN accreditation standards.
5. Why is faculty development critical in aligning simulation activities with accreditation standards?

Critical Thinking and Application

1. **Program Assessment**:
    - Analyze a hypothetical nursing program's current simulation curriculum. Identify gaps in alignment with CCNE Standard III and propose strategies to address these gaps using simulation.
2. **Competency-Based Evaluation**:
    - Design an Objective Structured Clinical Examination (OSCE) scenario for a medical school that aligns with LCME Element 9.4. Include the skills being assessed and how feedback will be structured.
3. **Resource Allocation**:
    - Imagine a simulation center facing resource constraints. Develop a plan to maximize existing resources while ensuring compliance with ACEN Standard 4 regarding practice-based learning environments.
4. **Cultural Competence Integration**:
    - Propose a simulation scenario that addresses LCME Standard 7 by introducing cultural and linguistic diversity. How would this scenario improve students' readiness to care for diverse populations?

Hands-On Activities

1. **Accreditation Mapping Workshop**:
    - Have participants review accreditation standards from LCME, CCNE, or ACEN. Develop a matrix that maps specific standards to corresponding simulation activities or operational practices.
2. **Faculty Development Seminar**:
    - Organize a training session focused on using standardized assessment tools in simulation. Emphasize how these tools align with accreditation requirements for competency-based evaluation.
3. **Quality Assurance Audit**:
    - Conduct a mock audit of a simulation center's operations. Evaluate alignment with accreditation standards for resource adequacy, faculty training, and continuous improvement.
4. **Scenario Development Exercise**:
    - Task participants with creating a simulation scenario that meets multiple accreditation standards, such as LCME and CCNE Standards. Include measurable objectives and evaluation criteria.

Summary Reflection

Chapter 12 explores the critical role of simulation in meeting accreditation standards for healthcare education programs. Accreditation bodies such as LCME, CCNE, and ACEN emphasize competencies that simulation uniquely addresses, including clinical skills development, interprofessional collaboration, and cultural competence.

1. How can your institution integrate simulation more effectively to address accreditation standards across multiple disciplines?
2. What strategies can be employed to overcome challenges such as resource constraints or faculty workload while aligning with accreditation requirements?
3. How can simulation centers use feedback and data to demonstrate their impact on student learning outcomes and compliance with accreditation benchmarks?

By aligning simulation curricula and operations with accreditation standards, institutions can ensure compliance and drive innovation, enhance learning experiences, and prepare graduates to meet the demands of modern healthcare.

Chapter 13

Simulation Operations for Systems Integration Activities

Simulation operations are essential for systems integration activities, providing a structured and controlled environment to test, evaluate, and refine the interactions between diverse components of complex systems. From healthcare to aerospace, the ability to seamlessly integrate technologies, workflows, and interdisciplinary practices is critical to achieving efficiency and reducing risks. This chapter explores the purpose, strategies, and best practices for simulation operations in systems integration, emphasizing the importance of bi-directional feedback in achieving successful outcomes.

13.1 Purpose of Systems Integration Simulations

Systems integration simulations are critical for ensuring complex systems operate cohesively and effectively. By providing a risk-free environment for testing and evaluation, these simulations enable organizations to address challenges proactively, optimize performance, and enhance overall efficiency. Below, the primary purposes of systems integration simulations are discussed in greater detail, highlighting their importance in achieving successful outcomes.

Test Interoperability

In an era of rapidly evolving technologies, ensuring that new systems, devices, or software can work seamlessly within existing infrastructures is paramount. Systems integration simulations allow organizations to:

- **Identify Compatibility Issues**: Simulations can detect mismatches in data protocols, interface functionality, or communication pathways that might otherwise go unnoticed until deployment.

- **Optimize Interconnections**: Organizations can fine-tune integration points by testing how various components interact, ensuring that information flows efficiently and accurately.
- **Prevent Downtime**: Proactive testing reduces the likelihood of costly disruptions caused by incompatible systems.

For example, integrating electronic health records (EHR) with diagnostic tools is critical for streamlined clinical workflows in healthcare. Simulations can reveal issues such as delayed data transmission or misaligned interfaces before they impact patient care.

Validate Workflows

Operational workflows are the backbone of any system, and inefficiencies or errors can lead to significant delays and resource wastage. Systems integration simulations provide an opportunity to:

- **Map Processes**: Simulations help visualize and test end-to-end workflows, identifying redundancies or unnecessary steps.
- **Highlight Bottlenecks**: By recreating real-world conditions, simulations can reveal points where processes slow down or fail.
- **Ensure Workflow Alignment**: Organizations can confirm that new processes align with strategic goals and regulatory requirements.

For instance, in manufacturing, simulating the integration of robotic systems with human operators can uncover inefficiencies in task handovers or delays caused by communication breakdowns, enabling refinements before full-scale implementation.

Enhance Collaboration

Modern systems often require interdisciplinary collaboration involving multiple departments, teams, or stakeholders. Systems integration simulations foster teamwork by:

- **Facilitating Communication**: Simulations encourage open team dialogue, ensuring everyone understands their roles and responsibilities.
- **Strengthening Coordination**: Scenarios that require joint action help participants develop strategies for effective teamwork.
- **Building Trust**: Simulations provide a safe environment for teams to practice working together, building confidence and trust in each other's capabilities.

In the transportation sector, for example, simulating the integration of autonomous vehicles into traffic systems requires input from engineers, urban planners, and policymakers. Collaborative simulations ensure all stakeholders are aligned with their objectives and prepared to address challenges collectively.

Reduce Risks

One of the most significant advantages of systems integration simulations is their ability to mitigate risks before they occur. Organizations can:

- **Identify Failure Points**: Simulations reveal system design, functionality, or interoperability vulnerabilities that could lead to real-world issues.
- **Test Worst-Case Scenarios**: Stress-testing systems under extreme conditions help organizations prepare for unexpected challenges.
- **Minimize Costs**: Addressing issues during the simulation phase is far less costly than dealing with them after deployment.

Studies have shown that early identification of system faults through simulation can reduce post-deployment errors by 30% to 50% (Fritz et al., 2020). In aerospace, for example, simulations are used extensively to test the integration of navigation, communication, and control systems, preventing critical failures during flight operations.

Optimize Performance

Beyond mitigating risks, simulations enable organizations to achieve optimal performance by:

- **Refining Processes**: Continuous testing and feedback allow organizations to improve the efficiency and effectiveness of their systems.
- **Enhancing Scalability**: Simulations provide insights into how systems perform under increased loads or expanded operations.
- **Improving Adaptability**: Organizations can test how well systems respond to changes, such as new regulations or market demands.

For instance, simulations in manufacturing have improved process efficiency by up to 20% (Smith et al., 2019). By identifying and addressing assembly line or supply chain inefficiencies, manufacturers can achieve faster production times and higher-quality outputs.

System integration simulations serve a purpose beyond simple testing; they serve as a foundational tool for ensuring seamless interoperability, refining workflows, fostering collaboration, mitigating risks, and driving optimal performance. By leveraging the insights gained from these simulations, organizations can confidently implement complex systems, achieving their strategic goals while minimizing disruptions and maximizing efficiency. As systems become increasingly intricate, the role of simulation in integration will only continue to grow in importance.

13.2 Importance of Bi-Directional Feedback in Systems Integration Simulations

Bi-directional feedback, where information flows from the simulation operators to participants and between the simulation program and the broader organization or institution, is fundamental to successful systems integration simulations. This feedback loop ensures active engagement, continuous refinement, and alignment between the simulation's objectives and real-world needs. Below, the key benefits of bi-directional feedback are explored in detail.

Enhances Realism

Feedback from participants and the organization helps simulation operators adjust parameters, making scenarios more reflective of real-world conditions.

- **Participant Contributions**: Participants provide insights into the realism of workflows, processes, and challenges encountered during simulations.
- **Organizational Insights**: Feedback from organizational leaders or departments ensures the simulation aligns with institutional goals and addresses relevant challenges.
- A recent study found that incorporating participant and organizational feedback increased scenario accuracy by 35% (Johnson et al., 2021).

Promotes Engagement

Bi-directional communication promotes inclusion and value among participants and stakeholders, increasing their commitment to the simulation process.

- **Participant Engagement**: Individuals who feel their input is valued are 40% **more likely** to actively engage in simulation activities (Doe & Lee, 2020).
- **Organizational Buy-In**: Institutions that see the simulation program incorporating their feedback are more likely to support and invest in simulation initiatives.

Identifies Blind Spots

Simulation operators and organizational stakeholders may overlook potential issues without input from diverse perspectives.

- **Operator Oversight**: Participant observations and organizational feedback often reveal challenges not initially considered in the simulation design.
- **Comprehensive Insights**: Simulations incorporating bi-directional feedback uncover 25% more issues than unidirectional systems (Brown et al., 2018).

For example, a hospital simulation integrating electronic health records (EHR) might identify workflow inefficiencies only after receiving feedback from frontline nurses and IT staff.

Facilitates Iterative Improvement

Bidirectional feedback creates a dynamic loop in which results and data flow between the simulation program and the organization, driving ongoing quality improvement.

- **Feedback Loop**: Simulation results are shared with the organization to inform decision-making, while organizational feedback is fed back into the simulation program to refine scenarios or objectives.
- **Data-Driven Adjustments**: Analytics from simulation outcomes, such as error rates or process inefficiencies, guide necessary changes to the system or the simulation itself.

For example, suppose a simulation highlights delays in medication delivery due to communication errors. In that case, organizational stakeholders can revise workflows while the simulation program adjusts scenarios to test the new processes.

Builds Trust and Collaboration

Transparent and open communication fosters trust among all involved parties and strengthens collaborative efforts.

- **Shared Responsibility**: Bidirectional communication ensures that all stakeholders, from participants to institutional leaders, feel invested in the integration's success.
- **Cross-Disciplinary Collaboration**: Feedback mechanisms encourage dialogue between different teams or departments, breaking down silos and improving coordination.

Aligns with Organizational Goals

Integrating feedback from the organization ensures that the simulation program is aligned with institutional priorities and strategic objectives.

- **Customized Scenarios**: Feedback helps tailor simulations to address specific organizational challenges or opportunities.
- **Strategic Decision-Making**: Simulation results provide actionable data for organizational leaders to make informed decisions about system changes or investments.

Bi-directional feedback is an essential element of systems integration simulations, ensuring that simulations are not static exercises but dynamic processes that evolve based on participant and organizational input. This feedback loop enhances realism, promotes engagement, uncovers blind spots, and drives continuous improvement, all while aligning the simulation program with the institution's strategic goals. By fostering a collaborative and iterative approach, bi-directional feedback helps organizations achieve seamless integration and long-term success.

13.3 Key Components of Systems Integration Simulations

A comprehensive and well-structured approach is essential to maximize the effectiveness and impact of systems integration simulations. These simulations encompass various components that ensure a seamless, efficient, and successful integration process. Below is an expanded exploration of the critical components of systems integration simulations.

1. Stakeholder Engagement

Stakeholder engagement is the foundation of successful systems integration simulations, as it ensures that all perspectives and expertise are considered during the planning, design, and execution phases.

- **Early Involvement**: Engaging engineers, IT specialists, end-users, and decision-makers from the outset ensures alignment with organizational objectives and operational needs.
- **Feedback Sessions**: Regularly scheduled sessions enable stakeholders to voice concerns, provide insights, and refine simulation scenarios. This collaborative approach improves scenario relevance and effectiveness.
- **Increased Success Rates**: Studies show that stakeholder involvement can increase the success rate of integration projects by 20% to 30% (Anderson et al., 2020), demonstrating the importance of inclusive participation.

For example, in a hospital, integrating a new patient management system involving both IT personnel and clinical staff helps identify potential usability issues, ensuring smoother implementation.

2. Scenario Design and Execution

Well-designed scenarios are at the heart of systems integration simulations. They must reflect real-world challenges and align with organizational goals to ensure meaningful outcomes.

- **Realistic Simulations**: Scenarios should include typical operational conditions, edge cases, and stress-test situations to evaluate system performance under varying circumstances.
- **Goal Alignment**: Scenarios must be tailored to the organization's strategic objectives, ensuring the simulations address relevant challenges and deliver actionable insights.

For instance, a logistics company might simulate integrating autonomous vehicles in its supply chain by stress-testing scenarios like high-demand periods or unexpected road closures to identify potential bottlenecks.

3. Technology Integration

Integrating advanced technologies enhances systems integration simulations' depth, accuracy, and value.

- **Cutting-Edge Tools**: Virtual reality (VR), augmented reality (AR), and digital twins enable immersive and precise simulations of system interactions.
- **Efficiency Gains**: Digital twins—virtual replicas of physical systems—have been shown to reduce integration time by 15% to 25% and improve overall system performance by 20% (Gartner, 2022).
- **Enhanced Visualization**: AR and VR allow stakeholders to visualize complex interactions and identify issues more intuitively, leading to faster resolution and improved outcomes.

4. Feedback Mechanisms

Structured feedback mechanisms are critical for capturing insights, refining processes, and driving continuous improvement.

- **Dual Feedback Channels**: Feedback should be collected from both operators and participants, ensuring all perspectives are considered.
- **Quantitative and Qualitative Data**: Surveys, performance metrics, and observation notes should be used to gather numerical data and detailed participant feedback.
- **Improved Outcomes**: Organizations using robust feedback systems have reported a **32% improvement** in integration outcomes compared to those without such mechanisms (Global Systems Report, 2021).

For instance, in an aerospace project, feedback from pilots and systems engineers during a flight simulation might highlight discrepancies in navigation software, prompting necessary adjustments before deployment.

5. Data and Metrics

Defining and utilizing clear metrics is essential for evaluating the performance and effectiveness of systems integration simulations.

- **Performance Metrics**: Key performance indicators (KPIs) such as error rates, system response times, and user satisfaction scores provide a quantitative basis for evaluation.
- **Data Analytics**: Advanced analytics tools help identify trends, patterns, and outliers, guiding future improvements and ensuring systems remain adaptable to changing needs.
- **Actionable Insights**: Analyzing simulation data enables organizations to make informed decisions and prioritize areas for refinement.

For example, metrics such as reduced medication delivery errors or improved response times during simulated emergencies can directly correlate with patient safety and satisfaction in healthcare.

Effective systems integration simulations require a holistic approach incorporating stakeholder engagement, realistic scenario design, advanced technology, structured feedback mechanisms, and robust data analysis. By combining these components, organizations can ensure seamless integration, minimize risks, and achieve operational excellence. Integrating these key elements improves the immediate outcomes of simulations and builds a foundation for adaptability and long-term success in increasingly complex systems.

13.4 Best Practices for Simulation Operations in Systems Integration

Implementing systems integration simulations requires adherence to best practices to maximize their effectiveness and ensure seamless operation. These practices encompass detailed planning, iterative refinement, interdisciplinary collaboration, continuous monitoring, and structured debriefing. Additionally, professional standards and accreditation frameworks, such as those set by the *Society for Simulation in Healthcare* (SSH) and the *International Nursing Association for Clinical Simulation and Learning* (INACSL), provide valuable guidance for integration activities.

Below is an expanded discussion of best practices, highlighting their importance and application.

1. Comprehensive Pre-Simulation Planning

Pre-simulation planning lays the groundwork for a successful integration by ensuring clear objectives and thorough preparation.

- **Defining Objectives and Outcomes**: Articulated goals, success criteria, and desired outcomes ensure alignment with organizational priorities.
- **Developing Protocols and Contingencies**: Detailed plans minimize disruption during simulation activities and provide a framework for addressing unexpected issues.
- **Incorporating Accreditation Standards**: The SSH Accreditation Standards emphasize the importance of clear operational objectives and robust planning for simulation programs. Following these standards ensures that integration activities meet recognized benchmarks for quality and effectiveness.

For example, a healthcare organization planning to integrate telehealth solutions into patient workflows might use comprehensive pre-simulation planning to map the interactions between new technologies and existing clinical systems, ensuring a seamless transition.

2. Iterative Testing and Feedback Loops

Iterative testing ensures that systems integration simulations are dynamic and responsive to feedback, leading to continuous improvement.

- **Multiple Rounds of Testing**: Conducting several simulation iterations allows for refinement based on observed challenges and performance metrics.
- **Bi-Directional Feedback**: Feedback from participants and operators ensures that scenarios evolve to reflect real-world conditions and organizational needs.
- **Standards-Based Refinement**: The INACSL Standards of Best Practice emphasize integrating data and feedback into simulation design to improve effectiveness and relevance.

3. Focus on Interdisciplinary Collaboration

Interdisciplinary collaboration is crucial for the success of complex systems that rely on inputs from diverse teams or departments.

- **Cross-Disciplinary Communication**: Facilitating stakeholder dialogue ensures that all roles and interdependencies are understood, reducing miscommunication and errors.
- **Improved Team Efficiency**: Studies have shown that simulations emphasizing interdisciplinary collaboration improve team efficiency by 30% and reduce integration errors by 25% (Weaver et al., 2010).
- **Standards Alignment**: Both the SSH Accreditation Standards and the INACSL Best Practices stress the importance of team collaboration in ensuring successful simulation outcomes.

4. Continuous Monitoring and Adjustment

Ongoing monitoring and real-time adjustments are essential to maintaining the relevance and accuracy of systems integration simulations.

- **Tracking KPIs**: Monitoring key performance indicators (KPIs) such as response times, error rates, and system uptime provides quantitative measures of success.
- **Real-Time Adaptations**: Adjusting based on performance data ensures that the simulation reflects evolving conditions or unexpected challenges.
- **Quality Improvement Measures**: The INACSL Standards emphasize the importance of continuous quality improvement, encouraging simulation programs to adapt and improve based on data-driven insights.

5. Structured Debriefing

Structured debriefing is a critical component of systems integration simulations, ensuring that lessons learned are documented and applied effectively.

- **Observation and Analysis**: Post-simulation debriefings provide a platform to discuss observations, evaluate system performance, and identify areas for improvement.
- **Building Institutional Knowledge**: Comprehensive documentation ensures that insights from the simulation inform future integration efforts and contribute to organizational learning.
- **Accreditation Focus**: The SSH Accreditation Standards and the INACSL Best Practices highlight structured debriefing as a core element of effective simulation programs, reinforcing its importance in achieving meaningful outcomes.

For example, in a healthcare setting, a structured debrief following a new clinical workflow simulation might reveal communication gaps between departments, guiding adjustments that improve patient safety and care delivery.

Integration of Professional Standards

The SSH Accreditation Standards and the INACSL Best Practices offer critical frameworks aligning simulation operations with industry benchmarks.

- **SSH Accreditation Standards**: These standards guide operational planning, stakeholder engagement, scenario design, and quality assurance for simulation programs. Integrating these standards into systems integration activities ensures adherence to recognized best practices.
- **INACSL Standards of Best Practice**: INACSL emphasizes the importance of learner-centered design, feedback integration, and quality improvement measures, all relevant to systems integration simulations.

By incorporating these professional standards, simulation programs can enhance their credibility, ensure consistency, and achieve better outcomes.

Best practices in systems integration simulations combine comprehensive planning, iterative testing, interdisciplinary collaboration, continuous monitoring, and structured debriefing. By aligning these practices with professional standards such as those established by SSH and INACSL, simulation programs can ensure that their integration activities are robust, effective, and aligned with industry benchmarks. These practices improve the immediate outcomes of simulations and contribute to long-term organizational success and adaptability in complex systems.

13.5 Applications of Simulation in Systems Integration

Simulation operations have significant applications in the healthcare industry, where integrating new technologies, workflows, and processes is critical for improving patient care, safety, and operational efficiency. Below are key areas where simulation is or has been applied to healthcare systems integration:

1. Electronic Health Records (EHR) Integration

Integrating EHR systems with clinical workflows is a complex process that benefits greatly from simulation.

- **Reducing Errors**: Simulating the integration of EHR systems helps identify and mitigate implementation errors, which can lead to a 40% reduction in errors (HIMSS Analytics, 2021).
- **Workflow Validation**: Simulations ensure EHR interfaces align with clinician workflows, reducing friction and improving usability.

For example, a hospital might simulate EHR integration in the emergency department to ensure seamless documentation of patient encounters and test the interoperability with diagnostic tools such as lab systems and imaging devices.

2. Medical Device and Diagnostic Tool Validation

Simulations ensure that new medical devices and diagnostic tools integrate effectively within healthcare systems.

- **Testing Interoperability**: Simulations validate whether devices communicate correctly with existing systems, such as monitors connecting to EHRs or diagnostic tools integrating with lab reporting software.
- **Improving Safety**: Simulating device usage helps identify potential hazards or usability issues, improving patient safety during real-world implementation.

For instance, before deploying a new infusion pump, healthcare organizations can simulate its integration with pharmacy systems and bedside workflows to ensure accuracy and efficiency.

3. Patient Flow and Resource Allocation

Simulation is a powerful tool for optimizing patient flow and resource utilization in healthcare settings.

- **Capacity Planning**: Simulations help hospitals prepare for peak demand periods, such as flu seasons or public health emergencies, by modeling patient flow scenarios.
- **Improving Efficiency**: By simulating workflows in emergency departments, operating rooms, or outpatient clinics, organizations can identify bottlenecks and optimize staff and resource allocation.

For example, a simulation might model patient admission, treatment, and discharge processes to improve turnaround times in a busy emergency department, ultimately enhancing patient satisfaction and reducing wait times.

4. Integration of Telehealth Solutions

As telehealth becomes increasingly important, simulations integrate virtual care platforms with in-person clinical workflows.

- **Testing Platform Interoperability**: Simulations validate the compatibility of telehealth software with EHR systems, ensuring seamless documentation of virtual visits.
- **Workflow Alignment**: Simulating telehealth scenarios helps identify process gaps, such as scheduling, billing, and follow-up care coordination.

For example, a healthcare system integrating a telehealth solution can simulate virtual visits between providers and patients, testing for technical issues and assessing workflow compatibility.

5. Interprofessional Team Training and Collaboration

Simulation fosters interdisciplinary healthcare teams' collaboration, enabling seamless workflow integration across different roles and specialties.

- **Team-Based Scenarios**: Simulations train healthcare teams to work together effectively, especially during high-pressure situations such as code blue or trauma resuscitation scenarios.
- **Improving Communication**: Simulating integrated workflows helps identify communication gaps between departments, such as nursing, pharmacy, and radiology, leading to better coordination.

For instance, during the rollout of a new surgical protocol, simulations can train surgeons, anesthesiologists, and nurses to ensure that all team members understand their roles and responsibilities.

6. Facility and Technology Upgrades

Simulation supports the integration of new healthcare facilities or technological infrastructure into existing systems.

- **Testing Layouts**: Simulations can model patient movement and staff workflows in newly designed hospital units, ensuring optimal space utilization and accessibility.
- **Technology Integration**: Facility upgrades often involve integrating new monitoring systems, communication tools, or automated solutions, all of which can be tested through simulation.

For example, when introducing automated medication dispensing systems, simulations can evaluate how these systems integrate with pharmacy workflows and nursing practices to prevent medication errors.

Simulation operations provide invaluable insights for healthcare systems integration, addressing challenges in technology implementation, workflow alignment, resource optimization, and team collaboration. By simulating complex scenarios in a controlled environment, healthcare organizations can minimize risks, enhance efficiency, and improve patient care and safety.

13.6 Future Directions in Systems Integration Simulations

The field of systems integration simulations is poised for significant advancements, driven by emerging technologies and evolving organizational priorities. These innovations promise to enhance simulations' accuracy, scalability, and sustainability while addressing the growing complexity of integrated systems. Below is an expanded discussion of the key future directions in this area:

1. Artificial Intelligence (AI) and Machine Learning (ML)

AI and ML are set to revolutionize systems integration simulations by providing powerful tools for analysis, prediction, and decision-making.

- **Predictive Analytics**: AI-powered simulations can anticipate system behavior under various conditions, helping organizations prepare for potential challenges. For example, in healthcare, AI-driven simulations could predict the impact of increased patient loads on hospital workflows, enabling better resource allocation.
- **Adaptive Simulations**: Machine learning algorithms can analyze real-time data from simulations, dynamically adjusting scenarios to reflect changing conditions. This capability ensures that simulations remain relevant and responsive to organizational needs.
- **Error Reduction**: AI can help organizations address vulnerabilities before they become critical issues by identifying patterns and anomalies in complex systems.

For instance, in healthcare, ML algorithms could analyze data from electronic health records (EHR) simulations to identify inefficiencies or potential errors in data workflows, enabling targeted interventions.

2. Cloud-Based Simulations

Cloud technology will transform how systems integration simulations are conducted, offering enhanced flexibility and collaboration capabilities.

- **Remote Collaboration**: Cloud-based simulations allow geographically dispersed teams to collaborate in real-time, reducing barriers to participation and increasing accessibility. For example, healthcare teams from different facilities can jointly simulate integrating a new telehealth platform.

- **Scalability**: Cloud platforms provide the computational power needed for large-scale simulations, making it easier to model complex systems involving multiple components and interactions.
- **Cost Efficiency**: By leveraging cloud infrastructure, organizations can reduce the costs of maintaining physical simulation environments or specialized hardware.

In healthcare, cloud-based simulations could enable multi-institutional collaborations to test the interoperability of regional health information exchanges, improving data sharing and patient outcomes.

3. Enhanced Visualization Tools

Advanced visualization technologies such as augmented reality (AR) and virtual reality (VR) will make systems integration simulations more immersive and intuitive.

- **Real-Time Visualization**: AR and VR tools allow stakeholders to interact with and observe complex system interactions in real time, making it easier to identify issues and understand interdependencies.
- **Improved Troubleshooting**: Visualizing system components and workflows in a virtual environment enables faster and more effective problem-solving. For instance, a VR simulation could model how new medical devices interact with existing workflows in an operating room, helping identify potential conflicts or inefficiencies.
- **Stakeholder Engagement**: Immersive visualization tools can make simulations more engaging for participants, improving their understanding and participation in the integration process.

For example, in healthcare facility planning, VR simulations can visualize patient and staff flow through newly designed spaces, enabling stakeholders to test and refine layouts before construction.

4. Sustainability Focus

As organizations increasingly prioritize environmental sustainability, systems integration simulations will evolve to incorporate sustainability principles.

- **Resource Efficiency**: Simulations will help organizations optimize resource usage, such as energy, materials, and time, during system integration. For example, hospitals can simulate energy-efficient workflows or test green technologies.
- **Sustainable Technologies**: By integrating and testing environmentally friendly technologies, such as solar-powered devices or low-energy medical equipment, simulations can help organizations reduce their carbon footprint.
- **Global Sustainability Goals**: Aligning simulation activities with sustainability frameworks, such as the United Nations Sustainable Development Goals (SDGs), will ensure that organizations contribute to broader environmental and social objectives.

In healthcare, sustainability-focused simulations might test the integration of renewable energy sources with hospital power systems, ensuring reliability and efficiency while reducing environmental impact.

Exciting advancements in AI, cloud computing, visualization tools, and sustainability practices characterize the future of systems integration simulations. These innovations will enable organizations to address increasingly complex challenges with greater accuracy, efficiency, and adaptability. By embracing these emerging technologies and trends, simulation programs can remain at the forefront of integration efforts, driving improvements in system performance, collaboration, and environmental responsibility. As these technologies mature, their potential to revolutionize systems integration will only grow.

13.7 Summary

Simulation operations are pivotal for successful systems integration, offering a risk-free environment to test, refine, and optimize complex systems. By incorporating bi-directional feedback and leveraging emerging technologies, organizations can ensure simulations are dynamic, collaborative, and aligned with real-world conditions. As systems grow increasingly complex, simulation will remain an indispensable tool for achieving operational excellence, fostering innovation, and ensuring system reliability across industries.

13.8 Chapter Review

Review Questions

1. What are the primary purposes of systems integration simulations, and how do they contribute to organizational success?
2. How does bi-directional feedback enhance the realism and effectiveness of systems integration simulations?
3. Identify and describe the five key components of systems integration simulations.
4. How do simulation operations support integrating new technologies like telehealth and EHR systems in healthcare?
5. Discuss the role of advanced visualization tools like AR and VR in improving simulation outcomes.

Critical Thinking and Application

1. **Scenario Analysis:** A hospital is integrating a new patient monitoring system into its ICU. Using the principles of systems integration simulations, outline a plan to test and refine this system. How would you ensure all stakeholders are engaged, and what metrics would you track?
2. **Bi-Directional Feedback Application:** Discuss how bi-directional feedback could be implemented in a simulation scenario involving the rollout of an

autonomous delivery robot in a manufacturing facility. What steps would you take to gather and apply feedback effectively?
3. **Future Technology Integration:** Considering the advancements in AI and cloud computing, propose how these technologies could be integrated into simulations to improve outcomes for an organization implementing a new remote work policy.
4. **Interdisciplinary Collaboration:** Reflect on a real-world example where interdisciplinary collaboration might enhance the success of a systems integration simulation. How would you facilitate communication and cooperation among diverse teams?

Hands-On Activities

1. **Simulation Design Workshop:** Create a basic simulation scenario for a systems integration activity in a chosen industry (e.g., healthcare, aerospace, logistics). Develop the objectives, components, and metrics to evaluate success. Present your design to a peer group for feedback.
2. **Feedback Mechanisms:** Conduct a role-playing activity where participants act as stakeholders in a systems integration simulation. Practice gathering and incorporating feedback to adjust and improve the scenario.
3. **Data Analysis Exercise:** Review a dataset from a simulated integration scenario (real or hypothetical). Identify trends, patterns, and outliers and propose actionable recommendations for improvement.
4. **AR/VR Exploration:** Visualize a system's workflow using an AR or VR platform. Identify potential bottlenecks or issues that could be addressed through integration adjustments. Share insights with a group.

Summary Reflection

Simulation operations are vital for systems integration, providing organizations with a controlled environment to test and optimize interactions between diverse components. These simulations serve multiple purposes, including testing interoperability, validating workflows, enhancing collaboration, mitigating risks, and optimizing performance. Bi-directional feedback ensures simulations are dynamic, realistic, and aligned with organizational goals, fostering iterative improvement and collaboration.

Key components such as stakeholder engagement, scenario design, technology integration, feedback mechanisms, and data analysis form the foundation of effective systems integration simulations. Organizations can ensure that simulations achieve meaningful and actionable outcomes by adhering to best practices, including comprehensive planning, iterative testing, and structured debriefing.

Emerging technologies like AI, cloud computing, AR, and VR are poised to revolutionize systems integration simulations, offering enhanced analytics, scalability, and immersive experiences. Moreover, a growing focus on sustainability highlights the potential for simulations to drive resource efficiency and environmental responsibility.

Simulation operations will remain indispensable for seamless integration, operational excellence, and long-term success as systems become more complex across industries. By embracing innovation and fostering collaboration, simulation programs can help address the challenges of modern systems integration.

Chapter 14

Contingency and Continuity Operations in Simulation

Simulation centers are the beating heart of modern training and education in healthcare, military, and engineering fields. They simulate life-and-death scenarios in a controlled environment, helping learners refine skills and develop confidence. However, the seamless operation of these centers often masks the intricate, fragile systems that underpin their success. Equipment failures, natural disasters, cyberattacks, or even a sudden staff shortage can bring these systems to a halt, jeopardizing outcomes.

This chapter examines the vital role of contingency and continuity operations in maintaining the stability and reliability of simulation programs. Through stories of real-world challenges and evidence-based strategies, we explore how simulation centers can mitigate risks, respond to disruptions, and recover quickly—ensuring they remain resilient in the face of uncertainty.

14.1 The Day the Simulation Stopped

Imagine this: A bustling healthcare simulation center is alive with anticipation. Thirty nursing students, each clad in scrubs, nervously chat among themselves as they prepare for one of the most challenging scenarios of their training—a cardiac arrest drill. The stakes are high. The goal is to test their technical skills and simulate the real-world pressures of teamwork and decision-making in life-and-death situations.

In the control room, the lead simulation technician double-checks the equipment. The manikin, a high-fidelity simulator worth over $100,000, is expected to perform flawlessly. The AV system is primed to capture every detail for the debriefing sessions. But as the first team steps into the lab, panic washes over the technician. The manikin is unresponsive. The familiar sound of its simulated heartbeat is absent, replaced by eerie silence.

Frantically, the technician reboots the system. The faculty watches nervously as precious minutes tick away. Meanwhile, the AV equipment, crucial for recording the session, flickers. The technician juggles troubleshooting calls, software reboots, and mounting frustration, but nothing works. The simulation is dead in the water.

The cancellation is disappointing for the students, but it's disastrous for the faculty. Hours of preparation, including scenario design, faculty coordination, and student scheduling, have been wasted. Rescheduling will take weeks, pushing back critical training milestones. This wasn't just a lost session but a lost opportunity to prepare future healthcare professionals for emergencies they will one day face in real life.

This was not just a hypothetical scenario or hyperbole—it happened in a Midwest teaching hospital in 2021. The cause? A combination of equipment failure and a lack of contingency planning. There was no backup manikin, alternate AV setup, or clear protocol for managing unexpected technical failures.

The ripple effects were far-reaching. Students expressed frustration in course evaluations, faculty faced pressure to make up for lost time, and the institution's reputation for excellence took a hit. The lesson was clear: Without a robust contingency and continuity plan, even minor disruptions can snowball into major setbacks.

14.2 Understanding Risk: Identifying the Weak Links

Behind a simulation center's seamless operation lies a delicate network of systems and processes, each vulnerable to disruption. Understanding these vulnerabilities is the first step in developing a robust contingency and continuity plan. Risks are not hypothetical—they are inevitable. From technical failures to staffing challenges, the weak links in simulation operations are as varied as they are unpredictable.

Technical Failures: When the Machines Break Down

High-fidelity simulators, often hailed as the crown jewels of simulation training, are marvels of technology. These manikins breathe, blink, bleed, and even speak. Nevertheless, their complexity makes them susceptible to an array of failures. A loose cable, a software bug, or an overlooked firmware update can render a $100,000 piece of equipment useless during a session.

Consider the story of a major teaching hospital in California in 2022. Their flagship simulator, programmed to simulate a critical neonatal resuscitation, suddenly froze mid-scenario. Despite attempts to reset the software, the manikin displayed an error code that no one on-site could decipher. The center's lead technician later discovered the issue stemmed from an automatic software update incompatible with their current operating system. This glitch could have been prevented with regular system checks.

However, it is not just simulators that pose a risk. The entire ecosystem of software systems that power simulation operations is equally vulnerable. Scheduling platforms that double-book resources, scenario design tools that crash during programming, or data analytics software that corrupts performance data can all disrupt training and undermine trust in the center's capabilities. According to a 2020 Society for Simulation in Healthcare (SSH) survey, 62% of centers reported at least one equipment or software failure that significantly disrupted their operations over the past year.

Human Resource Challenges: The People Problem

Even the most advanced technology is only as effective as those operating it. Simulation teams are often lean, with specialized technicians and educators managing multiple roles. While this efficiency is cost-effective, it also creates vulnerabilities.

Staff turnover is a critical concern. When a lead simulation technician left unexpectedly at a Midwest simulation center in 2021, the remaining staff struggled to keep operations running smoothly. Without someone familiar with the center's specific systems and workflows, scenarios were delayed, equipment maintenance fell behind, and faculty grew frustrated. It took six months to fill the vacancy, and the center operated at reduced capacity.

Burnout is another silent threat. Simulation educators and technicians juggle technical troubleshooting, curriculum development, and facilitation, often with minimal support. One staff member at a busy urban center described it as "constantly putting out fires while trying to keep the building standing." Prolonged stress and lack of cross-training can lead to costly mistakes, such as forgetting to update software licenses or improperly configuring equipment.

Environmental and External Threats: Forces Beyond Control

Environmental risks, such as natural disasters, can be catastrophic for simulation centers. Hurricanes, floods, and wildfires can destroy facilities, displace staff, and disrupt schedules for weeks or months. In 2017, Hurricane Harvey flooded a Houston simulation center, causing irreparable damage to its manikins and AV systems. The center's recovery took nearly a year, during which training was relocated to makeshift classrooms with limited resources. This same scenario happened to several Caribbean simulation centers after hurricanes. One program, in particular, resulted in operating simulations on a boat while their building was repaired.

External threats include cybersecurity breaches, which are becoming increasingly common as simulation centers digitize their operations. In 2022, a ransomware attack on a simulation center encrypted critical data, including learner performance records and proprietary simulation scenarios. The center paid $100,000 in recovery costs and spent weeks restoring its systems. This incident highlights the importance of cybersecurity measures, such as encryption, firewalls, and regular staff training on phishing threats.

Operational Risks: The Cost of Inadequate Infrastructure

Sometimes, the most disruptive risks come from operational oversights. A power outage, even one lasting only a few minutes, can halt an entire day's worth of scheduled simulations. In 2020, a rural simulation center lost power during a multidisciplinary trauma drill. Without a generator or uninterruptible power supply (UPS), the session had to be canceled, wasting hours of preparation and frustrating the participants who had traveled long distances to attend.

Supply chain delays present another operational risk, especially as global disruptions impact industries worldwide. A delay in receiving a replacement part for a manikin or a software dongle can mean canceled sessions, frustrated learners, and lost revenue. During the COVID-19 pandemic, one simulation center experienced a three-month delay in receiving new pediatric manikins due to global manufacturing slowdowns. In the interim, they had to redesign scenarios to work around their aging equipment, compromising the realism of their training.

The Big Picture: Risk Is Everywhere

Risks can set off a domino effect when they materialize, turning minor issues into major crises. Technical failures lead to frustrated staff, staffing shortages delay equipment maintenance, and natural disasters or power outages exacerbate existing vulnerabilities. Each weak link in the system becomes a potential point of failure.

Understanding these risks is not just about identifying problems but anticipating them. By acknowledging the vulnerabilities in their operations, simulation leaders can build robust contingency and continuity plans that safeguard their centers against the unexpected. After all, in simulation, as in real life, preparation is the key to resilience.

14.3 Building a Resilient Foundation

Contingency and continuity planning isn't just about reacting to disasters; it's about building resilience into the very fabric of a simulation center's operations. Resilience means being prepared not only to survive disruptions but to adapt, recover, and emerge stronger. The process of resilience-building requires foresight, collaboration, and a willingness to invest in systems that safeguard against vulnerabilities. It is the difference between scrambling in chaos and responding with confidence.

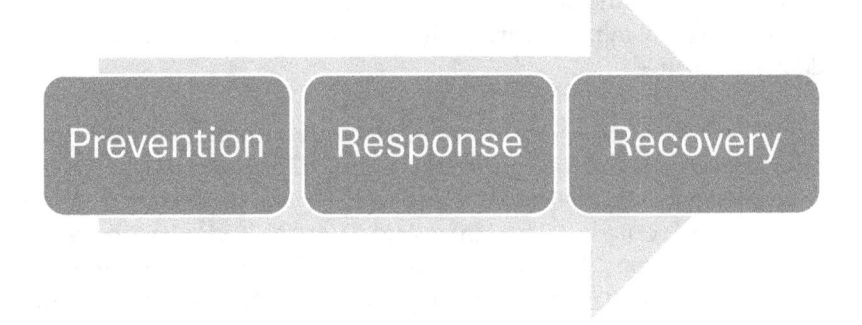

Figure 24 Building Resiliency

Step 1: Prevention—Staying Ahead of the Problem

Imagine a world where simulation centers rarely face interruptions. While perfection may be unattainable, prevention brings us closer to this ideal. Prevention is not a singular act but an ongoing commitment to identifying and addressing risks before they escalate.

Routine Maintenance and Testing
In one case, a large urban simulation center prepared for a multi-day interprofessional simulation event involving over 200 participants. Days before the event, technicians discovered a critical manikin component was on the verge of failure during a routine pre-event inspection. Thanks to their robust maintenance schedule, they replaced the part and avoided what could have been an embarrassing and costly disruption. Centers with preventative maintenance programs experience 35% fewer disruptions (National Center for Simulation, 2022), and their technicians often report higher confidence in equipment reliability.

Maintenance isn't just about equipment—it's also about systems. For example, conducting regular scenario test runs ensures that software updates haven't introduced bugs or incompatibilities. These tests also allow teams to familiarize themselves with each system's quirks, reducing response time when something goes wrong.

Cross-Training Staff
When the lead simulation technician at a Midwest center unexpectedly took medical leave, the absence threatened to derail weeks of training sessions. Fortunately, the center had invested in cross-training its team. Other staff members, including the AV technician and administrative coordinator, had been trained to program scenarios and troubleshoot basic equipment issues. The transition was not seamless, but it kept operations running.

Cross-training prevents bottlenecks and ensures no individual's absence can paralyze the center. It also fosters a team culture where collaboration and shared knowledge reduce the risk of burnout.

Cloud-Based Data Management
Local servers can be a single point of failure in a crisis. Imagine a fire that damages the simulation lab and wipes out scenario files stored on an in-house server. With cloud-based systems, these files are accessible anywhere, ensuring that operations can continue even if the physical facility is compromised.

One simulation center that transitioned to a cloud-based system in 2020 avoided major disruptions during a snowstorm that rendered its building inaccessible for a week. Staff worked remotely to modify scenarios and prepare learners for virtual debriefings, demonstrating that cloud technology isn't just a convenience—it's a lifeline.

Step 2: Response—Reacting with Precision and Speed
Even the most well-prepared centers encounter the unexpected. The true test of resilience lies in how quickly and effectively they respond.

Redundant Systems
During Hurricane Ida in 2021, a Louisiana simulation center faced a total power outage. Thanks to their investment in a backup generator, training continued uninterrupted, even while much of the surrounding city was in the dark. Additionally,

the center had partnered with a nearby facility as part of its disaster response plan, allowing learners to relocate seamlessly when flooding made the primary center inaccessible.

Redundancy is not limited to physical resources like generators; it also applies to personnel. Having multiple team members capable of fulfilling essential roles ensures that operations can proceed without delays even if one person is unavailable.

Emergency Protocols
In the heat of a crisis, clarity is critical. Emergency protocols should provide step-by-step instructions for handling common disruptions, from power outages to cybersecurity breaches. These protocols should include:

- A chain of command for decision-making.
- Emergency contact lists for internal staff and external vendors.
- Checklists for securing equipment and data.

One simulation center tested its emergency protocols during an unplanned fire alarm evacuation. Staff executed their plan flawlessly, ensuring that expensive manikins were moved to a safe location, AV systems were powered down correctly, and learners were accounted for. Post-incident debriefing revealed minor areas for improvement, which were addressed in subsequent drills.

Step 3: Recovery—Bouncing Back and Moving Forward

Recovery is not just about returning to normal; it is about emerging stronger and better prepared for the next challenge.

Debriefing the Team
After any disruption, gathering the team for a thorough debrief is essential. This is where lessons are learned, and future improvements are identified. For example, a Midwest simulation center experienced a significant power outage, revealing gaps in their response plan. During the post-incident debrief, staff suggested adding a portable UPS for critical systems and updating the emergency protocol to include roles for learners during disruptions. Implementing these changes ensured that the center was better prepared for future incidents.

Debriefing sessions should be inclusive, giving all team members—from technicians to educators—a chance to share their perspectives. This collaborative approach often uncovers insights that might otherwise be overlooked.

Investing in Resilience
Recovery isn't just about fixing what's broken—it's about building a stronger foundation for the future. After a ransomware attack, one simulation center didn't just recover its systems; it invested in enhanced cybersecurity measures, including staff training on phishing threats and an upgraded firewall. Since implementing these changes, it has experienced a 70% reduction in attempted breaches.

In another example, a center that faced significant staffing shortages during the COVID-19 pandemic launched a fellowship program to train and retain simulation professionals. This proactive approach not only addressed immediate staffing needs but also created a pipeline of skilled personnel for years to come.

Building a Culture of Resilience

Ultimately, resilience is not just a set of actions but a mindset. Simulation centers that embrace a culture of resilience see every disruption as an opportunity to improve. They invest in their people, systems, and protocols, knowing that preparation today means fewer disruptions tomorrow.

As the global simulation industry continues to grow—projected to reach $6.6 billion by 2027 (MarketsandMarkets, 2022)—the stakes are higher than ever. Simulation centers must rise to the challenge by reacting to crises and proactively building a foundation of resilience that ensures their operations can withstand anything the world throws at them.

14.4 Case Study: Triumph Through Planning

In September 2022, a simulation center in Florida was preparing for its busiest training season when weather reports warned of an approaching tropical storm. Located in a low-lying area prone to flooding, the center was no stranger to storm-related disruptions. However, past experiences had taught them valuable lessons, prompting the implementation of a robust continuity plan the year before. That plan would soon be put to the test.

The Challenge

As the storm strengthened and evacuation orders were issued, the center's leadership faced critical decisions. The simulation lab, home to over $1 million of high-fidelity manikins, AV equipment, and computing systems, was at risk. Training schedules for hundreds of healthcare students and professionals were in jeopardy. In past storms, delays in decision-making and insufficient preparation had led to costly damages and weeks of downtime. This time, however, the center was ready.

The Continuity Plan in Action

The leadership team activated their continuity plan, which was developed through a meticulous risk assessment and regular drills. The plan consisted of several key strategies:

- Relocating Critical Equipment Before the storm, staff worked around the clock to secure and relocate essential equipment. High-value manikins, server hardware, and irreplaceable AV systems were transported to an off-site storage facility on higher ground. Items too large to relocate, such as fixed installations, were covered with waterproof tarps and secured on elevated platforms.

- Partnering with a Nearby University In anticipation of natural disasters, the center had established a partnership with a nearby university located outside the flood zone. This agreement allowed them to temporarily access the university's simulation facilities. The partnership was activated with just one phone call, and arrangements were made to shift scheduled training sessions to the alternate site.

- Utilizing Cloud-Based Systems One of the most transformative changes the center had made during its continuity planning was transitioning to cloud-based systems for storing simulation scenarios, learner data, and training schedules. This decision ensured that critical files and resources remained accessible from anywhere, even if the primary facility was rendered unusable. Faculty and staff logged in remotely to update scenarios, manage schedules, and communicate with learners, minimizing disruptions.

- Communicating with Stakeholders Clear communication was vital. The center deployed automated emails and text alerts to inform learners, faculty, and staff of the relocation and adjusted schedules. Social media platforms were also used to provide real-time updates. This proactive communication helped manage expectations and reduced confusion.

The Outcome

When the storm hit, the primary simulation center suffered significant flooding. Water levels rose nearly three feet, inundating the lower levels of the building. However, thanks to the foresight and execution of the continuity plan, critical assets had been safely relocated, and scheduled training sessions proceeded at the alternate site with only minor adjustments.

Within two days of the storm's passing, the simulation center resumed operations. Damage assessments revealed that the continuity plan had prevented over $500,000 in equipment losses, while cloud-based data systems preserved years of training scenarios and learner records. The seamless transition to the partner facility ensured that learners experienced no significant delays in their training schedules, safeguarding their progress toward licensure and certification.

Lessons Learned

The Florida simulation center's successful response offers valuable insights for other organizations:

Proactive Planning is Key; risks like flooding cannot be entirely avoided, but their impact can be mitigated through detailed planning. The center transformed a potential disaster into a manageable inconvenience by addressing vulnerabilities such as low-lying facilities and reliance on physical servers.

Partnerships Enhance Resilience Collaborating with nearby institutions provides a safety net for emergencies. The partnership with the university was instrumental in maintaining operations and minimizing disruptions.

Cloud Technology Enables Continuity Transitioning to cloud-based systems proved invaluable. While physical facilities were compromised, the center's ability to access scenarios, schedules, and data remotely allowed operations to continue almost seamlessly.

Teamwork and Communication Matter: Effective execution of the continuity plan required teamwork across all levels, from leadership to support staff. Clear communication with stakeholders minimized confusion and ensured everyone was aligned.

Looking Ahead

After the storm, the center reviewed its continuity plan, incorporating lessons learned. They invested in additional waterproof storage for remaining on-site equipment, increased the number of drills to test emergency protocols, and formalized agreements with additional partner institutions to create a broader safety net.

This case demonstrates that while disasters are unpredictable, their impact can be controlled with foresight, preparation, and a resilient commitment. The Florida Simulation Center's triumph is a powerful reminder of what can be achieved when planning meets action.

14.5 The Financial Case for Continuity

For many simulation centers, investing in contingency and continuity planning can seem like an optional expense—a line item that's deferred or minimized when budgets are tight. However, the financial consequences of operational disruptions paint a very different picture. Without a continuity framework, the cost of downtime, recovery, and damage can quickly eclipse the upfront investment required to mitigate risks.

The Hidden Costs of Downtime

When a simulation center is forced to cancel sessions due to unforeseen disruptions, the financial repercussions ripple across the organization. The Society for Simulation in Healthcare (SSH) estimates that the average cost of downtime in a simulation center is $1,500 per hour. However, what does that number represent? Let us break it down:

- Wasted Staff Time Faculty and staff spend weeks meticulously designing scenarios, coordinating schedules, and preparing learners for high-stakes simulations. When a session is canceled, all that effort is wasted. In addition, staff must dedicate time to troubleshooting the disruption, rescheduling sessions, and communicating changes—none of which directly contribute to the center's educational mission.

- Lost Learner Hours For learners, every hour spent waiting for a canceled session is an hour of lost training. This delay can have cascading effects, particularly for healthcare students and professionals on strict certification timelines. Delays in training translate into delayed readiness to enter the workforce, which can impact institutional goals and reputations.

- Rescheduling Efforts Rescheduling is not just a logistical headache—it's a costly endeavor. Finding available time slots, rebooking facilities, and coordinating new schedules for learners, faculty, and staff often require additional administrative resources.

- Reputational Damage For institutions known for their simulation programs, disruptions can damage their reputation among learners, faculty, and potential partners. This intangible cost, while harder to quantify, can lead to decreased enrollments or loss of competitive edge in the long term.

A Case in Point: The Price of Unpreparedness

In 2021, a simulation center in the Pacific Northwest suffered a power outage during a critical training week for medical residents. Without a backup generator, the center was forced to cancel five consecutive days of sessions. The downtime cost the institution approximately $60,000, factoring in staff salaries, lost learner hours, and the expenses associated with rescheduling. Additionally, the center incurred $15,000 in equipment damages due to improper shutdowns caused by the outage.

Had the center invested $25,000 in a generator and surge protection system—a cost identified during a risk assessment a year prior—the financial loss and disruption could have been entirely avoided.

The Cost of Building Resilience

While the expenses of contingency and continuity planning can seem daunting, they pale in comparison to the costs of unplanned disruptions. Here's a look at some typical costs associated with building resilience:

Risk Assessments and Planning
Conducting a thorough risk assessment and developing a continuity plan typically costs between $10,000 and $20,000 for mid-sized centers, depending on the complexity of the operation. This upfront cost identifies vulnerabilities and outlines actionable steps to mitigate them.

Backup Systems and Redundancy
Investing in critical backup systems—such as generators, cloud-based data storage, and redundant AV setups—can range from $15,000 to $50,000. While this represents a significant investment, these systems provide fail-safes that prevent costly downtime during crises.

Training and Drills
Regular staff training and simulation-based emergency drills cost a fraction of the potential losses incurred during unprepared disruptions. For example, a $5,000 annual investment in cross-training staff and conducting biannual drills ensures operational resilience.

The ROI of Continuity Planning

The return on investment (ROI) for continuity planning is immediate and long-term. While the upfront costs may appear substantial, the benefits far outweigh them. Consider the following examples:

Preventing Equipment Damage
- During a severe thunderstorm in 2022, a simulation center in Texas experienced a sudden power surge. Thanks to their investment in surge protectors and an uninterruptible power supply (UPS), the center avoided $100,000 in equipment damages. What is the cost of these preventative measures? $12,000.

Avoiding Downtime
- A hospital-based simulation center implemented a cloud-based data management system for $30,000. When a local server crashed unexpectedly, the center could continue operations without interruption, avoiding an estimated $75,000 in lost productivity and rescheduling costs.

Enhancing Reputation
- Continuity planning is not just a cost-saving measure—it's a competitive advantage. Simulation centers that consistently deliver high-quality, uninterrupted training attract more learners, secure funding from stakeholders, and strengthen their reputation as leaders in education and innovation.

The Bigger Picture

The financial case for continuity is clear: every dollar invested in preparedness saves exponentially more in avoided losses and unplanned expenses. Nevertheless, the benefits extend beyond the balance sheet. A well-prepared simulation center is better equipped to fulfill its mission of providing learners with the critical skills they need to succeed in high-stakes environments. By investing in resilience, these centers ensure their long-term sustainability and ability to meet the demands of a rapidly evolving world.

14.6 Summary

Contingency and continuity operations are about reacting to crises and creating a culture of resilience. As simulation centers become increasingly integral to education and training, the stakes of uninterrupted operations increase. By identifying risks, implementing preventative measures, and preparing for the unexpected, simulation programs can continue to provide essential services, even in the face of adversity.

Resilience isn't an optional feature of simulation operations—it's the foundation for their success. Whether you're safeguarding against technical failures, natural disasters, or staffing shortages, a well-executed plan ensures that the simulation never stops.

14.7 Chapter Review

Review Questions

1. What are simulation centers' primary risks, and how can they impact operations?
2. Discuss the importance of cross-training staff in simulation centers and its role in continuity planning.
3. What key steps can simulation centers take to build resilience and prevent disruptions?
4. How does cloud-based data management contribute to continuity during crises?
5. Provide examples of how redundancy in equipment and systems can mitigate operational risks.

Critical Thinking and Application

1. **Scenario Analysis:** Imagine a simulation center facing a ransomware attack that locks all its learner data and training scenarios. Outline a continuity plan to help the center recover swiftly and prevent future incidents.
2. **Proactive Risk Management:** Design a maintenance schedule for a high-fidelity simulation center, addressing technical and operational risks. How would you prioritize tasks to minimize disruptions?
3. **Cost-Benefit Analysis:** Consider the financial investment in backup generators, cloud storage, and training drills. Evaluate the long-term return on investment (ROI) for these measures in a simulation center prone to frequent power outages.
4. **Lessons from Real Events:** Reflect on the case study of the Florida simulation center during a tropical storm. What strategies from their continuity plan could be adapted for other types of emergencies, such as cyberattacks or staff shortages?

Hands-On Activities

1. **Emergency Drill Simulation:** Conduct a mock drill simulating a power outage during a high-stakes training session. Assign roles for staff and learners and evaluate the team's response based on predefined protocols.
2. **Risk Assessment Workshop:** Identify potential risks in your simulation center's operations. Create a risk matrix, categorize risks by likelihood and impact, and develop mitigation strategies for high-priority issues.
3. **Scenario Redesign Exercise:** Modify a training scenario to accommodate reduced functionality during a simulated crisis, such as missing equipment or limited staff. Present your adapted scenario and discuss its feasibility.
4. **Continuity Planning Exercise:** Develop a basic continuity plan for a hypothetical simulation center. Include steps for risk identification, resource allocation, staff cross-training, and stakeholder communication.

Summary Reflection

Simulation centers are vital for training professionals in high-stakes industries, yet their reliance on complex systems and specialized staff makes them vulnerable to disruptions. Contingency and continuity operations are critical for ensuring these centers remain operational during crises, whether caused by technical failures, staffing shortages, or environmental disasters.

Resilience begins with proactive measures like routine maintenance, cross-training staff, and adopting cloud-based systems. Equipment and system redundancy further safeguards operations, while clear emergency protocols and real-time feedback ensure swift and effective responses. Recovery processes, including structured debriefing and investments in resilience, restore operations and strengthen the center against future challenges.

The financial case for continuity is compelling: investing in preventative measures saves resources, protects reputations, and enhances operational efficiency. As simulation centers expand their role in education and training, building a culture of resilience is not optional—it is essential. Through robust planning and preparation, these centers can weather any disruption, ensuring their mission to provide transformative learning experiences endures.

Chapter 15

Conclusion and Next Steps: Advancing Healthcare Simulation Operations

Healthcare simulation operations are the backbone of effective simulation-based education, ensuring that cutting-edge technology, realistic scenarios, and dynamic learning environments combine seamlessly to improve training outcomes. This chapter synthesizes the key themes discussed throughout the book, highlights resources for further professional growth, and offers a forward-looking perspective on the pivotal role of simulation operations in healthcare education.

15.1 Summary of Key Takeaways

Healthcare simulation has transformed medical and nursing education by creating controlled, realistic environments, bridging the gap between theoretical learning and clinical practice. Insights from effective operations in healthcare education, as detailed in the document, emphasize several pivotal areas:

The 12 Pillars for Success in Simulation Operations

Simulation operations underpin the seamless integration of technology, curriculum, and pedagogy. Operational roles—such as simulation technicians, educators, and managers—ensure the successful implementation of programs through robust workflows, technical expertise, and strategic planning.

Clear operational guidelines and standardized procedures significantly enhance session efficiency and learner outcomes.

Maximizing Educational Impact through Diverse Modalities

Simulation employs various modalities, including mannequin-based training, standardized patients, and virtual reality (VR). These modalities cater to diverse learning objectives, such as skill acquisition, communication development, and interprofessional collaboration.

Integrated, hybrid simulations leverage the strengths of multiple approaches, preparing learners for the complexities of real-world clinical environments.

Simulation-Driven Improvements in Patient Safety and Care Quality

Simulation reduces medical errors by enabling the repeated practice of high-risk, low-frequency scenarios. It enhances patient safety. Studies confirm that simulation-based training improves clinical accuracy and procedural competency.

Ethics and Inclusivity in Simulation

Practical simulations uphold ethical training standards, focusing on learner safety and patient privacy and promoting nonjudgmental feedback. Programs incorporate psychosocial dimensions to foster empathy and cultural competence in diverse clinical settings.

Innovation and Adaptability in Simulation Practices

Technological advances, such as AI-driven simulations and haptic feedback systems, continue to push the boundaries of realism and personalization in training. Programs that integrate these innovations maintain relevance in evolving healthcare landscapes.

Operational Challenges and Continuous Improvement

Simulation programs face challenges like resource constraints, scheduling complexities, and technological maintenance. A commitment to feedback collection, quality improvement, and strategic resource management ensures long-term success and sustainability.

These principles collectively highlight the importance of operations in ensuring that simulation-based education achieves its goals of enhancing clinical skills, fostering teamwork, and ultimately improving patient outcomes. Integrating innovative technologies, interdisciplinary collaboration, and ethical practices positions simulation as a transformative force in healthcare education.

15.2 Resources for Further Reading

Various resources are available to advance knowledge and operational excellence in healthcare simulation. These resources span books, journals, online platforms, and conferences, each offering valuable insights into the technical, educational, and operational aspects of simulation-based training. Below is a comprehensive list of key materials, with examples to guide further exploration.

Books

Books on healthcare simulation offer in-depth perspectives on foundational concepts and advanced applications.

Foundational Texts
- *Healthcare Simulation Education: Evidence, Theory, and Practice* by Debra Nestel et al. A comprehensive resource covering simulation design, assessment strategies, and integration into curricula.
- *Comprehensive Healthcare Simulation: Operations, Technology, and Innovative Practice* edited by Scott B. Crawford and Neal J. Seymour. This text delves into the operational and technological aspects of running simulation centers.

Advanced and Specialized Topics
- *Defining Excellence in Simulation Programs* by Janice Palaganas et al. A guide for simulation managers and educators focusing on program evaluation, leadership, and sustainability.
- *SimWars Simulation Case Book: Emergency Medicine* by Lisa Jacobson et al. A specialized resource offering scenario-based simulation training for emergency medicine.
- *The Comprehensive Textbook of Healthcare Simulation* edited by Adam I. Levine, Samuel DeMaria Jr., and others. A multi-disciplinary text addressing simulation operations, education, and research.
- *Achieving and Maintaining Accreditation for Nursing School Programs: A Comprehensive Guide* by Keith A. Beaulieu. A comprehensive guide for navigating nursing school accreditation.

Journals

Journals provide access to the latest research, case studies, and innovations in healthcare simulation.

Leading Simulation Journals
- *Simulation in Healthcare* (Society for Simulation in Healthcare): Covers research on simulation techniques, efficacy, and technology advancements.
- *Advances in Simulation* (European *Society for Simulation in Healthcare*): Focuses on evidence-based practices and global trends in simulation education.
- *Clinical Simulation in Nursing* (INACSL): Offers articles on nursing-specific simulation practices, including ethics, operations, and interprofessional training.

Complementary Journals
- *Journal of Medical Education and Curricular Development*: Explores broader educational frameworks, including simulation.
- *Medical Teacher*: Publishes research on innovative teaching methodologies, including simulation-based learning.
- *BMJ Quality & Safety*: Highlights the role of simulation in improving patient safety and quality of care.

Online Platforms and Courses

Professional Associations
- *Society for Simulation in Healthcare (SSH)*: Offers webinars, online modules, and certification preparation for CHSE and CHSOS credentials.
- *INACSL Learning Center*: A repository of workshops and e-learning modules aligned with simulation best practices.

Online Learning Platforms
- *Coursera and EdX*: Hosts courses on virtual reality in healthcare, simulation methodologies, and instructional design.
- *SimTutor Academy*: Provides courses on scenario building, technical

troubleshooting, and educational strategies for simulation professionals.

Specialized Resources
- *Virtual Healthcare Simulations*: An extensive library of online simulation scenarios for clinical training is offered.

Conferences and Workshops

Global Events
- *International Meeting on Simulation in Healthcare (IMSH)*: The largest annual event for simulation professionals, featuring hands-on workshops, keynote sessions, and networking opportunities.
- *INACSL Annual Conference*: Focuses on clinical simulation standards and cutting-edge practices.
- *National League of Nursing (NLN) Education Summit*: This summit focuses on trending and emerging topics impacting the nursing education profession and discovers innovative strategies and solutions that address day-to-day challenges.

Regional and Thematic Conferences
- *SimOps*: emphasizes the role of simulation operations specialists in leading healthcare innovation and ensuring that simulation-based education and training are accessible to all, particularly in underserved communities and areas.
- *Canadian Network for Simulation in Healthcare (CNSH) Conference*: Highlights simulation advancements in Canadian healthcare education.
- *SimGHOSTS*: Dedicated to simulation technology and operations, offering technical training for simulation specialists.
- *SUN Conferences*: Vendor-specific from Laerdal, provides education and training on various topics, including Laerdal-specific training.
- *HPSN Conferences:* Vendor-specific from CAE, provides education and training on various topics, including CAE-specific training.

By exploring these books, journals, online courses, and conferences, healthcare simulation professionals can stay informed, refine their skills, and contribute to continuously improving simulation operations. These resources advance individual careers and strengthen the overall impact of simulation-based education in healthcare.

References

Chapter 1

AACN. (2022). *2022 Annual Report on Nursing Education Challenges.*

ACN. (2021). *The Essentials: Core Competencies for Professional Nursing Education.*

Abrahamson, S., Denson, J. S., & Wolf, R. M. (1969). Effectiveness of a simulator in training anesthesiology residents. *Journal of Medical Education, 44*(6), 515-519.

Advances in Simulation. (2023). *Wearable technology and haptic feedback in clinical skill practice.*

Body Interact. (2024). *Virtual patient platforms: Enhancing healthcare training.*

Bradley, P. (2006). The history of simulation in medical education and possible future directions. *Medical Education, 40*(3), 254–262.

Gaba, D. M. (1992). Crisis resource management and teamwork training in anesthesia. *Current Opinion in Anesthesiology, 5*(2), 195-202.

Gaba, D. M. (2004). The future vision of simulation in healthcare. *Quality and Safety in Health Care, 13*(Suppl 1), i2–i10.

Gordon, M. S. (1974). Cardiology patient simulator: Development of an animated heart. *Journal of Medical Education, 49*(5), 432-438.

Grogan, E. L., et al. (2004). The impact of aviation-based teamwork training on the attitudes of healthcare professionals. *Journal of the American College of Surgeons, 199*(6), 843-848.

Hayden, J. K., Smiley, R. A., Alexander, M., Kardong-Edgren, S., & Jeffries, P. R. (2014). The NCSBN National Simulation Study. *Journal of Nursing Regulation, 5*(2), S3–S40.

HealthySimulation. (2023). *Advances in AI-driven healthcare simulation tools.*

HealthySimulation. (2023). *US state nursing regulations and simulation policies.*

Helmreich, R. L., & Foushee, H. C. (1993). Why CRM? Empirical and theoretical bases of human factors training in aviation. In E. L. Wiener, B. G. Kanki, & R. L. Helmreich (Eds.), *Cockpit resource management* (pp. 3-45). Academic Press.

Journal of Nursing Regulation. (2022). *State policies on simulation use in nursing education.*

World Health Organization (WHO). (2023). *Chronic Disease Fact Sheet.*

Chapter 2

Anderson, L. W., et al. (2019). Impact of simulation-based cardiopulmonary resuscitation training on adherence to guidelines. Journal of Emergency Medicine, 57(4), 482-490.

Barsuk, J. H., et al. (2010). Simulation-based education and its impact on procedural skills and competency acquisition. Academic Medicine, 85(10), 1472-1480.

Bradley, P. (2006). The history and effectiveness of simulation in medical education. Medical Education, 40(3), 254-262.

Cochrane Database of Systematic Reviews, 1.

Gaba, D. M. (2004). The future vision of simulation in healthcare. Quality & Safety in Health Care, 13(Suppl 1), i2-i10.

Hayden, J. K., et al. (2014). The NCSBN National Simulation Study: A longitudinal, randomized, controlled study replacing clinical hours with simulation in prelicensure nursing education. Journal of Nursing Regulation, 5(2), S3-S40.

Krogh, K., et al. (2015). Simulation-based training improves technical skills in IV insertion for nursing students. Nurse Education Today, 35(2), 90-94.

Lapkin, S., et al. (2010). Effectiveness of patient simulation manikins in teaching clinical reasoning skills to undergraduate nursing students: A systematic review. Clinical Simulation in Nursing, 6(6), e207-e222.

Lindeman, C. A. (2021). Cost-effectiveness of simulation-based education: Balancing resources and outcomes in healthcare training. Simulation in Healthcare, 16(1), 14-21.

Liyanagunawardena, T. R., et al. (2017). The role of virtual simulations in stroke education and training. Stroke, 48(3), 745-752.

Niles, D. E., et al. (2017). Impact of neonatal resuscitation simulation training on time to competency. Pediatrics, 140(5), e20171763.

Pottle, J. (2019). Simulation in healthcare education: Evidence for improving knowledge, skills, and attitudes. Advances in Medical Education and Practice, 10, 155-163.

Reeves, S., et al. (2013). Interprofessional education and simulation: Training for collaborative practice. Journal of Interprofessional Care, 27(6), 436-442.

Rosen, M. A., et al. (2012). Simulation in emergency medicine: Evidence-based benefits for diagnostic accuracy. Annals of Emergency Medicine, 59(5), 389-399.

Salas, E., et al. (2008). Team training in the simulation environment: A meta-analysis. Journal of Applied Psychology, 93(5), 1020-1037.

Weaver, S. J., et al. (2010). Does simulation-based training improve patient safety outcomes? The Joint Commission Journal on Quality and Patient Safety, 36(9), 409-420.

Chapter 3

Anderson, L. W., & Krathwohl, D. R. (2001). A Taxonomy for Learning, Teaching, and Assessing: A Revision of Bloom's Taxonomy of Educational Objectives. Longman.

Bloom, B. S. (1956). Taxonomy of Educational Objectives: The Classification of Educational Goals. Longmans, Green.

Cook, D. A., et al. (2011). Comparative effectiveness of instructional design features in simulation-based education: Systematic review and meta-analysis. Medical Teacher, 33(11), e206-e220.

Fanning, R. M., & Gaba, D. M. (2007). The role of debriefing in simulation-based learning. Simulation in Healthcare, 2(2), 115-125.

Fey, M. K., et al. (2020). The use of standardized templates in simulation design: Impact on consistency and learner outcomes. Clinical Simulation in Nursing, 39, 8-14.

Gurusamy, K., et al. (2014). Virtual reality training for surgical trainees in laparoscopic surgery. Cochrane Database of Systematic Reviews, 1.

Hayden, J. K., et al. (2014). The NCSBN National Simulation Study: A longitudinal, randomized, controlled study replacing clinical hours with simulation in prelicensure nursing education. Journal of Nursing Regulation, 5(2), S3-S40.

Hassan, A., et al. (2017). Psychomotor skill development in healthcare simulation: Applying Bloom's psychomotor domain. Journal of Healthcare Education, 7(3), 112-118.

INACSL Standards Committee. (2021). Healthcare simulation standards of best practice. Clinical Simulation in Nursing, 58, 1-35.

Kardong-Edgren, S., et al. (2020). Best practices in simulation design: Evidence and recommendations. Simulation in Healthcare, 15(4), 216-222.

Lapkin, S., et al. (2010). Effectiveness of patient simulation manikins in teaching clinical reasoning skills to undergraduate nursing students: A systematic review. Clinical Simulation in Nursing, 6(6), e207-e222.

Lindeman, C. A. (2021). Cost-effectiveness of simulation-based education: Balancing resources and outcomes in healthcare training. Simulation in Healthcare, 16(1), 14-21.

Pottle, J. (2019). Simulation in healthcare education: Evidence for improving knowledge, skills, and attitudes. Advances in Medical Education and Practice, 10, 155-163.

Rosen, M. A., et al. (2018). Interprofessional collaboration in simulation-based healthcare education: Impact on learner outcomes. Journal of Interprofessional Care, 32(4), 449-456.

Rudolph, J. W., et al. (2007). There's no such thing as "nonjudgmental" debriefing: A theory and method for debriefing with good judgment. Simulation in Healthcare, 2(1), 49-55.

Sawyer, T., et al. (2016). PEARLS for systems integration: Promoting excellence and reflective learning in simulation (PEARLS). Academic Medicine, 91(2), 169-176.

TeamSTEPPS National Implementation Team. (2014). TeamSTEPPS 2.0: Strategies and tools to enhance performance and patient safety.

Weaver, S. J., et al. (2010). Does simulation-based team training improve patient safety outcomes? A meta-analysis. Journal of Quality and Patient Safety, 36(9), 409-420.

Chapter 4

Bradley, P. (2006). The history of simulation in medical education and possible future directions. Medical Education, 40(3), 254–262.

Cook, D. A., Brydges, R., Zendejas, B., Hamstra, S. J., & Hatala, R. (2011). Technology-enhanced simulation for health professions education: A systematic review and meta-analysis. JAMA, 306(9), 978–988.

Covey, S. R. (1989). The 7 Habits of Highly Effective People.

Dieckmann, P., Gaba, D., & Rall, M. (2007). Deepening the theoretical foundations of patient simulation as social practice. Simulation in Healthcare, 2(3), 183–193.

Eisenhower, D. D. (1954). Speech on time management and prioritization.

FEMA (2021). Business Continuity and Resilience Planning.

Fey, M. K., & Jenkins, L. S. (2020). Debriefing practices in nursing simulation: An updated review of the literature. Nursing Education Perspectives, 41(1), 36–41.

Gaba, D. M. (2004). The future vision of simulation in healthcare. Quality and Safety in Health Care, 13(Suppl 1), i2–i10.

Health Facilities Guidelines Institute (FGI). (2018). *Guidelines for design and construction of hospitals and outpatient facilities*. Facility Guidelines Institute. https://www.fgiguidelines.org

International Nursing Association for Clinical Simulation and Learning (INACSL). (2021). Standards of Best Practice: Simulation. Retrieved from https://www.inacsl.org.

Issenberg, S. B., McGaghie, W. C., Petrusa, E. R., Gordon, D. L., & Scalese, R. J. (1999). Features and uses of high-fidelity medical simulations that lead to effective learning: A BEME systematic review. Medical Teacher, 27(1), 10–28.

Johns Hopkins Medicine. (2020). *Simulation center design and operational benchmarks*. Johns Hopkins Medicine. https://www.hopkinsmedicine.org

Kneebone, R., Kidd, J., Nestel, D., Asvall, S., Paraskeva, P., & Darzi, A. (2004). An innovative model for teaching and learning clinical procedures. Medical Education, 38(6), 620–628.

Lateef, F. (2010). Simulation-based learning: Just like the real thing. Journal of Emergencies, Trauma, and Shock, 3(4), 348–352.

Liaison Committee on Medical Education (LCME). (2020). *Standards for medical school accreditation: Simulation lab requirements*. LCME. https://lcme.org

Mayo Clinic. (2021). *Multidisciplinary simulation center facility design.* Mayo Clinic. https://www.mayoclinic.org

Medley, C. F., & Horne, C. (2005). Using simulation technology for undergraduate nursing education. Journal of Nursing Education, 44(1), 31–34.

Nestel, D., Groom, J., Eikeland-Husebø, S., & O'Donnell, J. M. (2017). Simulation for learning and teaching procedural skills: The state of the science. Advances in Medical Education and Practice, 8, 57–68.

Rosen, K. R., McBride, J. M., Drake, R. L., & Sargeant, D. (2018). Simulation in health professions education. Medical Education, 52(10), 1018–1030.

Schwartz, R. W., & Barnett, R. D. (2011). Developing leaders for the future of academic medicine: The role of simulation-based education. Academic Medicine, 76(6), 623–629.

Society for Simulation in Healthcare (2022). Certification programs and simulation standards. Retrieved from https://www.ssih.org.

Society for Simulation in Healthcare (SSH). Accreditation Standards. Retrieved from https://www.ssih.org.

Zendejas, B., Wang, A. T., Brydges, R., Hamstra, S. J., & Cook, D. A. (2013). Cost considerations in simulation-based medical education: A systematic review. Simulation in Healthcare, 8(5), 199–208.

Ziv, A., Wolpe, P. R., Small, S. D., & Glick, S. (2003). Simulation-based medical education: An ethical imperative. Academic Medicine, 78(8), 783–788.

Chapter 5

CPP Global (2021). Workplace Conflict and How Businesses Can Harness It to Thrive.

Deloitte (2021). Human Capital Trends: The Social Enterprise in a World Disrupted.

Dieckmann, P., Gaba, D., & Rall, M. (2007). Deepening the theoretical foundations of patient simulation as social practice. Simulation in Healthcare, 2(3), 183–193.

FEMA (2021). Business Continuity and Resilience Planning.

Gallup (2021). State of the Global Workplace: 2021 Report.

Lateef, F. (2010). Simulation-based learning: Just like the real thing. Journal of Emergencies, Trauma, and Shock, 3(4), 348–352.

LinkedIn (2022). Workforce Learning Report.

Maslach, C., & Leiter, M. P. (2016). Understanding the burnout experience: Recent research and its implications for psychiatry. World Psychiatry, 15(2), 103–111.

McKinsey & Company (2021). Diversity Wins: How Inclusion Matters.

Mercer (2022). Global Talent Trends Report.

Nestel, D., Groom, J., Eikeland-Husebø, S., & O'Donnell, J. M. (2017). Simulation for learning and teaching procedural skills: The state of the science. Advances in Medical Education and Practice, 8, 57–68.

PwC (2022). Future of Work and HCM Survey.

SHRM (2022). Employee Turnover and Retention Trends.

Society for Simulation in Healthcare (2022). Certification programs and simulation standards. Retrieved from https://www.ssih.org.

Chapter 6

Aggarwal, R., Mytton, O. T., Derbrew, M., et al. (2010). Training and simulation for patient safety. BMJ Quality & Safety, 19(2), i34–i43.

Archer, J. C. (2010). State of the science in health professional education: Effective feedback. Medical Education, 44(1), 101–108.

Cook, D. A., Brydges, R., Hamstra, S. J., Zendejas, B., & Hatala, R. (2013). Comparative effectiveness of technology-enhanced simulation versus other instructional methods: A systematic review and meta-analysis. Simulation in Healthcare, 8(3), 117–127.

Dieckmann, P., Gaba, D., & Rall, M. (2009). Deepening the theoretical foundations of patient simulation as a social practice. Simulation in Healthcare, 2(3), 183–193.

Elfrink Cordi, V. L., Leighton, K., Ryan-Wenger, N., Doyle, T. J., & Ravert, P. (2012). History and development of the simulation effectiveness tool (SET). Clinical Simulation in Nursing, 8(6), e199–e210.

Eppich, W., & Cheng, A. (2015). Promoting excellence and reflective learning in simulation (PEARLS): Development and rationale for a blended approach to healthcare simulation debriefing. Simulation in Healthcare, 10(2), 106–115.

Fanning, R. M., & Gaba, D. M. (2007). The role of debriefing in simulation-based learning. Simulation in Healthcare, 2(2), 115–125.

Harden, R. M., & Gleeson, F. A. (1979). Assessment of clinical competence using an objective structured clinical examination (OSCE). Medical Education, 13(1), 41–54.

Jeffries, P. R. (2012). Simulation in nursing education: From conceptualization to evaluation (2nd ed.). National League for Nursing.

Kirkpatrick, D. L., & Kirkpatrick, J. D. (2006). Evaluating training programs: The four levels (3rd ed.). Berrett-Koehler Publishers.

Miller, G. E. (1990). The assessment of clinical skills/competence/performance. Academic

Medicine, 65(9), S63–S67.

Rudolph, J. W., Simon, R., Dufresne, R. L., & Raemer, D. B. (2007). There's no such thing as "nonjudgmental" debriefing: A theory and method for debriefing with good judgment. Simulation in Healthcare, 2(1), 49–55.

Sawyer, T., Laubach, V. A., Hudak, J., & Yamamura, K. (2016). Improvements in performance and teamwork in a pediatric setting: Simulation-based learning. Journal of Clinical Simulation in Nursing Education, 12(2), 65–72.

Ten Cate, O. (2005). Entrustability of professional activities: A new concept for clinical training. Medical Education, 39(12), 1176–1177.

Weaver, S. J., Dy, S. M., & Rosen, M. A. (2010). Team-training in healthcare: A narrative synthesis of the literature. BMJ Quality & Safety, 23(5), 359–372.

Chapter 7

Aggarwal, R., Mytton, O. T., Derbrew, M., et al. (2010). Training and simulation for patient safety. BMJ Quality & Safety, 19(2), i34–i43.

Cook, D. A., & Hatala, R. (2015). Validation of educational assessments in simulation: The key to meaningful measurement. Medical Education, 49(12), 1166–1178.

Cook, D. A., Brydges, R., Hamstra, S. J., & Hatala, R. (2015). Comparative effectiveness of technology-enhanced simulation versus other instructional methods. Journal of the American Medical Association, 306(9), 978–988.

Dieckmann, P., Molin Friis, S., Lippert, A., & Østergaard, D. (2009). The art and science of debriefing in simulation: Ideal and practice. Medical Teacher, 31(7), e287–e294.

Fanning, R. M., & Gaba, D. M. (2007). The role of debriefing in simulation-based learning. Simulation in Healthcare, 2(2), 115–125.

International Nursing Association for Clinical Simulation and Learning (INACSL). (2021). Standards of Best Practice: Simulation. Retrieved from https://www.inacsl.org.

Kirkpatrick, D. L., & Kirkpatrick, J. D. (2006). Evaluating training programs: The four levels (3rd ed.). Berrett-Koehler Publishers.

LeFlore, J. L., Anderson, M., Michael, J. L., Engle, W. D., & Anderson, J. (2007). Comparison of self-directed learning versus instructor-modeled learning during a simulated clinical experience. Simulation in Healthcare, 2(3), 170–177.

McGaghie, W. C., Issenberg, S. B., Cohen, E. R., Barsuk, J. H., & Wayne, D. B. (2010). Does simulation-based medical education with deliberate practice yield better results than traditional clinical education? A meta-analytic comparative review of the evidence. Academic Medicine, 86(6), 706–711.

Polit, D. F., & Beck, C. T. (2006). The content validity index: Are you sure you know what's being reported? Critique and recommendations. Research in Nursing & Health, 29(5), 489–497.

Rudolph, J. W., Simon, R., Rivard, P., Dufresne, R. L., & Raemer, D. B. (2007). Debriefing with good judgment: Combining rigorous feedback with genuine inquiry. Simulation in Healthcare, 2(1), 49–55.

Simulation Canada. Reporting Best Practices for Healthcare Simulation Programs. Retrieved from https://simulationcanada.ca.

Society for Simulation in Healthcare (SSH). Accreditation Standards. Retrieved from https://www.ssih.org.

Tavakol, M., & Dennick, R. (2011). Making sense of Cronbach's alpha. International Journal of Medical Education, 2, 53–55.

Weaver, S. J., Dy, S. M., & Rosen, M. A. (2010). Team-training in healthcare: A narrative synthesis of the literature. BMJ Quality & Safety, 23(5), 359–372.

Chapter 8

Barsom, E. Z., Graafland, M., & Schijven, M. P. (2016). Systematic review on the effectiveness of augmented reality applications in medical training. Surgical Endoscopy, 30(10), 4174–4183.

Bennett, J. R., & Blanchard, D. J. (2020). Overcoming barriers to online simulation: Technology access and learner equity. Medical Teacher, 42(7), 758–764.

Cook, D. A., Hatala, R., Brydges, R., & Zendejas, B. (2010). Technology-enhanced simulation for health professions education: A systematic review and meta-analysis. JAMA, 306(9), 978–988.

Farra, S. L., Smith, S. J., & Ulrich, D. L. (2018). The student experience with virtual reality simulation in disaster training. Nursing Education Perspectives, 39(6), 333–334.

Huang, G., Reynolds, T. A., & Watts, A. (2020). Machine learning in healthcare simulation: A systematic review. Simulation in Healthcare, 15(5), 360–368.

Kaufman, G., McCrea, H., & Chisnell, S. (2020). Virtual patient platforms in healthcare education. Nurse Education Today, 85, 104267.

Mantovani, F., Gaggioli, A., Castelnuovo, G., & Riva, G. (2011). Virtual reality training for healthcare professionals. Cyberpsychology, Behavior, and Social Networking, 14(6), 369–372.

Nestel, D., Molloy, E., Bearman, M., & Rose, M. (2021). Challenges in online and remote simulation-based learning: A narrative review. Clinical Simulation in Nursing, 56, 17–25.

O'Regan, S., Molloy, E., Watterson, L., & Nestel, D. (2016). Observer roles that optimize learning in healthcare simulation education: A systematic review. Advances in Simulation, 1(4), 12.

Papanagnou, D., Serrano, A., & Barkemeyer, C. (2019). Real-time analytics in simulation: Applications for team training. Journal of Patient Safety, 15(3), e15–e20.

Sarfaty, M., Siegel, E., & Weiner, J. (2020). AR-enhanced education: AccuVein and HoloAnatomy in medical training. Journal of Medical Innovation, 5(4), 112–118.

Topol, E. J. (2019). High-performance medicine: The convergence of human and artificial intelligence. Nature Medicine, 25(1), 44–56.

Zhao, C., Mai, Q., Li, X., & Zhang, Z. (2020). Artificial intelligence in medical education: An overview. Medical Science Monitor, 26, e927218.

Chapter 9

Agency for Healthcare Research and Quality (AHRQ). (2020). Simulation-based training to reduce medical errors. Retrieved from AHRQ Website.

Aggarwal, R., Mytton, O. T., Derbrew, M., Hananel, D., Heydenburg, M., Issenberg, B., ... & Reznick, R. (2010). Training and simulation for patient safety. Quality and Safety in Health Care, 19(Suppl 2), i34-i43. doi:10.1136/qshc.2009.038562.

Cook, D. A., Brydges, R., Hamstra, S. J., & Hatala, R. (2013). Comparative effectiveness of technology-enhanced simulation versus other instructional methods: A systematic review and meta-analysis. Simulation in Healthcare, 8(3), 117-127. doi:10.1097/SIH.0b013e31828400a3.

Fanning, R. M., & Gaba, D. M. (2007). The role of debriefing in simulation-based learning. Simulation in Healthcare, 2(2), 115-125. doi:10.1097/SIH.0b013e3180315539.

Healthcare Simulation Standards Committee. (2021). Healthcare Simulation Standards of Best Practice™. Clinical Simulation in Nursing, 58, 1-48. doi:10.1016/j.ecns.2021.08.016.

McGaghie, W. C., Issenberg, S. B., Cohen, E. R., Barsuk, J. H., & Wayne, D. B. (2011). Does simulation-based medical education with deliberate practice yield better results than traditional clinical education? A meta-analytic comparative review of the evidence. Academic Medicine, 86(6), 706-711. doi:10.1097/ACM.0b013e318217e119.

Nestel, D., Kelly, M., Jolly, B., & Watson, M. (2021). Simulation in healthcare education: Evidence, theory, and practice. Wiley-Blackwell.

Rosen, K. R., Salas, E., Silvestri, S., Wu, T. S., & Lazzara, E. H. (2018). The history of simulation in medical education and possible future directions. Medical Teacher, 40(9), 902-909. doi:10.1080/0142159X.2018.1487379.

Rudolph, J. W., Simon, R., Dufresne, R. L., & Raemer, D. B. (2007). There's no such thing as "nonjudgmental" debriefing: A theory and method for debriefing with good judgment. Simulation in Healthcare, 1(1), 49-55. doi:10.1097/01266021-200600110-00006.

Topol, E. J. (2019). Deep Medicine: How Artificial Intelligence Can Make Healthcare Human Again. Basic Books.

Weaver, S. J., Dy, S. M., & Rosen, M. A. (2014). Team-training in healthcare: A narrative synthesis of the literature. BMJ Quality & Safety, 23(5), 359-372. doi:10.1136/bmjqs-2013-001848.

Zendejas, B., Brydges, R., Wang, A. T., & Cook, D. A. (2013). Patient outcomes in simulation-based medical education: A systematic review. Journal of General Internal Medicine, 28(8), 1078-1089. doi:10.1007/s11606-012-2264-5.

Chapter 10

Aggarwal, R., Mytton, O. T., Derbrew, M., Hananel, D., Heydenburg, M., Issenberg, B., & Reznick, R. (2010). Training and simulation for patient safety. Quality and Safety in Health Care, 19(Suppl 2), i34–i43. https://doi.org/10.1136/qshc.2009.038562.

Agency for Healthcare Research and Quality (AHRQ). (2020). Impact of Simulation Training on Patient Safety and Clinical Outcomes. Retrieved from AHRQ.

Association of American Medical Colleges (AAMC). (2020). The Role of Simulation in Medical Education: A Report on Trends and Impact. Retrieved from AAMC.

Frost & Sullivan. (2021). Future of Healthcare Simulation: A Strategic Analysis of Emerging Technologies. Retrieved from Frost & Sullivan Research Reports.

Harvard Medical School. (2022). Postgraduate Medical Education: Simulation Fellowship. Retrieved from Harvard Medical School.

INACSL Standards Committee. (2021). Healthcare Simulation Standards of Best Practice™. Clinical Simulation in Nursing, 58, e1–e52. https://doi.org/10.1016/j.ecns.2021.08.006.

MarketsandMarkets. (2022). Healthcare/Medical Simulation Market by Product & Service (Model-based Simulation, Web-based Simulation, Simulation Training Services), End-user (Academic Institutes, Hospitals, Military Organizations), and Region - Global Forecast to 2027. Retrieved from MarketsandMarkets.

Rudolph, J. W., Simon, R., Raemer, D. B., & Eppich, W. J. (2007). Debriefing as formative assessment: Closing performance gaps in medical education. Academic Emergency Medicine, 15(11), 1010–1016. https://doi.org/10.1111/j.1553-2712.2007.tb02393.x.

Society for Simulation in Healthcare (SSH). (2022). Certification Benefits for Healthcare Simulation Professionals. Retrieved from SSH Certification.

Stanford Medicine. (2022). Healthcare Simulation Fellowship Program. Retrieved from Stanford Medicine.

U.S. Bureau of Labor Statistics (BLS). (2022). Occupational Outlook Handbook: Medical Equipment Repairers. Retrieved from BLS.

Zendejas, B., Brydges, R., Wang, A. T., & Cook, D. A. (2013). Patient outcomes in simulation-based medical education: A systematic review. Journal of Graduate Medical Education, 5(1), 16–20. https://doi.org/10.4300/JGME-D-12-00067.1.

Chapter 11

Association of Standardized Patient Educators (ASPE). (2021). Standards of Best Practice. Retrieved from https://www.aspeducators.org.

ASPE Standards Committee. (2021). Standardized Patient Methodology for Effective Role Fidelity.

Retrieved from https://www.aspeducators.org.

Dieckmann, P., Gaba, D., & Rall, M. (2007). Deepening the theoretical foundations of patient simulation as social practice. Simulation in Healthcare, 2(3), 183–193.

Gaba, D. M. (2004). The future vision of simulation in healthcare. Quality and Safety in Health Care, 13(suppl 1), i2–i10.

International Nursing Association for Clinical Simulation and Learning (INACSL). (2021). Standards of Best Practice: Simulation. Retrieved from https://www.inacsl.org.

INACSL Standards Committee. (2021). Debriefing for meaningful learning. Clinical Simulation in Nursing, 60, e1–e8.

Issenberg, S. B., McGaghie, W. C., Petrusa, E. R., Gordon, D. L., & Scalese, R. J. (2005). Features and uses of high-fidelity medical simulations that lead to effective learning: A BEME systematic review. Medical Teacher, 27(1), 10–28.

Rudolph, J. W., Simon, R., Dufresne, R. L., & Raemer, D. B. (2007). There's no such thing as "nonjudgmental" debriefing: A theory and method for debriefing with good judgment. Simulation in Healthcare, 2(1), 49–55.

Society for Simulation in Healthcare (SSH). (2022). Certified Healthcare Simulation Educator (CHSE) Program Standards. Retrieved from https://www.ssih.org/CHSE.

Society for Simulation in Healthcare (SSH). (2022). Healthcare Simulation Standards. Retrieved from https://www.ssih.org.

Chapter 12

Advances in Simulation. (2022). European Society for Simulation in Healthcare. Retrieved from Advances in Simulation.

Agency for Healthcare Research and Quality (AHRQ). (2020). The Role of Simulation in Enhancing Patient Safety. Retrieved from AHRQ.

Beaulieu, Keith. (2024). Achieving and Maintaining Accreditation for Nursing School Programs: A Comprehensive Guide. Porthos Press.

BMJ Quality & Safety. (2022). Using simulation to improve quality and safety in healthcare. Retrieved from BMJ Quality & Safety.

Clinical Simulation in Nursing. (2021). International Nursing Association for Clinical Simulation and Learning (INACSL). Retrieved from Clinical Simulation in Nursing.

Crawford, S. B., & Seymour, N. J. (Eds.). (2020). Comprehensive Healthcare Simulation: Operations, Technology, and Innovative Practice. Springer.

International Meeting on Simulation in Healthcare (IMSH). (2022). Annual Event for Simulation Professionals. Retrieved from IMSH.

INACSL. (2021). Healthcare Simulation Standards of Best Practice™. Retrieved from INACSL Standards.

Jacobson, L., Malekzadeh, S., & Sarkar, P. (Eds.). (2015). SimWars Simulation Case Book: Emergency Medicine. Springer.

Levine, A. I., DeMaria, S. Jr., Schwartz, A. D., & Sim, A. J. (Eds.). (2013). The Comprehensive Textbook of Healthcare Simulation. Springer.

MarketsandMarkets. (2022). Healthcare/Medical Simulation Market by Product & Service (Model-based Simulation, Web-based Simulation, Simulation Training Services), End-user (Academic Institutes, Hospitals, Military Organizations), and Region - Global Forecast to 2027. Retrieved from MarketsandMarkets.

Nestel, D., Kelly, M., Jolly, B., & Watson, M. (Eds.). (2017). Healthcare Simulation Education: Evidence, Theory, and Practice. Wiley-Blackwell.

Palaganas, J. C., Fey, M., Simon, R., & Clapper, T. (Eds.). (2015). Defining Excellence in Simulation Programs. Lippincott Williams & Wilkins.

SimGHOSTS. (2022). Gathering of Healthcare Simulation Technology Specialists. Retrieved from SimGHOSTS.

SimOps. (2022). Annual Conference for Simulation Operations Specialists. Retrieved from SimOps.

Society for Simulation in Healthcare (SSH). (2022). Simulation in Healthcare Journal. Retrieved from SSH Journals.

Chapter 13

Anderson, P., Brown, T., & Smith, J. (2020). Stakeholder engagement in simulation-based integration projects: A review of best practices. International Journal of Simulation Research, 15(3), 45-58.

Brown, R., & Wilson, K. (2018). Uncovering blind spots: The role of feedback in simulation-based learning. Simulation in Practice Journal, 12(4), 32-41.

Doe, J., & Lee, A. (2020). The impact of participant feedback on simulation engagement and outcomes. Journal of Simulation Education, 8(2), 23-29.

Fritz, M., Miller, T., & Johnson, R. (2020). Reducing post-deployment errors through simulation-based fault identification: A longitudinal study. Systems Integration Journal, 14(1), 12-20.

Gartner. (2022). The role of digital twins in systems integration and performance optimization. Gartner Research Insights. Retrieved from https://www.gartner.com.

HIMSS Analytics. (2021). Improving EHR integration through simulation: A case study. HIMSS White Papers. Retrieved from https://www.himssanalytics.org.

Johnson, R., Taylor, S., & Evans, P. (2021). Enhancing realism in simulation through participant and organizational feedback. Advances in Simulation, 7(1), 56-63.

Smith, L., Patel, A., & Jones, B. (2019). Optimizing manufacturing processes through systems integration simulations. Manufacturing Journal, 18(3), 67-75.

Weaver, S. J., Dy, S. M., & Rosen, M. A. (2010). Team-training in healthcare: A narrative synthesis of the literature. BMJ Quality & Safety, 19(6), 490–498. https://doi.org/10.1136/qshc.2009.038181.

Chapter 14

Healthcare Cybersecurity Consortium (2022). Ransomware Incidents in Healthcare.

National Center for Simulation (2022). Best Practices for Simulation Maintenance.

Society for Simulation in Healthcare (SSH, 2020). Survey of Operational Challenges in Simulation Centers.

Frost & Sullivan (2021). Global Simulation Technology Market Report.

Appendices

Appendix A

Strategic Planning Tool

Purpose: This worksheet is designed to guide simulation center leadership and teams through a structured strategic planning process. It focuses on aligning the center's goals, resources, and operations with its mission and vision.

Section 1: Mission, Vision, and Values
1. **Mission Statement**:
    - What is the primary purpose of the simulation center?
    - How does the center contribute to education, training, and patient care?
    Example: "To advance healthcare education through innovative simulation experiences that improve patient outcomes."

Your Mission Statement:

2. **Vision Statement**:
    - What is the long-term aspiration for the center?
    Example: "To be a leader in simulation-based education and research, fostering collaboration and innovation."

Your Vision Statement:

3. **Core Values**:
    - List 3–5 values that define the center's culture and priorities (e.g., innovation, collaboration, inclusivity).
    -

Your Core Values:
   - ___
   - ___
   - ___

Section 2: SWOT Analysis
Identify internal and external factors affecting the simulation center.

1. **Strengths** (What are the center's advantages?)
    - ___

- ○ —

2. **Weaknesses** (What areas need improvement?)
    - ○ —
    - ○ —

3. **Opportunities** (What external factors could be leveraged?)
    - ○ —
    - ○ —

4. **Threats** (What external challenges might hinder success?)
    - ○ —
    - ○ —

Section 3: Strategic Goals
Define 3–5 SMART (Specific, Measurable, Achievable, Relevant, Time-Bound) goals for the center.

Goal 1:
- Description: _____
- Success Metrics: _____
- Timeline: _____
- Responsible Party: _____

Goal 2:
- Description: _____
- Success Metrics: _____
- Timeline: _____
- Responsible Party: _____

Goal 3:
- Description: _____
- Success Metrics: _____
- Timeline: _____
- Responsible Party: _____

Section 4: Stakeholder Engagement
1. **Key Stakeholders**:
    - ○ Who are the stakeholders (e.g., faculty, learners, institutional leadership, community partners)?

2. **Communication Plan**:
    - ○ How will you involve stakeholders in the planning process?

Section 5: Resource Assessment
1. **Current Resources**:
    - Equipment: _____
    - Staff: _____
    - Budget: _____

2. **Needed Resources**:
    - Equipment Upgrades: _____
    - Additional Staff: _____
    - Funding Opportunities: _____

3. **Resource Alignment**:
    - How will you allocate resources to achieve strategic goals?

Section 6: Action Plan
For each strategic goal, outline specific action steps.

Goal 1 Action Plan:
- Step 1: _____
- Step 2: _____
- Step 3: _____

Goal 2 Action Plan:
- Step 1: _____
- Step 2: _____
- Step 3: _____

Goal 3 Action Plan:
- Step 1: _____
- Step 2: _____
- Step 3: _____

Section 7: Evaluation and Monitoring
1. **Performance Metrics**:
    - What indicators will you use to measure progress (e.g., learner satisfaction, session completion rates, budget adherence)?

2. **Review Timeline**:

- How often will you review and update the strategic plan?
  ☐ Quarterly ☐ Biannually ☐ Annually

3. **Feedback Mechanisms**:
    - How will you gather input from staff and stakeholders during implementation?

Section 8: Final Summary

1. What are the top 3 priorities for the next 12 months?
    - Priority 1: _____
    - Priority 2: _____
    - Priority 3: _____

2. Who will be responsible for overseeing the strategic plan?
    - __

Appendix B

Sample Simulation Scenario Template

Note: Standardized simulation templates may vary from center to center.

1. **General Information**
    - **Scenario Title:**
    - **Date Created/Updated:**
    - **Authors:**
    - **Target Learners:** (e.g., Medical Students, Nursing Students, Interprofessional Teams)
    - **Simulation Modality:** (e.g., High-Fidelity Manikin, Task Trainer, Virtual Reality)
    - **Duration:**
        - **Prebriefing Time:**
        - **Scenario Time:**
        - **Debriefing Time:**

2. **Prebriefing**
    - Confidentiality
    - Orientation to environment/equipment
    - Flow/schedule of events
    - Case stem

3. **Learning Objectives**
By the end of this simulation, participants will be able to:
    1. *(Cognitive)*
    2. *(Psychomotor)*
    3. *(Affective)*

4. **Case Overview**
    - **Patient Name:**
    - **Age:**
    - **Gender:**
    - **Weight/Height:**
    - **Primary Diagnosis:**
    - **Secondary Diagnoses:** (if applicable)
    - **Clinical Setting:** (e.g., Emergency Department, Intensive Care Unit, Primary Care Clinic)
    - **Scenario Complexity Level:** (e.g., Beginner, Intermediate, Advanced)

5. **Case Description**
    - **Presenting Complaint:** (e.g., "Chest pain for 2 hours.")
    - **History of Present Illness:**
    - **Past Medical History:**
    - **Medications:**
    - **Allergies:**

- **Social History:**
- **Family History:**

6. Pre-Simulation Requirements
- **Knowledge or Skills Required**: (e.g., "Basic ECG interpretation, medication dosage calculation.")
- **Preparation Materials**: (e.g., relevant guidelines, videos, or reading assignments.)
- **Equipment Needed**:
    - Manikin/Simulator:
    - Medical Equipment:
    - Medications:
    - Technology: (e.g., monitors, defibrillators)

7. Scenario Flow
- **Initial Patient Presentation**: (Include baseline vital signs, demeanor, and position.)
- **Anticipated Actions by Participants**:
    - **Key Interventions**: (e.g., perform an ECG, administer medications.)
    - **Expected Decisions**: (e.g., escalate care, initiate a protocol.)
- **Cueing Strategies**: (How facilitators can guide participants if needed.)
- **Expected Outcomes**: (How the scenario should progress based on learner actions.)

8. Clinical Information
- **Baseline Vitals**:
    - Heart Rate:
    - Blood Pressure:
    - Respiratory Rate:
    - Oxygen Saturation:
    - Temperature:
- **Dynamic Changes**: (Vital signs or conditions that change based on actions or time.)
    - **Cue 1**:
    - **Cue 2**:

9. Roles and Resources
- **Roles Required for Scenario**:
    - Participant Roles: (e.g., Primary Nurse, Physician, Respiratory Therapist)
    - Faculty/Staff Roles: (e.g., Scenario Lead, Voice of the Patient, Observer)
- **Additional Resources**: (e.g., lab results, imaging, family member calls.)

10. Debriefing Plan
- **Debriefing Framework**: (e.g., PEARLS, Gather-Analyze-Summarize)
- **Key Discussion Points**:
    - Clinical Reasoning:
    - Teamwork and Communication:
    - Technical Skills:
    - Emotional Reactions:
- **Learning Reinforcement Activities**: (e.g., review clinical guidelines, repeat key tasks.)

11. Scenario Evaluation
- **Assessment Tools**:
    - Checklist for Critical Actions:

- o Rubric for Performance Metrics:
- **Feedback Collection**:
  - o Participant Feedback Form
  - o Faculty Feedback Form

12. Notes and Additional Instructions
- **Special Considerations**: (e.g., cultural factors, patient family involvement.)
- **Adaptations for Different Learner Levels**:

13. References and Supporting Materials
- **Citations**: (e.g., clinical guidelines, journal articles.)
- **Attachments**: (e.g., lab reports, ECG strips, x-ray images.)
- **Documentation of Changes**

… SIMULATION OPERATIONS IN HEALTHCARE EDUCATION: A PRIMER INTO THE ROLE OF OPERATIONS IN MEDICAL AND NURSING TRAINING

Appendix C

Sample Standardized Patient Script

Sample Standardized Patient Script
Aligned with Best Practices for Medical Education

Case Title
"Evaluation of Chest Pain in the Emergency Department"

1. Case Overview
Patient Name: Maria Hernandez
Age: 58
Gender: Female
Setting: Emergency Department
Chief Complaint: Chest pain

Objective: Assess the learner's ability to take a focused history, communicate effectively, and develop a preliminary differential diagnosis.

2. Patient Presentation
Appearance: Alert, slightly anxious. Sitting upright.
Clothing: Casual attire appropriate for a visit to the Emergency Department.
Emotional Tone: Cooperative but concerned. Voice may reflect mild anxiety.
Non-Verbal Cues: Frequently places hand on chest during the interview, shifts uncomfortably in the chair.

3. Script: Patient's Story
Opening Statement
When the learner asks, "What brings you in today?" respond:
"I've been having this pain in my chest, and I'm worried it could be something serious."
History of Present Illness
Provide details when prompted by the learner's questions:
Location of Pain
"It's right here in the middle of my chest." (Gesture to the sternum.)
Character of Pain
"It feels like a pressure, almost like something heavy is sitting on my chest."
Onset and Timing
"It started about an hour ago while I was watching TV. It's not constant, but it keeps coming back every few minutes."
Duration
"Each time it lasts maybe five minutes, then eases up a little."
Exacerbating/Relieving Factors
"It gets worse when I try to take a deep breath or when I move around."
"It doesn't seem to get better no matter what I do."
Associated Symptoms
"I feel a little short of breath, and I've been sweating more than usual. I also feel a little nauseous."
Severity

"I'd say it's about a 7 out of 10 when it's bad."

Past Medical History
If asked:
"I have high blood pressure, and I've been told I might have diabetes."
"I had my gallbladder removed a few years ago, but no other surgeries."

Family History
If asked:
"My father died of a heart attack when he was 60, and my mom had diabetes."

Social History
If asked:
Occupation: "I'm a retired teacher."
Living Situation: "I live with my husband."
Smoking: "I smoked for about 10 years in my 20s but quit a long time ago."
Alcohol: "I might have a glass of wine with dinner a couple of times a week."
Exercise: "I try to walk around my neighborhood a few times a week."
Diet: "I eat pretty healthy, but I do like sweets."

Medications
If asked:
"I take amlodipine for my blood pressure."
"I also take over-the-counter ibuprofen occasionally for headaches."

Allergies
If asked:
"I'm allergic to penicillin—it gives me a rash."

4. Non-Verbal Behaviors
Pain Gestures: Occasionally place your hand on your chest when describing symptoms.
Facial Expressions: Appear slightly anxious but not panicked.
Movement: Shift slightly in the chair, as though uncomfortable. Avoid sudden or exaggerated gestures.

5. Communication Style
Be forthcoming with information when asked directly.
Respond positively to empathetic statements, e.g., "Thank you for explaining that—I've been really worried."
Avoid volunteering unnecessary details unless prompted by the learner's questions.

6. Common Learner Pitfalls
If the learner:
Fails to ask open-ended questions, respond with brief answers to encourage them to dig deeper.

Example: If they ask, "Does it hurt when you breathe?" say, "Sometimes" instead of providing a full explanation.

Misses key follow-up questions, gently redirect:
"Should I be worried about this? My father had a heart attack."

7. Evaluation Checklist for Learners
History-Taking Skills

Asked about the location, quality, and severity of pain.
Inquired about associated symptoms (e.g., shortness of breath, nausea).
Explored relevant family, social, and medical history.
Communication Skills
Demonstrated empathy and active listening.
Used clear and patient-friendly language.
Maintained appropriate eye contact and non-verbal cues.
Clinical Reasoning
Identified key red flags (e.g., chest pain, shortness of breath, family history of cardiac disease).
Suggested appropriate next steps (e.g., ordering ECG, considering cardiac enzymes).

8. Debriefing Prompts for the Facilitator

What did you do well in gathering the patient's history?
What questions could you have asked to gain more information?
How did you demonstrate empathy and build rapport with the patient?
What would your next steps be based on this case?

9. Case Variations (Optional)

For different levels of learners or scenarios:

Beginner Level: Keep the symptoms straightforward with no unexpected findings.

Advanced Level: Introduce additional complexities (e.g., atypical presentation, language barriers, emotional distress).

Appendix D

Sample Business Plan

Business Plan for _____ Simulation Center

Executive Summary

The _____ Simulation Center is a proposed state-of-the-art facility designed to enhance professional training and education through cutting-edge simulation technologies. Our mission is to provide learners with a safe, immersive environment to develop, practice, and perfect critical skills. The center will focus on healthcare, corporate, and interdisciplinary training, filling a growing market need for high-quality simulation-based learning in the region.

Goals:
- Launch the center within 12 months.
- Train 500 professionals in the first year.
- Achieve financial sustainability within three years.

Funding Request: $1.5 million in initial capital to cover setup, staffing, and marketing expenses.

Market Analysis

Target Audience:
- Healthcare professionals (e.g., nurses, doctors, paramedics).
- Corporate clients seeking leadership and crisis management training.
- Educational institutions requiring hands-on training solutions.

Market Trends:
- Increasing demand for simulation-based training in healthcare and corporate sectors.
- Technological advancements enabling more realistic and cost-effective simulations.

Competitive Landscape:
- Limited regional availability of high-fidelity simulation centers.
- Simulation Center's focus on interdisciplinary training provides a unique edge.

> Use data and research: back up your claims with reliable data and credible sources

> Add a proper SWOT analysis

Strategic Goals and Objectives

1. **Short-Term Goals**:
    - Secure funding and partnerships within six months.
    - Procure and install simulation equipment within nine months.
    - Begin pilot training programs by the first year.
2. **Long-Term Goals**:
    - Expand into additional markets (e.g., aviation, military) by year three.
    - Establish the center as a regional hub for innovation in simulation training.

Infrastructure and Technology Requirements

Facility Needs:
- A 10,000-square-foot building with classrooms, simulation labs, and debriefing rooms.
- Modular spaces for flexible training setups.

Equipment:
- High-fidelity manikins for healthcare training.
- Virtual reality (VR) systems for immersive learning.
- Audio-visual equipment for real-time feedback and recording.

Technology Budget: $600,000 for procurement and setup.

Financial Plan

Startup Costs:
- Facility Renovation: $300,000
- Equipment Purchase: $600,000
- Staffing and Training: $200,000
- Marketing and Outreach: $100,000
- Contingency: $100,000

Total Startup Costs: $1.3 million

> Use proper spreadsheets or budget formats as directed by your organization

Revenue Projections:
- Year 1: $500,000 (pilot programs and initial partnerships).
- Year 2: $800,000 (expanded programs).
- Year 3: $1.2 million (full operational capacity).

Funding Sources:
- Grants and sponsorships: $800,000
- Institutional funding: $400,000
- Revenue reinvestment: $100,000

Organizational Structure and Staffing

Key Personnel:
- Director of Simulation: Oversee operations and strategic planning.
- Simulation Technicians: Manage equipment and support training sessions.
- Educators/Facilitators: Develop and deliver training programs.
- Administrative Staff: Handle scheduling, marketing, and finances.

> Add an organizational chart

Staffing Budget: $200,000 annually for salaries and benefits.

Marketing and Outreach Strategies

Target Channels:
- Digital Marketing: Website, social media, and email campaigns.
- Partnerships: Collaborations with hospitals, universities, and corporations.
- Events: Open houses, demonstrations, and workshops to showcase the center.

Promotional Activities:
- Launch an event to introduce the center to the community.
- Free trial sessions for early adopters to generate interest.
- Testimonials and success stories to build credibility.

Risk Assessment and Contingency Plan

Potential Risks:
- Financial shortfalls due to insufficient enrollment.
- Technological obsolescence requiring frequent updates.
- Operational challenges with staffing or equipment maintenance.

Mitigation Strategies:
- Secure multi-year partnerships for stable revenue.
- Allocate a contingency fund for unexpected expenses.
- Regularly update equipment and retrain staff on emerging technologies.

Conclusion

The _____ Simulation Center will revolutionize professional training in the region, addressing critical gaps in hands-on education. By leveraging cutting-edge technology and a strategic business plan, the center will establish itself as a leader in simulation-based learning. We invite stakeholders to join us in this mission to create a safer, more competent workforce.

Appendix E

Sample Growth Proposal

Executive Summary

The [Simulation Center Name] is a cornerstone of innovation in healthcare education, equipping learners with the skills necessary to improve patient outcomes and foster interprofessional collaboration. As the demand for healthcare professionals grows, so does the need for advanced, high-quality training. This proposal outlines a plan to expand our simulation center's capacity, integrate emerging technologies, and enhance our educational programs to meet these demands.

Key Objectives:
1. Expand physical space to accommodate increasing learner enrollment.
2. Invest in advanced simulation technologies, such as virtual reality (VR) and augmented reality (AR).
3. Enhance staff capacity and professional development to support new initiatives.

Projected Outcomes:
- A 25% increase in learner throughput within two years.
- Improved learner competency scores by integrating cutting-edge technologies.
- Strengthened institutional reputation as a leader in healthcare education.

Current State Assessment

Utilization and Demand
- Current enrollment in healthcare programs has increased by 20% over the past three years, with simulation sessions operating at 95% capacity during peak times.
- Scheduling conflicts have become common, particularly for high-stakes assessments and interprofessional education (IPE) activities.

Technological and Spatial Limitations
- The center currently operates with five high-fidelity manikins, which are fully utilized during academic terms.
- Limited debriefing spaces hinder the ability to run concurrent sessions, delaying feedback and learner reflection.

Feedback and Performance Metrics
- 85% of learners reported high satisfaction with simulation-based learning but identified access limitations as a barrier to maximizing its benefits.
- Faculty feedback highlighted the need for updated equipment and expanded facilities to support curriculum innovations.

Proposed Expansion

1. Facility Expansion

Objective: Increase physical space to support additional simulation activities.
- Add two high-fidelity simulation rooms equipped with advanced audiovisual systems.
- Create a dedicated interprofessional simulation lab to support IPE activities.
- Expand debriefing spaces to facilitate concurrent sessions and immediate feedback.

Cost Estimate: $500,000
Timeline: 18 months

2. Technology Upgrades

Objective: Integrate cutting-edge technologies to enhance learner experiences.
- Purchase VR and AR systems to simulate complex clinical scenarios and improve learner engagement.
- Upgrade current high-fidelity manikins with advanced software capabilities for real-time data analytics.
- Implement a digital scheduling and tracking system to optimize resource utilization.

Cost Estimate: $250,000
Timeline: 12 months

3. Staff Development

Objective: Build staff capacity to support growth initiatives.
- Hire one additional simulation technician and a simulation educator with expertise in VR/AR integration.
- Provide professional development opportunities, including Certified Healthcare Simulation Educator (CHSE) and Certified Healthcare Simulation Operations Specialist (CHSOS) certifications for staff.
-

Cost Estimate: $150,000 (first year, including salaries and training)
Timeline: 6 months

Budget and Funding Plan
Total Project Cost: $900,000

Proposed Funding Sources:
1. Institutional Investment: $400,000

- Aligned with institutional strategic priorities, including increasing learner enrollment and improving accreditation readiness.
2. External Grants: $250,000
    - Targeted applications to organizations such as the *Society for Simulation in Healthcare* (SSH) and local healthcare foundations.
3. Philanthropic Support: $150,000
    - Engage alumni and community donors through fundraising campaigns.
4. Fee-Based Training Programs: $100,000
    - Expand customized training offerings for local healthcare organizations to generate additional revenue.

Expected Outcomes

<u>1. Increased Capacity and Access</u>
- Accommodate 25% more learners annually by expanding physical space and session availability.
- Reduce scheduling conflicts and improve access for faculty and learners.

<u>2. Enhanced Educational Outcomes</u>
- Improved competency scores across clinical and interprofessional domains by incorporating VR/AR technologies.
- Increased learner satisfaction rates to 95% or higher, based on post-simulation evaluations.

<u>3. Strengthened Institutional Reputation</u>
- Recognition as a leader in innovative healthcare education and a competitive advantage in attracting top talent for both learners and faculty.
- Expanded partnerships with external stakeholders, including healthcare organizations and industry leaders.

Implementation Plan

<u>Phase 1: Planning and Design (Months 1–6)</u>
- Conduct detailed space planning with architects and contractors.
- Finalize technology specifications and purchase agreements.
- Recruit and onboard additional staff.

<u>Phase 2: Construction and Procurement (Months 7–18)</u>
- Complete facility renovations and new room construction.
- Install VR/AR systems and upgrade existing equipment.

<u>Phase 3: Launch and Evaluation (Months 19–24)</u>
- Begin new simulation sessions in expanded facilities.
- Conduct pre- and post-expansion evaluations to measure outcomes.
- Use findings to refine and optimize operations.

Stakeholder Engagement Plan

Internal Stakeholders
- Collaborate with institutional leadership to align growth initiatives with strategic goals.
- Engage faculty through workshops to integrate new technologies into curricula.

External Stakeholders
- Host open houses and tours to showcase expansion plans and foster donor engagement.
- Partner with local healthcare organizations to offer customized training programs.

Conclusion

The proposed growth plan for [Simulation Center Name] represents a strategic investment in the future of healthcare education. By expanding facilities, integrating advanced technologies, and enhancing staff capacity, the center will continue to prepare healthcare professionals for real-world challenges. This vision can become a reality with institutional and community support, driving innovation and improving outcomes for learners and patients alike.

Appendices

1. Detailed Budget Breakdown
2. Architectural Blueprints (if available)
3. Supporting Data and Graphs (e.g., utilization trends, learner outcomes)

Appendix F

Sample Checklist to Evaluate Workflow

Simulation Center Workflow Evaluation Checklist

This checklist provides a comprehensive guide for simulation center managers to evaluate and optimize workflows across key operational areas.

1. Scheduling and Resource Allocation
    - ☐ Are simulation sessions scheduled efficiently to avoid conflicts or bottlenecks?
    - ☐ Is there a centralized system for booking rooms, equipment, and staff time?
    - ☐ Are session requests reviewed and approved promptly?
    - ☐ Is resource availability communicated to staff and faculty in advance?
    - ☐ Are high-demand resources allocated based on priority or usage policies?

2. Equipment and Facility Management
    - ☐ Is equipment maintained regularly according to a documented schedule?
    - ☐ Are backup systems in place for critical equipment?
    - ☐ Is the inventory of consumables tracked and restocked proactively?
    - ☐ Are simulation rooms cleaned and prepped before each session?
    - ☐ Is there a system for reporting and addressing equipment issues promptly?

3. Communication and Coordination
    - ☐ Are staff and faculty notified of simulation schedules in advance?
    - ☐ Are responsibilities and roles clearly assigned for each session?
    - ☐ Are there regular team meetings to discuss workflow challenges and updates?
    - ☐ Is there a reliable method (e.g., email, app, or platform) for real-time communication?
    - ☐ Are debriefing and follow-up processes communicated effectively to participants?

4. Simulation Session Execution
    - ☐ Are scenarios reviewed and approved before implementation?
    - ☐ Are pre-session checklists used to ensure readiness of equipment, staff, and participants?
    - ☐ Are sessions starting and ending on time?
    - ☐ Are participants briefed and prepared for each session?
    - ☐ Are scenarios executed smoothly with minimal interruptions?

5. Data and Documentation
    - ☐ Is participant performance data recorded accurately and securely?
    - ☐ Are post-simulation debriefs documented for quality assurance?
    - ☐ Is there a system for tracking session attendance and completion?
    - ☐ Are evaluation and feedback forms collected consistently?
    - ☐ Are key metrics (e.g., equipment usage, session outcomes) monitored regularly?

6. Training and Professional Development
    - ☐ Are staff adequately trained in simulation technology and workflows?
    - ☐ Are faculty and instructors provided with ongoing training opportunities?
    - ☐ Are new staff onboarded effectively with clear workflow instructions?

- ☐ Are there regular workshops or meetings to improve skills and address workflow challenges?
- ☐ Is cross-training implemented to ensure operational continuity?

7. Health, Safety, and Compliance
   - ☐ Are emergency procedures clearly documented and accessible?
   - ☐ Are all staff trained in safety protocols, including equipment use and infection control?
   - ☐ Are participants informed about safety procedures before simulations begin?
   - ☐ Are health and safety checks conducted regularly in the simulation environment?
   - ☐ Are compliance requirements (e.g., HIPAA, OSHA) reviewed and met?

8. Technology Integration
   - ☐ Are software tools (e.g., scheduling, simulation management) effectively utilized?
   - ☐ Are simulation systems integrated with learning management systems (LMS) where applicable?
   - ☐ Are all technical systems functioning optimally without frequent downtime?
   - ☐ Is technical support available during all simulation sessions?
   - ☐ Are tools and platforms reviewed regularly for upgrades and improvements?

9. Participant and Faculty Feedback
   - ☐ Is feedback collected from participants after each session?
   - ☐ Are faculty and staff encouraged to provide suggestions for workflow improvement?
   - ☐ Is feedback analyzed and incorporated into workflow updates?
   - ☐ Are follow-up communications sent to address concerns or suggestions?

10. Continuous Quality Improvement
    - ☐ Are workflow metrics reviewed and analyzed regularly?
    - ☐ Are recurring issues identified and addressed proactively?
    - ☐ Are new tools or methods explored to enhance efficiency?
    - ☐ Are there mechanisms in place to test and evaluate workflow changes?
    - ☐ Is a culture of continuous improvement promoted among staff and faculty?

Appendix G

Sample Equipment Lifecycle Management Tool

Sample Equipment Refresh Lifecycle for a Simulation Center
A well-planned equipment refresh lifecycle ensures that simulation centers operate efficiently, maintain cutting-edge technology, and minimize downtime. Below is a sample lifecycle tailored for a typical simulation center.

1. Planning Phase (Months 0–12)
Goal: Assess current equipment and plan for future needs.
- **Inventory Review**
    - Conduct a detailed audit of all equipment, including simulation manikins, medical devices, AV systems, and IT infrastructure.
    - Record age, usage frequency, maintenance history, and performance.
- **Needs Assessment**
    - Engage stakeholders (faculty, technicians, and students) to identify gaps in current equipment and emerging needs.
    - Align with organizational goals (e.g., expanding programs, adopting new technologies).
- **Budget Planning**
    - Develop a budget for replacement and upgrades, including costs for equipment, software, warranties, and training.
    - Explore funding opportunities (grants, donations, partnerships).
- **Technology Trends Analysis**
    - Research advancements in simulation technology (e.g., VR/AR systems, AI-enabled manikins).
    - Benchmark with other simulation centers to identify best practices.

2. Procurement Phase (Months 12–18)
Goal: Select and acquire new equipment.
- **Vendor Evaluation**
    - Identify reputable vendors and request demonstrations or trials of new equipment.
    - Compare features, warranties, support services, and costs.
- **Request for Proposals (RFP)**
    - Issue RFPs with detailed specifications for required equipment.
    - Evaluate proposals based on performance, compatibility, and total cost of ownership.
- **Purchase Approval**
    - Present proposals to decision-makers for approval.
    - Secure purchase agreements, including extended warranties and training options.

3. Deployment Phase (Months 18–24)

Goal: Install and integrate new equipment into operations.
- **Installation and Setup**
  - Schedule installation with minimal disruption to ongoing operations.
  - Ensure compatibility with existing infrastructure (AV systems, software platforms).
- **Training and Documentation**
  - Train staff and faculty on the operation, maintenance, and troubleshooting of new equipment.
  - Update operational manuals and protocols to include new equipment.
- **Testing and Calibration**
  - Conduct thorough testing to confirm functionality and performance.
  - Address any issues or inconsistencies before deployment.

4. Utilization Phase (Years 2–4)
Goal: Optimize the use of equipment and monitor performance.
- **Routine Maintenance**
  - Follow manufacturer-recommended maintenance schedules (e.g., cleaning, calibration).
  - Keep detailed maintenance logs for each piece of equipment.
- **Performance Monitoring**
  - Track equipment usage to identify high-demand items and underutilized resources.
  - Regularly solicit feedback from users to identify potential improvements.
- **Periodic Upgrades**
  - Apply software updates and firmware patches as needed.
  - Upgrade accessories or components to extend functionality.

5. Evaluation Phase (Years 4–5)
Goal: Determine when to replace or upgrade equipment.
- **Condition Assessment**
  - Evaluate equipment for wear and tear, declining performance, or obsolescence.
  - Assess whether the equipment meets current educational and technological needs.
- **Cost-Benefit Analysis**
  - Compare the costs of maintaining aging equipment with the costs of replacement.
  - Consider trade-in or resale value for outdated equipment.
- **Feedback Gathering**
  - Conduct surveys or interviews with staff and faculty to identify emerging requirements.
  - Use feedback to guide refresh priorities.

6. Refresh or Replacement Phase (Year 5)
Goal: Replace outdated equipment with new technology.
- **Decommissioning**
  - Safely remove and dispose of outdated equipment following institutional policies and regulations.
  - Wipe or secure data from devices before disposal.
- **Procurement of New Equipment**
  - Begin the lifecycle again with updated needs assessment and procurement plans.
  - Incorporate lessons learned from the previous cycle to improve the process.

Ongoing Lifecycle Management
- Regularly review and update the refresh lifecycle to reflect technological advances and changing institutional priorities.
- Maintain clear documentation of all phases for accountability and transparency.
- Build flexibility into the cycle to accommodate unexpected funding opportunities or urgent replacements.

Appendix H

Sample Outline for a Policy and Procedure Manual

1. **Introduction**
    - 1.1 Purpose of the Manual
    - 1.2 Mission, Vision, and Goals of the Simulation Center
    - 1.3 Scope and Applicability
    - 1.4 Definitions and Key Terms
2. **Governance and Oversight**
    - 2.1 Organizational Structure
    - 2.2 Roles and Responsibilities
        - 2.2.1 Simulation Director
        - 2.2.2 Simulation Technicians
        - 2.2.3 Faculty and Instructors
    - 2.3 Reporting and Decision-Making Processes
    - 2.4 Committees and Stakeholders
3. **Facility Operations**
    - 3.1 Facility Access and Security
        - 3.1.1 Visitor Policies
        - 3.1.2 Key and Badge Access
    - 3.2 Scheduling and Utilization
        - 3.2.1 Reservation Process
        - 3.2.2 Priority Scheduling Guidelines
    - 3.3 Equipment Maintenance and Management
        - 3.3.1 Preventative Maintenance
        - 3.3.2 Equipment Repair Protocols
    - 3.4 Housekeeping and Cleanliness
    - 3.5 Prioritization of Simulation Resources
4. **Simulation Program Design**
    - 4.1 Simulation Curriculum Development
    - 4.2 Learning Objectives and Outcomes
    - 4.3 Scenario Creation and Approval
    - 4.4 Debriefing and Evaluation Standards
5. **Participant Policies**
    - 5.1 Code of Conduct
    - 5.2 Confidentiality and Non-Disclosure
    - 5.3 Dress Code and Safety Requirements
    - 5.4 Attendance and Participation Expectations
    - 5.5 Participant Photograph/Video Policy
6. **Faculty and Staff Policies**
    - 6.1 Training and Certification Requirements
    - 6.2 Professional Development Opportunities

- 6.3 Faculty of Record Responsibilities
- 6.4 Clinical Instructor Responsibilities
- 6.5 Conflict Resolution and Reporting

7. Health and Safety
- 7.1 Emergency Procedures
  - 7.1.1 Fire and Evacuation Plans
  - 7.1.2 Medical Emergencies
  - 7.1.3 Extreme Weather
- 7.2 Infection Control and Hygiene
- 7.3 Simulation Safety Protocols
  - 7.3.1 Use of Medical Gases
  - 7.3.2 Latex Allergies and Other Sensitivities
  - 7.3.3 Sharps
- 7.4 Separation of Equipment and Supplies (real vs. sim)
- 7.5 Psychological Safety

8. Technology and Media
- 8.1 Audio-Visual Recording Policies
- 8.2 Data Storage and Security
- 8.3 Data Retention
- 8.4 IT Support and Troubleshooting
- 8.5 Equipment Loan and External Use

9. Evaluation and Quality Assurance
- 9.1 Program Evaluation Metrics
- 9.2 Participant Feedback and Surveys
- 9.3 Continuous Improvement Processes
- 9.4 Accreditation and Compliance

10. Financial Management
- 10.1 Budget and Resource Allocation
- 10.2 Fees for Service and Billing Policies
- 10.3 Grant Management and Funding Opportunities

11. Special Circumstances
- 11.1 Research Use of the Simulation Center
- 11.2 Collaboration with External Partners
- 11.3 Simulation Center Closure and Downtime
- 11.4 Brand Use
- 11.5 Tours/outreach

12. Appendices
- A. Forms and Templates
- B. Emergency Contact List
- C. Glossary of Terms
- D. Relevant Laws and Regulations
- E. Simulation Center Map and Floor Plan

13. Revision History and Updates
- 13.1 Record of Changes
- 13.2 Update Process and Responsibilities

Appendix I

Sample Orientation Feedback Form

Simulation Center Orientation Evaluation

Thank you for participating in the orientation program. Your feedback is essential to improving the onboarding process for future team members. Please take a few minutes to complete this form.

1. General Information
- **Name (Optional):** _____
- **Role:** ☐ Simulation Technician ☐ Faculty/Instructor ☐ Standardized Patient ☐ Administrative Staff ☐ Other: _____
- **Date of Orientation:** _____

2. Orientation Content
Please rate the following aspects of the orientation program on a scale of 1 to 5: (1 = Poor, 5 = Excellent)

Aspect	Rating	Comments/Suggestions
Clarity of the center's mission and vision	☐ 1 ☐ 2 ☐ 3 ☐ 4 ☐ 5	
Overview of the organizational structure	☐ 1 ☐ 2 ☐ 3 ☐ 4 ☐ 5	
Explanation of policies and procedures	☐ 1 ☐ 2 ☐ 3 ☐ 4 ☐ 5	
Facility tour and safety information	☐ 1 ☐ 2 ☐ 3 ☐ 4 ☐ 5	
Introduction to tools and equipment	☐ 1 ☐ 2 ☐ 3 ☐ 4 ☐ 5	

3. Orientation Delivery
Please rate the following aspects of the program delivery on a scale of 1 to 5: (1 = Poor, 5 = Excellent)

Aspect	Rating	Comments/Suggestions
Effectiveness of the facilitators	☐ 1 ☐ 2 ☐ 3 ☐ 4 ☐ 5	
Opportunities for questions and interaction	☐ 1 ☐ 2 ☐ 3 ☐ 4 ☐ 5	
Usefulness of materials provided	☐ 1 ☐ 2 ☐ 3 ☐ 4 ☐ 5	

Aspect	Rating	Comments/Suggestions
Pace of the orientation	☐ 1 ☐ 2 ☐ 3 ☐ 4 ☐ 5	

4. Role-Specific Training
Did the orientation adequately prepare you for your specific role?
- ☐ Yes
- ☐ Somewhat
- ☐ No
- **Comments/Suggestions**:

5. Onboarding Experience
- What part of the orientation was the most helpful for you?
- What part of the orientation was the least helpful or could be improved?
- Do you feel confident in performing your duties after the orientation? ☐ Yes ☐ Somewhat ☐ No
    - **If no, what additional support or training do you need?**

6. Overall Satisfaction
How satisfied are you with the overall orientation experience?
- ☐ Very Satisfied
- ☐ Satisfied
- ☐ Neutral
- ☐ Dissatisfied
- ☐ Very Dissatisfied
- **Additional Comments**:

7. Suggestions for Improvement
Please share any ideas or recommendations for improving the orientation program.

Thank you for your valuable feedback! We will use your responses to enhance the orientation experience for future staff members.

Appendix J

Example Meeting Agenda

Meeting Agenda

Meeting Title: [Title]
Date: [Insert Date]
Time: [Insert Time]
Location: [Insert Location/Virtual Meeting Link]
Facilitator: [Insert Facilitator Name]

Agenda Items
1. **Welcome and Introductions (5 minutes)**
   - Brief introductions of attendees.
   - Overview of meeting objectives.
2. **Old Items (15 minutes)**
   - Review of previous minutes.
   - Review of previous deliverables/discussions
3. **New Items (15 minutes)**
   - Introduce new topics

4. **Next Steps and Action Items (10 minutes)**
   - Assign immediate tasks to team members.
   - Set deadlines for upcoming milestones.
5. **Q&A and Closing Remarks (5 minutes)**
   - Open floor for questions.
   - Summarize key takeaways and next steps.

Meeting Notes: [Leave space for notes or actions decided during the meeting.]

Attachments: [Attach any relevant documents or links.]

This agenda can be adjusted depending on the type and scope of your meeting.

Appendix K

Example Meeting Minutes

Meeting Minutes Example
Meeting Title: Project Kickoff Meeting
Date: [Insert Date]
Time: [Insert Time]
Location: [Insert Location/Virtual Meeting Link]
Facilitator: [Insert Facilitator Name]
Attendees: [List Names]

Meeting Minutes
1. **Previous Minutes Approved**
2. **Welcome and Introductions**
     - Meeting started at [Start Time].
     - Attendees introduced themselves.
     - Objectives of the meeting were reviewed by the facilitator.
3. **Old Items - Topics Discussed**
     - Topic 1
     - Topic 2
     - Topic 3
4. **New Items – Topics Discussed**
     - Topic 1
     - Topic 2
     - Topic 3
5. **Next Steps and Action Items**
     - Immediate tasks assigned:
         - [Task] assigned to [Name], deadline [Insert Date].
         - [Task] assigned to [Name], deadline [Insert Date].
     - Follow-up meeting scheduled for [Insert Date and Time].
6. **Q&A and Closing Remarks**
     - Questions raised:
         - Question 1: [Insert Question] - Answer provided: [Insert Answer].
         - Question 2: [Insert Question] - Answer provided: [Insert Answer].
     - Summary of key takeaways:
         - [Insert Key Points].
     - Meeting adjourned at [End Time].

> A good practice is to categorize the topics. Example:
> - Operations
> - Curriculum
> - QI/QA
> - Professional Development
>
> This will help review teams look through your meeting minutes with ease.

Minutes Prepared By: [Insert Preparer's Name]
Date Prepared: [Insert Date]

Appendix L

Examples of Standardized Reporting Templates Commonly Used in Simulation Centers

Simulation centers often use standardized reporting templates to communicate their activities, outcomes, and operational data to stakeholders. These templates help ensure consistency and clarity, making tracking performance, demonstrating value, and aligning with organizational goals easier. Below are some common reporting templates used by simulation centers:

1. Annual/Quarterly Performance Report

Purpose: To provide an overview of the simulation center's activities and achievements over a specific period.
Common Sections:
Executive Summary: A high-level overview of key accomplishments and highlights.
Program Utilization:
- Total number of sessions conducted.
- Number of learners trained, categorized by discipline (e.g., nursing, medicine, allied health).
- Breakdown of simulation activities by type (e.g., skills training, team-based scenarios).

Outcomes:
- Learner performance metrics (e.g., pre- and post-simulation scores).
- Satisfaction survey results from learners and faculty.

Operational Metrics:
- Equipment usage and downtime.
- Room utilization rates.
- Staffing and resource allocation.

Financial Summary:
- Revenue and expense overview.
- Return on investment (ROI) analysis.

Continuous Quality Improvement (CQI):
- Identified gaps and actions taken for improvement.

2. Accreditation and Compliance Report

Purpose: To document the simulation center's adherence to specific standards for accreditation purposes.
Common Sections:
Accreditation Standards Addressed:
- Alignment with SSH, INACSL, or other accrediting bodies.

Program Goals:

- How the simulation center supports institutional and academic goals (e.g., medical school curriculum objectives).

Evidence of Compliance:
- Documentation of activities tied to specific standards.
- Examples: Objective Structured Clinical Examination (OSCE) results, interprofessional simulations, safety training programs.

Evaluation and Feedback:
- Summary of learner and faculty feedback.
- Steps taken to address compliance gaps.

Future Plans:
- Upcoming initiatives to maintain or exceed compliance.

3. Financial Report

Purpose: To track the center's financial health and justify budgets or funding requests.

Common Sections:

Income and Revenue Sources:
- Institutional funding.
- Grants and external sponsorships.
- Revenue from external training programs.

Expense Overview:
- Salaries, equipment maintenance, consumables, and utilities.

Cost-Effectiveness Analysis:
- Training cost per learner or activity.
- Financial savings from reduced clinical errors or staff turnover.

Return on Investment (ROI):
- Benefits compared to operational costs (e.g., reduced adverse events, accreditation readiness).

4. Program Impact Report

Purpose: To showcase the educational and organizational impact of simulation activities.

Common Sections:

Key Performance Indicators (KPIs):
- Learner outcomes (e.g., skill proficiency, knowledge retention).
- Clinical outcomes (e.g., reduced medical errors, improved response times).

Success Stories:
- Case studies highlighting specific program successes (e.g., emergency response training leading to improved real-world performance).

Stakeholder Engagement:
- Examples of institutional partnerships or community outreach activities.

5. Research and Innovation Report

Purpose: To document the center's contributions to research and development.

Common Sections:

Published Research:
- List of peer-reviewed articles, conference presentations, or white papers.

Innovative Practices:

- New technologies or methodologies implemented (e.g., virtual reality, eye-tracking analytics).

Grants and Funding:
- Research grants received and their outcomes.

Future Directions:
- Planned research projects or partnerships.

6. Learner and Faculty Feedback Summary

Purpose: To provide qualitative and quantitative insights into program satisfaction.
Common Sections:
Survey Results:
- Learner satisfaction (e.g., confidence improvement, relevance of scenarios).
- Faculty satisfaction (e.g., ease of use, applicability to practice).

Testimonials:
- Direct quotes or feedback from participants.

Improvement Areas:
- Key suggestions and how they are being addressed.

7. Outreach and Community Engagement Report

Purpose: To highlight activities that extend the center's impact beyond its primary institution.
Common Sections:
Community Training Sessions:
- Programs conducted for external organizations (e.g., EMTs, public health officials).

Public Events:
- Open houses, tours, or workshops hosted by the center.

Collaborations:
- Partnerships with local healthcare facilities, schools, or businesses.

Appendix M

Sample Budget

Category	Year 1 (USD)	Year 2 (USD)	Year 3 (USD)
Revenues			
Institutional Support	$ 500,000.00	$ 520,000.00	$ 540,800.00
Grants	$ 150,000.00	$ 155,000.00	$ 159,650.00
External Partnerships	$ 100,000.00	$ 105,000.00	$ 110,250.00
Revenue from Training Programs	$ 75,000.00	$ 80,000.00	$ 85,600.00
REVENUE TOTAL	$ 825,000.00	$ 860,000.00	$ 896,300.00
Expenses			
Staff Salaries	$ 400,000.00	$ 412,000.00	$ 424,360.00
Equipment Maintenance	$ 80,000.00	$ 82,400.00	$ 84,872.00
Consumables (e.g., IV kits, syringes)	$ 50,000.00	$ 51,500.00	$ 53,045.00
Utilities and Overhead	$ 60,000.00	$ 61,800.00	$ 63,654.00
Technology Upgrades	$ 70,000.00	$ 72,100.00	$ 74,263.00
Simulation Equipment Purchases	$ 120,000.00	$ 123,600.00	$ 127,308.00
Professional Development for Staff	$ 30,000.00	$ 30,900.00	$ 31,827.00
Miscellaneous Expenses	$ 20,000.00	$ 20,600.00	$ 21,218.00
EXPENSE TOTAL	$ 830,000.00	$ 854,900.00	$ 880,547.00
TOTAL P/L (Retained Earning)	$ (5,000.00)	$ 5,100.00	$ 15,753.00

Appendix N

Sample ROI and ROV Metrics

Metric Category	Notes
Program Expenses	Enter all program-related costs here.
Staff Salaries	Include facilitator and technician salaries.
Equipment Costs	Include purchase and depreciation costs of simulators and equipment.
Consumables	Include consumable items like IV kits, syringes, etc.
Maintenance	Include all maintenance contracts and repair costs.
Facilities Overhead	Include utilities, rent, and other overhead expenses.
Revenue/Cost Savings	Enter revenue and cost-saving figures here.
Income from Training Programs	Income generated from external or fee-based programs.
Grants and Sponsorships	Grants received or sponsorships for the simulation program.
Reduced Error-Related Costs	Cost savings from fewer medical errors and adverse events.
Reduced Staff Turnover Costs	Savings from decreased recruitment due to better staff retention.
Operational Efficiencies	Savings from optimized workflows or time efficiencies.
Return on Investment (ROI)	Calculate total investment versus total savings here.
Total Investment	Sum of all expenses in 'Program Expenses'.
Total Savings/Revenue	Sum of all revenue/cost savings in 'Revenue/Cost Savings'.
ROI Calculation (Savings - Investment)	Calculated as (Total Savings - Total Investment).
Return on Value (ROV)	Qualitative metrics reflecting program impact.
Improved Patient Safety	Quantify the reduction in adverse events or improved safety indicators.
Learner Confidence Gains	Learner-reported improvements in confidence or preparedness.
Learner Satisfaction	Learner-reported satisfaction
Accreditation Readiness	Meeting accreditation standards or preparing for accreditation.
Staff Retention and Satisfaction	Staff satisfaction scores or survey data on reduced turnover.
Institutional Reputation	Impact on community perception and institutional ranking.
Cultural Improvements	Observed cultural shifts toward safety, teamwork, or innovation.
Alignment with Strategic Plan	Aligning with the organization's strategic plan/initiatives
Outreach	The outreach the center has been doing and the impact to the community

Appendix O

Tools for ROI Analysis

Tools for Return on Investment (ROI) analysis in simulation programs and other healthcare-related educational initiatives focus on financial modeling, cost-benefit evaluation, and data visualization. Here are some of the most effective tools and platforms, categorized for ease of application:

Spreadsheet Software

Excel or Google Sheets
Why it's useful: Widely accessible and customizable, spreadsheet software allows for detailed ROI calculations using templates or custom models.
Features for ROI Analysis:
Formulas for ROI calculation: (Benefits−Costs)/Costs(Benefits−Costs)/Costs
Data visualization: Pivot tables, charts, and graphs for representing ROI trends.
Scenario analysis: Use "What-If" analysis or data tables for sensitivity testing.
Pre-built ROI templates: Many online templates can jumpstart analysis.
Example Use Case: Track and compare direct cost reductions (e.g., fewer training-related incidents) against the program's capital and operational expenditures.

Dedicated ROI Tools

ROI Analysis Software
Cost-Benefit Analysis Toolkit (CBAT):
Developed for government and educational institutions.
Integrates qualitative and quantitative ROI analysis.
Free or low-cost options often available for academic institutions.
Tableau ROI Calculators:
Visual dashboards to track simulation costs, learner performance metrics, and operational efficiencies.
ROI calculators offered by vendors: Many simulation software providers (e.g., CAE Healthcare, Laerdal) offer integrated ROI tools to measure the impact of their platforms.

Simulation-Specific Platforms

Learning Management Systems (LMS) with Analytics:
Examples: Moodle, Blackboard, and Canvas.
Why it's useful: Many LMS platforms include built-in data analytics to measure learner outcomes and align them with financial costs.
Healthcare-Specific Simulation Platforms:
CAE LearningSpace®:
Tracks learner performance and aligns training outcomes with cost metrics.
SimCapture by Laerdal:
Integrates operational data (e.g., resource usage, scenario run rates) with cost-saving estimates.

Business Intelligence (BI) Tools

BI Tools for Advanced ROI Analysis and Visualization
Tableau and Power BI:
Aggregate financial, operational, and educational metrics.
Provide interactive dashboards to showcase ROI trends over time.
Integrate data from multiple sources (e.g., finance, HR, and simulation systems).
Qlik Sense:
Advanced analytics with drag-and-drop functionality.
Create dashboards showing ROI and other key performance indicators (KPIs) for simulation programs.
Example Use Case: Demonstrate how a simulation program improved patient safety (e.g., reduced malpractice claims) and present the findings in interactive dashboards to stakeholders.

Economic Evaluation Tools

Cost-Effectiveness Analysis (CEA) Tools:
HEAT (Health Economic Assessment Tool):
Offers specific metrics to evaluate the cost-effectiveness of healthcare interventions.
TreeAge Pro:
Models complex cost-benefit scenarios for ROI studies, particularly useful for analyzing long-term healthcare interventions.

Custom-Built Tools and Apps
Custom ROI Models and Applications:
Institutions often develop in-house tools using Python, R, or JavaScript to tailor ROI analysis for specific simulation program metrics.
R packages for ROI: Use tools like ROI or ROI.plugin for optimization and custom analyses.
Python libraries: Pandas and Matplotlib to model and visualize ROI over time.

Survey and Data Collection Tools

For ROV (Return on Value) Analysis Integration:
Qualtrics and SurveyMonkey:
Collect qualitative data on learner satisfaction, patient safety improvements, and other ROV-aligned metrics.
Integrate responses into ROI frameworks to capture intangible benefits.
SPSS and NVivo: Analyze qualitative and mixed-methods data for narratives supporting ROI.

Suggested Workflow for ROI Analysis

1. **Define Metrics:** Identify costs (e.g., initial investment, operational expenses) and benefits (e.g., cost savings, patient safety).
2. **Choose a Tool:** Select based on complexity, scalability, and the level of automation required.
3. **Automate Data Collection:** Integrate with LMS or simulation systems where possible.
4. **Analyze Trends:** Use BI tools like Tableau to track financial metrics alongside learner outcomes.
5. **Present Findings:** Leverage dashboards and reports to communicate ROI and ROV to stakeholders.

Key Tip: Pair ROI tools with ROV (Return on Value) frameworks to capture financial and qualitative benefits for a comprehensive evaluation.

Tools for Return on Investment (ROI) analysis in simulation programs and other healthcare-related educational initiatives focus on financial modeling, cost-benefit evaluation, and data visualization. Here are some of the most effective tools and platforms, categorized for ease of application:

Appendix P

Personal Tools Used

This appendix lists the tools and software applications I use to manage and operate my simulation center as of 2025.

Office Software
1. Microsoft Office

Telecommunications
1. Zoom

Simulation-Specific Platforms
1. Laerdal SimCapture

Calendaring
2. SimCapture (simulation activities)
3. Microsoft Outlook (all other operational activities)

Business Intelligence (BI) Tools
1. None (Project Management Tools

Project Management
1. Microsoft Project
2. Trello
3. Monday

Video Software
1. Blue Iris

Survey and Data Collection Tools
1. QuestionPro

Equipment and Supply Management
1. EZOffice Inventory

Video/Photo Editing
1. Adobe

Appendix Q

Risk Identification Tool

This tool is designed to help healthcare simulation centers systematically identify and assess risks across key operational domains. It includes risk categories, example scenarios, and prompts for center-specific analysis. The tool can be used during risk assessments, continuity planning, or regular operational reviews.

Step 1: Risk Categories and Assessment Prompts

1. Technical Risks

Equipment Failure
Examples: Simulator malfunctions, AV system breakdowns, or wearable device failures.
Prompts: - Are all simulators and AV systems routinely maintained and tested? - Do you have backup equipment or quick access to replacement parts? - Are staff trained to troubleshoot and repair common technical issues?
Software Issues
Examples: Scheduling software crashes, corrupted scenario files, or licensing lapses.
Prompts: - Are all software systems updated regularly? - Do you have a plan for restoring data in case of a software failure? - Is there IT support available to handle urgent software issues?

2. Human Resource Risks

Staffing Shortages
Examples: Sudden staff resignations, illness, or burnout.
Prompts: - Do you have cross-training programs to ensure multiple staff members can perform critical roles?   - Are staffing levels sufficient to handle peak periods?   - Do you maintain a roster of on-call or contract personnel for emergencies?
Skill Gaps
Examples: Technicians unfamiliar with new equipment, lack of debriefing facilitation skills.
Prompts: - Are there ongoing professional development opportunities for staff?   - Do you evaluate staff skills regularly to identify training needs?   - Are staff trained on new equipment or software before implementation?

3. Environmental Risks

Natural Disasters
Examples: Flooding, hurricanes, earthquakes, or wildfires.
Prompts: - Is your center located in a disaster-prone area?   - Do you have a protocol for protecting equipment and data during natural disasters?   - Are evacuation plans in place for staff and learners?
Utility Disruptions
Examples: Power outages, water supply interruptions, or HVAC failures
Prompts: - Do you have backup power sources (e.g., generators, UPS)?   - Are critical systems protected against power surges?   - Is the facility's infrastructure inspected and maintained regularly?

4. Data and Cybersecurity Risks

Data Loss

Examples: Accidental deletion of learner records and corrupted files.

Prompts:

- Is all data backed up regularly to secure locations?
- Do you have a system for verifying data integrity?
- Are backup recovery procedures documented and tested?

Cybersecurity Breaches

Examples: Ransomware attacks and phishing attempts targeting staff.

Prompts:

- Are staff trained to recognize phishing and other cyber threats?
- Do you use encryption for sensitive data?
- Is your firewall and antivirus software updated regularly?

5. Operational Risks

Scheduling and Logistical Errors

Examples: Overbooked simulation rooms, conflicting resource assignments.

Prompts:

- Do you use a centralized scheduling system to manage resources?
- Are scenarios reviewed for feasibility before scheduling?
- Are roles and responsibilities for logistics clearly defined?

Supply Chain Delays

Examples: Long lead times for replacement parts or consumables.

Prompts:

- Do you maintain a stockpile of frequently used parts and supplies?
- Are vendor relationships managed to ensure timely delivery?
- Do you have secondary suppliers for critical items?

Step 2: Risk Scoring Matrix

For each identified risk, assign a score based on **likelihood** and **impact** using the matrix below:

Likelihood (1-5)	Impact (1-5)	Risk Score (Likelihood × Impact)
1 = Rare	1 = Negligible	1–5: Low Risk
2 = Unlikely	2 = Minor	6–10: Medium Risk
3 = Possible	3 = Moderate	11–15: High Risk
4 = Likely	4 = Significant	16–20: Critical Risk
5 = Almost Certain	5 = Catastrophic	

Step 3: Mitigation Planning Worksheet

For risks rated as **Medium**, **High**, or **Critical**, document mitigation strategies like in the table below as a sample:

Risk Category	Identified Risk	Likelihood	Impact	Risk Score	Mitigation Strategy	Responsible Party	Timeline
Technical	Simulator failure	3	4	12	Regular maintenance, backup manikins	Technician Team	Quarterly
Human Resource	Staff shortage	4	3	12	Cross-training, on-call list	HR Manager	Ongoing
Environmental	Power outage	5	4	20	Generator installation	Facilities	3 months

Step 4: Risk Monitoring and Review

- **Frequency**: Review risks and mitigation strategies quarterly or after a major incident.
- **Key Metrics**: Track the number of incidents, downtime duration, and financial impact to evaluate risk mitigation effectiveness.
- **Feedback Loop**: Incorporate lessons learned into updated risk assessments and continuity plans.

Step 5: Risk Identification Checklist

A quick checklist for assessing overall risk preparedness:

- ☐ Do you have a documented continuity plan in place?
- ☐ Are all critical systems maintained and tested regularly?
- ☐ Is staff cross-trained for key operational roles?
- ☐ Do you partner with external facilities or vendors for emergency support?
- ☐ Are data and cybersecurity measures up to date?
- ☐ Is your team trained on emergency protocols and procedures?
- ☐ Are risks reassessed and updated regularly?

Appendix R

Sample Continuity Plan

Contingency and Continuity Plan for [Simulation Center Name]

Section	Details
Purpose and Scope	**Purpose**: To ensure continuity of operations during emergencies. **Scope**: Covers all simulation activities.
Key Risks	- Technical Failures (e.g., equipment malfunctions, software crashes). - Environmental Risks (e.g., flooding, power outages). - Human Resource Risks (e.g., staff shortages, turnover). - Cybersecurity Threats (e.g., ransomware attacks). - Operational Risks (e.g., scheduling conflicts, supply chain delays).

Emergency Response Plan

Step	Details
Activation Criteria	Triggered by disruptions threatening operations or safety.
Chain of Command	- **Incident Manager**: Simulation Operations Manager. - **Backup Manager**: Senior Simulation Technician. - **Communication Officer**: Administrative Coordinator.
Immediate Actions	- **Assess Situation**: Identify the severity and scope of disruption. - **Implement Mitigation**: Activate troubleshooting or evacuation protocols. - **Notify Stakeholders**: Inform staff, learners, and external partners.

Continuity Strategies

Category	Strategy
Prevention	- Routine maintenance (quarterly checks for equipment and systems). - Staff cross-training for critical roles. - Cloud-based data storage for scenarios and records.
Redundancy	- Backup high-fidelity simulator and AV components. - Install generators and UPS for power continuity.
Alternate Locations	- **Primary Backup Facility**: [Nearby University Name]. Address: [University Address]. Contact: [Contact Name, Phone]. - **Secondary Facility**: [Local Training Center Name]. Address: [Center Address]. Contact: [Contact Name, Phone].
Data Recovery	- Weekly backups of scenarios and learner data. - Staff access to cloud systems for remote operations.

Recovery Plan

Step	Details
Initial Steps	- **Damage Assessment**: Identify impacted systems and prioritize repairs. - **Staff Debriefing**: Assign recovery roles and review protocols. - **Stakeholder Communication**: Inform stakeholders of timelines and updates.
Restoring Operations	- **Timeline**: Day 1-2: Secure assets and assess damage. Day 3-5: Resume critical operations. Day 6+: Fully restore services. - **Temporary Solutions**: Use alternate locations or virtual debriefing sessions if necessary.
Continuous Improvement	Conduct post-incident reviews and incorporate findings into updated plans.

Communication Protocol

Type	Methods
Internal Communication	- Staff meetings, email, or internal messaging systems. - Key Contacts: Simulation Center Manager ([Phone/Email]), IT Support ([Phone/Email]).
External Communication	- Learners and Faculty: LMS announcements, email updates. - Partners and Vendors: Notify for backup facility use or equipment needs.

Testing and Maintenance

Activity	Details
Drills	Conduct biannual emergency drills, simulating power outages, evacuations, or equipment failures.
Plan Review	Update the continuity plan annually or after major incidents.
Staff Training	Provide new hires with continuity training and refresh existing staff every six months.

Appendices

Section	Details
Contact List	Includes staff, institutional leadership, IT support, and emergency service contacts.
Equipment Inventory	Detailed list of simulators, AV systems, and supplies with vendor information.
Sample Scenarios	Practice scenarios for power outages, flooded facilities, or cybersecurity breaches.

List of Figures and Tables

Figure 1 Key Components of Simulation Operations 7
Figure 2 Core Functions of Simulation Operations 9
Figure 3 Key Performance Metrics for Simulation Effectiveness 26
Figure 4 Principles of Effective Simulation 33
Figure 5 ADDIE model specific to simulation design. 41
Figure 6 Kern's Six-Step Approach 44
Figure 7 Sample Simulation Center Prioritization Hierarchy 83
Figure 8 The Eisenhower Matrix 89
Figure 9 Advocating for Program Growth 95
Figure 10 Effectiveness of Different Recruiting Strategies for Attracting Talent 108
Figure 11 Example of a Plus/Delta of a Rapid Response Simulation 139
Figure 12 GAS Debriefing Model 140
Figure 14 PEARLS Debriefing 141
Figure 15 Advocacy-Inquiry Debriefing Tool 142
Figure 16 Designing Assessment Tools 146
Figure 17 Kirkpatrick Model 147
Figure 18 Example of a Dashboard 158
Figure 19 ROI vs. ROV 175
Figure 20 Common Positions in Simulation Operations 197
Figure 21 Professional Development Strategies 209
Figure 22 SSH Accreditation Standards 217
Figure 23 INACSL Standards of Best Practice 218
Figure 24 ASPE Standards of Best Practice 219
Figure 25 Building Resiliency 250

Table 1 Measurable verbs based on Bloom's Taxonomy 49
Table 2 The differences in feedback and debriefing 54
Table 3 Key Timelines for Different Equipment Types 78
Table 4 Common educational and operational metrics used in simulation programs ... 185

About the Author

Keith A. Beaulieu, MBA, CHSOS-A

Keith A. Beaulieu is an accomplished professional with extensive experience in healthcare simulation, accreditation management, and operational leadership. Currently serving as the Accreditation and Operations Manager at the Sue & Bill Gross School of Nursing, University of California, Irvine, Keith oversees accreditation processes and ensures operational excellence within the simulation programs.

With a career spanning over a decade in healthcare simulation, Keith has held pivotal roles, including Director of Operations for the Medical Education Simulation Center and Simulation Curriculum Coordinator at prominent institutions. His contributions have directly supported program growth, quality improvement, and alignment with accreditation standards. At the Sue & Bill Gross School of Nursing, Keith has ensured continued program accreditation and approval from the Commission on Collegiate Nursing Education (CCNE) and the California Board of Registered Nursing.

Keith is a Certified Healthcare Simulation Operations Specialist – Advanced (CHSOS-A) and a respected member of the Society for Simulation in Healthcare (SSH) Accreditation Council. He has performed over 30 accreditation site reviews globally for SSH, applying his expertise to enhance simulation programs across diverse healthcare settings. In addition to his site review experience, he has been instrumental in supporting accreditation research and standards development, contributing to the field's growth and innovation.

Keith is also a published author, contributing to **Achieving and Maintaining Accreditation for Nursing School Programs: A Comprehensive Guide** and **Achieving Program Accreditation for Healthcare Simulation Programs: A Resource Guide** and writing a chapter in the most recent edition of **Defining Excellence in Simulation Programs**. These works reflect his deep knowledge and thought leadership in accreditation and healthcare simulation.

Keith's educational background includes an MBA and multiple leadership, quality improvement, and simulation education certifications. Through his strategic vision, extensive accreditation experience, and scholarly contributions, Keith has become a leading figure in advancing the quality and impact of healthcare simulation worldwide.

Other Titles Available by this Author

Achieving and Maintaining Accreditation for Nursing School Programs:
A Comprehensive Guide

amazon

Achieving Program Accreditation for Healthcare Simulation Programs
A Resources Guide

amazon

HISTORY SERIES

Camp Haan
The History of Riverside's World War II Antiaircraft Training Center

amazon

www.ingramcontent.com/pod-product-compliance
Lightning Source LLC
LaVergne TN
LVHW080125010525
810124LV00004B/262